AFRICA IN WORLD POLITICS

FIFTH EDITION

AFRICA IN WORLD POLITICS

Engaging a Changing Global Order

EDITED BY **JOHN W. HARBESON** AND **DONALD ROTHCHILD**

WESTVIEW
PRESS

A Member of the Perseus Books Group

Westview Press was founded in 1975 in Boulder, Colorado, by notable publisher and intellectual Fred Praeger. Westview Press continues to publish scholarly titles and high-quality undergraduate- and graduate-level textbooks in core social science disciplines. With books developed, written, and edited with the needs of serious nonfiction readers, professors, and students in mind, Westview Press honors its long history of publishing books that matter.

Find us on the World Wide Web at www.westviewpress.com.

Every effort has been made to secure required permissions for all text, images, maps, and other art reprinted in this volume.

Westview Press books are available at special discounts for bulk purchases in the United States by corporations, institutions, and other organizations. For more information, please contact the Special Markets Department at the Perseus Books Group, 2300 Chestnut Street, Suite 200, Philadelphia, PA 19103, or call (800) 810-4145, ext. 5000, or e-mail special.markets@perseusbooks.com.

Designed by Trish Wilkinson
Set in 10.5 point Minion Pro

Library of Congress Cataloging-in-Publication Data

Africa in world politics : engaging a changing global order / edited by John W. Harbeson and Donald Rothchild. — 5th ed.
    p.   cm.
    Includes bibliographical references and index.
    ISBN 978-0-8133-4845-2 (pbk. : alk. paper) — ISBN 978-0-8133-4846-9 (e-book)
1. Africa—Politics and government—1960–   2. World politics—1989–
I. Harbeson, John W. (John Willis), 1938–   II. Rothchild, Donald S.
DT30.5.A3544 2013
960.33—dc23   2012032305

10 9 8 7 6 5 4 3 2 1

Contents

Tables and Figures

Tables

Figures

Africa

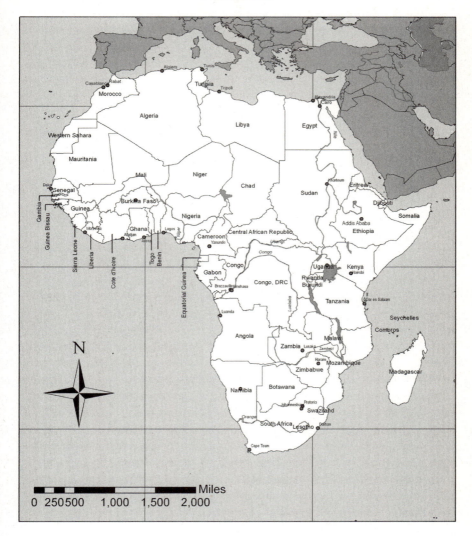

Acronyms

ACP	African, Caribbean, and Pacific States group
ADB	African Development Bank
ADFL	Alliances of Democratic Forces for the Liberation of the Congo
AEF	French Equatorial Africa
AFRICOM	US Africa Command
AfDB	African Development Bank
AGOA	African Growth and Opportunity Act (US)
AIAI	Al Itihaad al Islaami
AIPPA	Access to Information and Protection of Privacy Act (Zimbabwe)
AMIS	Africa Union Mission
AMU	Arab Mahgreb Union
ANC	African National Congress (South Africa)
AOF	French West Africa
APF	Africa Union Peace Fund
APRM	African Peer Review Mechanism
AU	African Union
AUHLIP	African Union High Level Implementation Panel
BRICS	Brazil, Russia, India, China, and South Africa
CDR	Coalition for the Defense of the Republic (Rwanda)
CEAO	West African Economic Community
CEEAC	Economic Union of the States of Central Africa
CfA	Commission for Africa (Blair Commission)
CFA	Communauté Financière Africaine
CFSP	Common Foreign and Security Policy (Europe)
CJTF-HOA	Combined Joint Task Force–Horn of Africa

COMESA	Common Market of East and Southern Africa
CPA	Comprehensive Peace Agreement
CSSDCA	Conference on Security, Stability, Development, and Cooperation in Africa
DANIDA	Danish International Development Authority
DATA	Debt, AIDS, Trade, Africa report
DFID	British Department of International Development
DRC	Democratic Republic of the Congo (Kinshasha)
EACU	East African Customs Union
ECA	Economic Commission for Africa
ECOMOG	West African Military Observer Group
ECOWAS	Economic Commission of West African States
EPAs	Economic Partnership Agreements
EPLF	Eritrean People's Liberation Front
EPRDF	Ethiopian People's Revolutionary Democratic Front
ESCE	Economic Security and Cooperation in Europe
ESDI	Europe's Common Security and Defense Identity
EU	European Union
EUCOM	US European Command
EUFOR	European Force
FDC	Forum for Democrfatic Change (Uganda)
FNLA	National Front for the Liberation of Angola
FOMWAN	Federation of Muslim Women's Associations of Nigeria
FRELIMO	Mozambique Liberation Front
FTAs	Free trade areas
G8	Group of eight leading industrial economies
GDA	Global Development Alliance
GFATM	Global Fund to fight AIDS, Tuberculosis, and Malaria
GLPF	Great Lakes Policy Forum
GPRA	Provisional Government of the Republic of Algeria
GSPC	Salafist Group for Preaching and Combat
HIPC	Highly Indebted Poor Countries
IBRD	International Bank for Reconstruction and Development (World Bank)
ICG	International Crisis Group
IFIs	international financial institutions
IGAD	Inter-Governmental Agency for Development
IGADD	Inter-Governmental Agency on Drought and Development
IMF	International Monetary Fund
LIFG	Libyan Islamic Fighting Group

MDG	UN Millennium Development Goals
MDRI	Multilateral Debt Relief Initiative
MOSOP	Movement for the Survival of the Ogoni People
MSF	Medicin Sans Frontieres (Doctors Without Borders)
NANGO	National Association of Non-Governmental Organizations (Zimbabwe)
NANGOF	Namibian Nongovernmental Organization Federation
NATO	North Atlantic Treaty Organization
NCP	National Congress Party (Sudan)
NEPAD	New Partnership for African Development
NIF	National Islamic Front (Sudan)
OAU	Organization of African Union (predecessor of AU)
ODA	Official Development Assistance
OECD	Organization for Economic Cooperation and Development
OIC	Organization of the Islamic Conference
ONLF	Ogaden National Liberation Front
OOTW	Operations Other than War
OSCE	Organization for Security and Cooperation in Europe
PAGAD	People Against Gangsterism and Drugs (South Africa)
PEPFAR	Presidential Emergency Program for AIDS Relief
PMLA	Popular Movement for the Liberation of Angola
POSA	Public Order and Security Act (Zimbabwe)
PRSP	Poverty Reduction Strategy Paper
PSFU	Private Sector Foundation of Uganda
PSI	Policy Support Instrument
PTA	Preferential Trade Area
RBAs	Rights Based Approaches
RENAMO	Mozambique National Resistance Organization
RUF	Revolutionary United Front (Sierra Leone)
SACU	Southern African Customs Union
SADC	Southern African Development Council
SADR	Sahrawi Democratic Republic
SIDA	Swedish International Development Authority
SNA	Somali National Alliance
SPLM/A	Sudan People's Liberation Movement Army
SRSG	Special Representative of the Secretary General
SSA	Sub-Saharan Africa
SSLM	Southern Sudan Liberation Movement
SST	states sponsoring terrorism
TCSTI	Trans-Saharan Counter Terrorism Initiative

TFG	Transitional Federal Government (Somalia)
TRIPS	Trade-Related Aspects of International Property Rights
UDEAC	Customs Union of the Central African States
UEAC	Economic Union of Central Africa
UEMOA	West African Monetary and Economic Union
UIC	Union of Islamic Courts (Somalia)
UNAIDS	Joint UN Program on HIV/AIDS
UNESCO	United Nations Educational, Scientific, and Cultural Organization
UNCTAD	UN Conference on Trade and Development
UNDP	United Nations Development Program
UNDRD	United Nations Declaration on the Right to Development
UNFPA	United Nations Population Fund
UNICEF	United Nations Children's Fund
UNITA	Union for the Total Independence of Angola
UNITAF	United Nations Task Force (Somalia)
UNODC	UN Office on Drugs and Crime
UNOSOM	United Nations Operations in Somalia
USAID	United States Agency for International Development
WHO	World Health Organization
WILDAF	Women in Law and Development in Africa
WTO	World Trade Organization

Preface

The dramatic changes in the contours of African politics in the past few years led to the decision to launch this fifth edition of *Africa in World Politics* more closely following the previous edition than might otherwise have been the case. Among the most prominent of these developments have been the rapid expansion of China's economic engagement, the markedly improved rates of economic growth for many countries, and the troubled birth of the continent's newest independent country, the Republic of South Sudan. More generally, the core focus of this edition is upon the numerous and complex interconnections between Africa's emergence from marginalization to greater economic prominence on the world stage and the transformation of the global economic and political order itself heralded by the growing power of many G-20 countries.

A central concern of this volume, however, is the fundamental question of to what extent Africa's growing prominence on the world stage will translate into greater and more sustainable well-being for the continent in political, socioeconomic, environmental, and cultural terms. Not yet clear is to what degree more rapid economic growth, if it proves sustainable, will both substantially reach all countries on the continent and include diminished poverty and inequality and broadly improved quality of life for most of the continent's peoples.

The essays in this volume also attest to the profound elusiveness of the goal of building stronger and reformed states given their deeply rooted manifestations of weakness and ineffectiveness arising from decades of postcolonial authoritarian and corrupt stewardship. Continuing manifestations are present in the fragile, tentative easing of the Great Lakes crisis, uneven and still fragile democratization, pervasive clientelism, and the responsibility to protect honored in the breach.

Notwithstanding all these profound challenges, this edition of *Africa in World Politics,* like its predecessors, is born of resilient optimism, which I believe all the authors share, that the seeds of genuine and sustainable political, economic, and cultural well-being still grow in African soils, and even offer more fresh and encouraging hints of an attainable bountiful harvest than in the past.

Our late, wonderful colleague and friend, Don Rothchild, is not with us on paper in this volume but for all of us he remains a model and an inspiration, and in that sense he has been very much with us in spirit in planning this volume and in preparing the chapters that follow.

The publication of this fifth edition is an appropriate time to recognize and express my great appreciation to each and every one of the scholars and friends who have written chapters for one or more of these editions. In addition to the authors of chapters in this fifth edition, the other members of the *Africa in World Politics* family have included Thomas Callaghy, Naomi Chazan, Herman Cohen, Larry Diamond, Kenneth Grundy, Jeffrey Herbst, Gilbert Khadiagala, Carol Lancaster, Rene Lemarchand, Victor LeVine, Guy Martin, Rob Mortimer, Marina Ottaway, Anokhi Parikh, John Ravenhill, Donald Rothchild, Denis Tull, Nicolas van de Walle, Vitaley Vasikov, and Alan Whiteside.

The late Don Rothchild and I have greatly appreciated the encouragement, assistance, and friendship of the editors at Westview with whom we have had the pleasure of working. I want especially to thank my Westview editor for this edition, Anthony Wahl, for all his support and encouragement and especially his flexibility in working with me on the challenges we have encountered in launching this edition. Finally, Don and I greatly appreciate the feedback we have received from our readers and those who have adopted editions of this book in their courses. My thanks to Westview and to everyone who responded to the readers' survey conducted in preparation for this edition for the recommendations it produced, several of which I have attempted to incorporate.

My colleagues and I offer this fifth edition of *Africa in World Politics* in hopes that in some small way it will broaden and deepen understanding of the human condition in Africa and, thereby, to a brighter future for its peoples and their countries.

John W. Harbeson
BETHESDA, MARYLAND

ENGAGING A CHANGING GLOBAL ORDER

one

Engaging a Changing Global Order

JOHN W. HARBESON

In the first decades of the twenty-first century, a new era of intense, significantly broadened international political and economic competition for preeminence has profoundly influenced sub-Saharan Africa's own continuing struggles with weak states, democratization, and chronically underdeveloped economies. Nearly three decades of international pressure on African states to liberalize their economies has made them increasingly attractive to a growing number of increasingly strong economies, led by the BRICS, some of whose rapidly expanding investments in African countries have represented both recognition of new opportunities and calculated strategies to further their own growth and global influence.* Overall, African economies have grown more rapidly, albeit unequally, in the first decade of the twenty-first century than at any time since the first years of independence in the 1960s, although rates of poverty and inequality have remained very high. They have done so while unprecedented, also unequal, rates of democratization on the continent since the end of the Cold War have shown signs of diminished momentum, even regression in some cases.

The fulcrum on which these diverse, convergent external and domestic patterns and political and economic change hinge is their implications for the condition of the African state. Reform of the state has been a centerpiece of

---

*Brazil, Russia, India, China, and more recently South Africa.

efforts to promote political and economic development since the first days of African independence in the 1960s. Initially the leaders of African independence movements undertook to reform and refocus the colonially imposed Western conception of the state with a view to mobilizing resources and energies for rapidly realizing socioeconomic development. By the 1980s, however, agendas for reforming the African state have been set externally, by circumventing states to direct development assistance to the needs of poor majorities via NGOs and local organizations, and implicitly to build grassroots pressure upon states from below for development with equity. At the same time, in the 1980s, international financial institutions and bilateral donors insisted on dramatically shrinking state-led promotion of development to comport with neoclassical theories of political economy. In the 1990s, the external agenda for state reform broadened to include a greater focus on the poor, while global civil society initiatives built broad support for substantial debt relief for African countries.* In 2000 the United Nations launched the fifteen-year Millennium Development Goals project to reduce dramatically the causes of poverty in developing countries, on the optimistic premise that less than fully reformed African states and donor countries alike would facilitate these objectives wholeheartedly and single-mindedly.

Since the 1990s, the focus of international campaigns to reform the state has expanded from seeking to align developing countries with changing socioeconomic development agendas to include reforming of the state itself. In the afterglow of the Cold War, strong international support for democratization converged with vigorous civil society pressure, perhaps stimulated by the earlier development emphases, to promote democratization. Virtually every sub-Saharan African state has conducted multiple competitive, multiparty elections of sharply varying quality. By the second decade of the new century, however, most African countries remained hybrid varieties of partial democratization and residual authoritarian practices while a few countries evidenced markedly broader and potentially sustainable if still fragile democratic institutions. The coup and secessionist insurgency in Mali in 2012, for nearly two decades a model sub-Saharan African democracy, supplied stark evidence, however, that unless actively maintained and extended, democratization may not necessarily prove to be synonymous with either strengthening or reforming the state.

The events of September 11, 2001, have appeared to set as markedly distinct and at least partially contradictory the international agendas for reforming the

---

*Thomas Callaghy and John Ravenhill, eds., *Hemmed In: Responses to Africa's Decline* (New York: Columbia University Press, 1993).

state in sub-Saharan Africa and other developing countries. Liberal initiatives continued apace to reform the state, by more fully democratizing it even as some slowing of democratic momentum, including retreats, has occurred in sub-Saharan Africa. At the same time, the impacts upon democratization, not to mention sustainable economic development, of greatly expanded G-20 investments have remained uncertain. Less noted, along with the continent's expanding global economic importance but significant in its own right, has been Africa's expanding global prominence as a center, solely in terms of numbers of adherents, of Arab, Islamic, and Christian, as well as francophone, culture, each of which originated from "invaders" over the course of Common Era African history.*

Meanwhile, international efforts to reconstruct failed states and heal those rent by civil war, impose sanctions upon and prosecute in the International Criminal Court those accused of genocide and crimes against humanity, strengthen states against domestic insurgencies, and oblige states to adhere to their responsibility to protect their citizens as a condition of their sovereignty have coexisted uneasily. The degree to which these initiatives, individually and collectively, have in fact actually strengthened chronically weak and failing states in sub-Saharan Africa and those fractured by civil war has remained an issue for legitimate debate, hinging to some degree on conceptualizations of the state and the degree to which the strengthening of states and regimes can be, and have been, distinguished from one another.

This fifth edition of *Africa in World Politics* explores the nature and the interconnections among all the foregoing patterns and issues as sub-Saharan Africa enters the second decade of the twenty-first century. Our inquiries begin with a reprise of the profound and, to varying degrees, continuing footprint of colonial experience upon the continent, half a century into its independent era. More than two decades after democracy's Third Wave reached African shores, residual authoritarian practices, corruption, or reformulations of those established in colonial times continue to resist strong civil society initiatives for democratic reform.** These efforts have continued to be compromised, as Crawford Young observes in Chapter 2, by clientelist networks upon which authoritarian regimes have continued to rely to connect with their citizen constituencies, and which have weakened whatever strengths colonial state structures may have acquired.

---

*Mazrui, Chapter 4.
**John W. Harbeson, Donald Rothchild, and Naomi Chazan, eds., *Civil Society and the State in Africa* (Boulder, CO: Lynne Rienner Publishers, 1994).

Africa's economic prominence early in the new century has derived from sharply increased rates of economic growth affecting more than a third of the countries. Among seven partially overlapping groups of countries tracked by the International Monetary Fund, sub-Saharan Africa moved from last place among them in the 1990s (2.4 percent) to more than doubling to become third in the first decade of the twenty-first century (5.7 percent), trailing only developing Asian and emerging developing economies as a group but surpassing Latin American and Caribbean, Middle Eastern and North African, newly industrializing Asian, and Commonwealth of Independent States economies.*

For 2001 through 2011, Table 1.1 records that nineteen sub-Saharan African countries averaged growth rates of 5.0 percent or better, where only four of this group also did so during the 1990s: Equatorial Guinea, Mozambique, Uganda, and Cape Verde. Equatorial Guinea's presence at the top of the list is attributable entirely to its expanding oil output, without regard to the fact that it is one of the most corrupt and authoritarian states in the continent. The factors involved in these surging growth rates prominently have included the attractiveness of several countries with important oil reserves and other important mineral deposits for investors from China and other rapidly expanding G-20 economies. Also important have been belated steps by African countries to liberalize their economies, a measure that international financial institutions first began to demand early in the 1980s. The "implicit bargain" that the IFIs struck with countries receiving their heavily conditional economic assistance, that expanded external investment would accompany African countries' adhering to these requirements, has been realized, but from a significantly wider array of sources than anticipated at the time.

Yet, as Todd Moss observes in Chapter 3, sub-Saharan Africa's engagement with international capital remains problematic, as it has throughout the independence era. Even today he projects that the growth of African economies will diverge markedly between those that embrace their new attractiveness to expanded external investment and trade and those that remain reluctant to do so. This faster growth, fueled by domestic private as well as external investment, is still too new to fully and accurately chart the likely socioeconomic and political outcomes. As has been the case for all of the world's strongest economies, the manner in which governments promote the early stages of economic growth has been of critical importance.

---

*International Monetary Fund data as published in *World Economic Outlook 2011*, http://mdgs.un.org/unsd/mdg/Resources/Static/Products/Progress2011/11-31330 %20(E)%20MDG%20Report%202011_Progress%20Chart%20LR.pdf.

Table 1.1. Fastest-Growing Sub-Saharan African Economies, 1990–2011

	2000s	1990s
Equatorial Guinea	17.3	32.9
Angola	10.8	1.4
Sierra Leone	9.3	−6.4
Nigeria	8.9	2.9
Chad	8.4	2.9
Ethiopia	8.3	3.1
Mozambique	7.9	6.1
Rwanda	7.7	1.9
Uganda	7.3	6.3
Tanzania	6.9	3.3
Ghana	6.5	4.4
Cape Verde	6.0	6.2
Sao Tome/Principe	5.9	1.2
Sudan	5.9	4.3
Burkina Faso	5.7	4.8
Zambia	5.7	−0.1
Mali	5.6	3.8
Niger	5.4	0.9
Dem. Rep. Congo	5.1	−5.6

Source: International Monetary Fund: *World Economic Outlook 2011*

For African countries and their governments, important precepts from their own histories as well as those of other developing countries are readily discernible. These include, first, the political as well as economic risks of failing to see that investment patterns support economic diversification, specifically to escape the resource curse syndrome experienced by the petro states and other extractive-industry-dependent economies. Second, sub-Saharan African countries continue to sustain very high levels of inequality and poverty, and it has long been well established that equitable growth in relief of these conditions is not a predictable by-product of more rapid growth. Third, some countries' leasing of large tracts of land for externally funded agro-industry initiatives puts at some risk the socioeconomic well-being of communities of small-scale local farmers and businessmen, recalling also ample evidence that these entrepreneurs have been the most effective utilizers of scarce investment resources.* Fourth, in the absence of adequate standards of transparency, still generally lacking in sub-Saharan Africa, governments have found ways to use expanded resources for development for their own political purposes and to reward allies and exclude others. Finally, the most effective deployment of expanded investment resources is substantially a function of the extent to which transparent governance processes have diminished the scope of clientelistic political networks, which are still prominent in sub-Saharan Africa.

As with its new prominence on the world stage as a region of economic opportunity, sub-Saharan Africa's evolution as a center of global cultures emanating from outside its borders is also not without its complications and challenges. Ali Mazrui's chapter notes that Africa has been as receptive to the diffusion of major global cultural currents as any region on the planet, a receptivity that has enabled the continent to become the center of those very cultures by virtue of the numbers of African adherents to them. But he concludes that, by the same token, Africa has important challenges to overcome from conflicts between and within these cultural currents. Pan-Africanism underwrote much of the continent's early drive to redress imperial conquest, its influence waning as national independence movements claimed center stage. In what is now one of the fastest-growing regions for both Islam and Christianity, and for Arab and francophone cultures, these cultural currents have been caught up with centrifugal political insurgencies. In Chapter 4, Mazrui appears to beckon to a distant shore wherein the spirit of foundational pan-Africanism, cultural rapprochement, synthesis, and coexistence may ultimately come to reign in Africa.

In a sense, all the chapters in Parts Three and Four of this book revolve around important dimensions of what has continued to be principally an internationally driven pursuit of responsible sovereignty centered on the states of sub-Saharan Africa and others in the developing world. Francis M. Deng, as both scholar and United Nations envoy, has helped to advance that agenda, which he examines in the concluding chapter. Preceding but especially since the end of the Cold War, international forged regimes have acquired visibility and strength in support of democracy and the basic human rights of every state's citizens, modifying the principle of unbounded state sovereignty on which the United Nations, and indeed international law itself since 1648, was founded.

---

*Ward Anseeuw, Mathieu Boche, Thomas Breu, Markus Giger, Jann Lay, Peter Messerli, and Kerstin Nolte, *Transnational Land Deals for Agriculture in the Global South,* http://landportal.info/landmatrix/media/img/analytical-report.pdf. Land Matrix is a cooperative venture of six European NGOs and think tanks.

Each of the chapters in Parts Three and Four bears witness in some way to the principle of responsible sovereignty, examines challenges rendering its realization elusive in sub-Saharan Africa, and notes the shortcomings of African initiatives in pursuit of responsible sovereignty. Fundamental prior issues underlie what may be entailed in actually reforming states, let alone in causing them to be responsible and responsive to their citizens. Chapter 5 suggests that apparent slowing of democratization momentum in sub-Saharan Africa may be attributable to insufficient engagement of citizens not just in competitive electoral processes but also in more collaborative ways of asserting themselves. In Chapter 6, Aili Mari Tripp makes somewhat the same point in charting the progress as well as points of contestation in civil society's efforts to extend the scope of human rights in Africa to social and economic rights as well as political and civil liberties, based on the combined thrusts of United Nations resolutions ordaining not just human rights in general but also specifically development as a right.

The chapters by Will Reno, I. William Zartman, and Ulf Engel examine African efforts to shore up the foundations of their weak and failing states, in an international context that is supportive of these efforts but in which the interests of individual states have added to the complexities of doing so. On the one hand, as Engel writes, African states have made significant strides in building regional cooperation and self-reliance in undergirding with externally supported security infrastructure combined with peer review in holding states responsible for the treatment of their citizens. Amid contrasting visions of a more unified, peaceful, integrated, governmentally accountable Africa, Engel traces the African Union Commission's increasing role as an international actor in its own right in relation to member states and regional economic communities in the areas of peace and security and governance. In Chapter 8, Zartman emphasizes that the original artificially constructed boundaries of states, a much-cited dimension of their weakness, have in fact increasingly become false mantras. He writes that today they are no more artificial than any other boundaries and, indeed, the relatively few changes that have occurred are exceptions proving the rule that for practical purposes they are now permanent. He concludes that a stable future is best ensured by facilitating and accepting small boundary rectifications and adjusting them to be more user-friendly where circumstances merit them.

On the other hand, regional organizations have reflected as much as they have compensated for underlying, uncertain state strength and commitment to democracy in member countries' governance practices. IGAD has been weakened by ongoing animosity between Ethiopia and Eritrea following their 1998–2000 war and stalled implementation of their United Nations–brokered postwar Algiers accords. Preoccupation with upholding state sovereignty won at independence has limited the effectiveness of SADC, especially South Africa, in addressing Zimbabwe's descent into autocracy and economic disarray. At the same time, the African Peer Review Mechanism, established to further the African Union's NEPAD goals of democratic governance, transparent and effective economic and corporate governance, and enhanced socioeconomic development, through country review mission teams has undertaken assessments and counsel in thirty countries since 2001 with varying degrees of effectiveness. Less clear is how much has changed in the countries benefitting from these APRM inquiries. Meanwhile, in early April 2012 ECOWAS successfully asserted collective leadership in persuading the coup leaders in Mali to step aside, though as this is written, what steps will be taken concerning the assertion of an independent Tuareg state of Azawad, carved out of northern and eastern Mali, remains unclear.

Reno's chapter chronicles the core problem of building strong, capable states on the foundations weakened by decades of pervasive postcolonial authoritarian and corrupt rule. His analysis implicitly illuminates important senses in which efforts to reform states democratically and to restore them following civil war or collapse is analogous to the proverbial construction of houses upon sand rather than rock as long as the clientelist networks that have sustained them remain in place. In particular, he observes that external efforts to strengthen either reigning regimes or their adversaries can easily animate these networks in counterproductive ways. In so doing his analysis lays bare both the implicit weakness of Africa-led efforts in many circumstances to eradicate these networks and the open question of precisely what steps might be taken to supplant them with sturdy, accountable, and transparent foundations of stateness.

Finally, the essays in Part Four articulate the challenges in enabling weak states to meet the standards of responsible sovereignty, defined as responsibility to protect the fundamental rights and welfare of citizens. In Chapter 12, Filip Reyntjens examines in depth the major components of the complex and enduring Great Lakes crisis centered on the essentially failed Democratic Republic of the Congo state but engaging also, principally, Rwanda, Uganda, Burundi, Zimbabwe, and Angola. He reports that while the worst of the crisis has subsided, the elements of its renewal remain in place, implicit testimony to the limits and failings as much as the achievements of UN missions in the region.

Princeton Lyman's chapter examines dimensions of the Sudan civil war resulting in the 2011 independence of South Sudan, but with resolution of few of the explosive issues underlying hostility between the now-independent states. Failures to facilitate coaxing of the two states to accommodation on these outstanding issues, he projects, may require the formulation of solutions by mediators, which, he observes, can also be effective only if backed by unanimous and total support by all the relevant external actors. A comparative examination of the roles of multilateral and bilateral actors in the cases of Liberia, Rwanda, and Mozambique lead Carrie Manning and Louis-Alexandre Berg to conclude in Chapter 10, however, that bilateral actors possess the resources and engagement to nudge African states to accept adoption costs of conflict settlements that multilateral actors alone lack. Indispensability of bilateral actors, collaborating with multilateral actors in mediating conflicts in African states, however, opens the door to possibly counterproductive pursuit by bilateral actors of their particular interests.

Lastly, Ian Taylor's account of China's extensive recent role in Africa points to potential long-term risks as well as the evident near-term benefits of this expanding relationship, a calculus extending by implication to other rising G-20 economies also increasingly engaged in the continent. An implicit premise of neoliberal economic reform mandated by the international financial institutions beginning in the 1980s that became more evident in the 1990s was that, to the extent enacted, these reforms would synchronize with primarily Western-sponsored post–Cold War democratic political reform. Less than clear in the new century's second decade is the extent to which that premise will be sustained in the era of expanded G-20 interventions in African economies.

PART II

HISTORICAL PARAMETERS

The chapters that follow in this section trace Africa's evolving engagement with changing global political and economic orders from the colonial era to the present. They blend a wide range of perspectives on these developing relationships in order to situate the continent properly, in all its diversity, within the family of nations. All three essays in this section reflect on the continuing legacies and burdens of the colonial era, a half century after most sub-Saharan African countries gained independence, even as they attest to glimmerings of significant progress in recent decades, progress that carries the potential to enable African nations to gain stature, respect, and influence in international affairs, leaving behind legacies of dependence and marginalization that most nations of the region have endured since independence.

Ali Mazrui's chapter on conquest and counter-conquest examines what has been arguably one of the most significant as well as one of the least noted measures of Africa's gradually but quietly acquired prominence in global affairs. As he observes, Africa has been singularly receptive to external cultural influences throughout its history. In what he describes as a "boomerang" effect, building upon the tolerance of non-proselytizing practice of indigenous African cultures, by dint of both numbers of converts and the creativity of their elites, he envisions Africa as an emerging global center of the very cultures that have "invaded" it over the centuries: Arabism, Islam, and Christianity, and even French civilization. While civil war and genocide have dogged the continent throughout its history, Mazrui reminds us that Africa has produced more Nobel laureates influenced by Gandhi's teaching than India itself. And yet he notes that Africa still must conquer itself, enabling cultures of peace, tolerance, and inclusiveness to prevail over conflict spurred as much by its adopted cultures as by its indigenous ones.

13

Africa has experienced no such boomerang effects with respect to the political legacies of colonial rule, which the leaders of Africa's independence movements projected with their visions of African socialism and one-party democracy. They have proven profoundly resistant to transformation and reform throughout the continent's half century of independence, even as welcome and hopeful glimmerings of reform and progress have appeared in the post–Cold War era. The Western conception of the state itself is a core legacy of imperialism, as Francis M. Deng reminds us in the book's concluding chapter. In his authoritative accounts of the colonial state in Chapter 2, Crawford Young observes that the "colonial legacy cast its shadow over the emergent African state system to a degree unique among the major world regions." Of central importance, "bureaucratic authoritarianism," he concludes, was "the institutional essence of the colonial state." He finds its perpetuation after independence, in the forms of single-party and military regimes, inter alia, that profoundly weakened whatever strengths colonial states had exhibited, sustained only by corrupting encrustation of networks of clientelism that have remained pervasive.

In Chapter 3, Todd Moss observes that during the twenty-first century African countries have their best opportunity since the first years of their independence to "boomerang" their economies from postcolonial global economic marginalization, poverty, and dependence to sustainable economic growth, equity, and global significance. This opportunity comes on the heels of what he terms the "lost decades of growth" for which, implicitly, donors as well as African countries have shared responsibility, first with their common belief that rapid transformation of African economies was possible, and then through IFI-imposed conditions that he concludes were a "total failure." Debt relief since the mid-1990s, inspired by the civil society efforts at a global level (Callaghy, 2008), has allowed African countries a fresh start fueled by continued IFI lending and delayed fulfillment of an IFI "implicit bargain" struck in the 1980s that private as well as public investment would attend IFI-imposed reforms (Callaghy and Ravenhill, 1993). While significantly expanded private investment in recent years is welcome, and an important factor in healthy growth rates for at least some countries, it is problematic, as Moss notes, for reasons that include its concentration in a few countries and less than full transparency about its terms especially when emanating from China and new G-20 sources. Moreover, the impact of this new private investment may be divisive, for Moss predicts that "international capital will help to drive that wedge between the next generation of emerging markets and those left behind." Not yet clear either is to what extent and in what ways, if at all, African governments will be encouraged and/or able to ensure that the resulting growth includes all segments of the population and is accompanied by significant reductions in poverty and inequality.

two

The Heritage of Colonialism

CRAWFORD YOUNG

Africa, in the rhetorical metaphor of imperial jingoism, was a ripe melon awaiting carving in the late nineteenth century. Those who scrambled fastest won the largest slices and the right to consume at their leisure the sweet, succulent flesh. Stragglers snatched only small servings or tasteless portions; Italians, for example, found only arid deserts on their plate. In this mad moment of imperial atavism—in Schumpeterian terms, the objectless disposition to limitless frontier expansion—no one imagined that a system of states was being created. Colonial rule, assumed by its initiators to be perpetual, later proved to be a mere interlude in the broader sweep of African history; however, the steel grid of territorial partition that colonialism imposed appears permanent. Although the patterns of disorder and state collapse that emerged in the 1990s led some to call for a reconsideration of the existing territorial system, the stubborn resilience of the largely artificial boundaries bequeathed by the colonial partition remains astonishing.[1]

Colonial heritage is the necessary point of departure for analysis of African international relations. The state system—which is, transnational vectors notwithstanding, the fundamental structural basis of the international realm—inherits the colonial partition. A few African states have a meaningful precolonial identity (Morocco, Tunisia, Egypt, Ethiopia, Burundi, Rwanda, Madagascar, Swaziland, Lesotho, and Botswana), but most are products of the competitive subordination of Africa—mostly between 1875 and 1900—by seven European powers (Great Britain, France, Germany, Belgium, Portugal, Italy, and Spain).

15

AFRICAN COLONIAL HERITAGE COMPARED

The colonial system totally transformed the historical political geography of Africa in a few years' time, and the depth and intensity of alien penetration of subordinated societies continues to cast its shadow.[2] The comprehensive linkages with the metropolitan economies in many instances were long difficult to disentangle. In the majority of cases in which decolonization was negotiated, the colonizer retained some capacity to shape the choice of postcolonial successors and often—especially in the French case—enjoyed extensive networks of access and influence long after independence was attained. The cultural and linguistic impact was pervasive, especially in sub-Saharan Africa, where the language of the colonizer continues to enjoy official status. Embedded in the institutions of the new states was the deep imprint of the mentalities and routines of their colonial predecessors. Overall, colonial legacy cast its shadow over the emergent African state system to a degree unique among the major world regions.

In Latin America, although colonial administrative subdivisions shaped the state system, Spain and Portugal swiftly ceased to be major regional players after Creole elites won independence in the nineteenth century. Great Britain and, later, the United States were the major external forces impinging upon the region. In Asia, the first target and long the crown jewel of the colonial enterprise, imperial conquest tended to follow the contours of an older state system; not all Asian states have a historical pedigree (the Philippines, Pakistan, Indonesia), but a majority do. The circumstances surrounding Asian independence, the discontinuities imposed by the Japanese wartime occupation of Southeast Asia, and the larger scale of most Asian states and the greater autonomy of their economies all meant that the demise of the colonial order there was far more sharp and definitive than was the case in Africa.

Perhaps the closest parallel to Africa in terms of durable and troubled colonial impact on regional international relations is found in the Middle East. The partition of the Ottoman domains in the Levant between Great Britain and France and the imperial calculus employed in territorial definitions and structures of domination left in their wake a series of cancerous conflicts. The duplicity of incompatible World War I promises to Arabs and Zionists bore the seeds of inextricable conflict over whether the Palestine mandate awarded to Great Britain by the League of Nations would develop as a Jewish homeland or an Arab state; Great Britain invented Jordan as a territory for its wartime ally Prince Abdullah; Lebanese borders were drawn so as to maximize the zone of dominance for Maronite Christians; Sunni Arab nationalism in Syria was countered by heavy recruitment of minority Alawites for the colonial militia, and Kurdish state demands were denied so that oil-rich zones could be attached to the British-Iraqi mandate.[3] The unending turbulence in this region provides daily confirmation of the colonial roots of many intractable contemporary conflicts. But even here, colonial penetration of Middle Eastern Arab societies and economies was much less than was the case in Africa, and the erstwhile colonial connections weigh less heavily.

In the African instance, the shadow of the colonial past falls upon the contemporary state system in several critical features. The sheer number of sovereign units and the weakness and vulnerability of many due to their small scale are the most obvious. At the same time, the struggle for territorial independence always had an associated pan-African vision, which became a permanent vector in African international relations. The continuing importance of former economic and political colonial linkages, most of all for the twenty states formerly under French rule, significantly shapes regional politics—both as an active channel of influence and as a negative point of reference. Finally, and perhaps most important, the bureaucratic authoritarianism, which was the institutional essence of the colonial state, quickly resurfaced in the guise of single-party or military regimes, whose failure led to the widespread state crisis by the 1980s.[4] In this chapter, I will consider these components of the colonial heritage in turn.

FRAGMENTATION OF AFRICA

The African continent in 2011 (and its offshore islands) contained no fewer than fifty-four sovereign units (using UN membership as the criterion)—nearly one-third of the world total.[5] Although this large number has some advantages in guaranteeing a voice in international forums where the doctrine of sovereign equality ensures equal voting rights for states large and small, this is little compensation for the disabilities of being tiny. Sheer economic weakness is one disadvantage. Most African states had a GNP less than the Harvard University endowment or the profits of a major multinational corporation. The limits of choice imposed by a narrow national market and circumscribed agricultural and mineral resource bases rendered most states highly vulnerable to the vagaries of commodity markets and the workings of the global economic system. Although some minuscule mercantile states elsewhere have achieved prosperity—Singapore is an obvious example—and tiny sovereignties perched on vast oil pools may accumulate enormous wealth—Kuwait, Bahrain, and Qatar are illustrations, now joined by Equatorial Guinea in Africa, of the microstates among Africa's fifty-four polities, only Mauritius, Equatorial Guinea, Cape Verde, and Seychelles have prospered.

The full scope of the fragmentation of independent Africa was not apparent until the virtual eve of independence. Most of the vast sub-Saharan domains under French domination were joined in two large administrative federations: Afrique Occidentale Française (AOF) and Afrique Equatoriale Française (AEF). Political life, however, germinated first at the territorial level; the crucial 1956 *Loi-cadre* (framework law) located the vital institutions of African political autonomy at this echelon. Although some nationalist leaders dreamed of achieving independence within the broader unit, especially in the AOF, the wealthier territories (Ivory Coast, Gabon) were strongly opposed. In the final compressed surge to independence, the interaction of divisions among nationalist leaders and movements, combined with French interests, resulted in twelve states of modest size rather than two large ones.[6] In the 1950s, Great Britain did promote federations of its colonial possessions as a formula for self-government in the West Indies, the United Arab Emirates, and Malaysia, as well as in east and central Africa, but with indifferent success. In east and central Africa, the fatal flaw was linking the project of broader political units to the entrenchment of special privilege for the European settler communities. Thus contaminated, the federation idea was bound to fail as a framework for independence, although the dream of an East African Federation was revived in the 1960s, and again at the turn of the twenty-first century.[7] In instances in which large territories had been governed as single entities—Nigeria, Sudan, Congo-Kinshasa— independence as one polity was possible, although all three countries have at times been beset by separatist pressures, and in 2011 Sudan broke in two.

Since sovereignty gave life to colonial territories as independent nations, the African state system has proven to be singularly refractory to broader movements of unification. The 1964 amalgamation of Tanganyika and Zanzibar to form Tanzania and the 1960 unification of British Somaliland and Italian-administered Somalia at the moment of independence remain the sole such cases. At times the Tanzania union with Zanzibar has been questioned, and in the wake of the collapse of a Somali state in 1991, Somaliland reemerged, although unrecognized by the international community, as a separate and functioning unit, in contrast to the prolonged anarchy in the rest of Somalia.

DREAM OF AFRICAN UNITY

The dream of a broader African unity persists, first nurtured by intellectuals of the diaspora and expressed through a series of pan-African conferences beginning in 1900, then embraced by the radical wing of African nationalism in the 1950s, above all, by Kwame Nkrumah of Ghana. The Organization of African Unity (OAU) was created in 1963 to embody this dream, but even its charter demonstrated its contradictions. The OAU was structured as a cartel of states whose territorial integrity was a foundational principle. Rather than transcending the state system, the OAU consolidated it. Although the vocation of African unity was reaffirmed with the 2002 official launch of the African Union to replace an OAU deemed moribund, the ascendancy of states remains.

The urgency of regional and ultimately continental unification is nonetheless repeatedly endorsed in solemn documents. Innumerable regional integration schemes have been launched, of which the most important are the (moribund) Union du Maghreb Arabe, the Economic Community of West African States, the Southern African Development Community, the various customs and monetary unions of the francophonic West African states, and renewed efforts to build an East African Federation. But the goal of effective integration remains elusive; the impact of the colonial partition remains an enduring obstacle.

The colonial origins of most African states weighed heavily upon the consciousness of postindependence rulers. Initially the fundamental illegitimacy of the boundaries was a central tenet of pan-African nationalism; the 1945 Manchester Pan-African Congress excoriated "the artificial divisions and territorial boundaries created by the Imperialist Powers." As late as 1958, the Accra All-African Peoples' Conference denounced "artificial frontiers drawn by the imperialist Powers to divide the peoples of Africa" and called for "the abolition or adjustment of such frontiers at an early date."[8] But once African normative doctrine was enunciated by the states rather than by nationalist movements, the tone changed, and the sanctity of colonial partition frontiers was asserted. The consensus of the first assembly of African independent states—also in Accra in 1958—was expressed by Nkrumah, the leading apostle of African unification: "Our conference came to the conclusion that in the interests of that Peace which is so essential, we should respect the independence, sovereignty and territorial integrity of one another."[9]

The OAU charter referred to territorial integrity no fewer than three times; at the Cairo OAU summit in 1964, the assembled heads of state made the commitment even more emphatic by a solemn pledge to actively uphold existing borders, a level of responsibility that goes significantly further than the mere passive recognition of the inviolability of frontiers.[10] Although a certain number of boundary disputes have arisen in independent Africa, the principle of the sanctity of colonial partition boundaries—the juridical concept of *uti possidetis*—remains a cornerstone of a solidifying African regional international law.[11] Most of the disputes have been resolved by negotiation, applying the colonial treaties as the point of juridical reference.[12] The enduring fear of the fragility of the African state system paradoxically endows the artificial, colonially imposed boundaries with astonishing durability. The one apparent exception—the independence of Eritrea from Ethiopia in 1993—can be said to prove the point. Eritrean nationalists grounded their claim to self-determination in the argument that Eritrea, as a former Italian colonial territory, should have had the opportunity for independence like all other former colonies, rather than being forcibly joined (in the Eritrean view) to Ethiopia by the international community. The same argument is advanced by the Western Saharan independence movement to contest Moroccan annexation justified by precolonial historic claims.

The colonial system profoundly reordered economic as well as political space. During their seventy-five years of uncurbed sovereignty, colonial powers viewed their African domains as veritable *chasses gardées* (private preserves). Metropolitan capital enjoyed privileged access; to varying degrees, other foreign investment was viewed with reserve or even hostility (especially by the Portuguese until the final colonial years). The security logic of the colonial state joined the metropolitan conviction that the occupant was entitled to exclusive economic benefits in return for the "sacrifice" of supplying governance services to foster trade and investment linkages, which tied African territories to metropolitan economies as subordinated appendages. Territorial infrastructures, particularly the communications systems, were shaped by the vision of imperial integration; road networks ran from the centers of production to the ports and colonial capitals. Although over time a shrinkage of the once-exclusive economic ties with the erstwhile colonizers has occurred, these bonds were so pervasive that they have been difficult to disentangle. It is no accident that regional economic integration schemes joining states once under different colonial jurisdictions have had only limited success; the most resilient mechanism of regional economic cooperation has been the Communauté Financière Africaine (CFA) franc zone, a product of the economic space defined by the former French empire in sub-Saharan Africa.

INFLUENCE OF FORMER COLONIZERS

The colonial occupation of Africa, which occurred relatively late in the global history of imperial expansion, was comparatively dense and thorough. The multiplex apparatus of domination was constructed to ensure the "effective occupation" stipulated by the 1884–1885 Berlin Conference as a condition for the security of the proprietary title and to extract from the impoverished subjects the labor service and fiscal tribute to make alien hegemony self-financing. As metropolitan finance ministries required, this apparatus was unlikely to dissolve instantly once the occupying country's flag was lowered on independence day. Over time, the many linkages—both manifest and submerged—binding the decolonized state to the former metropole have slowly eroded. They were a central dimension in the international relations of new states, especially in the early years of independence. Even five decades later, especially in the case of France, colonial connections still play a role.

Several factors influence the importance of ties with former colonizers. In those cases in which independence was won through armed liberation struggles rather than bargaining, the power transfer brought initial rupture (Algeria, Guinea-Bissau, Mozambique, Angola). In some other cases (Guinea, Congo-Kinshasa), the circumstances of independence brought immediate crisis and discontinuity in relationships; even though relations were ultimately restored, the degree of intimacy between the two countries could never be the same. Generally, the smaller erstwhile colonial powers played a less visible role than did the two major imperial occupants, Great Britain and France.

Italy was largely eliminated by being on the losing side in World War II. Although it regained a ten-year trust territory mission in Somalia in 1950, Rome was never permitted to return to Libya and Eritrea and quickly ceased to be a factor in either territory. Spain was the last country to enter the colonial scramble, and it had only a superficial hold on its territories in northwest Africa (former Spanish Morocco, Ifni, Western Sahara) and Equatorial Guinea. Its minor interests were swallowed up in postcolonial turmoil in its erstwhile domains (the Moroccan annexation of Western Sahara, the Macías Nguema capricious tyranny in Equatorial Guinea from its independence in 1968 until 1979). Emblematic of Spain's elimination from Africa was the affiliation of Equatorial Guinea with the French-tied CFA franc zone after Macías Nguema was overthrown in 1979.[13]

Belgium retained a role in its small former colonies of Rwanda and Burundi, but its economic interests in these states were not large. In Congo-Kinshasa, where the financial stake was considerable, relationships were punctuated with repeated crises.[14] The sudden and aborted power transfer left inextricably contentious disputes over the succession to the extensive colonial state holdings in a wide array of colonial corporations. These disputes were seemingly resolved several times, only to reemerge in new forms of contention.[15]

In the Portuguese case, an imperial mythology of the global Lusotropical multiracial community was a keystone of the corporatist authoritarianism of the Salazar-Caetano *Estado Novo*. However, the utter discrediting of this regime by its ruinous and unending colonial wars in Africa from 1961 to 1974 brought it repudiation.[16] More broadly, in the postcolonial era, a common element for the minor participants in the African partition was an abandonment of earlier notions that overseas proprietary domains validated national claims to standing and respect in the international arena.

Particularly intriguing has been the relative effacement over time of Great Britain on the African scene. Great Britain has long seen itself as a great power, although the resources to support such a claim silently ebbed away because of imperial overreach, according to one influential analysis.[17] In the 1950s, as the era of decolonization opened for Africa, conventional wisdom held that Great Britain was the most likely of the colonizers to maintain a permanent role in its vast colonial estates because of the flexible framework for evolution supplied by the British Commonwealth. This illusion proved to be based upon false inferences deduced from the older constellation of self-governing dominions, which had remained closely bound in imperial security relationships with London. Many thought the Commonwealth could preserve a British-ordered global ensemble beyond the formal grant of sovereignty in Asia and Africa. The illusion of permanence in which British imperialism had so long basked dissipated slowly.[18] The doctrine enunciated at the 1926 Imperial Conference still dominated official thinking as the African hour of self-government approached. This document perceived the future as incorporating "autonomous communities within the British Empire, equal in status, in no way subordinate one to another in any aspect of their domestic or external affairs, though united by a common allegiance to the Crown and freely associated as members of the British Commonwealth of Nations."[19] As one of its commentators then wrote: "The British Empire is a strange complex. It is a heterogeneous collection of separate entities, and yet it is a political unit. It is wholly unprecedented; it has no written constitution; it is of quite recent growth; and its development has been amazingly rapid."[20] Membership is even open to countries never under British rule, such as Mozambique and Rwanda, which joined after 1995.

These lyrical notions of a global commonwealth operating in a loose way as a political unit in world affairs so that Great Britain's claim to major power status might survive the decolonization of the empire eroded slowly. India's independence in 1947 was a crucial turning point; with the country as the true jewel in the imperial crown, its metamorphosis from the pivot of empire security to a self-assertive "neutralist" Asian power should have ended the illusion that an enlarged commonwealth could remain in any sense a "political unit." Yet when African members of the Commonwealth began joining with Ghanaian independence in 1957, some of the old mystique still persisted.

For most former British territories, joining the Commonwealth formed part of the *rite de passage* of independence; only Egypt and Sudan declined to enter its ranks.[21] Paradoxically, as Commonwealth membership became numerically dominated by Asian, African, and Caribbean states, it ceased to serve as a loose-knit, worldwide, British-inspired combine, and its meetings became occasions for heated attacks on British policy in Rhodesia and South Africa.

Instead of the ingenious instrument for the subtle nurture of British global influence its designers imagined, the Commonwealth thus seemed by the 1970s a funnel for unwelcome pressures upon British diplomacy. Even imperial nostalgia could not stave off recognition of these facts; waning British interest removed the Commonwealth's energizing center. In the words of one influential study, "The Commonwealth has survived only in [a] very attenuated form. . . . [It is] still a useful argumentative forum for its governments, offering a place for small states to be heard, extending benefits (albeit on a modest scale) to its members, and providing opportunities for discussion of problems of common interest."[22] This adjustment in the British images of the Commonwealth goes hand in hand with the gradual reduction of London's self-perception—from global hegemon to middle-size European power.

The diminishing mystique of the Commonwealth as the vessel for a global British role helps to explain the relative effacement of Great Britain on the African scene. In the first years of African independence, British disposition for intervention was still visible. In the army mutinies that swept Uganda, Kenya, and Tanganyika in 1964, British troops intervened to check the mutineers, at the request of the embattled regimes. In Nigeria, Great Britain initially had a defense agreement; however, this was annulled in 1962 due to Nigerian nationalist pressure. In a number of cases, national armies remained under British command for a few years after independence; in 1964, the British commander of the Nigerian army refused the solicitation of some Nigerian leaders to intervene after scandal-ridden national elections brought the country to the brink of disintegration. Security assistance and economic aid in modest quantities continue, and in a few cases—most notably Kenya—influence remains significant. But since 1970, the relatively subdued role of Britain, if set against the expectations of 1960, is what stands out. One striking recent exception was the energetic British military intervention under a UN cover in 1999–2000 in Sierra Leone, which put a final end to the macabre atrocities of the rebel Revolutionary United Front of Foday Sankoh.

THE FRENCH CONNECTION

The case of France, which has played a pervasive role in the seventeen sub-Saharan states formerly under its rule, is completely different from that of Great Britain. The political, cultural, economic, and military connection Paris has maintained with the erstwhile *bloc africain de l'empire* has been frequently tutelary, often intrusive, and sometimes overtly interventionist. The intimacy and durability of these linkages are as surprising as the eclipse of the United Kingdom. When African independence loomed on the horizon, France still suffered from its World War II humiliation and bitter internal divisions. The country was weakened by the chronic instability of the Fourth Republic, with one-third of its electorate aligned with the antiregime Stalinist French Communist Party and its army locked in unending and unwinnable colonial wars—first in Indochina, then in Algeria. *France Against Itself* was the title of the most influential portrait of the epoch.[23] Few anticipated the recapture of its European status and sub-Saharan role as regional hegemon under the Fifth Republic.

In grasping the pervasive African role of the resurrected postcolonial France, one first must draw a sharp distinction between the Maghreb and sub-Saharan Africa, which is sometimes overlooked in the fascination with the French connection. In reality, French influence was shattered in what had been the most important parts of the former empire: North Africa and Indochina. In terms of the size of the economic stake, AOF (French West Africa federation) and especially AEF (French Equatorial Africa federation) were far behind the core regions of the imperial era. Psychologically, the heart of overseas France was Algeria, whose northern portions were considered to be full French departments. The savagery of the eight-year war for Algerian independence, especially the self-destructive fury of its final phases, compelled the exodus of most of the one million French settlers and the abandonment of much of their stranglehold on the Algerian economy.[24] The independent Algerian state pursued a consistently radical anti-imperial foreign policy until the 1990s, rendered financially possible by its relatively ample oil and natural gas revenues. Although Tunisia and Morocco were less assertive in international politics and leaned toward Western positions in their nonalignment, neither accepted the degree of French tutelage that was common in sub-Saharan Africa.

Several factors explain the comprehensive nature of the French relationship with sub-Saharan states formerly under its domination.[25] The terminal colonial effort in this zone to construct an elusive "federalism" as permanent institutional bonding, although failing in its manifest goal of defining political status short of independence, had important consequences. The representation accorded emergent African leaders in the Fourth and (briefly) the Fifth Republics in French institutions, especially the Parliament, but also the cabinet of ministers, drew much of the sub-Saharan independence generation into the heart of French political processes. In the Algerian instance, Paris representation was dominated by settler interests and a small number of collaborating Algerians; Tunisia and Morocco, which had a different international legal status, were not given parliamentary seats.

Sub-Saharan Africans elected to French Parliament were far more representative of emergent political forces than the few Algerians who served in the

Paris Legislative Assembly. As early as the 1946 constitutional deliberations, Léopold Senghor of Senegal played an influential role. By the late Fourth Republic, African leaders held ministerial positions as well (for example, future presidents Félix Houphouët-Boigny of Ivory Coast, Modibo Keita of Mali). Until literally the eve of independence, the "federal" formula the Fifth Republic Constitution sought to institutionalize had the assent of most of the current francophone African political class, with the exception of the more radical intelligentsia—especially the students. The referendum approving the Fifth Republic Constitution in 1958, which proposed keeping the French-ruled sub-Saharan territories within a French sovereign framework, drew large, usually overwhelming majorities in all territories except Guinea, reflecting the strong wishes of the African leadership for its approval. Jarring as his words now sound, Houphouët-Boigny spoke for a political generation in his often-quoted 1956 statement: "To the mystique of independence we oppose the reality of fraternity." The degree of incorporation of the sub-Saharan African political elite into the French political world in the 1940s and 1950s has no parallel, and it left a lasting imprint on the texture of postcolonial relationships.[26] Successive French presidents from Charles de Gaulle to Jacques Chirac brought to office long-standing intimate ties with many sub-Saharan political leaders, linkages notably absent with former President Nicolas Sarkozy.

The original Fifth Republic concept of sub-Saharan territorial autonomy with an array of core sovereign functions (defense, money, and justice, for example) vested in the France-centered French community swiftly vanished.[27] In its place emerged an array of devices giving institutional expression to intimacy. Some form of defense accord was negotiated with fourteen sub-Saharan former colonies;[28] French troops were permanently garrisoned in Djibouti, the Central African Republic, Gabon, the Ivory Coast, and Senegal; and a reserve intervention force earmarked for swift African deployment was held in readiness in France. Except for Guinea, Mali, Mauritania, and Madagascar, all these ex-colonies remained within a French currency zone (and Guinea and Mali eventually sought reentry).

By the 1970s, Franco-African summit conferences became a regular and lavish part of the diplomatic landscape; often these attracted more heads of state than the OAU or AU summits. *Francophonie* as a cultural instrument finds expression in the French educational systems and linguistic policies; the nurture of the French language enjoys a priority in French diplomacy that is unique among former colonizers. In the Maghreb, *francophonie* competes with the active policies of affirmation of the Arab language and culture; in sub-Saharan Africa (excepting Madagascar and Mauritania), retention of French as the primary state vehicle has been internalized as a political value by most of the state class.[29] Even a populist socialist leader such as Alphonse Massemba-Débat of Congo-Brazzaville exclaimed in the late 1960s that the Congolese and the French were "Siamese twins," separable only by surgery.[30] Senghor, who was the most intellectually brilliant member of the independence political generation, summed up the pervasive relationship as *francité* (Frenchness, France-hood).[31] His induction into the Académie Française was, in his own eyes, a crowning achievement in a splendid career. A neologism such as *francité* has plausible resonance in the Franco-African case, but its analogues would be preposterous in characterizing any other postcolonial ties.

A singular form of tutelary, or dependent, linkages results from this broad set of connections, not all of which are well captured in the visible aspect of politics or in the asymmetrical core-periphery economic flows to which "dependency theory" draws attention. The francophonic African community counts upon the senior French partner to defend its interests within the European Union and among the international financial institutions, both public and private. Priority access to French aid is assumed, including periodic budgetary bailouts for the more impoverished states.[32] French willingness to occasionally intervene militarily to protect clients is of crucial importance; between 1960 and 2003, Victor Le Vine tallied fifteen major instances of such intervention.[33] As then-president Valéry Giscard d'Estaing stated, "We have intervened in Africa whenever an unacceptable situation had to be remedied."[34] Perhaps even more critical to the nurture of tutelary standing are French security services of a more clandestine nature. French intelligence services provide invaluable protection to rulers by their capacity to monitor and penetrate opposition groups and to foil potential conspiracies by providing early warning to incumbents. These security operations have always enjoyed high-level attention in Paris through such presidential advisers as the late éminence grise Jacques Foccart, master manipulator of the shadowy *réseaux* (networks) that provided the sinews of *Françafrique* from 1960 until his death in 1987. The absence of a full replacement is one measure of the slow decline of *Françafrique* itself.

In the early years of the twenty-first century, there are signs that the silken threads binding francophonic Africa to France are fraying. France made no move to prevent the overthrow of Hissène Habré by armed insurgents enjoying Libyan support in Chad at the end of 1990, although French troops in Chad could have easily prevented the takeover, and French air power did block an effort by armed insurgents to oust his successor, Idriss Déby Itno. Nor did France lift a finger to avert the overthrow of Ivory Coast ruler Henri Bédié in December 1999 when he was forced out by a military coup, although French contingents served under a UN mandate to separate the parties to a 2002–2003 civil war, and also in the final action on behalf of the AU and UN to oust usurper Laurent Gbagbo in 2011, and install the elected president, Al-lasane Ouattara.[35]

Supporting the CFA franc zone is more expensive and less profitable than it once was, and France engineered a large devaluation in 1994, in the face of heated opposition by a number of African clients. Protection of friendly incumbents appears to have lost some of its attraction, as in early 1990, France softened its long-held view that single-party rule, with its corollary of life presidency, was the most "realistic" political formula for Africa. But the closely woven fabric of the French connection is too sturdy to quickly unravel, and France was more ambivalent toward democratization than the other former colonial powers.

STRUGGLE TO ELIMINATE COLONIAL INFLUENCE

The importance of the colonial past in shaping contemporary African international relations is thus beyond dispute. At the same time, the colonial system serves—paradoxically—as a negative point of reference for the African concert of nations. The legitimacy of the first generation of African regimes was rooted in the regimes' achievement—by conquest or negotiation—of independence. The two transcendent unifying principles of the pan-African movement from its inception have been opposition to both colonialism and racism, evils that were joined on the African continent. The independent states that assembled to create the OAU in 1963 were divided on many questions of ideology and interpretation of nonalignment; all could rally behind the combat to complete the liberation of Africa from colonial occupation and regimes of white racial domination. The elemental notion of African solidarity arose out of the shared experience of racial oppression, a point made explicit by W. E. B. DuBois many years ago:

> There is slowly arising not only a curiously strong brotherhood of Negro blood throughout the world, but the common cause of the darker races against the intolerable assumption and insults of Europeans has already found expression. Most of humanity are people of color. A belief in humanity means a belief in [people of color]. The future world will in all reasonable possibility be what colored men make of it.[36]

Nearly five decades later, Julius Nyerere translated these thoughts into African nationalist language: "Africans all over the continent, without a word being spoken, either from one individual to another, or from one African country to another, looked at the European, looked at one another, and knew that in relation to the European they were one."[37]

Indeed, at the moment of the OAU's creation, many of the most arduous independence struggles still lay ahead, such as those in the Portuguese territories, Zimbabwe, and Namibia, as well as the mortal combat with apartheid in South Africa. The OAU had a mediocre record in coping with conflicts within Africa (Somalia, Liberia, Eritrea, Western Sahara, the Nigerian civil war, the Congo rebellions, and Chad-Libya, for example). However, its anticolonial role has been important in providing a continental focus for African liberation diplomacy.

Within their own territorial domain, independent states faced a compulsion to demarcate themselves from their colonial past, to render visible the new status. The superficial symbolic accoutrements of independence—flags and postage stamps—might serve for a time. Africanization of the state apparatus might help as well, although over time, the perception could arise that the real benefits of this change accrued above all to state personnel.

The imperative of demarcation eventually spread to the economic realm. In the 1970s, a wave of seizures of foreign assets with potent colonial connotations swept through Africa: Idi Amin's "economic war" against the Asian community in 1972, Mobutu Sese Seko's "Zairianization" (Congolization) and "radicalization" campaigns of 1973 and 1974, Tanzania's socialization measures after the 1967 Arusha Declaration, the 1972 and 1976 Nigerian "indigenization decrees," the copper-mine nationalizations in Zambia and Congo-Kinshasa, and parallel measures in many other countries. Measures of expropriation of foreign assets almost exclusively affected holdings associated with the colonial past. This partly reflected a distinction often made between postindependence investments, which involved contractual commitments (presumably) freely made by the African state, and those made under alien sovereignty, which lacked moral standing (and doubtless had been well amortized). More important, moves to indigenize the economy reflected pressures to move beyond purely political independence, which would be denatured if all the structures of economic subordination remained intact. By the 1980s, this surge of economic demarcation had run its course; the deepening economic crisis and heightened vulnerability to external pressures made such measures unfeasible. In addition, the measures were frequently discredited by the chaotic improvisation of their implementation and consequent dislocations (Congo-Kinshasa, Uganda) or by the perception that only narrow politico-mercantile classes had benefited (Nigeria).[38]

The compulsion for demarcation from the colonial past was driven by psychological as well as political and economic factors. Particularly in sub-Saharan Africa, the colonial era brought a broad-front assault upon African culture that was far more comprehensive than similar experiences in the Middle East and Asia. The "colonial situation," to borrow Georges Balandier's evocative concept,[39] was saturated with racism. African culture was, for the most part, regarded as having little value, and its religious aspect—outside the zones in which Islam was well implanted—was subject to uprooting through intensive Christian evangelical efforts, which were often state-supported. European languages supplanted indigenous ones for most state purposes; for the colonial subject, social mobility required mastering the idiom of the colonizer. In innumerable ways, colonial subjugation in Africa brought not only political oppression and economic exploitation but also profound psychological humiliation. In the nationalist response to colonialism, psychological themes are prevalent to a degree unique in Third World anti-imperialist thought. Frantz Fanon, the Martinique psychiatrist who supplied so powerful a voice to the Algerian revolution, was only the most eloquent such spokesman.[40] Such doctrines as *négritude* and "African personality" were central components in nationalist thought, asserting the authenticity and value of African culture. This dimension of African nationalism gave a special emotional edge to the postcolonial quest for demarcation, as well as to the fervor of African state reaction to racism and colonialism.

Colonial heritage as a negative point of reference also influenced the contours of Cold War intrusion into Africa. The United States and the Soviet Union both represented themselves as alternatives to exclusive reliance of African nations upon the erstwhile colonizers for succor and support, as has China more recently. Particularly in the early phases of independence, visible Soviet linkages served as a badge of demarcation. The extravagant fears of all colonizers—and of the West generally—regarding "Communist penetration" of Africa enhanced the value of Soviet relations, even if Soviet economic assistance was minimal. For those states that wanted (or felt compelled to undertake) a more comprehensive break with the Western colonial system, for a short period in the early 1960s and again in the 1970s, the Soviet bloc appeared to offer an alternative. The bargain proved to be rather fruitless, however, as the Soviet Union began to disengage from Africa in the early 1980s.[41]

AUTHORITARIAN LEGACY OF THE COLONIAL STATE

Finally, the defining attribute of the colonial state in Africa until its final years was the monopoly of central authority enjoyed by its almost entirely European top administration. The structures of a postindependence polity were grafted onto the robust trunk of colonial autocracy, which proved a much more enduring legacy than the hastily created and weakly rooted democratic institutions normally assembled at the final hour before independence. The command habits and authoritarian routines of the colonial state were in most countries soon reproduced in single-party or military-political monopolies.

In the final colonial years after World War II, the superstructure of imperial rule had become well professionalized, its European cadres trained in specialized institutes, and its chiefly African intermediaries now requiring literacy and competence as well as customary qualifications. The imperial administration enjoyed exceptional insulation from an emergent African civil society denied organizational scope till the eve of independence by repressive colonial legislation. The African colonial state was a pure model of bureaucratic authoritarianism.

Swelling postwar colonial revenues fueled by the global commodity boom, and for the first time significant metropolitan public investment, yielded rapid expansion of state services and social infrastructure in the final colonial decade. Though some authors, notably Jeffrey Herbst, argue that the colonial state was weak,[42] in my reading, in the form bequeathed to the African independence elite generation, the late colonial state was a robust and effective hegemonic apparatus habituated to a command relationship with its subject population. The African state weakness stressed in the introductory chapter is rather a product of political itineraries since 1960 than an immediate consequence of colonial legacy.[43]

Postcolonial rulers, inspired by a vision of high modernity to be swiftly realized, sought a rapid expansion in the mission and scope of the state.[44] African independence coincided with a moment of peak confidence in state-led development; the example of apparent centrally planned transformation of the Soviet Union and China stood as potent models. To release the developmental state from the constraints of democratic process, the fragile representative institutions belatedly created by the withdrawing colonizer for the transition to independence were set aside in favor of single parties or, when these lost public favor, military regimes restoring the colonial legacy of authoritarian rule.

However, effective centralization and monopolization of power and political space did not suffice to ensure the unhindered hegemony of the postcolonial state, which could never match the autonomy from society enjoyed by the imperial bureaucracy. The command state could not operate on the basis of impersonal authority and coercive force alone; indispensable were supplementary mechanisms translating state rule into personalized linkages with key intermediaries and their ramifying networks of clientele. By subtle metamorphosis the bureaucratic authoritarianism of the colonial state legacy became the patrimonial autocracy almost everywhere ascendant by the 1970s. As numerous works attest,[45] this pathway led to the economic and political bankruptcy afflicting most states by the calamitous 1980s, and the battered, delegitimated—and weak—state that faced the democracy moment of 1990, a tale beyond the scope of this chapter.

Thus, in various ways, the colonial heritage intrudes into postindependence African international relations. Perhaps more than five decades after the great surge to independence in 1960, the colonial shadow begins to fade, overwritten by the turbulent history of the postindependence years. Important new trends that may tug colonial legacy further into the background will have a critical impact as the new century unfolds.[46] The end of the Cold War has already had a profound influence. A widening consensus that regional integration that bridges the old colonial divisions is indispensable to overcoming them, which may lead to innovations in the state system that will begin to transcend the colonial partition. For the first half century of African independence, however, colonial heritage has powerfully shaped the African international system.

NOTES

1. Jeffrey Herbst, *States and Social Power in Africa: Comparative Lessons in Authority and Control* (Princeton, NJ: Princeton University Press, 1994).

2. For a more extended argument on the pathology of the African colonial state, see Crawford Young, *The African Colonial State in Comparative Perspective* (New Haven, CT: Yale University Press, 1994).

3. In the extensive literature on these themes, I have found especially useful Charles Issawi, *An Economic History of the Middle East and North Africa* (New York: Columbia University Press, 1972); Peter Sluglett, *Britain in Iraq, 1914–1932* (London: Ithaca Press, 1976); William Roger Louis, *The British Empire in the Middle East, 1945–1951: Arab Nationalism, the United States, and Postwar Imperialism* (Oxford: Clarendon Press, 1984); George Antonius, *The Arab Awakening* (New York: Capricorn Books, 1965); and Mary C. Wilson, *King Abdulla, Britain and the Making of Jordan* (Cambridge: Cambridge University Press, 1987).

4. This argument is advanced in detail in Young, *The African Colonial State*.

5. This total does not include Western Sahara, which is recognized as a member state by the Organization of African Unity but not by the United Nations. Eritrea and South Africa were added in the 1990s.

6. The most careful political history of this process of fragmentation is Joseph-Roger de Benoist, *La Balkanisation de l'Afrique Occidentale Française* (Dakar, Senegal: Nouvelles Editions Africaines, 1979). His study clearly demonstrates that the balkanization was less a product of Machiavellian French design than the outcome of a complicated interplay of African political competition and French improvised response. Resentment of the distant bureaucratic despotism of the AOF French administrative headquarters was common in the outlying territories. Those nationalist leaders who at various times fought to preserve the unit—Léopold Senghor, Sékou Touré, Modibo

Keita—were constrained both by their own rivalries and by the absence of a strong popular attachment to the AOF as a geographical entity.

7. Among the works on this subject, see Arthur Hazlewood, ed., *African Integration and Disintegration* (London: Oxford University Press, 1967); Joseph S. Nye, *Pan-Africanism and East African Integration* (Cambridge: Cambridge University Press, 1965); Patrick Keatley, *The Politics of Partnership* (Harmondsworth, UK: Penguin Books, 1964); Philip Mason, *Year of Decision: Rhodesia and Nyasaland in 1960* (London: Oxford University Press, 1960); and Donald S. Rothchild, *Toward Unity in Africa: A Study of Federalism in British Africa* (Washington, DC: Public Affairs, 1960).

8. Saadia Touval, *The Boundary Politics of Independent Africa* (Cambridge, MA: Harvard University Press, 1972), pp. 22–23, 56–57.

9. Ibid., p. 54.

10. Onyeonoro S. Kamanu, "Secession and the Right of Self-Determination: An O.A.U. Dilemma," *Journal of Modern African Studies* 12, no. 3 (1974), pp. 371–373.

11. *Uti possidetis* is derived from a Roman private law concept that holds that pending litigation, the existing state of possession of immovable property is retained. Translated into international law, the phrase means that irrespective of the legitimacy of the original acquisition of territory, the existing disposition of the territory remains in effect until altered by a freely negotiated treaty. For a passionate attack on this doctrine by a Moroccan jurist, see Abdelhamid El Ouali, "L'uti possidetis ou le non-sens du principe de base de l'OUA pour le règlement des différends territoriaux," *Le mois en Afrique* 227–228 (December 1984–January 1985), pp. 3–19.

12. For major studies on African boundary issues, see, in addition to the previously cited Touval work, Ricardo René Larémont, *Borders, Nationalisms, and the African State* (Boulder, CO: Lynne Rienner Publishers, 2005); Carl Gosta Widstrand, ed., *African Boundary Problems* (Uppsala, Sweden: Scandinavian Institute of African Studies, 1969); A. I. Asiwaju, *Partitioned Africans: Ethnic Relations Across Africa's International Boundaries, 1884–1984* (London: C. Hurst, 1984); Ian Brownlie, *African Boundaries: A Legal and Diplomatic Encyclopedia* (Berkeley: University of California Press, 1979); and Markus Kornprobst, "Border Disputes in African Regional Subsystems," *Journal of Modern African Studies* 40, no. 2 (2002), pp. 360–394.

13. On the limited nature of Spanish rule, see Ibrahim Sundiata, *Equatorial Guinea* (Boulder, CO: Westview Press, 1989); and Tony Hodges, *Western Sahara: The Roots of a Desert War* (Westport, CT: Lawrence Hill, 1983).

14. For thorough detail, see Gauthier de Villers, "Belgique-Zaire: Le grand affrontement," *Cahiers du CEDAF* 1–2 (1990).

15. For detail on the contentieux, see Crawford Young and Thomas Turner, *The Rise and Decline of the Zairian State* (Madison: University of Wisconsin Press, 1985), pp. 276–325. By the turn of the twenty-first century, the large corporations that had dominated the colonial economy had entirely redeployed their capital, and no longer had a Congo presence.

16. Patrick Chabal et al., *A History of Postcolonial Lusophone Africa* (Bloomington: Indiana University Press, 2002). In the revolutionary moment in Portugal following the coup in 1974 and 1975, some radical Portuguese leaders dreamed of a Marxist federation linking Portugal in an ideological federation to its former colonies; this vision was short-lived.

17. Paul Kennedy, *The Rise and Fall of the Great Powers: Economic Change and Military Conflict from 1500 to 2000* (New York: Vintage Books, 1987).

18. The phrase is drawn from the intriguing study by Francis G. Hutchins, *The Illusion of Permanence: British Imperialism in India* (Princeton, NJ: Princeton University Press, 1967).

19. Cited in Cecil J. B. Hurst et al., *Great Britain and the Dominions* (Chicago: University of Chicago Press, 1928), p. 9.

20. Ibid., p. 3.

21. South Africa, which had been a member since its accession to "dominion" status in 1910, quit in 1961 in the face of increasing attacks from the swelling ranks of African members but rejoined after the fall of the apartheid regime.

22. Dennis Austin, *The Commonwealth and Britain* (London: Routledge & Kegan Paul, 1988), pp. 62, 64.

23. Herbert Luthy, *France Against Itself* (New York: Meridian Books, 1959).

24. For a graphic account of the holocaust during the final year of the Algerian war, with a mutinous army and a murderous settler force—the Organization de l'Armée Secrète—see Paul Henissart, *Wolves in the City: The Death of French Algeria* (New York: Simon & Schuster, 1970).

25. Useful studies on this topic include Stephen Smith, *Voyage en postcolonie: Le nouveau monde franco-africain* (Paris: Bernard Grasset, 2010); Edward Corbett, *The French Presence in Black Africa* (Washington, DC: Black Orpheus Press, 1972); Guy Martin, "Bases of France's African Policy," *Journal of Modern African Studies* 23, no. 2 (1985), pp. 189–208; George Chaffard, *Les carnets secrets de la décolonisation* (Paris: Calmass-Levy, 1965); Pierre Pean, *Affaires africaines* (Paris: Fayard, 1983); and Charles-Robert Ageron, *Les chemins de la décolonisation de l'empire français, 1936–1956* (Paris: Editions du CNRS, 1986).

26. Victor T. Le Vine, *Politics in Francophone Africa* (Boulder, CO: Lynne Rienner Publishers, 2004), pp. 61–102.

27. For a painstaking account by a highly informed French observer, see Joseph-Roger de Benoist, *Afrique Occidentale Française de 1944 à 1960* (Dakar, Senegal: Nouvelles Editions Africaines, 1982).

28. Martin, "Bases of France's African Policy," p. 204.

29. One encounters some exceptions among the intelligentsia; one example was the late Cheikh Anta Diop of Senegal, a cultural nationalist of great influence who strongly urged promotion of the most widely spoken Senegalese language, Wolof. But overall, the commitment to French as the cultural medium is far more entrenched in the former French sub-Saharan territories than anywhere else in Africa.

30. Corbett, *The French Presence,* p. 66.

31. Léopold Sédar Senghor, *Ce que je crois: Négritude, francité et civilisation de l'universel* (Paris: B. Crasset, 1988).

32. In theory, financial injections to meet budgetary crises—most commonly, payments to civil servants—have long ceased; in practice, they continue to occur. For fascinating details on the process and its political importance, see Raymond Webb, "State Politics in the Central African Republic," PhD diss., University of Wisconsin–Madison, 1990.

33. Le Vine, *Politics in Francophone Africa,* pp. 380–381.

34. Martin, "Bases of France's African Policy," p. 194.

35. Thomas J. Bassett and Scott Straus, "Defending Democracy in Côte d'Ivoire," *Foreign Affairs* 90, no. 4 (2011), pp. 130–140.

36. Quoted in Victor Bakpetu Thompson, *Africa and Unity: The Evolution of Pan-Africanism* (London: Longman, 1969), p. 36.

37. Lecture by Julius Nyerere at Wellesley College, Wellesley, MA, April 1961; from my notes attending the lecture.

38. For details, see Crawford Young, *Ideology and Development in Africa* (New Haven, CT: Yale University Press, 1982).

39. Georges Balandier, "The Colonial Situation," in Pierre van den Berghe, ed., *Africa: Social Problems of Change and Conflict* (San Francisco: Chandler Publishing, 1965), pp. 36–57.

40. See, for example, Frantz Fanon, *Black Skin, White Masks* (New York: Grove Press, 1967). On this theme, see also O. Mannoni, *Prospero and Caliban: The Psychology of Colonization* (London: Methuen, 1956), and A. Memmi, *Portrait du colonisé, précédé du portrait du colonisateur* (Paris: Buchet-Chastel, 1957).

41. Arnold Hughes, ed., *Marxism's Retreat from Africa* (London: Frank Cass, 1992).

42. Herbst, *States and Social Power.*

43. For a more extended argument, see Young, *The African Colonial State.*

44. James C. Scott, *Seeing Like a State: How Certain Schemes to Improve the Human Condition Have Failed* (New Haven, CT: Yale University Press, 1998).

45. Among other sources, see Achille Mbembe, *On the Postcolony* (Berkeley: University of California Press, 2001); Mark R. Beissinger and Crawford Young, eds., *Beyond State Crisis? Postcolonial Africa and Post-Soviet Eurasia in Comparative Perspective* (Washington, DC: Woodrow Wilson Center Press, 2002); Patrick Chabal and Jean-Pascal Daloz, *Africa Works: Disorder as Political Instrument* (Oxford: James Currey, 1999); and Jean-François Bayart, *The State in Africa: The Politics of the Belly* (New York: Longman, 1993).

46. For analysis of some such trends, see Thomas Callaghy, Ronald Kassimir, and Robert Latham, eds., *Intervention and Transnationalism in Africa* (Cambridge: Cambridge University Press, 2001).

three

Reflections on Africa's Rocky Love-Hate Relationship with International Capital

TODD MOSS

Sub-Saharan Africa's rocky and volatile relationship with international capital markets has moved into a new phase. Private capital flows are rocketing upward just at a time when public sector aid flows are leveling off, and are expected to start declining. Overall, Africa should expect to make a transition soon, as happened in Asia and Latin America, where private capital becomes much more important than public aid. (If the data were better, it is possible we would know for sure whether this threshold has in fact already been crossed.) This trend not only represents a major financial watershed for the continent, but will also signify an important historical and political shift. This chapter outlines some of the key trends driving international public and private investment with the subcontinent, and highlights a few of the key policy agendas—and constraints—that remain.

LOST DECADES OF GROWTH

The starting point for any discussion of Africa's relationship with the global economy is the continent's dismal economic performance over the past half century. At independence, Africa's economic prospects were believed to be very bright. Both private and public investment flowed into the continent to support ambitious plans for rapid industrialization—on the widely held assumption that in the wake of investment flows, economic growth and indeed modernization would naturally follow. Most newly independent countries, supported by external donors, believed that the economic foundations in mining and farming could be quickly transformed, via robust government action and capital investment, into broad economic gains. Instead, most African economies faltered miserably. Several decades of postindependence investment and aggressive policy intervention were almost universally a dismal failure (Easterly and Levine 1997; Collier and Gunning 1999; van de Walle 2001; Easterly 2001). The subsequent period of adjustment and reflection has been equally long and, still today, the results are largely ambiguous. Even among those economies that have recovered the most ground and made the most improvements, few have successfully transitioned beyond the skeleton of the inherited colonial economy. (Copper, for instance, still accounts for more than three-quarters of Zambia's exports.)

Africa's headline economic growth rates—as measured by changes in real GNI (gross national income)—in the immediate postindependence period was fairly positive, with income per capita rising about 2.6 percent per year during the 1960s. But this slowed to just 0.9 percent per year in the 1970s and then turned sharply negative. The 1980s—often called the "lost decade" for Africa—saw average incomes decline by 1 percent per year. The 1990s were still a time of moving backward, albeit at only half the pace, with income per capita losing only 0.4 percent per year. Underneath these broad macroeconomic trends for the continent as a whole, there is of course great variance for individual countries. But of the thirty-three countries for which reasonable data are available, sixteen were poorer in 2000 than in 1970. The growth failure led to several outcomes: plunging incomes, mounting external debt burdens, and severe capital flight. This put Africa on a course for substantial financial dependence on a cartel of Western donors (Callaghy and Ravenhill 1993), which is only today being (selectively) broken.

THE RISE OF PUBLIC-SECTOR AID DEPENDENCY

By the early 1980s, many countries had hit bottom and had little choice but to continue to turn to the international financial institutions (IFIs) and Western donors for assistance. The donors almost always agreed to provide new capital, but only if the African governments promised to fix what donors viewed as the policy shortcomings that had caused the trouble in the first place. Although the economic problems across countries were diverse, there was a general agreement that many of the aggressive policies pursued by African governments were failing and that the state was not facilitating economic growth but rather strangling it.

A crucial aspect of the donor strategy was the promise of policy changes by recipients in exchange for aid—what came to be called "conditionality." A prerequisite for receiving new loans was agreeing with the lender on what the recipients would do differently. The centerpiece of this approach is the letter of intent written by a finance minister to the International Monetary Fund (IMF) outlining reform plans. At the time, such promises seemed reasonable given the poor economic performance and the long list of identifiable problems. The basket of macroeconomic reforms, based on changes adopted by Latin American countries facing their own not-dissimilar debt problems, came to be known as the "Washington Consensus" (see box). For the receiving governments, making a long series of promises seemed a fair price to pay for low-interest money to fill their budget gaps and to enable them to service their debt obligations. In practice, of course, conditionality was itself a near-total failure. Even if the policies the donors asked for seemed reasonable on paper, governments had little reason to actually implement policy changes and plenty of latitude to manipulate the system. In hindsight, it was also obvious that the dynamics of aid and bureaucratic inertia also provided donors few reasons to ever enforce their previous demands (Mosley 1992; Collier 1997).

The "Washington Consensus"

In 1990 economist John Williamson coined the phrase the "Washington Consensus" to describe (but not necessarily advocate) a list of the policies most commonly given as advice to Latin American countries in the late 1980s:

1. *Fiscal discipline.* Shrink large budget deficits that may create balance-of-payments crises and drive inflation.
2. *Reorder public expenditure priorities.* Switch spending away from the unproductive (e.g., subsidies, bloated civil services) to the productive (e.g., health, education, infrastructure).
3. *Tax reform.* Build a fair and effective tax system.
4. *Liberalize interest rates.* Encourage savings by lifting state control of interest rates.
5. *Liberalize the exchange rate.* End currency manipulation (which tended to favor imports at the expense of export competitiveness).
6. *Liberalize trade.* Reduce barriers to exchange of goods.
7. *Liberalize inward investment.* Reduce barriers to foreign investors.
8. *Privatization.* Sell state-owned industries, starting with those draining the treasury.
9. *Deregulation.* Reduce legal barriers to private business operations.
10. *Property rights.* Enforce contracts and encourage landownership.

SOURCE: John Williamson, 1990

The end result was nonetheless clear: steadily rising dependence of most African economies on publicly funded capital and on the advice from the providers of that very same aid. Despite a downturn in the immediate aftermath of the end of the Cold War, aid flow into Africa has been strong. Indeed, contemporary sub-Saharan Africa is by far the most aid-dependent region of the globe in history. By the late 2000s, at least twenty countries received total aid in excess of 10 percent of GDP. (By comparison, the US Marshall Plan to reconstruct postwar Europe never rose above 3 percent of any recipient European economy.) The ideological peak of the global aid movement was likely the 2005 summit of the Group of Eight at Gleneagles in Scotland when then–British prime minister Tony Blair extracted aggressive new commitments from all members, including pledges to double aid to Africa.

While the traditional donors have been increasing flows, new actors have also arrived. China's rapid and dramatic push into Africa has shaken much of the aid community (Brautigam 2010). China has long been involved in Africa, for example, building most of the stadiums and railroads constructed after independence. Yet, in recent years, China's engagement on the continent has accelerated spectacularly. The anecdotes are compelling: Chinese companies and workers are building major infrastructure projects in almost every African country, and China has announced enormous financing package deals for new projects (such as $9 billion in the Democratic Republic of the Congo and $13 billion in Ghana).

The true extent of Chinese investment, however, is largely unknown for several reasons. First, China does not have an "aid" program like other countries. Various agencies within the Chinese government and many state-owned companies engage in activities that appear aid-like, but also often have commercial purposes. (If a Chinese company builds a road from a Chinese mine to the port using subsidized credit from a Chinese bank, is that "aid"?) Second, China does not report its aid spending in any manner that allows comparison. The World Bank guesses Chinese aid is about $2 billion per year. Third, China is still very secretive with many of its activities, so it is difficult from the outside to know the terms of an announced deal (is the loan soft or hard?) or whether it is even real (as for all donors, announcements don't always lead to actual projects). Lastly, there is much speculation that many of the aid packages are part of larger deals, such as cheap loans in exchange for mining or oil concessions for Chinese companies.

These characteristics have sometimes put China and occasionally other new entrants, such as India or Saudi Arabia, in apparent conflict with other donors, who may be trying to promote transparency (of aid and natural resource contracts) or who deny aid to rogue regimes, such as those in Khartoum or Harare.

However, most of the mainstream donors have shifted resources to health and education and gotten out of funding roads, ports, and bridges. Thus the Chinese reasonably argue they are responding to demand from Africa for large infrastructure investments and are often seen on the continent as filling that need rather than displacing traditional donors.

THE BEGINNING—AND END—OF THE DEBT CRISIS

The buildup of the aid business over the decades—combined with repeated investments in projects that never led to the increased exports required to generate hard currency to repay foreign loans—eventually contributed to the debt crisis. Africa's debt became a significant problem in the 1980s when the total debt started to mount up at the same time that countries encountered problems paying back older loans. The total amount the continent owed grew from just $6 billion in 1970 (or about $22 billion in today's dollars, after adjusting for inflation) to nearly $200 billion by the mid-1990s. This debt represented less than 15 percent of the continent's total GDP in 1970 but jumped to over 100 percent by the 1990s. More important, it was clear that for many African countries these debts were unpayable and that the rising level of debt itself was becoming a barrier to progress on other fronts.

As early as the 1970s, bilateral creditors began writing off debts to some low-income countries or at least agreeing to easier repayment plans (Easterly 2002). For some creditors, it was merely another way to transfer resources to countries, either as another form of aid or to help a strategic ally. But it was also part of a growing realization that much of the old lending was lost. The past projects financed by old loans were probably not going to generate returns sufficient to enable repayment. The major bilateral official creditors organized into the Paris Club to provide a framework for renegotiating old debts. Even though various forms of debt relief were available in the 1980s and early 1990s, advocates began to call for more widespread and systematic debt relief. Campaigns, such as the Jubilee Movement, began to urge the rich-country creditors not just to reduce but also to erase the debts poor countries owed.

One problem was that the World Bank and IMF were not legally allowed to provide debt relief. As bilateral and other credit was dealt with, the multilateral financial institutions were left as the major sticking point. So in 1996, at the behest of their major shareholders, the IMF and World Bank created the heavily indebted poor countries (HIPC) initiative, which for the first time tackled multilateral credit. The HIPC process calls for countries to first seek a Paris Club deal, then, assuming their debt numbers are still too high, they can apply for HIPC, which determines eligibility based on debt sustainability and some record of good performance. In 1999 the initiative was enhanced and the terms were softened further, including 90 percent bilateral relief on Cologne terms and further multilateral debt reductions through HIPC.* In 2005 the major economic powers agreed to even further cuts among the HIPC-qualified countries, with up to 100 percent debt reduction for the qualified countries. The so-called multilateral debt relief initiative (MDRI) expanded the HIPC program to completely erase the remaining debt owed to the World Bank, the IMF, and the regional African Development Bank.

SEEDS OF A NEW DEBT CRISIS?

These efforts effectively made debt a passé problem (with the exception of a handful of countries, such as Myanmar or Zimbabwe, who were left out of the process, for a variety of reasons). However, countries that go through HIPC and have their books cleaned usually want to borrow again. Such countries frequently ask the IMF for more "flexibility" in deciding when they should be allowed to borrow again and how much new debt they can assume responsibly. The IMF, under growing pressure from borrowers, tweaked the formulas used to determine debt sustainability. In effect, HIPC has—as some critics of the program charged it would—not only erased the debt problem but also cleared the decks for countries to start borrowing again. While MDRI was supposed to be the final answer, some have asked whether we might just be back with the same problem in a few years.

In fact, there are already some worrying signs. First, many of the same financial institutions (the World Bank, IMF, and African Development Bank) have been relending to the very same countries. Surprisingly, the lending has been at a similar rate: in the years immediately before MDRI, lending to all HIPC countries was about $4 billion per year; in the years after MDRI, the lending volume was roughly the same (Leo 2009). During the financial crisis of 2008–2009, new lending volumes went even higher as part of a fiscal stimulus aimed at preventing recession. While most bilateral donors have shifted to giving grants instead of loans to these low-income countries, a few bilaterals (France, Spain, Japan) still mostly lend.

Second, borrowing from new creditors, such as China, Iran, India, and Saudi Arabia, has grown just as the HIPCs are finally getting out from under

---

*Cologne terms featured up to 90 percent reduction added in 1999 for HIPC countries. These terms followed those forged in Naples (67 percent) and preceded the Evian terms (up to 100 percent).

their debts. For example, within a few years of Ghana's receiving nearly $4 billion in debt relief under HIPC/MDRI, the country agreed to a $13 billion credit line with two Chinese banks. Some countries didn't even wait for the ink to dry: the Democratic Republic of the Congo finalized a $9 billion line of credit agreement with China at the same time it was completing the HIPC process. Though some of these new loans are for construction projects that may very well turn out to be good investments (thus justifying the new borrowing), these new lenders typically do not reveal the terms of their loans, and the deals are often shrouded in secrecy—which raises all kinds of new worries.

Finally, several HIPC countries have started borrowing from commercial markets again as well. Less than a year after receiving debt relief for its old close-to-zero-interest loans, Ghana issued a $750 million Eurobond with an interest rate of 8.75 percent. Other countries, such as Senegal, Uganda, and Tanzania, have also either floated commercial bonds or plan to do so soon. One interpretation of this trend is a new market confidence that these countries will be better placed to grow and repay these debts. However, if these new loans aren't much more productive than the old loans were, these same countries could find themselves once again in debt distress.

THE RETURN OF PRIVATE CAPITAL

The vast majority of development policy debates remain stuck in the public sector, the role of the African state in promoting (or hindering) development, and what rich-world governments can do to help (or hurt). But the history of capitalism and the transition from poverty to wealth in other regions of the globe has mostly been about private actors. Progress in wealth and humankind has generally come not from politicians at home or abroad but from the activities of farmers, investors, small businesses, and big corporations. The development community has increasingly, if a bit belatedly, recognized that the private sector and private capital can each play a vital role in promoting economic progress in Africa as well. African governments have taken some steps to try to attract foreign investment, while many of the donors have created programs to try to boost Africa's indigenous entrepreneurs and to help catalyze private-capital flows to the continent. Although recent signs have been encouraging, the private sector often remains a marginal player in many countries. This is a shame because if Africa is going to grow out of poverty and create a more prosperous future, it is unavoidable that these economies will need more and bigger businesses.

Several broad trends are currently defining the private investment landscape. First, private capital flows to Africa have been rising (Figure 3.1). Foreign

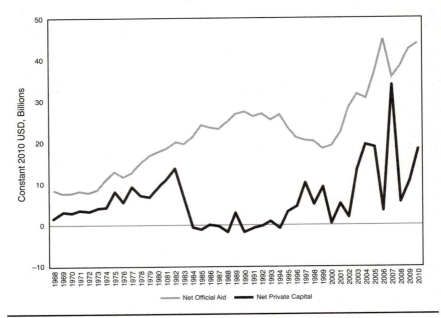

Figure 3.1. Private Capital Flows vs. Official Aid to SSA, 1968–2010

direct investment (FDI) in particular has been growing from around $1 billion per year in the 1970s and 1980s to $4 billion per year in the 1990s, and an average of more than $20 billion per year for the 2000s. Portfolio flows (investments via publicly traded stocks or bonds or minority private equity stakes) have also grown from close to zero in the 1970s to several billion dollars per year in recent years. Despite the big gains in attracting new investment, the continent has largely missed out on a global investment boom that has seen flows to other regions accelerate even faster. As a result, Africa's relative share of global FDI, which averaged around 5 percent in the early 1970s, fell to just 1–2 percent by the early 1980s and has recovered to only around 3 percent in recent years.

Second, the continent-wide aggregates mask major heterogeneity among countries. Indeed, private investment to Africa has clustered very strongly in a handful of countries and sectors. Over the period 2005–2008, for example, Nigeria and Angola alone accounted for more than half of all FDI to the continent. The top ten countries received 84 percent, leaving less than 5 percent of the total for the bottom twenty-five countries (see Table 3.1). At the same time, there has been a long-standing concentration in the extractive sectors, particularly petroleum. In five of the top six recipients (Nigeria, Angola, Su-

Table 3.1. Inward FDI: Sub-Saharan Africa, 2005–2008 (Average Annual)

Rank		Net flows (in millions of dollars)	% of SSA total	Cumulative %
1	Nigeria	12,917	28.9%	28.9%
2	Angola	10,300	23.0%	51.9%
3	South Africa	5,203	11.6%	63.6%
4	Sudan	2,721	6.1%	69.7%
5	Republic of Congo	1,718	3.8%	73.5%
6	Equatorial Guinea	1,636	3.7%	77.2%
7	Ghana	939	2.1%	79.3%
8	Zambia	809	1.8%	81.1%
9	Madagascar	659	1.5%	82.6%
10	Uganda	636	1.4%	84.0%
–	–	–	–	–
23	Kenya	223	0.5%	95.1%
24–28	Bottom 25 countries	2,202	4.9%	100.0%

Source: Author calculations based on UNCTAD data.

dan, Congo, and Equatorial Guinea) nearly all of the investment is oil-related, with much of this invested in offshore facilities. In addition, much of the foreign investment in Ghana, Zambia, and South Africa has been in large enclave mining projects.

Another significant trend, although one that is not always apparent in much of the available data, is that FDI and other private capital inflows are coming from a range of new sources. The traditional sources of FDI—large corporations in upper-income Western countries—are now joined by major investors from other emerging regions, especially Asia. Chinese investment in particular—both by private Chinese companies and by projects financed through quasi-public Chinese banks—is among the largest sources of new capital flowing into Africa (Brautigam 2010). One of the main channels for Chinese investment in Africa is through the China Export-Import Bank, a state agency that directs capital to support trade and investments by Chinese companies. China Ex-Im is similar to the export credit agencies in the United States or in Europe, but the scale is very different: China Ex-Im is larger than all of the export credit agencies of all the OECD countries combined. Recent commitments from China Ex-Im to African projects are estimated at some $6 billion–$7 billion per year. Through Ex-Im and other quasi-official banks, significant Chinese investments have been made in infrastructure (especially roads, telecommunications, and power), manufacturing, mining, fisheries, and agribusiness. In 2007, the Industrial and Commercial Bank of China bought a major stake in one of South Africa's largest banks, Standard Bank, expanding Chinese influence in the African financial sector.

The full picture of Chinese investments in Africa, however, is complicated by a lack of regular reporting about deals. The Chinese government tends not to share information about such matters. If this is true for aid, it is even more so for investment flows where commercial propriety may be valuable. Of course, much of what is called "private" is actually by state-owned banks or companies that may be partly directed by government policy or, at a minimum, have some kind of relationship to state entities. This confusion is furthered by the mechanisms often used to avoid taxation or to hide the true ownership. Much of the truly private investment, such as that by small or medium-size companies, is done through intermediaries in tax havens that intentionally obscure the origin of the capital. Finally, local press reports often declare major investments by Chinese firms, but project implementation is another matter. For example, in 2006 the local Nigerian press announced with fanfare that a not yet completed massive Chinese-financed and -operated project would soon connect all thirty-six state capitals by railway.

THE RISE OF AFRICAN STOCK MARKETS AND DOMESTIC CAPITAL MOBILIZATION

Africa has also attempted to attract private capital via stock exchanges. The subcontinent now has nineteen stock markets with nearly 1,000 publicly listed companies. Most of these markets have opened only since 1989, part of the wave of reform that coincided with the emerging-markets boom of the 1990s (see Table 3.2). South Africa dominates the market, accounting for more than 90 percent of the total capitalization (i.e., the value of all the companies listed on the market). But even without South Africa, more than five hundred African companies are publicly listed whose shares are traded. In 1998, the stock exchange in Abidjan became Bourse Régionale des Valeurs Mobilières (BRVM), the first official regional market. (Cameroon claims to be the central African regional market, but Gabon wants to open a competing market.) More important, many of the markets have begun to cross-list companies from other exchanges, such as the appearance of Kenya Airways and East African Breweries on all three East African exchanges (Kenya, Tanzania, and Uganda). Several South African companies are also listed on exchanges in Namibia, Botswana, Zimbabwe, Malawi, and Zambia.

Table 3.2. Sub-Saharan Africa's Stock Markets

	Year Opened	Market Capitalization (end-2011, US$bn)
Botswana	1989	4.4
Cameroon	2006	na
Cape Verde	2005	na
Côte d'Ivoire (BRVM)	1976	7.3
Ghana	1989	3.5
Kenya	1954	10.3
Malawi	1996	1.5
Mauritius	1996	8.1
Mozambique	1999	na
Namibia	1992	na
Nigeria	1961	46.3
Rwanda	2008	na
South Africa	1887	478.1
Sudan	1994	na
Swaziland	1990	na
Tanzania	1997	3.7
Uganda	1997	0.7
Zambia	1994	2.3
Zimbabwe	1946	4.0

Source: Standard and Poor's

Despite their relatively small size, African stock markets were established with the strong support of governments and remain fairly popular. Political and national pride factors clearly are behind some of the minor markets, but there are also real economic benefits. Most immediately, the stock markets have been useful vehicles for spreading ownership during privatization. In Tanzania, for example, almost all of the listings are former state-owned companies, and listing these firms on the Dar es Salaam exchange has allowed trading by small-holders and encouraged wider shareholding.

In the long term, it is hoped that the markets will be used by more domestic firms to mobilize capital for expansion, a trend that seems to be emerging already in countries such as Botswana and Kenya. However, many of the markets remain dominated by local subsidiaries of foreign multinationals, which are able to access capital more easily and more cheaply by turning to the parent company. Over time, as firms become more comfortable with the idea of public ownership and a greater number make the leap in size, more companies may turn to the local market. Similarly, the markets have not yet become a major destination for either local or global investors, but as the markets grow this should also change.

Remittances, the private money sent home by Africans living abroad, are another important source of private capital for Africa that is often forgotten. There is no hard data on such flows because most of these transactions take place outside formal banking channels (and out of sight of tax collectors). As a result, we have only a rough idea of the size and role of remittances (one World Bank estimate puts the inflow to sub-Saharan Africa at $12 billion in 2007). Regardless of their exact size, remittances are thought to be very substantial for countries with large populations living overseas, such as Cape Verde, Ghana, Nigeria, and Zimbabwe. Remittances are likely to be particularly important in poverty reduction because they are cash sent directly to families. Because much higher wages can be found in the rich world (even for the same job), there is a strong incentive for both temporary and permanent emigration—an option taken by millions of Africans—and many of these migrants continue to support family members in their country of origin. For the recipient families, remittances can be a crucial source of income for everyday household spending and investments in schooling, housing, or a business. For the countries involved, it is a source of foreign exchange, and the migrants, if they return, often bring back capital, ideas, and new skills. Some development agencies are trying to find ways to channel remittances for even greater impact on poverty, for example, linking them to financial services, such as banking.

A LINGERING SKEPTICISM?

These trends in investment flows are relevant to development because such flows are believed to bring major benefits. At the macroeconomic level, FDI by definition is new investment capital, contributing to the balance of payments, adding to the country's capital stock, and (assuming the money is used at least moderately productively) contributing to future economic growth. There is some evidence that foreign investment can contribute to raising exports for a country and help the economy integrate into global economic networks. At the microeconomic level there is also a range of possible benefits, especially higher productivity through new investment in physical and human capital (machines and training), increased job creation, better management, and new technology introduced into the country. Foreign investment also is thought to have important follow-on effects on local companies, or spillovers, through supply and distribution chains, trading, and outsourcing (Moran, Graham, and Blomström 2005).

FDI is sometimes considered more development-friendly than portfolio flows because it is more stable and can often be visibly linked to things such as jobs, buildings, and tax payments. But portfolio flows are also potentially beneficial because they still represent money flowing into a country. To the extent that this raises stock prices or lowers the yield on bonds, it makes money cheaper for companies to use to expand. There are also indirect gains from having portfolio investor interest, such as the impact on corporate governance and helping to link economies into the global financial network, giving access to money for local businesses, and lowering the overall cost of capital.

Despite the growing competition for private investment and Africa's ability to attract only modest amounts outside of the extractive industries, the continent still has a strong historical skepticism toward foreign capital (Moss, Ramachandran, and Shah 2005). Much of the prevailing attitude toward foreign investment is rooted in history, ideology, and the politics of the postindependence period. Africa's early experiences with foreign companies continue to affect official and public perceptions of FDI. The arrival of European capitalism in West Africa, first by the Portuguese in the fifteenth century, and later by the Dutch, French, and British, is indelibly linked in the public mind to the slave trade and as a precursor for colonialism. The use of European companies as proxies for sovereign powers has helped to link in the public mind international business with imperial expansion. In 1652 Jan van Riebeeck arrived in the Cape on behalf of the Dutch East India Company. In the late nineteenth century, Cecil Rhodes claimed swathes of southern Africa on behalf of the British South Africa Company. Through the company, Rhodes secured mining concessions in gold, copper, and diamonds, playing the dual roles of entrepreneur and representative of the British crown. Harsh conditions and treatment of laborers added to the connection between foreign companies and exploitation, such as in the mines (e.g., under the Witwatersrand Native Labor Association) or plantations (see, e.g., Hochschild 1999 for conditions on rubber plantations in the Belgian Congo). As with the United Fruit Company in Latin America, foreign companies in Africa frequently are thought of as agents of imperialism and exploitation. Although the colonial period ended more than a generation ago, it has remained a central factor in Africa's skepticism over joining the global economy.

Second, and perhaps just as important, most of Africa's anticolonial movements were heavily supported by the Soviet Union and its satellites. This encouraged the spread of socialism—or rather African variants on socialism—and a general ideological predilection against Western capital. This was closely complemented by dependency theory, which argued that capitalism in general, and foreign companies in particular, were agents of underdevelopment and merely continuing colonialism in another guise (Leys 1975; Rodney 1981). Although dependency theory has been widely discredited, it continues to flourish among certain academic circles, in many NGOs, and in some political circles and contributes to a lingering climate of distrust of foreign investors. Although there has been substantial turnover of political leadership in Africa over the past decade, many of the current decision makers (including those frequently hailed as reformers) have held political positions for decades and were trained on the socialist model steeped in anti–foreign investment ideology. Even as most of Africa's finance ministers have become increasingly convinced that economic openness can be beneficial for their countries and fluent in the language of international capitalism, many of their cabinet colleagues remain unreconstructed economic nationalists.

Third, ideas of economic nationalism affected sentiment toward foreign investment, and they continue to influence policy today. Kenneth Kaunda's "political independence is meaningless without economic independence" shaped not only Zambian investment policy but also the policies of his entire generation of leaders (Tangri 1999). On the one hand leaders frequently sought a symbolic break with foreign players that were closely identified with colonialism or external control. On a more practical level, political elites also did not want to be constrained by foreigners who might control key strategic sectors of the economy or their access to foreign exchange. Although FDI may be considered more stable than other types of capital flows, the flip side is that foreign investors with a greater stake in the long term might be more inclined to get involved in influencing policy or, in the extreme, supporting opposition political groups.

THE NEW "BUSINESS ENVIRONMENT" AGENDA

The phrases "business environment" or "investment climate" refer to a broad range of microeconomic conditions that affect entrepreneurs (Ramachandran, Gelb, and Shah 2009). It has become increasingly apparent that these conditions are particularly unfriendly to business in much of Africa. These include legal restrictions (such as requiring multiple licenses), lack of property protection (the state can seize assets), excessive regulations of all kinds, and colossal amounts of red tape and other headaches. The combined effect on business operations is onerous and confusing, and can become absurd. In Senegal, for example, an investor trying to open a factory and meet all of the legal hurdles must submit twenty-three applications and get clearance from thirty-one different agencies, and the process can take up to three years just to clear the paperwork. The worst part is that Senegal is neither unique in Africa nor even close to the worst case. The World Bank has undertaken several efforts to try to document such barriers (such as average number of days to start a business or time spent with officials), not to embarrass governments so much as to give them the information to better make policy as they try to revive the private sector and attract more investment. The results have nevertheless been discomfiting. The bank's "Doing Business" surveys have found massive administrative barriers (see Table 3.3). The net effect of these obstructions is to scare away foreign investors, squash local entrepreneurs, and force many small businesses into the informal black market.

Although much attention has been focused on foreign investment, it is also clear that local businesses, especially budding entrepreneurs, face considerable barriers. (Anyone who doubts that Africa has entrepreneurial potential should visit the huge Bakara market in Mogadishu and Roque Santeiro in Luanda where, even during periods of conflict, almost anything can be found.) Large foreign companies seeking to expand business may get access to high officials, including the president, who may help facilitate their entry. But the average small businessperson in Africa has no such luxury and often is vulnerable to extortion by local officials. Perhaps just as important, most domestic businesses in Africa have little access to credit, fewer resources to buy their way out of problems (such as buying a generator to get around electricity blackouts), and generally lower skills and less management experience.

Table 3.3. Slow Business in Africa

Number of Days to . . .	Nigeria	Chad	Uganda	Africa average	OECD average
Start a business	31	75	25	46	13
Get licenses	350	181	143	261	157
Register property	82	44	77	81	25
Export	25	75	37	34	11
Import	41	100	34	39	11
Enforce a contract	457	743	510	644	462

Source: Doing Business 2010

CONCLUDING COMMENT ON DIVERGENCE

Africa's interaction with international capital has been volatile and complex, often infused not just with the changing norms of economic policymaking, but also with the emotional and political implications of economic change and power. The broad trends have been driven by a combination of external conditions and internal reforms that leave Africa today in perhaps the strongest position since independence to take advantage of international capital to promote its own development. Some African leaders clearly have recognized this and are actively seeking ways to engage with international actors—in both the public and private sectors—to invest in their countries' futures. Other leaders do not seem to have adjusted yet to the emerging world and their countries are destined to lag. As such, the dominant macroeconomic and macropolitical trend is one of intraregional divergence. Whatever the rocky relationship holds, international capital will help to drive that wedge between the next generation of emerging markets and those left behind.

CITED WORKS

Brautigam, Deborah. 2010. *The Dragon's Gift: The Real Story of China in Africa.* Oxford: Oxford University Press.

Callaghy, Thomas, and John Ravenhill, eds. 1993. *Hemmed In: Responses to Africa's Economic Decline.* New York: Columbia University Press.

Collier, Paul. 1997. "The Failure of Conditionality." In *Perspectives on Aid and Development,* edited by C. Gwyn and J. Nelson. Washington, DC: Overseas Development Council.

Collier, Paul, and Jan Willem Gunning. 1999. "Why Has Africa Grown Slowly?" *Journal of Economic Perspectives* 13, no. 3 (Summer): 3–22.

Easterly, William. 2001. *The Elusive Quest for Growth: Economists Adventures and Misadventures in the Tropics.* Cambridge, MA: MIT Press.

———. 2002. "How Did Heavily Indebted Poor Countries Become Heavily Indebted? Reviewing Two Decades of Debt Relief." *World Development* 30, no. 10: 1677–1696.

Easterly, William, and Ross Levine. 1997. "Africa's Growth Tragedy: Policies and Ethnic Divisions." *Quarterly Journal of Economics* 112 (November): 1203–1250.

Hochschild, Adam. 1999. *King Leopold's Ghost: A Story of Greed, Terror, and Heroism in Colonial Africa.* Boston: Houghton Mifflin.

Leo, Benjamin. 2009. "Will World Bank and IMF Lending Lead to HIPC IV? Debt Déjà-Vu All Over Again." *CGD Working Paper 193.* Washington, DC: Center for Global Development.

Leys, Colin. 1975. *Underdevelopment in Kenya: The Political Economy of Neo-Colonialism.* Nairobi, Kenya: General Printers Ltd.

Moran, Theodore, Edward Graham, and Magnus Blomström, eds. 2005. *Does Foreign Direct Investment Promote Development?* Washington, DC: Institute for International Economics.

Mosley, Paul. 1992. "How to Confront the World Bank and Get Away With It: A Case Study of Kenya." In *Policy Adjustment in Africa,* edited by Chris Milner and A. J. Rayner. London: Macmillan.

Moss, Todd, Vijaya Ramachandran, and Manju Shah. 2005. "Is Africa's Skepticism of Foreign Capital Justified? Preliminary Evidence from Firm Survey Data in East Africa." In *Does Foreign Direct Investment Promote Development?,* edited by T. Moran, E. Graham, and M. Blomstrom. Washington, DC: Institute for International Economics.

Ramachandran, Vijaya, Alan Gelb, and Manju Kedia Shah. 2009. *Africa's Private Sector: What's Wrong with the Business Environment and What to Do About It.* Washington, DC: Brookings Press/Center for Global Development.

Rodney, Walter. 1981. *How Europe Underdeveloped Africa.* Washington, DC: Howard University Press.

Tangri, Roger. 1999. *The Politics of Patronage in Africa: Parastatals, Privatization, and Private Enterprise in Africa.* Oxford: James Currey Ltd.

van de Walle, Nicolas. 2001. *African Economies and the Politics of Permanent Crisis, 1979–1999.* New York: Cambridge University Press.

Williamson, John. 1990. *Progress of Policy Reform in Latin America.* Policy Analyses in International Economics, Issue 28. Washington, DC: Institute for International Economics.

four

Africa and Other Civilizations
Conquest and Counter-Conquest

ALI A. MAZRUI

One of the most intriguing aspects of the historical sociology of Africa since the early twentieth century has been its remarkable cultural receptivity. For example, Christianity has spread faster in a single century in Africa than it did in several centuries in Asia.[1] European languages have acquired political legitimacy in Africa more completely than they have ever done in formerly colonized Asian countries, such as India, Indonesia, and Vietnam. Indeed, while nobody talks about "English-speaking Asian countries" or "francophone Asia," African countries are routinely categorized in terms of which particular European language they have adopted as their official medium (Lusophone, English-speaking, and francophone African states).

If we examine the preceding millennium, not only were North Africa and much of the Nile River valley converted to the Muslim religion; millions of the inhabitants were linguistically transformed into Arabs. Elsewhere in Africa the Muslim faith has continued to make new converts despite the competitive impact of Euro-Christian colonial rule following the Berlin conference of 1884–1885.[2]

Linguistic nationalism in favor of indigenous languages in postcolonial Africa has been relatively weak. Only a handful of African countries allocate much money to developing African languages for modern needs. These include Tanzania, Somalia, and of course Ethiopia. On the other hand, most African governments south of the Sahara give high priority to the teaching of European languages in African schools.[3] It is yet to be seen whether African universities will be giving degrees in Chinese before the end of the twenty-first century.

No African country has officially allocated a national holiday in honor of the gods of indigenous religions. All African countries, on the other hand, have a national holiday either in favor of Christian festivals (especially Christmas) or Muslim festivals (e.g., Eid al-Fitr) or *both* categories of imported festivals. The Abrahamic religions (Christianity and Islam) are nationally honored in much of Africa; the indigenous religions are at best ethnic occasions rather than national ones.

TOWARD CONQUERING THE CONQUERORS

Africa's readiness to welcome new cultures is both its strength and its weakness. There is an African preparedness to learn from others, but there is also the persistent experience of Africa's dependency and intellectual imitation.

What has so often been overlooked is the third dimension of this equation. Africa's cultural receptivity can over time make others dependent on Africa. A cyclic dynamic is at play. Those who have culturally conquered Africa have, over time, become culturally dependent upon Africa. The biter has sometimes been bitten; the conqueror has sometimes been counter-conquered. This essay is about this boomerang effect in acculturation and assimilation. Africa has sometimes counter-penetrated the citadels of its own conquerors.

This process of Africa's counter-penetration has sometimes been facilitated by Africa's political fragmentation in the egalitarian age. The majority of the members of the nonaligned movement were from Africa. The largest single group of members of the Organization of the Islamic Conference are African and also members of the African Union. Much of the agenda of the Commonwealth of Nations from the 1960s to the 1990s was set by its African members—as they used the "Britannic" fraternity to help liberate southern Africa, dismantle apartheid, and address the challenges of globalization, such as the debt crisis. Although African countries compose about a third of the commonwealth members, they have been by far the most influential regional group in shaping its agenda and its decisions. For a while in the 1990s African influence was enhanced by the election of the first African secretary-general of the commonwealth, Chief Eleazar Emeka Anyaoku of Nigeria. South Africa's readmission under majority rule brought the whole story full circle. And when Mozambique was admitted in 1995, the commonwealth ceased to be an exclusively Anglophone club.

In the United Nations, countries from Africa were also almost a third of the total global membership until the Soviet Union and Yugoslavia collapsed into multiple republics, and Czechoslovakia split into separate UN members. Africa's fragmentation in an egalitarian age had for a while helped Africa's voting power in the General Assembly. Postcolonial partitions include the secessions of Eritrea and South Sudan. But Africa's percentage of the total membership has declined in the 1990s—closer to a quarter of the membership.[4]

On the other hand, Africa has had two successive secretaries-general of the United Nations—Boutros Boutros-Ghali and Kofi Annan—partly as a result of the wider rivalries of world politics. On the negative side, the United States and Great Britain also succeeded in hounding out of power the first African director-general of UNESCO, Amadou-Mahtar M'Bow of Senegal.[5] Even in this relatively egalitarian age in human history, real power continues to be decisive—when there is enough at stake to invoke it. In the first half of this twenty-first century, will Africa provide another director-general of UNESCO? In 2012 Nigeria's finance minister, Ngozi Okonjo-Iweala, became the most serious female and sub-Saharan nominee ever for the presidency of the World Bank. Ironically, she was defeated by a Korean American nominee of the first black president of the United States. All World Bank presidents since 1945 have been US citizens.

Even Africa's weakness has—on other occasions—been a source of power. As we indicated, Africa's territorial fragmentation has translated into voting influence even in UNESCO, despite what happened to Dr. M'Bow. And the UN General Assembly continues to take into account the liberation and egalitarian concerns of the African group.

Similarly, Africa's cultural receptivity—though often excessive and a cause of Africa's intellectual dependency—has sometimes become the basis of Africa's counterinfluence on those who have conquered it. This report about Africa's counter-penetration is supposed to be illustrative rather than exhaustive. We shall examine Africa's relationship with two interrelated civilizations—*Arab* and *Islamic*. We shall then examine the *French* connection as an illustration of Africa's potential in counterinfluencing the Western world. We then examine Africa's interaction with *India*—with special reference to the legacies of Mahatma Gandhi and Jawaharlal Nehru. We shall conclude with Africa's conquest of Africa—the full circle of autocolonization. The big question to be resolved is whether Christianization should be counted as part of Westernization or counted separately.

The Arab factor in Africa's experience is illustrative of the politics of *identity*. The Islamic factor is illustrative of the politics of *religion*. With the French connection we enter the politics of *language*. We examine the Afro-Indian interaction through the politics of *liberation*. Finally, we examine the future politics of *self-conquest*. Let us now turn to the four case studies (Afro-Arab, Afro-Islamic, Afro-French, Afro-Indian, and Afro-African) in greater detail.

AFRICA CONQUERS THE ARABS

In the seventh century CE, parts of Africa were captured by the Arabs in the name of Islam. Three factors speeded up the Arabization of North Africa and the Lower Nile Valley. One factor was indeed Africa's cultural receptivity—a remarkable degree of assimilability. The second factor that facilitated Arabization was the Arab lineage system, and how it defined the offspring of mixed marriages. The third factor behind Arabization was the spread of the Arabic language and its role in defining what constitutes an Arab. In the Maghreb across the centuries millions of "Berbers" became Arabs. In Egypt over an even longer period, millions of Coptic Christians became Muslims.

At first glance the story is a clear case of how the Arabs took over large chunks of Africa. But on closer scrutiny the Afro-Arab saga is a story of both conquest and counter-conquest.

But there is one important difference in the case of reciprocal conquest between the Arabs and the Africans. The actual creation of *new Arabs* continues in the Maghreb, northern Sudan, and elsewhere. Let us examine more closely this remarkable process of "Arab formation" in Africa across the centuries.

The Arab conquest of North Africa in the seventh and eighth centuries initiated two processes: Arabization (through language) and Islamization (through religion). The spread of Arabic as a native language created new Semites (the Arabs of North Africa). The diffusion of Islam created new monotheists, but not necessarily new Semites. The Copts of Egypt are linguistically Arabized but of course they are not Muslims. On the other hand, the Wolof and Hausa are preponderantly Islamized—but they are not Arabs.

The process by which the majority of North Africans and northern Sudanese became Arabized was partly biological and partly cultural. The biological process involved intermarriage and was considerably facilitated by the upward lineage system of the Arabs. Basically, if the father of a child is an Arab, the child is an Arab—regardless of the ethnic or racial origins of the mother. This lineage system could be described as *ascending miscegenation*—since the offspring ascends to the status of the more privileged parent.

This is in sharp contrast to the lineage system of, say, the United States, where the child of a white father and a black mother *descends* to the status of the less privileged race of that society. Indeed, in a system of descending miscegenation, like that of the United States, it does not matter whether it is the father or the mother who is black. An offspring of such racial mixture descends to black underprivilege. The American system does not therefore co-opt "impurities" upward across the racial barrier to high status in ethnic identity. It pushes "impurities" downward into the pool of disadvantage.

However, Barack Obama is considered a black president although his mother was white.

It is precisely because the Arabs have the opposite lineage system (*ascending* miscegenation) that North Africa was so rapidly transformed into part of the Arab world (and not merely Muslim world). The Arab lineage system permitted considerable racial co-optation. "Impurities" were admitted to higher echelons as new full members—provided the father was an Arab. And so the range of colors in the Arab world is from the whites of Syria and Iraq to the browns of Yemen, from blond-haired Lebanese to the black Arabs of Sudan. Since their 1952 revolution, Egyptians have had two presidents whose mothers were black—Muhammad Neguib and Anwar Sadat. These presidents were accepted as fully Arab.

Within Africa the valley of the White Nile is a particularly fascinating story of evolving Arabization. The Egyptians were of course not Arabs when the Muslim conquest occurred in the seventh century CE. The process of Islamization in the sense of actual change of religion took place fairly rapidly after the Arab conquerors had consolidated their hold on the country.

On the other hand, the Arabization of Egypt turned out to be significantly slower than its Islamization. The Egyptians changed their religious garment from Christianity to Islam more quickly than they changed their linguistic garment from ancient Egyptian and ancient Greek to Arabic. And even when Arabic became the mother tongue of the majority of Egyptians, it took centuries for Egyptians to begin to call themselves Arabs. The height of pan-Arabism in Egypt was under the leadership of Gamal Abdel Nasser (1953–1970). Abdel Nasser led not only the Egyptian revolution of the 1950s but also the first postcolonial Arab awakening.

But this is all relative. When one considers the pace of Arabization in the first millennium of Islam, it was still significantly faster than average in the history of human acculturation. The number of people in the Middle East who called themselves Arabs expanded dramatically in a relatively short period. This was partly because of the exuberance of the new religion, partly because of the rising prestige of the Arabic language, and partly due to the rewards of belonging to a conquering civilization. Religious, political, and psychological factors transformed Arabism into an expansionist culture that absorbed the conquered into the body politic of the conquerors. In the beginning there was an island or a peninsula called Arabia. But in time there were far more Arabs outside Arabia than within. At the end of it all there was an "Arab world."

Along the valley of the White Nile, northern Sudan was also gradually Islamized—and more recently has been increasingly Arabized. But as the crisis of Darfur illustrated, many northern Sudanese may learn the Arabic language as a second language—and fall short of seeing themselves as Arabs.[6]

But other Sudanese people who were not originally Arabs have come to see themselves more and more as Arabs.

The question that arises is whether there is a manifest destiny of the White Nile—pushing it toward further Arabization. It began with the Egyptians and their gradual acquisition of an Arab identity. The northern Sudanese have been in the process of similar Arabization. Are more and more southern Sudanese the next target of the conquering wave of Arabization within the next hundred to two hundred years, despite the secession of the south? Will linguistic Arabization continue in South Sudan despite the current intense separatism? Will the twin forces of *biological mixture* (intermarriage between northerners and southerners) and *cultural assimilation* transform some Dinkas and Nuers of today into black Arabs of the metaphorical day after tomorrow? A version of Arabic is already a lingua franca in the South despite the secession. Southerners often need Arabic among themselves.

It is for this reason that southern Sudanese are nevertheless the only sub-Saharan Africans who are being linguistically Arabized faster than they are being religiously Islamized. This is in sharp contrast to the experience of such sub-Saharan peoples as the Wolof, the Yoruba, the Hausa, and even the Somali—among all of whom the religion of Islam has been more triumphant than the language of the Arabs. The southern Sudanese could become Sudan's equivalent of the Copts of Egypt—a Christian minority community whose mother tongue is getting Arabized.

Nevertheless, racial ambivalence will maintain a linkage with Africanity. Indeed, the southern Sudanese are bound to be the most negritudist (in the sense of pride in blackness) of all Sudanese—even if they do become culturally Arabized in proximity. There is a precedent of black nationalism even among northern Sudanese. It is not often realized how much negritude sentiment (black cultural nationalism) there is among important sectors of northern Sudanese opinion. Muhammad al-Mahdi al-Majdhub has been described as "probably the first Sudanese poet to tap the possibility of writing poetry in the Arabic language with a consciousness of a profound belonging to a 'Negro' tradition."[7]

Muhammad Miftah al-Fayturi is another Arab negritudist. Information about his ancestry is somewhat contradictory. His father was probably Libyan and his mother Egyptian but of southern Sudanese black ancestry. In his words:

> *Do not be a coward*
> *Do not be a coward*
> *say it in the face*
> *of the human race:*

My father is of a Negro father,
My mother is a Negro woman,
and I am black.[8]

In some notes about al-Fayturi's early poetic experiences there is the anguished cry: "I have unriddled the mystery, the mystery of my tragedy: I am short, black and ugly." Needless to say, ugliness has never defined Africanity. Indeed, some have argued that "black is beautiful."

Arab black nationalists can also be defiant and angrily defensive about their racial mixture. Salah A. Ibrahim, in his piece on "The Anger of the Al-Hababy Sandstorm," declared:

Liar is he who proclaims:
"I am the unmixed . . ." Yes, a liar![9]

In the two Sudans of the future there may be even less room for such "lies" than there is at present. After all, Arabization is, almost by definition, a process of creating mixture.

It is worth reminding ourselves that the majority of the Arab people are in Africa. Over 60 percent of the population of the Arab world is now west of the Red Sea on African soil. The largest Arab country in population is Egypt, an important actor in pan-African politics. Meanwhile the African Union has since replaced the Organization of African Unity as Africa's Afro-Arab continent-wide association.

The largest city in the Arab world is located on its African side. The population of Cairo is more than the native population of Saudi Arabia as a whole.

Cairo also has become the cultural capital of the Arab world and a magnet for African Muslims. The greatest singers and musicians of the Arab world—including the incredible Umm Kalthoum, affectionately known as the "Star of the East"—used to mesmerize the Middle East from the studios of the Voice of the Arabs Broadcasting System in Cairo. She remains popular in part of Muslim sub-Saharan Africa.

The most famous Arab musical composer of the twentieth century has also come from the African side of the Arab world. Al-Ustadh Muhammad Abdul Wahab took Egyptian music into new levels of cross-cultural complexity. He developed new styles of Arab orchestral and even symphonic music. He was doing all this innovative work from the African side of the Arab world.

Culture has its technological and professional infrastructure. Egypt is by far the most important filmmaking country in both Africa and the Arab world. Egyptian shows feature prominently on cinema screens and television programs on both sides of the Red Sea.

Reaching much further into history, in the year 639 CE the Arabs had crossed into Africa and conquered Egypt. By the second half of the twentieth century Egypt had become the most important pillar of the military defense of the Arab world. History has once again played its cyclic boomerang game in the interaction between Africa and its conquerors. The ancestral home of the Arabs in Asia is now heavily dependent culturally and militarily on the African side of the Arab nation. Of course, Egypt has been *African* for thousands of years longer than it has been *Arab*. Egypt's African identity is permanently continental; her Arab identity is less than two millennia old.

AFRICA: THE FIRST ISLAMIC CONTINENT?

Why do Islam and Christianity continue to spread so fast in sub-Saharan Africa? Why has *religious* receptivity in Africa been so remarkable?

The spread of Christianity during Africa's colonial period was particularly spectacular. The Christian gospel spread faster in a single century in Africa than it did in several centuries in such places as India and China. Indeed, Christianity in southern India is virtually 2,000 years old—going back to the days of the disciples of Jesus himself. Yet to the present day the Christian population in the whole of India is little more than 50 million in a country that has a total population of over a billion.[10]

When we turn to Islam, there is just the chance that Africa will become to Islam what Europe has been to Christianity—the first continent to have a preponderance of believers.

Since independence, two issues have been central to understanding both Christianity and Islam: expansion and revivalism. Expansion is about the spread of religion and its scale of new conversions. Revivalism is about the rebirth of faith among those who are already converted. Expansion is a matter of geography and populations—in search of new worlds to conquer. Revivalism is a matter of history and nostalgia—in search of ancient worlds to reenact. The spread of the two Abrahamic faiths in postcolonial Africa is basically a peaceful process of persuasion and consent. But revivalism leads to fundamentalism and often militancy in both traditions.

In Arab Africa there is little Islamic expansion taking place and limited Christian evangelism—although some Egyptian Muslim militants regard the Coptic Church as a historical anachronism that ought to end.[11] For North Africa as a whole, Islamic revivalism is the main issue but it sometimes becomes anti-Western and a risk to Christians and political moderates. It probably cost President Anwar Sadat his life in 1981 and has sometimes threatened the ruling regimes of Tunisia, Algeria, and Morocco. On the other hand, following the Arab Spring revolutions in Tunisia and Egypt in 2011–2012,

Islamist parties in both countries have enjoyed popularity. The first freely elected president in thousands of years of Egyptian history belongs to the Muslim Brotherhood.

Outside Arab Africa the central issue concerning Islam and Christianity is not merely religious revival—it is also the speed of its expansion. We are back to the issue of receptivity. It is not often realized that there are more Muslims in Nigeria than there are Muslims in any Arab country, including Egypt.[12] Ethiopia, Nigeria, and Congo (Kinshasa) are the largest concentrations of Christians in Africa. The rivalry continues.

Of the three principal religious legacies of Africa (indigenous, Islamic, and Christian), the most tolerant on record must be counted to be the indigenous tradition. It is even arguable that Africa did not have religious wars before Christianity and Islam arrived. Indigenous religions were neither *universalist* (seeking to convert the whole of the human race) nor *competitive* (in bitter rivalry against other creeds). Christianity and Islam, on the other hand, were both universalist and competitive—perhaps especially in black Africa. In that arena south of the Sahara, Christianity and Islam have often competed for the soul of the continent. Rivalry has sometimes resulted in conflict.[13]

Indigenous African religions, on the other hand, are basically communal rather than universalist. Like Hinduism and modern Judaism—and unlike Christianity and Islam—indigenous African traditions have not sought to convert the whole of humankind. The Yoruba do not seek to convert the Igbo to Yoruba religion—or vice versa. Nor do either the Yoruba or the Igbo compete with each other for the souls of a third group, such as the Hausa. By not being proselytizing religions, indigenous African creeds have not fought with one another. Over the centuries Africans have waged many kinds of wars with each other—but hardly ever *religious* ones before the universalist creeds arrived.

But what has this to do with cultural receptivity in contemporary Africa? The indigenous toleration today has often mitigated the competitiveness of the imported Abrahamic religions (Christianity and Islam). Let us illustrate with Senegal, which is over 90 percent Muslim.[14] The founding president of this predominantly Islamic society was Léopold Sédar Senghor. A Roman Catholic, he presided over the fortunes of postcolonial Senegal for two decades (1960–1980), in basic political partnership with the Muslim leaders of the country, the Marabouts.[15]

Senghor's successor as president (partly sponsored by him) was Abdou Diouf, a Muslim ruler of a Muslim society at last. But the tradition of ecumenical tolerance continued in Senegal. The first lady of the country—Madame Elizabeth Diouf—was Roman Catholic. And from time to time several of the new president's ministers were Christian.

Senegalese religious tolerance has continued in other spheres since then. What in other Islamic countries elsewhere in the world might be regarded as provocative, in Senegal it has been tolerated. There have been occasions when a Christian festival like the First Communion—with a lot of feasting, merry-making, and singing—has been publicly held in Dakar right in the middle of the Islamic fast of Ramadan. The feast has coexisted with the fast. And the Christian merrymakers have been left undisturbed.[16]

Tanzania's triumph has been in implementing a religiously rotating presidency—a Christian president was followed by a Muslim president, and succeeded by another Christian, and followed again by a Muslim head of state.

When we place Islam in the context of the African continent as a whole, the cultural cyclic boomerang effect is once again discernible. The most influential Islamic university in the world—Al-Azhar University—is on the African continent. Al-Azhar in Cairo is credited with some of the most important fatwas under the *shar'ia* (legal opinions under Islamic law) in the past six hundred years.

Al-Azhar was founded by the Fatimids more than 1,000 years ago, in 970 CE. This makes it one of the oldest and most durable universities in the world. The basic program of studies through the ages has been Islamic law, theology, and the Arabic language. More recently other subjects have been added, especially since the nineteenth century. Women have been admitted since 1962, earlier than Princeton University started admitting female undergraduates. Al-Azhar University has continued to attract Muslim students from as far afield as China and Indonesia. It is widely regarded as the chief center of Islamic learning in the world.[17]

Islamic modernism has also been led from the African side of the Muslim world. The Egyptian thinker Muhammad Abduh (1849–1905) is still widely acclaimed as the chief architect of the modernization and reform of Islam. Born in the Nile delta, he was later influenced by the great pan-Islamic revolutionary Jamal al Din al-Afghani, who had settled in Cairo before being expelled for political activity in 1879. Abduh himself also suffered exile more than once. He lived to become the leading jurist of the Arab world, a professor at Al-Azhar University, and eventually mufti of Egypt (chief Islamic chancellor). His doctrinal reforms included freedom of will in Islam, the harmony of reason with revelation, the primacy of ethics over ritual and dogma in religion, and the legitimacy of interest on loans under Islamic law.[18]

But Muslim modernists have often been vulnerable to Muslim fundamentalists. A much more recent disciple of Abduh and al-Afghani was the Sudanese scholar Mahmoud Muhammad Taha. Taha's own version of Islamic modernism in Sudan earned him a punishment more severe than what Abduh and al-Afghani suffered in nineteenth-century Egypt. Under the presidency of Jaafar el-Nimeiry in Sudan, Mahmoud Muhammad Taha was executed in his old age in January 1985 on charges of apostasy and heresy.[19] This execution aggravated Nimeiry's unpopularity, and a few months later he was overthrown in a popular uprising in Khartoum.

While this history of Islamic modernism includes personal tragedy as well as intellectual originality, there is no doubt about Africa's role in the reformation of Islam. Africa has often been the very vanguard of Islamic innovation and doctrinal review. Taha's lectures interpreted Islam in a pro-feminist direction, using the Qur'an as evidence.

Africa's remarkable presence in the global Islamic equation includes the scale of Africa's membership of the Organization of the Islamic Conference (OIC). Until the collapse of the Soviet Union, almost half of the members of this global Islamic organization were also members of the Organization of African Unity (later succeeded by the African Union). Africa has produced some of the leaders of the OIC. Ahmed Sékou Touré of Guinea (Conakry) was chair of the Islamic Conference when he attempted to mediate between Iraq and Iran in the earlier phases of their own Gulf war.

The fastest rates of increase of both the Christian and the Muslim populations of the world are currently in Africa. This is partly because Africa is undergoing the fastest rate of Christian and Islamic conversions of any major region on earth. However, because natural fertility rates in Africa are higher than anywhere else—and Muslims in Africa are reproducing at a faster rate than most other Africans—Islamic expansion has an edge.[20]

There is evidence not only that Muslim women are married significantly earlier than other women in developing countries,[21] but also that Muslim women aspire to have more children. Kenya has slowed down its population growth, but until the concluding decades of the twentieth century, average Muslim women aspired to a family size of 8.4 children: this was the highest of any religious grouping, with Catholic women preferring 7.1 children and Protestant women an average of 7.0 children.[22]

While Asia still has many more millions of Muslims than Africa, the demographic indicators show that the African continent is narrowing the gap dramatically. In the twenty-first century Africa may already have become the only continent with an absolute Muslim majority.[23] This second-largest continent on earth geographically may have become the first in Muslim preponderance. A part of Asia (the Arabian Peninsula) once conquered Africa in the name of Islam. Africa is now repaying the debt by overshadowing Asia in the fortunes of Islam. The cultural boomerang effect has once again been at work.[24] Once again we have a full circle.

History is in the process of playing out a remarkable prophetic destiny. The first great muezzin of Islam was a black man—the great Bilal, son of Rabah of Ethiopian extraction. In more recent history, we might compare his great voice with that of Paul Robeson. Bilal called Muslim believers to prayer in seventh-century Arabia.[25] His credentials were a combination of faith, virtue, and voice. He is buried in Damascus.

EURAFRICA: THE FRENCH CONNECTION

France invented the concept of "Eurafrica"—asserting an organic relationship between Europe and Africa, deep enough to transform the two continents into a single integrated international subsystem. That was the long-term dream. How does this concept relate to the French language?

The majority of French-speaking people are in the Western world—mainly in France itself. However, the majority of French-speaking *states* are in Africa. Over twenty members of the African Union have adopted French as an official language.[26]

Without Africa the French language would be almost a provincial language. The Democratic Republic of the Congo (formerly Zaire) is, as we said, the largest French-speaking country after France in population—and destined to be the largest absolutely by about the middle of the twenty-first century.[27] If Congo succeeds in stabilizing itself and in assuming effective control over its resources, it may one day become France's rival in influence and power in French-speaking Africa as a whole.[28]

Over the course of the twentieth century several major factors resulted in the decline of the French language in the Global Northern Hemisphere, but our concern in this chapter is with factors that have contributed to its expansion in the Global South.

What must be emphasized in the first instance is that the southern expansion is mainly in Africa. On the whole the distribution of the French language is *bicontinental*—a large number of French-speaking *individuals* in Europe, and large number of French-speaking *states* in Africa. Europe and Africa are by far the primary constituencies of the French language.

Factors that have favored expansion in Africa have included the type of states that French and Belgian imperialism created during the colonial period. These were often multi-ethnic countries that needed a lingua franca. Colonial policy had chosen the French language, and the entire educational system and domestic political process consolidated that linguistic choice.[29]

A related factor was the assimilationist policy of France as an imperial power. This created an elite mesmerized by French culture and civilization. A surprising number still retained dual citizenship with France even after independence. If President Jean-Bédel Bokassa was anything to go by, some African heads of state may secretly still be French citizens. Annual holidays in France continue to be part of the elite culture of francophone West and North Africa.

With some subsidies and technical assistance, the French language also features in more and more classrooms in Anglophone Africa. Before independence British educational policymakers were more committed to promoting indigenous African languages than to promoting the rival French legacy in British colonies. Nor were French offers of language teachers for schools in British colonies welcome.

The global French fraternity of Francophonie has a secretariat in Paris that was for a while headed by Boutros Boutros-Ghali, an Egyptian. Membership of the Francophonie club now enlists countries that have not adopted French as a national language, but that can be persuaded to teach more French in their schools. Such states tend to be lovers of French culture. The cultural elite of Ethiopia and Eritrea in the twentieth century often combined Italian with French.

The difference that Africa's independence has made partly consists in greater readiness on the part of Anglophone governments to accept France's offers of teachers of the French language. Many an African university in the Commonwealth of Nations has been the beneficiary of technical assistance and cultural subsidies from the local French embassy or directly from France. However, the spread of English in francophone Africa has been despite France.

France's policy in Africa is consolidated partly through an aggressive cultural diplomacy. Considerable amounts of money are spent on French-style syllabi and curricula in African schools, and on the provision of French teachers, advisers, and reading materials. A residual French economic and administrative presence in most former French colonies has deepened Africa's orientation toward Paris.

In addition, every French president since Charles de Gaulle has attempted to cultivate special personal relations with at least some of the African leaders. There is little doubt that French-speaking African presidents have greater and more personalized access to the French president than their anglophone counterparts have had to either the British prime minister or the British head of state, the queen, despite commonwealth conferences.

Here again is a case of reciprocal conquest. There is little doubt that the French language and culture have conquered large parts of Africa. Many decisions about Africa's future are being made by people deeply imbued by French values and perspectives. Ironically, Africa's influence on Paris is often exercised through the Francophonie organization.

Moreover, French is expanding its constituency in Africa, despite reverse trends in Algeria and Rwanda. It is true that the postcolonial policy of re-Arabization in Algeria is designed to increase the role of Arabic in schools and public affairs at the expense of the preeminent colonial role of the French language. The rise of Islamic militancy in Algeria may pose new problems to aspects of French culture. It is also true that Mobutu Sese Seko's policy of promoting regional languages in the former Zaire (Lingala, Kikongo, Tchiluba, and Kiswahili) was partly at the expense of French in Zairean (now Congolese) curricula. African languages are more respected in former Belgian than former French Africa. Since 1994 French has also suffered a setback in Rwanda, led by anglophone Tutsi originally educated in Uganda. Rwanda has promoted Kiswahili also. But such setbacks for French in Africa are the exception rather than the rule. On the whole French is still on the ascendancy in Africa, though the speed of expansion has drastically declined. Postapartheid South Africa has also been reviewing its language policies, in addition to adopting eleven official languages.

However, when all is said and done, France's aspiration to remain a global power requires a cultural constituency as well as an economic one. It seems likely that within the new European Union France's *economic* priorities are now in favor of the new pan-European opportunities of an enlarged European Union and against the older investments in Africa. But it seems equally certain that a more open Europe after the end of the Cold War will favor the English language at the expense of the French language even within France itself. As custodian of the fortunes of French civilization, France could not afford to abandon the cultural constituency of Africa entirely in favor of the more open Eastern Europe. The collapse of the Soviet empire has been a further gain for the English language. France may need Africa more *culturally,* but less *economically.*

Because France's cultural constituency in Europe has been declining, its cultural constituency in Africa is more valuable than ever. A remarkable interdependence has emerged—still imperfect and uneven, but real enough to make Africa indispensable for the recognition of France as a truly global power, and the acceptance of the French language as a credible *world* language. Eurafrica as a concept gets its maximum meaningfulness in the destiny of the French language. But is there also a concept of "Afrindia" worth exploring? And how does this relate to the legacies of Gandhi and Nehru?

AFRINDIA: BETWEEN GANDHI AND NEHRU

It is perhaps not entirely accidental that the two most important Indian contributions to African political thought in the twentieth century were the doctrines of nonviolence and nonalignment. In a sense they were almost twin doctrines. Mohandas Gandhi (the Mahatma) contributed passive resistance to one school of African thought; Nehru contributed nonalignment to almost all African countries in the twentieth century. We should note how Uganda's President Milton Obote put it in his tribute to Nehru on his death in 1964: "Nehru will be remembered as a founder of nonalignment. . . . The new nations of the world owe him a debt of gratitude in this respect."[30] However, Gandhi and Nehru both taught Africa and learned from it.

But how related are the two doctrines in their assumptions? For India itself Gandhi's *nonviolence* was a method of seeking freedom, while Nehru's *nonalignment* came to be a method of seeking peace. And yet nonalignment was, in some ways, a translation into foreign policy of some of the moral assumptions that underlay passive resistance in the domestic struggle for India's independence.

With Nehru as independent India's first prime minister, his *armed* ejection of Portuguese colonialism from Goa in 1961 had a different impact on Africa. India's Foreign Minister Krishna Menon, when speaking in the UN, described colonialism as "permanent aggression."[31] Particularly "permanent" was the colonialism of those who regarded their colonies as part of the metropole—as Portugal had pretended to do. In such a situation when colonialism threatened to be more durable than even "permanent," the military solution was a necessary option.

Nehru's use of armed force against the Portuguese in Goa set a grand precedent for an Africa still shackled by Portuguese imperialism in Angola, Mozambique, and Guinea-Bissau. Had Gandhi's *Satyagraha* (soul force) been replaced in 1961 by Nehru's *satya-Goa*? Was there a Hegelian negation of the negation? Was Nehru's negation of nonviolence a legitimation of the violence of liberation?[32]

If Gandhi had taught Africa civil disobedience, had Nehru taught Africa armed liberation? Had the armed ejection of Portugal from the Indian subcontinent strengthened Africa's resolve to eject Portugal from Angola, Mozambique, and Guinea-Bissau?

The impact of India upon twentieth-century Africa went beyond even such towering figures as Mahatma Gandhi and Jawaharlal Nehru. More recently, Prime Minister Manmohan Singh led India into a new, more dynamic twenty-first century. But there is no doubt about the special significance for Africa of Gandhi's strategies of civil disobedience and Nehru's principles of both nonalignment and armed liberation. Gandhi's *Satyagraha* inspired African political figures as diverse as Nobel laureate Albert Luthuli of South Africa and Ivorian President Houphouet-Boigny. Nehru's ideas about what used to be called "positive neutralism" helped to shape African approaches to foreign policy in the early decades of the postcolonial era.

AFRICA'S REVERSE IMPACT ON GANDHI AND NEHRU

What has seldom been adequately examined is the reverse flow of influence *from* Africa *into* both Gandhi's vision of *Satyagraha* and Nehru's concept of nonalignment. Experience in the southern part of Africa must be counted as part of the genesis of Gandhi's political philosophy. And the 1956 Suez war in the northern part of Africa was probably a major influence on Nehru's vision of nonalignment.

South Africa was the *cradle* and threatened to be the *grave* of passive resistance as a strategy of Africa's liberation. Gandhi first confronted the problem of politicized evil in the context of racism in South Africa. He lived in South Africa for over twenty years—from 1893 to 1914. Racial humiliation in that part of the continent helped to radicalize him[33]—and therefore helped to prepare him for his more decisive historical role in British India from 1919 onward.

Gandhi's political philosophy developed from both the world of ideas and the world of experience. Moreover, in the realm of ideas he relied heavily on both Western liberalism and Indian thought. But what helped to radicalize Gandhi's own interpretation of those ideas was the power of experience. And within that crucible of experience we have to include Gandhi's exposure to sustained segregation in South Africa—a deeper form of racism than even the racist horrors of British India at that time.[34]

Under the stimulus of activated evil and the need to combat it, Gandhi reinterpreted in radical ways important concepts in Indian thought. For example, he reinterpreted *Ahimsa* (non-injury)—transforming it from non-resistance to passive resistance.

If Gandhi's *Satyagraha* was a response to the moral confrontation between good and evil, Nehru's nonalignment was a response to the militarized confrontation in the twentieth century between capitalism and socialism. If Gandhi's political philosophy was originally a response to racial intolerance, Nehru's nonalignment was originally a response to ideological intolerance. The regime in South Africa became the symbol of racial bigotry for Gandhi. The Cold War between East and West became the essence of ideological bigotry for Nehru.

South Africa as an inspiration for Gandhi is well documented. North Africa as an inspiration for Nehru's nonalignment has been less explored.

Two wars in North Africa in the 1950s were particularly important in Afro-Asian interaction. The Algerian war from 1954 to 1962 took African resistance beyond the passive level into the militarized active domain.[35] African Gandhism was in crisis. Had *Satyagraha* been rejected as no longer relevant for the struggle against colonialism?

The second great war in North Africa in the 1950s was the Suez conflict of 1956.[36] If the Algerian war marked a possible end to *Satyagraha* as a strategy for African liberation movements, the Suez war marked a possible *birth* of nonalignment as a policy of the postcolonial era. Gamal Abdel Nasser of Egypt was economically punished by the United States, Britain, and the World Bank for purchasing arms from the communist bloc. Washington, London, and the bank reneged on their commitment to help Egypt build the Aswan Dam on the Nile. Nasser's nationalization of the Suez Canal was an assertion of self-reliance; revenue from the canal was going to help Egypt construct the Great Dam. Egypt's sovereign right to purchase arms from either East or West was not for sale. In retrospect, Nasser's nationalization of the Suez Canal was a kind of unilateral declaration of nonalignment. This was before the non-aligned movement itself was formally constituted.[37]

At that time, Suez was the most dramatic test of a Third World country's being invaded by two members of the North Atlantic Treaty Organization (NATO), France and Britain. Never before had a Third World country been the subject of aggression by *two* members of NATO—and yet with the leader of NATO, the United States, protesting against its allies. Nehru was both a teacher over Suez and a learner from the experience.

What all this eventually meant was that while Mahatma Gandhi had, in the first half of the twentieth century, inspired many Africans to pursue the path of passive resistance, Nehru's liberation of Goa in 1961–1962 converted still more Africans south of the Sahara to the possibilities of military action. Gandhi was the prophet of nonviolence; Nehru became the symbol of armed struggle. Were the two Indians contradicting each other in the corridors of history? Or were passive resistance and armed struggle two sides of the same coin of liberation?

The answer probably lay in the final struggle in the Republic of South Africa in the concluding years of the twentieth century. Both armed struggle and nonviolence played a part in South Africa—and the two forms of struggle appeared to be at once complementary and contradictory. We have noted that in a sense, South Africa was the cradle of Gandhi's *Satyagraha*. Was it about to become the graveyard of passive resistance, as racial violence loomed larger? Or would *Satyagraha* receive a new moral validation in the process of dismantling apartheid? Both liberation theology and armed struggle operated in South Africa. Political apartheid has been abandoned, but economic apartheid is alive and well. Can "soul force" end economic apartheid?

The answer lies in the womb of history. Only two things about South Africa were in any case totally predictable. When the fires of struggle were put out, a new *black-led* republic would join the community of nations. Almost equally predictable was the foreign policy the new Republic of South Africa would adopt. It would be *nonalignment* in principle in the sense of Third World solidarity. When the republic joined the shadowy nonaligned movement, Gandhi's heritage and Nehru's legacy were at last fused on the very continent on which they were once separately born. Morally, "Afrindia" was about to be vindicated. The end of the Cold War had extinguished the rationale of nonalignment in terms of East–West relations. But there was still a need for Third World solidarity in terms of North–South relations.

South Africa is indeed the last testing ground. If India was the brightest jewel of the British crown, Africa is now the richest source of all jewels.

And seven black males and four women of color have won the Nobel Peace Prize:

Ralph Bunche (1950)
Albert Luthuli (1960)
Martin Luther King Jr. (1964)
Anwar Sadat (1978)
Desmond Tutu (1984)
Kofi Annan (2001)
Wangari Muta Maathai (2004)
Mohamed ElBaradei (2005)
Ellen Johnson Sirleaf (2011)
Leymah Gbowee (2011)
Tawakkol Karman (2011)

By a strange twist of fate, Mahatma Gandhi himself never won the Nobel Prize, despite having been nominated. But his black disciples did win the prize.

Africa's capacity to turn weakness into a form of influence has found a new arena of fulfillment. Fragmentation and excessive cultural receptivity are weaknesses. And weakness is not an adequate currency in the marketplace of power.

But quite often the power of the weak is, in human terms, less dangerous than the weakness of the powerful—their arrogance and all.

And yet, when all is said and done, the ultimate conquest is Africa's conquest of itself. The ultimate colonization is *self-colonization* under the banner of *Pax Africana*—an African peace enforced by Africans themselves. It is to this ultimate full circle that we must now turn.

TOWARD AN AFRICAN CONQUEST OF ITSELF

The issue has arisen as to whether colonization and decolonization are unilinear. We had previously assumed a neat sequence. There was a precolonial period covering millennia of African history. Then there was about a century of European colonial history, of immense economic, political, and cultural consequences. And then there would be the postcolonial period, ostensibly extending into infinity.

Western imperialism had previously resided in separate European powers: Britain, France, Portugal, Belgium, and so on. Has the imperial soul transmigrated to NATO, as in the case of the intervention in Libya in 2011? Or is the soul of imperialism trying to decide whether to settle in the bosom of the United States or become part of the UN Security Council? Is this a period of cosmic imperial indecision between NATO and the United Nations as voices of "the world community"? The United States has vastly expanded its military presence in Africa. Is Barack Obama the new absentee emperor of the continent of his Kenyan father?

The next phase of colonialism can be *collective* rather than through individual powers. It may indeed be the transmigration of the soul of the UN Trusteeship Council to the Atlantic Alliance or to some new UN decision-making machinery. The UN is better than *Pax Americana*. Will Africa play a role both as guardian and as ward?

The section of this new form of UN trusteeship started in 1960 when things fell apart in the former Belgian Congo as the imperial power withdrew: on that occasion, the UN intervened to oppose Katanga's secession from Congo. Officially, the United Nations ceased to be a trusteeship power in Africa as recently as 1990, when Namibia became independent. In Somalia since the 1990s the UN has ignored the self-proclaimed separatist Republic of Somaliland, which has declared its independence from the rest of Somalia. The attempted partition of Mali in 2012 has also been rejected so far. But if the problem of stability and anarchy in Somalia turns out to be insurmountable, the sanctity of Somalia's borders may one day be reexamined. Separatist Somaliland may yet survive to enjoy a legitimate UN seat—if not this time around, then after the next collapse of the Somali political patchwork. External recolonization under the banner of humanitarianism is entirely conceivable. Such countries as Congo (Kinshasa), Somalia, and Sierra Leone, where central control has collapsed, have in the past invited inevitable external intervention. But by whom in the future? That is the basic question.

Although colonialism may be resurfacing, it is likely to look rather different this time around. Imperialism does not have to be a military alliance. The

People's Republic of China is presenting itself as Africa's trustee for its resources and infrastructure. A future trusteeship system will be more genuinely international and less Western than under the old guise. NATO cannot masquerade as Africa's trustee, as it pretended in Libya in 2011. Administering powers for the trusteeship territories could come from Africa and Asia, as well as from the rest of the UN membership. For example, might the UN officially invite Uganda to administer a fragile Rwanda? Might Nigeria be officially invited to administer Sierra Leone for a while on behalf of the United Nations or on behalf of a reconstituted African Union?

Ethiopia was once a black imperial power, annexing neighboring communities. But Ethiopia cannot be a trustee of Somalia for historical reasons. The future may hold a more benign imperial role for other neighbors, though this may take a century to evolve. The recolonization of the future will not be based on "the white man's burden" or the "lion of Judah." It may instead be based on a shared human burden: Ethiopia as an administering power on behalf of the UN or the African Union to help nurture the sovereignties of its smaller neighbors. But can Ethiopia be trusted to be altruistic when it intervenes in Somalia?[38] China's energy needs have put the Chinese uncomfortably between the two Sudans.

However, regional hegemonic power can lose influence as well as gain it. Just as there is *subcolonization* of one African country by another, there can be sub-*decolonization* as the weaker country reasserts itself.

This is part of what has happened between Egypt and Sudan in the 1990s. Sudan under the Bashir Islamic regime started asserting greater independence of Egypt than anything that has happened since the Mahdiyya movement under Seyyid Muhammad el Mahdi in the nineteenth century. Since then President Omar al-Bashir has been indicted by the International Criminal Court at The Hague for alleged atrocities in Darfur. Is it counterproductive to indict an incumbent head of state?

Relations between Somalia and Egypt in the era after Siad Barre might also have been a case of *sub-decolonization*—the reassertion of the weaker country (Somalia) against the influence of its more powerful brother (Egypt). When he was UN Secretary-General, Boutros-Ghali's problems with Muhammad Farah Aideed were perhaps part of the same story of sub-decolonization. Boutros-Ghali was seen more as an Egyptian than as the chief executive of the world body.

If subcolonization of one African country by another is possible, and sub-decolonization has also been demonstrated, what about sub-*recolonization*? Will Egypt reestablish its Big Brother relationship with Sudan and Somalia? Will there be another full circle? As the Arabs would affirm: *Allahu Aalam* (only God knows).

In West Africa the situation is especially complex. Nigeria is a giant of about 160 million people. Its real rival in the region was never Ghana under Kwame Nkrumah, or Libya under Muammar Qaddafi or distant South Africa. The real rival to postcolonial Nigeria has all along been France. By all measurements of size, resources, and population in West Africa, Nigeria should rapidly have become what India is in South Asia or South Africa has been in southern Africa—a hegemonic regional power. Nigeria was marginalized not only by civil war in 1967–1970 but also by its own chronic instability and incompetence and by the massive French presence in West Africa, mainly in its own former colonies but also in Nigeria itself.

In this twenty-first century, France has been withdrawing from West Africa as it gets increasingly involved in the affairs of Eastern, Central, and Western Europe and in the financial politics of the euro zone. France's West African sphere of influence will be filled by Nigeria—a more natural regional hegemonic power in West Africa. It will be under those circumstances that eventually Nigeria's own boundaries are likely to begin threatening the Republic of Niger (the Hausa link), the Republic of Benin (the Yoruba link), and conceivably Cameroon (part of which in any case nearly became Nigerian in a referendum in 1959).

The case of postapartheid South Africa also raises questions about a regional hegemonic power. On the positive and optimistic side, this will make it possible to achieve regional integration in southern Africa. Regional unification is easier where one country is more equal than others—and can provide the leadership. Will South Africa eventually federate with Namibia, Lesotho, Botswana, and Swaziland?

On the negative side, postapartheid South Africa could be a kind of sub-imperial power—and questions of subcolonization, sub-decolonization and sub-recolonization may become part of the future historical fate of smaller countries of southern Africa. Another full circle.

Another African giant is the Democratic Republic of the Congo. It is already the largest French-speaking country in the world after France; in the course of the twenty-first century, it will become, as we indicated, absolutely the largest French-speaking country in the world in population. In mineral resources it is already the richest French-speaking country. If Congo attains stability, it may become the magnet for the whole of French-speaking Africa. Will its boundaries remain the same? Congo (Brazzaville) may work out a federal relationship with Congo (Kinshasa) in the course of the twenty-first century. It would help the transition now that Zaire has reverted to its own older name of Congo (Kinshasa). A confederal relationship of the former Zaire, Burundi, and Rwanda is also conceivable later in the twenty-first century. All three were once ruled by Belgium. However, a more stable federation may be between Burundi, Rwanda, and Tanzania, rather than Congo.

If I have presented some frightening possibilities, it is because some African countries may need to be temporarily controlled by others. The umbrella of *Pax Africana* is needed—an African peace enforced by Africans themselves. Africa may have to conquer itself.

Indeed, a thousand lives a day were being lost in the civil war in Angola at one time. If South Africa was already black-ruled, South Africa could have intervened—benevolent subcolonization could have been attempted for the greater good. It would have been comparable to India's intervention in East Pakistan in 1971 when the Pakistani army was on the rampage against its own Bengali citizens. India intervened and helped to create Bangladesh. But India had a vested interest in dividing Pakistan, whereas a postapartheid South Africa could intervene in a civil war in Angola for humanitarian and pan-African reasons, and still preserve the territorial integrity of its smaller neighbors. South Africa's intervention in Lesotho in 1998 was bungled and inept, but the basic principle of *Pax Africana* behind it was sound.

New possibilities are on the horizon. We may yet learn to distinguish between benevolent intervention and malignant invasion in the years ahead. Africa could conquer itself without colonizing itself. The Arab Spring in North Africa may have unleashed the forces of democratization in Tunisia, Egypt, and conceivably even Libya. And did the free and fair 2012 elections of Senegal constitute a new Black African Spring? History holds its breath as Africa waits for longer-term consequences.

CONCLUSION

We have sought to demonstrate in this essay the paradox of counter-penetration and the cyclic boomerang effect in Africa's interaction with other civilizations. Africa's cultural receptivity to its Arab conquerors has tilted the demographic balance and changed the Arab cultural equation. The majority of the Arabs are now in Africa—and the African side of the Arab world has become the most innovative in art and science. It may be significant that the Arab Spring started in Arab Africa (Tunisia and Egypt).

Africa's receptivity to Islam may make Africa the first truly Islamic continent. What Europe was to Christianity may turn out to be what Africa becomes to Islam—the first continent to have at least a plurality of believers. African Islam since the nineteenth century has also been the vanguard of the Islamic reformation and modernism—especially since the Egyptian thinker Muhammad Abduh. The fatal martyrdom of Mahmoud Muhammad Taha in

Numeiry's Sudan in 1985 is part of the story of the risky and daring innovation within the African constituency of the Islamic *ummah* (the worldwide Muslim community, basically followers of Sunni or Shi'a denominations, who account for more than 90 percent of the world's Muslim population).

Africa's cultural receptivity to the French language and culture has already made Africa the second–most important home of French civilization after France itself. The majority of French-speaking countries are already in Africa. And Congo (Kinshasa) stands a chance of one day becoming a rival to France in leading the French-speaking part of the world. Congo (Kinshasa) is in the process of closing the population gap and the resource gap with France.

Africa's response to Gandhian ideas, reinforced by Christian pacifism, has already given Africa more Nobel Prizes for peace than India. Gandhi himself had once predicted that the torch of *Satyagraha* (soul force) would one day be borne by the black world. Black winners of the Nobel Peace Prize in the second half of the twentieth century have included South Africans, Egyptians, Liberians, Americans, a Ghanaian, and a Kenyan.

Africa's response to Nehru's ideas of nonalignment in the twentieth century did result in a plurality of the nonaligned countries' being from Africa. Africa was in fact the first continent to become almost completely nonaligned as a form of diplomatic autonomy. If nonalignment once penetrated Africa, Africa had now truly penetrated the nonaligned movement. But this movement is now about North–South relations and no longer about East–West confrontations. When led wisely, Africa can still be a vanguard of such Third World solidarity.

But in the future Africa's *cultural receptivity* has to be more systematically moderated by *cultural selectivity*. Counter-penetrating one's conquerors may be one worthy trend. But at least as important for Africa is a reduced danger of being excessively penetrated by others.

Perhaps one day the sequence of cultural penetration will be reversed. Instead of Africans' being Arabized so completely that the majority of Arabs are in Africa, the Arabian Peninsula may become increasingly Africanized. Oman and the Gulf emirates are responding to Swahilization. Instead of the Democratic Republic of the Congo's being the largest French-speaking nation after France, Brazil will be counted the second-largest "African country" after Nigeria.

Meanwhile, Africa must conquer itself if it is to avoid further colonization by others. Africa needs to establish a *Pax Africana*—an African peace promoted and maintained by Africans themselves. One day each African person will look in the mirror—and recognize the human species triumphant. If African history has been a process of "paradise lost," will Africa's future be a process of "paradise regained"? The effort continues.

NOTES

1. For an overview of Christianity in Africa, see Bengt Sundkler and Christopher Steed, *A History of the Church in Africa* (Cambridge and New York: Cambridge University Press, 2000).

2. On this conference, consult H. L. Wesseling, *Divide and Rule: The Partition of Africa, 1880–1914,* trans. Arnold J. Pomerans (Westport, CT: Praeger, 1996), pp. 113–119.

3. On the resistance to African languages by the elite and their attraction to foreign languages, see M. Ekkehard Wolff, "Language and Society," in *African Languages: An Introduction,* ed. Bernd Heine and Derek Nurse (Cambridge and New York: Cambridge University Press, 2000), p. 342.

4. Montenegro's becoming the 192nd member of the United Nations in July 2006 seemed to cap the explosion of UN membership among the former states of the Soviet Union and Yugoslavia. There are 53 member states of the African Union.

5. The United States was of course the real power in this conflict; a discussion of US interaction with UNESCO may be found in W. Preston Jr., E. S. Herman, and H. I. Schiller, *The United States and UNESCO, 1945–1985* (Minneapolis: University of Minnesota Press, 1989).

6. The confusion over the identity politics of Darfur is exacerbated by several examples of intermarriage between those considered Arab and those considered African, as illustrated in a story by Emily Wax, "A Family Torn by Sudan's Strife," *Washington Post,* September 29, 2004.

7. See Muhammad Abdul-Hai, *Conflict and Identity: The Cultural Poetics of Contemporary Sudanese Poetry,* African Seminar Series No. 26 (Khartoum, Sudan: Institute of African and Asian Studies, University of Khartoum, 1976), pp. 26–27.

8. Cited by Abdul-Hai, *Conflict and Identity,* pp. 40–41.

9. *Ghadhbat al Hababy* (Beirut, Lebanon: Dar al Thaqafah, 1968), and Abdul-Hai, *Conflict and Identity,* p. 52.

10. V. A. Panadiker and P. K. Umashaker, "Politics of Population Control in a Diverse, Federal Democratic Polity: The Case of India," conference paper presented at the international symposium on "The Politics of Induced Fertility Change," sponsored by the University of Michigan, Villa Serbelloni, Rockefeller Foundation Conference Center, Bellagio, Italy, February 19–23, 1990.

11. Relatedly, see Daniel Williams, "Attacks on Copts Expose Egypt's Secular Paradox," *Washington Post,* February 23, 2006.

12. Because of religious and political issues over the implications of population numbers, the estimation of the numbers of Muslims in Nigeria is quite contentious. Moreover, population estimates are quite unreliable. However, based on the US State Department's *2006 Report on International Religious Freedom,* the Muslim population of Nigeria may be between 70 million and 75 million, while Egypt's is estimated to be about 67 million.

13. For an earlier elaboration of this thesis, see Ali A. Mazrui, "African Islam and Competitive Religion: Between Revivalism and Expansion," *Third World Quarterly* 10, no. 2 (April 1988): 499–518.

14. One estimate of the percentage of Muslims in OIC countries puts the Senegalese figure at 97 percent; see Saad S. Khan, *Reasserting International Islam: A Focus on the Organization of the Islamic Conference and Other Islamic Institutions* (Karachi, Pakistan: Oxford University Press, 2001), p. 325.

15. On Senghor and Senegalese accommodation with Islam, consult Janet G. Vaillant, *Black, French, and African: A Life of Léopold Sédar Senghor* (Cambridge, MA: Harvard University Press, 1990), and Robert Fatton, *The Making of a Liberal Democracy: Senegal's Passive Revolution, 1975–1985* (Boulder, CO: Lynne Rienner, 1987).

16. Consult Susan MacDonald, "Senegal: Islam on the March," *West Africa* 3494 (August 6, 1984): 1570.

17. On this venerable university, consult Bayard Dodge, *Al-Azhar: A Millennium of Muslim Learning* (Washington, DC: Middle East Institute, 1974).

18. For a discussion of this important figure in modern Islamic intellectual history, consult Mahmudul Haq, *Muhammad Abduh: A Study of a Modern Thinker of Egypt* (Aligarh, India: Institute of Islamic Studies, Aligarh Muslim University, 1970).

19. See Mahmud Muhammad Taha's book, *The Second Message of Islam* (Evanston, IL: Northwestern University Press, 1987).

20. Brian Nichiporuk said at a Pew Forum on Religion and Public Life on "The Coming Religious Wars? Demographics and Conflict in Islam and Christianity" (May 18, 2005), "Muslim regions tend to have significantly higher fertility rates than many other parts of the world" but also pointed to the complex and diverse nature of these fertility rates. The event transcript is available at http://www.pewforum.org/Politics -and-Elections/The-Coming-Religious-Wars-Demographics-and-Conflict-in-Islam -and-Christianity.aspx, accessed September 17, 2012. An earlier study demonstrated that the single most remarkable demographic aspect of Islamic societies is the nearly universal high level of fertility—the average of childbearing in Islamic nations is 6 children per woman. Fertility rates are highest for those Islamic nations in sub-Saharan Africa—an average of 6.6 births per woman. Furthermore, African Islamic nations south of the Sahara have higher fertility on average than do other developing nations in that region. John R. Weeks, "The Demography of Islamic Nations," *Population Bulletin* (publication of the Population Reference Bureau) 43, no. 4 (December 1988): 15.

21. More than a quarter (28.75 percent) of women in African Muslim countries between the ages of fifteen and nineteen are married, according to statistics from the United Nations, "Statistics and Indicators on Women and Men," at the site http://unstats.un.org/unsd/demographic/products/indwm/ww2005/tab2a.htm, accessed February 2, 2007.

22. John R. Weeks, "The Demography of Islamic Nations," *Population Bulletin* (publication of the Population Reference Bureau) 43, no. 4 (December 1988): 20.

23. According to an estimate of the UAE Ministry of Islamic Affairs and Awaqf, 59 percent of Africa's population (in 1996) was Muslim; see www.fedfin.gov.ae/moia /english/e_growingreligion.htm, accessed May 28, 2004.

24. It is widely believed in African Muslim circles that Islam is already the majority religion on the African continent. This claim was often repeated at an international conference on Islam in Africa held in Abuja, Nigeria, in November 1989. See "Islam in Africa," *Africa Events* 6, no. 2 (February 1990): 23–37.

25. A biography of this towering figure in Islam may be found in H. A. L. Craig, *Bilal* (London and New York: Quartet Books, 1977).

26. These are Algeria, Benin, Burundi, Chad, Cameroon, Central African Republic, Comoros, Congo-Brazzaville, Côte d'Ivoire, Djibouti, Burkina Faso, Gabon, Guinea, Malagasy, Mali, Mauritania, Morocco, Niger, Rwanda, Senegal, Réunion, Togo, Tunisia, and Congo-Kinshasa. This list is drawn from Banks and Muller, eds., *Political Handbook of the World* (Washington, DC: Congressional Quarterly Press, 2012), and David Crystal, ed., *The Cambridge Encyclopedia of Language* (Cambridge: Cambridge University Press, 1997).

27. See the map in Dennis Ager, *Identity, Insecurity, and Image: France and Language* (London: Multilingual Matters, 1997), p. 157.

28. Notably, even French public policy accepts that the demographic future of French rests in Africa; see Agers, *Identity, Insecurity, and Image,* p. 175.

29. For a portrait of French colonialism in Africa in the early part of the twentieth century, see Jean Suret-Canale, *French Colonialism in Tropical Africa, 1900–1945* (London: C. Hurst, 1971).

30. See *Uganda Argus,* May 29, 1964, and Ali A. Mazrui, *Africa's International Relations: The Diplomacy of Dependency and Change* (London: Heinemann Educational Books, and Boulder, CO: Westview Press, 1977), pp. 117–121.

31. Menon's view of the Goa affair and Western criticism of Indian action is described in Michael Brecher, *India and World Politics: Krishna Menon's View of the World* (New York: Praeger, 1968), pp. 121–136.

32. For two views on the Goa affair, see P. D. Gaitonde, *The Liberation of Goa: A Participant's View of History* (London and New York: C. Hurst and St. Martin's Press, 1987), and P. N. Khera, *Operation Vijay: The Liberation of Goa and Other Portuguese Colonies of India* (New Delhi, India: Ministry of Defence, 1974).

33. Some of the early incidents of Gandhi's encounters with racist South Africans are described in J. N. Uppal, *Gandhi: Ordained in South Africa* (New Delhi, India: Ministry of Information and Broadcasting, 1995), pp. 23–30.

34. In addition to Uppal, *Gandhi: Ordained in South Africa,* also see Shanti Sadiq Ali, *Gandhi and South Africa* (New Delhi, India: Hind Pocket Books, 1994), and Maureen Swan, *Gandhi: The South African Experience* (Johannesburg, South Africa: Ravan Press, 1985).

35. The bloody war between France and Algeria is described in John E. Talbott, *The War Without a Name: France in Algeria, 1954–1962* (New York: Random House, 1980).

36. A full treatment of the Suez crisis can be found in a collection of essays edited by William Roger Louis and Roger Owen, *Suez 1956: The Crisis and Its Consequences* (Oxford: Clarendon, 1989).

37. The first conference of the group of countries that would later become the non-aligned movement was held in Bandung, Indonesia, in April 1955.

38. Relatedly, see Stephanie McCrummen, "Ethiopia Finds Itself Ensnared in Somalia," *Washington Post,* April 27, 2007.

PART III

AFRICAN STATES AND THE STATE SYSTEM

The essays in this section are about the contemporary condition of sub-Saharan states. They have been pervasively weak throughout the independence era, owing both to the manner in which the state took shape during the colonial era and to the effects of predominantly authoritarian rule during much of the independence era. At the same time, both failed African state–led developments and shortcomings of international financial institution campaigns to reform African political economies along neoliberal lines have borne some responsibility for their continuing weakness. The essays to follow explore dimensions of a second era of reform dating roughly from and significantly influenced by the end of the Cold War.

To a significant degree, postindependence sub-Saharan African ruling regimes were sustained by external support. Membership in the United Nations conveyed external recognition of African states and a measure of legitimization to ruling regimes. The Cold War protagonists bolstered weak, corrupt regimes in their efforts to maintain and strengthen their global alliances, props that disappeared with the end of the Cold War in the late 1980s. Meanwhile, the 1980s witnessed the emergence of powerful grassroots and nongovernmental organization movements for democracy that brought regime change first in southern Europe and Latin America, and then, dramatically, in Eastern Europe and the then–Soviet Union. Christened democracy's Third Wave by Samuel Huntington, these movements revived the idea of civil society as the womb from which modern democracy emerged, especially in theory and practice in late seventeenth-century England.[1]

In sub-Saharan Africa, Third Wave democratization introduced almost unprecedented competitive multiparty elections and unprecedented pressure for observance of basic human rights by newly emboldened civil societies, backed by increasingly strong international regimes in support of those rights. Singularly in sub-Saharan Africa, however, democratization exposed the vulnerability of states, weakened by decades of authoritarian and corrupt rule, making the 1990s a season of serious instability and civil war in many countries. Meanwhile, in this new environment, the international financial institutions and the United Nations turned their attention increasingly to alleviating poverty and advancing basic social and economic as well as political rights.

The chapters in this section examine progress, shortfalls, and core issues in meeting the triple challenges of democratization, state strengthening, and reform against the background of socioeconomic empowerment initiatives centered since 2000 on the United Nations' Millennium Challenge Goals. Chapter 5 examines the significant overall democratization progress for sub-Saharan Africa as a whole since 1990, markedly divergent trajectories of progress among the individual countries, and indications of democratic retreats in several countries and possibly slowing democratization momentum overall since about 2005. Chapter 6 by Aili Tripp surveys progress and issues in broadening the scope of rights to include social and economic rights in Africa, bolstered by UN declarations ordaining development as a right. In Chapter 9, Ulf Engel explores African initiatives to reinforce peace and security and accountable governance through the African Union Commission's increasing authority as an independent actor in these areas.

To date, the scope of civil wars in sub-Saharan Africa has been sharply reduced in the twenty-first century, including notable successes in state restoration and reform in Liberia and Sierra Leone. But the question remains to what extent sub-Saharan Africa's predominantly weak states have actually been strengthened as well as reformed with the aid of democratization processes, a question highlighted by the 2012 coup and fracturing of Mali, for two decades a model African democracy. In Chapter 8, I. William Zartman writes that famously arbitrary, colonial-imposed state boundaries have gained substantial de facto permanence, implicitly adding to the viability of the states they encompass, aided by small, negotiated, user-friendly adjustments where these are merited. Will Reno's Chapter 7, however, draws attention to continuing and pervasive clientelism and corruption perpetuating state weakness, sometimes further weakened rather than strengthened by external efforts.

NOTES

1. Samuel Huntington, *The Third Wave: Democratization in the Late Twentieth Century* (Norman: University of Oklahoma Press, 1991); John Keane, *Civil Society*

and the State: New European Perspectives (London: Verso, 1988); Guillermo O'Donnell and Philippe C. Schmitter, *Transitions from Authoritarian Rule: Tentative Conclusions About Uncertain Democracies* (Baltimore, MD: Johns Hopkins University Press, 1986); John W. Harbeson, Donald Rothchild, and Naomi Chazan, eds., *Civil Society and the State* (Boulder, CO: Lynne Rienner Publishers, 1994).

complex trajectories. Common to all the major indices, however, is evidence of, at best, only limited continuing momentum in sub-Saharan Africa for substantial, rapid democratic advances.

Second, striking and even profound changes in sub-Saharan African socioeconomic, technological, and cultural contexts in the first years of the twenty-first century have appeared destined to influence democratization in African states for better and/or for worse in likely complex ways, including perhaps helping to explain why by some measures democratization has appeared to recede and/or to lose momentum. For several years, much of sub-Saharan Africa has experienced markedly increased rates of economic growth. Meanwhile, levels of external economic investment have increased dramatically, especially by China and other G-20 countries, accompanied by changing trade patterns—delayed outcomes of neoliberalism imposed by the World Bank–IMF beginning in the 1980s. At the same time, however, inequalities and widespread poverty have persisted, and UN-sponsored Millennium Development Goals generally are not expected to be reached by the 2015 target date. Moreover, rapidly albeit unevenly expanding information and communications technology carries the potential of transforming relations between citizens and their governments in ways and with long-term consequences that have yet fully to take shape. Additionally, the international political order in which sub-Saharan Africa participates has been radically transformed by the rise of China, other BRICS, and a number of G-20 economies, and by post–September 11, 2001, counterterrorism agendas juxtaposed with emergent radical cultural and/or religious insurgencies.[2]

At the same time, evolving Western-inspired international regimes upholding fundamental liberties, sanctioning crimes against humanity, and mandating responsible exercises of state sovereignty have gained traction, including with the African Union and regional organizations, such as ECOWAS. How these strengthened international human rights and democracy regimes may impact and/or be impacted by the extent, outcomes, and drivers of strengthened economic development is a question of central importance that will likely become clearer during the second and third decades of the new millennium.

Third, both trajectories of democratic progress and retreat to date, and the still-uncharted political implications of the foregoing international and societal transformations on sub-Saharan Africa, must be understood against the background of deeply troubled evolving and, in some important respects, singular contours of a half century of postindependence political development in the region. In the broadest terms, European powers ceded independence to African nationalist movements in such a way that they inherited arbitrarily constructed and imposed colonial states without significantly transforming or reconstructing them. Early on, perpetuation of their authoritarian structures and practices well into the independence era established their fundamental weakness, demonstrated by a season of military coups and counter-coups that dissolved most designs for one-party democratic socialism regimes, African style, within a decade and a half.[3] Authoritarian regimes presiding over weak postcolonial states prevailed thereafter.

From the 1970s until the end of the Cold War, international financial institutions and bilateral donors stepped into the breach created by sub-Saharan African political disarray and development failure. They substantially influenced African agendas for political and economic development thereafter. They centered first on circumventing overbearing authoritarian governments, by promoting equitable development from below via networks of international NGOs and domestic local organizations.[4] Then in the 1980s, because of the developing nations' debt crisis, the international financial institutions (IFIs) and bilateral donors turned to conditioning development assistance to African countries upon their governments, sharply diminishing their efforts to manage the development of their economies. In so doing, however, they largely overlooked the continuing underlying weakness of inherited, essentially unreconstructed postcolonial states, just when influential academic research sought to rescue and strengthen state autonomy from reductionist treatment of the state in modernization and dependency literatures.[5] Privatized and, to a significant extent, flourishing informal economies helped to shrink the scope of African governments' economic writs and threatened to bankrupt them, while incubating pressures to extend economic liberalism into the political sphere that would occur in the final decade of the twentieth century with the end of the Cold War.[6]

The central purpose of this chapter is to consider the existing levels of post–Cold War sub-Saharan African democratic progress in the context of these foundational historical and profoundly changing contemporary international and domestic circumstances. The fundamental question, especially in these complex circumstances, is to what extent and in what ways democratization may be enabling sub-Saharan African peoples to realize their ultimate rationale: to determine how, by whom, and to what ends they are to be governed. Specifically, to what extent and in what ways is the era of democratization that some have characterized as the region's "second independence" actually enabling sub-Saharan peoples to determine for themselves what democracy is to mean and how it is to be defined, thereby reclaiming development agenda–setting authority that the IFIs and bilateral donors have exerted for nearly four decades? Still more specifically, to the extent that the era of the Third Wave has enabled sub-Saharan African countries to assert the self-determination that is the essence of democratization, the question becomes by whom and how is it to be claimed within these countries?

A corollary fundamental and very difficult-to-address question then becomes to what extent, viewed through the lenses of conventional working conceptualizations of democratization, is it possible to gauge what African peoples actually make of democratization, so understood, in the contexts of these changing circumstances coursing across their continent? A key bargain with African governments implicit in IFI demands for neoliberal economic reform throughout the 1980s and 1990s, and into the new millennium, has been that principally *Western* private investment would adhere to those demands, joining liberated domestic investment, to spur long-awaited economic development.[7] That bargain was at best imperfectly fulfilled, at least initially, but sweetened considerably by debt relief demanded by an emergent global civil society and then by a new IFI focus on pro-poor development initiatives.[8] These initiatives were then crowned in 2000 by the fifteen-year UN-sponsored Millennium Development Goals project to reduce comprehensively the principal manifestations of citizen-level poverty that now appear likely to be only partially and unevenly met.

A further fundamental implicit but rarely articulated presumption of the original implicit bargain has been that any resulting economic development in sub-Saharan Africa, spurred by increased external and internal investment and resulting from neo-economic reform, would all occur within the liberal democratic framework supplied by the emergence of Third Wave democracy that animates prevailing working conceptions of democracy and democratization employed by policymakers and in the academy. That extension of the original implicit bargain has been challenged by waves of new external investment, especially from China, spurring recent levels of strong economic growth in many African countries that may or may not be shaped and focused ways to support, strengthen, and realize broad purposes implicit in these working conceptualizations of democracy. The extent to which they do, or do not, will in turn have an important bearing upon the extent to which sub-Saharan African countries uphold or undermine the strengthened and increasingly explicit international regimes undergirding democratic accountability, human rights, and the rule of law.

The core hypothesis of this chapter is that evidence of democratic retreats but, perhaps more fundamentally, plateauing of momentum for further democratization leaves the future of democratization in sub-Saharan Africa hanging in the balance. It is indeterminate at this point to what extent and in what ways sub-Saharan African countries will seize the fundamental underlying self-determination mandate implicit in the idea of democratization in such a way as not only to strengthen its institutions and processes as conventionally understood but also to shape new resources and opportunities of socioeconomic development in conventional and/or innovative ways consistent with those understandings. A meta-level question then becomes how political leaders and citizens relate to one another in determining how democratization is to take place and to what socioeconomic as well as political ends.

Much of the democratization assessment emphasis necessarily continues to center on how leaders deal with democratization, as development literature has all along with how and in what ways they conduct economic reform. The core contention of this chapter, however, is that by definition, after all, ordinary citizens as well as elites are also key drivers of democratization and, therefore, that democratization's prospects hinge also upon how citizens assess and respond to democratization as it has emerged for them over the past two decades. The evidence of democratic retreat and limited ongoing democratization momentum suggested by much of the data that this chapter will summarize, of course, calls into question the political commitments of leaders. Also, however, insufficiently explored to date has been the extent to which such democratization has occurred, limited and still fragile as it appears to be, and has satisfied the aspirations of citizens at tipping-point levels sufficient to empower and motivate them to seek its further advancement, or discouraged them from doing so. How these crucial assessments form is likely to hinge not only upon how citizens evaluate democracy as an end as they have experienced it but also, critically, upon the extent to which it is employed instrumentally in venues to help citizens to gain the skills and resources, and to generate the requisite incentives and commitment to assert both their interests in inclusive economic development and in defending and advancing democratization.

How the trajectories of democratization emerge as these fundamental questions are worked out and yield discernible empirical outcomes carries potentially fundamentally important theoretical implications as well. To the extent that sub-Saharan African citizens take ownership of democracy and restore momentum to press for full democratic states, the terms "democracy" and "state" may logically take on new meanings in these settings. Working conceptualizations of democracy have tacitly tended to shrink the roles of citizens to voting and to asserting fundamental liberties requisite to free and fair elections. Relatively overlooked have been their necessary roles *between elections* and, more broadly in societies and economies, in pressing for realization of *all* the fundamental dimensions of a democratic state in an era when the opportunity to do so for the first time has been most attainable. Further, an important dimension of this opportunity, to the extent it is seized, is to establish citizens as key players as well as rulers in the structure of the state itself in ways that prevalent implicitly Weberian working conceptions of the state have tended to overlook.

This chapter will review several influential indices that assess the current status of sub-Saharan African democratization. More than two decades into sub-Saharan Africa's era of Third Wave democratization, the issue of sustainability, as well as further advancement, becomes increasingly central. While sustainability ultimately depends not only on what leaders do about democracy but also on what citizens do *with* it, the analysis in this chapter concentrates on how democratization indices appraise the status of their empowerment to seize the full measure of their democratic opportunity. In this, the chapter picks up the thread of an important work on both the inculcation and maintenance of sustainable cultures of constitutionalism that appears to have been largely overlooked since it was advanced by John Ferejohn and his colleagues some years ago.[9]

ASSESSMENTS OF SUB-SAHARAN DEMOCRATIC PROGRESS

Assessment systems for worldwide comparative gauging of patterns and degrees of democratic progress have proliferated over two decades of what some have termed sub-Saharan Africa's "second independence." These opportunities for democratic progress generally did not exist when most of these countries first became independent, or afterward, until the post–Cold War arrival of the Third Wave. The major assessment systems have included those of Freedom House, Cingranelli and Richards (CIRI), the Economic Intelligence Unit, Polity IV, the World Bank Institute, and the Mo Ibrahim Foundation.[10] This section offers a comprehensive overview in some depth of their findings on sub-Saharan African countries' progress toward becoming democratic states.

In 1972 Freedom House began assessing the extent to which countries worldwide upheld basic civil and political liberties, preceding late twentieth-century democratization in central and southern Europe, Latin America, and Africa. The Polity project also originated in the 1970s, but its current form, Polity IV, took shape in the 1990s, although it projects its estimates of democracy for almost all countries back to 1800. The World Bank Institute established its "Governance Matters" assessments for all countries biennially in 1996, and more recently annually. The Economic Intelligence Unit began its worldwide comparative country estimates of democratic practice in 2006. The respected CIRI index, created by David Cingranelli and David Richards began worldwide assessments of respect for democratic liberties in 1981, but with an expanded list of countries added since 2000. The Mo Ibrahim Foundation initiated its assessments of socioeconomic as well as democratic progress for all African countries in 2006.

A common and defining feature of all these assessment systems is that they all quantify estimates of country observance of key elements of democracy that have been distilled from centuries of scholarship and from constitutional norms of the world's mature, well-established democracies. The methodological complexities and difficulties involved in constructing these indices are intuitively evident but are beyond the purview of this chapter to consider in any depth apart from the observation that surveys have been criticized, inter alia, for multicollinearity that, to varying degrees, has been found in estimates of variables included in the surveys. Reliance upon these quantitative estimates of democratic practice has, nonetheless, been all but universal among scholars and practitioners alike for the simple reason that they have supplied the only readily available putatively objective bases for systematic worldwide country comparisons of the extent and forms of actual democratic practice and the resulting conditions of states. How, then, does one gauge the validity and reliability of these estimates? In broad terms, one may hypothesize that scholars and policymakers have generally exhibited confidence in them to the extent that, especially in the aggregate, the estimates seem broadly to correspond to their overall impressions, based on their research, of the status of democracy in the countries and regions they know best, the author being no exception.[11]

These assessments of democratic practice have undertaken to gauge performance in terms of many of the same indicators of democracy, but they all have featured distinctive emphases as well. Broadly speaking, the assessments fall into two groups: (1) those that while assessing democracy generally, concentrate on the extent and quality of personal liberties; (2) those that, while including liberties, are more concerned with the quality of democratic governance. In the first group, Freedom House has focused on observance of fundamental civil and political liberties while also estimating observance of more systematic factors, including the rule of law and governmental electoral accountability and protection of pluralism. CIRI assessments focus on liberties but pay special attention to measures empowering women, the extent of personal safety, and judicial independence. The Economic Intelligence Unit's assessments offer a more encompassing conception of democracy that incorporates many of the concerns of the governance group.

Assessments that focus more on the quality of democratic governance include the Polity IV indices on the presence of restraints on executive power, on openness and freedom to compete for executive office, and on rule-based governance of political competition. The World Bank's "Governance Matters" assessments, which also incorporate measures of voice and accountability, embrace a more comprehensive conception of democratic governance, including indicators of state stability, corruption control, competent governmental performance, and the rule of law. The Mo Ibrahim Index not only assesses democratic governance but also blends in indices of human development and economic progress outcomes. The bank's indices build on the findings of the other indices considered in this chapter.

Democratic Liberties

By far the most widely cited and perhaps most influential assessments have been those by Freedom House of governmental observance of fundamental civil and political liberties.[12] Best known have been its 1–7 rankings of both civil and political liberties, where rankings of 1 and 2 establish a country as free, those of 3–5 indicate a "partly free" country, and those of 6 and 7 a country still "unfree." Between 1990 and 2011, overall sub-Saharan African countries collectively advanced from "unfree" to "partly free" on political rights and from borderline "unfree/partly free" to "partly free" on civil liberties (Table 5.1).[13]

Thirty-two sub-Saharan African countries were adjudged "unfree" by Freedom House in 1990, diminishing to nineteen in 2011 (Table 5.2). During this period, thirty countries registered overall gains while five regressed. Eight countries qualified as "free" in 2011 by contrast to four in 1990. Twenty-two countries were in the hybrid category in 2011, more than double the ten in that category in 1990. However, as Table 5.1 also indicates, Freedom House has recorded that sub-Saharan African countries, as a group, regressed on both political rights and civil liberties between 2005 and 2011, interrupting fifteen years of steady progress in both categories.[14] The observed African declines account for virtually all of the worldwide declines that Table 5.1 also indicates.

Less attended have been more detailed Freedom House estimates based on twenty-five specific questions, the scores for which are sorted into seven categories (as seen in Table 5.3): electoral process (category A), pluralism and participation (B), government functioning and accountability (C), freedom of expression and belief (D), associational and organizational rights (E), rule of

Table 5.1. Sub-Saharan African Progress on Political Rights and Civil Liberties, 1990–2011

		1990	1995	2000	2005	2011
Africa	Political Rights	5.50	4.56	4.48	4.23	4.44
	Civil Liberties	5.00	4.58	4.40	3.98	4.22
World	Political Rights	3.14	3.32	3.23	3.12	3.34
	Civil Liberties	3.05	3.50	3.31	2.95	3.24

Source: Freedom House

Table 5.2. Sub-Saharan Advances in Liberties, 1990–2011

	1990		2011		Change		
	Pol. Rights	Civil Libs.	Pol. Rights	Civil Libs.	Pol Rights	Civil Libs.	Total Change
Ghana	6	5	1	2	5	3	5
Liberia	7	7	3	4	4	3	4
Cape Verde	5	5	1	1	4	4	4
Benin	6	4	2	2	4	2	4
Mali	6	5	2	3	4	2	4
Malawi	7	6	3	4	4	2	4
Niger	6	5	3	4	3	1	3
Lesotho	6	5	3	3	3	2	3
Sao Tome & Principe	5	5	2	2	3	3	3
South Africa	5	4	2	2	3	2	3
Sierra Leone	6	5	3	3	3	2	3
Seychelles	6	6	3	3	3	3	3
Tanzania	6	5	3	3	3	2	3
Zambia	6	5	3	4	3	1	3
Guinea-Bissau	6	5	4	4	2	1	2
Burundi	7	6	5	5	1	1	2
Kenya	6	6	4	3	2	3	2
Togo	6	6	4	5	2	1	2
Comoros	5	5	3	4	2	1	2
Mozambique	6	6	4	3	2	3	2
Mauritania	7	6	6	5	1	1	1
Burkina Faso	6	5	5	3	1	2	1
Angola	7	7	6	5	1	2	1
Mauritius	2	2	1	2	1	0	1
Nigeria	5	5	4	4	1	1	1
Guinea	6	5	5	5	1	0	1
Uganda	6	5	5	4	1	1	1
Central African Republic	6	5	5	5	1	0	1
Senegal	4	3	3	3	1	0	1
Ethiopia	7	7	6	6	1	1	1

continues

Table 5.2. Sub-Saharan Advances in Liberties, 1990-2011 *continued*

	1990		2011		Change		
	Pol. Rights	Civil Libs.	Pol. Rights	Civil Libs.	Pol Rights	Civil Libs.	Total Change
Rwanda	6	6	6	5	0	1	0
Somalia	7	7	7	7	0	0	0
Sudan	7	7	7	7	0	0	0
Zimbabwe	6	4	6	6	0	-2	0
Namibia	2	3	2	2	0	1	0
Congo (Kinshasa)	6	6	6	6	0	0	0
Cameroon	6	6	6	6	0	0	0
Chad	7	6	7	6	0	0	0
Congo (Brazzaville)	6	6	6	5	0	1	0
Côte d'Ivoire	6	4	6	5	0	-1	0
Djibouti	6	5	6	5	0	0	0
Equatorial Guinea	7	7	7	7	0	0	0
Swaziland	6	5	7	5	-1	0	-1
Gabon	4	4	6	5	-2	-1	-2
Botswana	1	4	3	2	-2	0	-2
Madagascar	4	4	6	4	-2	0	-2
Gambia, The	2	2	6	5	-4	-3	-4
Somaliland			5	5			
Eritrea			7	7			
South Sudan			6	5			
African Average	5.50	5.00	4.44	4.22			
World Average	3.14	3.05	3.34	3.24			

Source: Freedom House

law (F), and personal autonomy and individual rights (G) in such areas as travel freedom and right to hold property. Tallies for each of these seven categories, published by Freedom House since 2005, are aggregated to establish overall scores of 0 to 100, 40 for the first three categories of political rights and 60 for the remaining four categories for civil rights.[15]

Freedom House has focused especially upon the extent to which countries meet the standards of an electoral democracy, which it defines as one achieving scores of at least 7 out of 12 on electoral process and 20 out of 40 for the three political rights categories. Of all countries worldwide, 60 percent met the Freedom House electoral democracy standard in 2011, but only 18 of 49 (37 percent) of sub-Saharan countries so qualified. However, if democracy is defined more broadly by *total* Freedom House scores, 15 countries exceeded the worldwide average of 61.3 in 2011, up from 13 in 2005—Kenya fell out of this group in 2011, while Sierra Leone—restored from civil war—Tanzania, and Zambia joined it. This group includes both countries in the "free" category and a few at the high end of the hybrid group By the same measure, however, Freedom House found that over the same period 29 of 48 countries experienced declining scores. Overall scores for sub-Saharan African countries for this period declined from 49.0 to 45.5 while, excluding African countries, average scores worldwide edged up slightly from 65.8 to 66.3.[16]

It is important to observe, however, that the sub-Saharan African declines have been concentrated among the hybrids and the already undemocratic countries, by Freedom House standards, to a far greater extent than among the dozen or so pacesetting democracies. Losses of the eight pacesetters that suffered retreats averaged only 1.8 points while twenty-one of the other thirty-five that declined did so by an average of 8.7 points. Table 5.3 shows scores for each of the seven areas as percentages of perfect scores. The table shows that the declines, overall, occurred in five of the seven broad categories, excluding electoral process and personal autonomy rights. Declines were somewhat greater in the civil liberties categories than in political rights. These declines were found in rule-of-law observance but also in two categories on which sub-Saharan African performance has been the strongest over time: freedom of expression and associational rights.

The Cingranelli and Richards indices (CIRI; Table 5.4) concentrate on particular clusters of citizen rights that are implicitly covered by the Freedom House surveys but are not singled out specifically.[17] CIRI rates most countries worldwide on fourteen separate indicators, scoring them 2 if the rights are generally fully respected, 0 if they are not, and 1 if it's a mixed picture. The fourteen indicators are aggregated into four groups. The CIRI index is distinctive in centering in some depth on rights to physical integrity. These include not being subjected to disappearance, torture, extrajudicial killing, and imprisonment for one's political views. In the category of empowerment rights, the seven CIRI indicators correspond roughly to those of freedom of expression and association rights in the Freedom House indices while pinpointing freedom to travel externally and domestically, which are included in Freedom House measures of personal autonomy. In addition, CIRI specifically gauges workers' and women's socioeconomic and political rights. It singles out judicial independence for its importance in guaranteeing the upholding of those rights.

Table 5.3. Freedom House: Sub-Saharan African Liberties Scores, 2005–2011

					2011			
	Tot.	A	B	C	D	E	F	G
Cape Verde	90	100	94	83	94	92	88	81
Mauritius	90	100	94	92	94	100	81	75
Ghana	84	100	94	83	88	92	75	63
South Africa	82	100	88	67	94	100	63	69
Benin	81	67	100	67	94	92	81	63
Sao Tome	80	92	88	67	94	83	75	63
Namibia	76	83	69	75	88	100	69	56
Botswana	75	83	69	67	81	83	75	69
Mali	72	75	81	75	100	83	50	44
Senegal	71	75	75	58	88	83	63	56
Lesotho	69	75	69	67	88	58	69	56
Sierra Leone	67	83	69	58	81	67	50	63
Seychelles	67	67	63	58	69	75	69	69
Tanzania	64	75	75	58	69	58	63	50
Zambia	63	75	81	58	69	58	50	50
Liberia	60	75	69	50	69	67	44	50
Mozambique	59	50	63	58	75	58	50	56
Malawi	57	58	69	58	63	50	56	63
Kenya	57	50	63	42	88	67	44	44
Niger	56	75	63	58	69	67	31	38
Comoros	55	75	69	42	63	50	50	38
Burkina Faso	51	42	44	33	81	67	38	50
Nigeria	49	50	56	50	56	67	25	44
Guinea-Bissau	45	75	44	17	63	67	25	31
Togo	44	42	50	33	50	50	38	44
Uganda	42	25	44	25	69	42	38	44
Madagascar	39	8	31	8	63	58	38	56
C.A.R.	39	58	44	25	63	42	19	25
Burundi	35	33	38	25	50	33	25	38
Guinea	34	42	50	8	44	42	25	25
Gabon	34	17	25	25	63	33	38	31
Mauritania	33	25	19	42	56	33	25	31
Djibouti	29	25	19	25	44	25	25	38
Angola	29	25	38	8	50	33	25	19
Congo-Brazzaville	29	8	19	25	50	50	13	38
Rwanda	25	17	13	33	25	17	25	44

A=electoral process
B=political pluralism & participation
C=accountable transparent government
D=freedom of expression and belief

	2005						
Tot.	A	B	C	D	E	F	G
90	100	94	83	94	92	88	81
91	100	94	92	94	100	88	75
84	100	94	83	88	92	75	63
88	100	88	83	94	100	81	75
78	67	88	67	94	92	75	63
80	92	88	67	94	83	75	63
77	83	75	75	94	100	63	56
78	92	69	75	88	83	81	63
74	75	75	75	94	75	69	56
76	100	75	75	94	75	63	56
74	83	75	75	94	67	69	56
60	75	63	33	75	67	50	56
68	67	69	58	69	75	69	69
58	50	63	50	69	58	0	0
56	42	69	50	69	67	50	44
56	75	63	33	69	58	44	50
56	58	69	58	63	58	38	50
57	68	63	50	69	67	50	44
66	75	69	50	88	75	50	56
62	83	63	58	69	58	63	44
48	58	50	25	63	50	50	38
53	42	50	33	81	75	38	50
49	58	50	50	69	58	25	38
59	75	63	50	75	67	50	38
25	17	19	17	44	25	6	44
45	25	38	42	69	50	44	44
60	67	56	58	63	67	56	56
44	58	44	25	63	75	19	31
49	75	69	42	56	42	25	38
32	17	31	17	50	42	25	38
40	17	31	25	69	50	44	38
38	17	38	25	63	50	38	31
35	33	31	25	44	42	31	38
29	17	31	8	50	50	25	19
37	25	31	33	56	67	13	38
32	25	19	42	44	25	38	31

E =associational/organizational freedom
F =rule of law observance
G=personal autonomy (travel, gender, econ. opp.)

continues

Table 5.3. Freedom House: Sub-Saharan African Liberties Scores, 2005–2011 *continued*

	2011							
	Tot.	A	B	C	D	E	F	G
Côte d'Ivoire	24	42	25	17	25	42	0	25
Gambia	24	17	31	0	31	33	13	38
Cameroon	23	17	19	17	44	25	13	25
Chad	21	25	6	8	44	33	13	19
Swaziland	21	0	6	0	50	25	31	25
Zimbabwe	20	17	25	17	25	25	6	25
Congo-Kinshasa	20	25	25	17	44	25	0	6
Ethiopia	19	8	13	33	25	0	19	31
Sudan	10	17	19	8	19	8	0	0
Eq.Guinea	8	0	6	0	25	0	0	19
Eritrea	6	0	6	8	6	0	0	19
Somalia	1	0	0	0	6	0	0	0
Africa Avg.	45.5	47	48	39	60	50	37	41
World Avg.	61.3	64	63	53	71	64	53	60
Afr./World-i	75	73	76	74	85	80	71	69
World-Afr.	65.9	70	68	58	73	68	57	66
Afr./World-o	69	67	71	67	82	74	65	62

A=electoral process
B=political pluralism & participation
C=accountable transparent government
D=freedom of expression and belief

Table 5.4. CIRI: Sub-Saharan African Liberties, 1990–2010

	Total			Physical Integrity			Empowerment Rights
	World	Africa	%	World	Africa	%	World
2010	16.9	14.2	0.37	5.0	4.1	0.34	8.2
2005	17	15.1	0.40	5.1	4.3	0.36	8.4
2000	13.5	12.6	0.46	4.5	3.9	0.41	8.3
1990	11.2	10.9	0.49	4.4	3.7	0.39	7.8

CIRI=Cingranelli and Richards

2005							
Tot.	A	B	C	D	E	F	G
21	17	13	17	31	25	19	25
49	50	44	33	63	50	50	50
27	25	31	25	44	25	13	25
26	25	13	25	44	50	13	19
21	0	6	0	50	25	25	31
15	8	24	0	31	25	6	6
20	8	31	17	38	42	0	6
36	42	38	33	44	25	31	38
11	0	25	8	25	8	0	6
10	0	6	0	31	0	6	19
14	0	6	17	13	0	19	38
15	0	25	33	19	8	19	0
49.0	47	49	41	63	55	40	41
61.8	64	63	56	73	67	54	60
79	73	78	75	87	83	76	69
65.4	68	69	60	74	70	58	66
75	69	71	68	85	79	69	62

E =associational/organizational freedom
F =rule of law observance
G=personal autonomy (travel, gender, econ. opp.)

	Africa	%	Women's Rights			Judicial Independence		
			World	Africa	%	World	Africa	%
	7.0	0.39	3.3	2.8	0.36	0.9	0.5	0.32
	7.2	0.39	3.1	2.9	0.45	1.1	0.7	0.31
	7.2	0.40	2.4	2.4	0.49	1.1	0.8	0.34
	6.1	0.34	1.9	1.9	0.49	1.2	0.9	0.35

CIRI assessments (Table 5.4) record the same trajectories as do those of Freedom House assessments: steady increases in the observance of all four categories of rights from 1990 to 2005 followed by noticeable declines by 2010, except for women's rights, which lost ground by 2010 only relative to worldwide scores. Raw scores for each category and total scores are also normed to indicate their relationship to worldwide CIRI index averages.

Table 5.5. CIRI: Liberties in Sub-Saharan Africa, 2010

	Total	%	Phyisical Integrity		Empower Rights		Women's Rights		Judicial Independence	
Cape Verde	25	0.85	7	0.81	13	0.87	3	0.41	2	0.89
Sao Tome	24	0.82	8	0.90	12	0.82	3	0.41	1	0.54
Mauritius	24	0.82	6	0.67	12	0.82	4	0.70	2	0.89
Lesotho	22	0.74	6	0.67	10	0.67	4	0.70	2	0.89
Botswana	22	0.74	7	0.81	10	0.67	3	0.41	2	0.89
Namibia	21	0.70	6	0.67	10	0.67	3	0.41	2	0.89
Malawi	21	0.70	5	0.50	11	0.75	3	0.41	2	0.89
Seychelles	20	0.65	8	0.90	8	0.48	4	0.70	0	0.16
Burkina Faso	20	0.65	5	0.50	12	0.82	3	0.41	0	0.16
Mali	19	0.60	5	0.50	11	0.75	3	0.41	0	0.16
Ghana	19	0.60	4	0.33	11	0.75	3	0.41	1	0.54
Comoros	19	0.60	8	0.90	8	0.48	2	0.16	1	0.54
Djibouti	19	0.60	7	0.81	8	0.48	3	0.41	1	0.54
Niger	18	0.56	5	0.50	8	0.48	4	0.70	1	0.54
Congo-Brazzaville	18	0.56	5	0.50	10	0.67	3	0.41	0	0.16
South Africa	18	0.56	2	0.10	11	0.75	4	0.70	1	0.54
Liberia	18	0.56	5	0.50	10	0.67	3	0.41	0	0.16
Guinea-Bissau	17	0.51	6	0.67	9	0.58	2	0.16	0	0.16
Gabon	17	0.51	6	0.67	8	0.48	3	0.41	0	0.16
Gambia, The	16	0.45	4	0.33	8	0.48	4	0.70	0	0.16
Sierra Leone	16	0.45	5	0.50	8	0.48	2	0.16	1	0.54
Benin	16	0.45	4	0.33	8	0.48	3	0.41	1	0.54
Mozambique	16	0.45	5	0.50	7	0.39	4	0.70	0	0.16
Tanzania	15	0.40	5	0.50	7	0.39	3	0.41	0	0.16
Zambia	15	0.40	4	0.33	8	0.48	3	0.41	0	0.16
Mauritania	14	0.36	5	0.50	6	0.30	3	0.41	0	0.16
Rwanda	13	0.31	3	0.19	5	0.22	4	0.70	1	0.54
Senegal	13	0.31	4	0.33	7	0.39	2	0.16	0	0.16
Guinea	13	0.31	4	0.33	7	0.39	2	0.16	0	0.16

continues

Table 5.5. CIRI: Liberties in Sub-Saharan Africa, 2010 *continued*

	Total	%	Phyisical Integrity		Empower Rights		Women's Rights		Judicial Independence	
Burundi	12	0.27	2	0.10	7	0.39	3	0.41	0	0.16
Angola	12	0.27	4	0.33	5	0.22	3	0.41	0	0.16
Swaziland	12	0.27	4	0.33	5	0.22	2	0.16	1	0.54
Chad	12	0.27	4	0.33	6	0.30	2	0.16	0	0.16
Kenya	11	0.23	4	0.33	5	0.22	2	0.16	0	0.16
Eq. Guinea	11	0.23	3	0.19	5	0.22	3	0.41	0	0.16
Togo	10	0.19	3	0.19	4	0.16	3	0.41	0	0.16
Côte d'Ivoire	10	0.19	2	0.10	5	0.22	3	0.41	0	0.16
C.A.R.	10	0.19	2	0.10	5	0.22	3	0.41	0	0.16
Madagascar	9	0.16	2	0.10	4	0.16	3	0.41	0	0.16
Uganda	8	0.13	2	0.10	4	0.16	2	0.16	0	0.16
Sudan	8	0.13	1	0.04	4	0.16	3	0.41	0	0.16
Ethiopia	7	0.11	2	0.10	3	0.11	2	0.16	0	0.16
Cameroon	7	0.11	3	0.19	2	0.07	2	0.16	0	0.16
Congo-Kinshasa	5	0.07	1	0.04	2	0.07	2	0.16	0	0.16
Nigeria	5	0.07	0	0.01	3	0.11	2	0.16	0	0.16
Zimbabwe	3	0.04	1	0.04	0	0.03	2	0.16	0	0.16
Eritrea	2	0.03	0	0.01	0	0.03	2	0.16	0	0.16
Africa Avg.	14.2	0.37	4.1	0.34	7	0.39	2.8	0.36	0.5	0.32
World Avg.	16.9	0.50	5	0.50	8.2	0.50	3.3	0.50	0.9	0.50

In general, the CIRI 2010 (Table 5.5) assessments find the same sub-Saharan countries to be above average by global standards as has Freedom House, although scores for Burkina Faso and to some extent Malawi are higher, while those for South Africa and especially Benin are noticeably lower because of low scores in the physical integrity category. Only perfect scores placed a country more than one standard deviation above the mean, scores approached only by the three island countries of Cape Verde, Mauritius, and Sao Tome. By contrast, nearly a quarter of sub-Saharan countries scored more than a standard deviation below worldwide norms. Particularly noteworthy is the number of countries rating scores of 3 or 4 out of 4 on women's rights and scores of 2 for only six countries on a crucial safeguard for the upholding of liberties: judicial independence. CIRI found generally independent judiciaries only in Cape Verde, Mauritius, Lesotho, Botswana, Namibia, and Malawi.

The Economist Intelligence Unit (EIU) has conducted surveys of democratic performance worldwide since 2006 that appear to fairly closely resemble those of Freedom House.[18] EIU scores countries from 0 to 0.5 to 1 on sixty questions that it tallies up scores in five categories: electoral process and pluralism (A), governmental functioning (B), political participation (C), political culture (D), and civil liberties (E), yielding scores of 0 to 10 in each category (Table 5.6). The EIU regards scores of 8 to 10, overall and in each category, as evidence of full democracy, those between from 6 up to 8 as indicating flawed democracy, those from 4 up to 6 as those of hybrid regimes and scores below 4 as autocracies.

Table 5.6. Economist Intelligence Unit: Democracy Scores, 2011–2006

	2011					
	Total	A	B	C	D	E
Worldwide	5.49	5.97	4.97	4.72	5.54	6.26
Africa	4.28	4.15	3.46	3.96	5.04	4.80
Mauritius	8.04	9.17	8.21	5.00	8.13	9.71
Cape Verde	7.92	9.17	7.86	7.22	6.25	9.12
South Africa	7.79	8.75	8.21	7.22	6.25	8.53
Botswana	7.63	9.17	7.14	5.56	6.88	9.41
Mali	6.36	8.25	6.43	4.44	5.63	7.06
Lesotho	6.33	7.42	5.71	6.11	5.63	6.76
Namibia	6.24	5.67	5.00	6.67	5.63	8.24
Zambia	6.19	7.92	5.00	4.44	6.25	7.35
Benin	6.06	7.33	6.43	4.44	5.63	6.47
Ghana	6.02	8.33	5.00	5.00	5.00	6.76
Malawi	5.84	7.00	5.71	5.56	5.63	5.29
Tanzania	5.64	7.42	4.29	5.56	5.63	5.29
Senegal	5.51	7.00	4.29	4.44	5.63	6.18
Uganda	5.13	5.67	2.86	5.00	6.25	5.88
Liberia	5.07	7.83	0.79	5.56	5.00	6.18
Mozambique	4.90	4.83	4.64	5.56	5.63	3.82
Kenya	4.71	3.92	4.29	4.44	5.63	5.29
Sierra Leone	4.51	7.00	1.86	2.78	5.63	5.29
Mauritania	4.17	3.42	4.29	5.00	3.13	5.00
Niger	4.16	7.50	1.14	2.78	4.38	5.00
Burundi	4.01	3.42	3.29	3.89	5.63	3.82
Madagascar	3.93	2.17	2.14	5.00	5.63	4.71
Nigeria	3.83	5.67	3.21	3.33	3.13	3.82
Ethiopia	3.79	0.00	3.93	5.00	5.63	4.41
Burkina Faso	3.59	4.00	3.57	2.22	3.75	4.41

Generally the same countries topped the EIU surveys of democratic performance as those of Freedom House and CIRI. The EIU adjudged only Mauritius, among sub-Saharan African countries, to be a full democracy in both 2006 and 2011. The number of flawed democracies increased from six to nine with the addition of former hybrids Mali, Zambia, and Ghana. The ranks of hybrids diminished from thirteen to eleven as Gambia and Ethiopia sank back into autocracy, while autocracies in Sierra Leone, Mauritania, and Niger became hybrids.

2006					
Total	**A**	**B**	**C**	**D**	**E**
5.52	6.02	4.98	4.45	5.82	6.32
4.21	4.00	3.54	3.38	5.42	4.72
8.04	9.17	8.21	5.00	8.13	9.71
7.43	9.17	7.86	5.00	6.88	8.24
7.91	8.75	7.86	7.22	6.88	8.82
7.60	9.17	7.86	5.00	6.88	9.12
5.99	8.25	5.71	3.89	5.63	6.47
6.48	7.92	6.43	4.44	6.25	7.35
6.54	4.75	4.00	6.67	8.75	8.53
5.25	5.25	4.64	3.33	6.25	6.76
6.16	6.83	6.43	3.89	6.88	6.76
5.35	7.42	4.64	4.44	4.38	5.88
4.97	6.00	5.00	3.89	4.38	5.59
5.18	6.00	3.93	5.06	5.63	5.29
5.37	7.00	5.00	3.33	5.63	5.88
5.14	4.33	3.93	4.44	6.25	6.76
5.22	7.75	2.14	5.00	5.63	5.59
5.28	5.25	5.71	4.44	6.88	4.12
5.08	4.33	4.29	5.56	6.25	5.00
3.57	5.25	2.21	2.22	3.75	4.41
3.12	1.83	4.29	2.22	3.13	4.12
3.54	5.25	1.14	1.67	3.75	5.88
4.51	4.42	3.29	3.89	6.25	4.71
5.82	5.67	5.71	5.56	6.88	5.29
3.52	3.08	1.86	4.44	4.38	3.82
4.72	4.00	3.93	5.00	6.25	4.41
3.72	4.00	1.79	2.78	5.63	4.41

A=electoral process and pluralism
B=govt. functioning
C=political participation
D=culture
E=liberties

continues

Table 5.6. Economist Intelligence Unit: Democracy Scores, 2011–2006 *continued*

	2011					
	Total	A	B	C	D	E
Comoros	3.52	3.92	2.21	3.89	3.75	3.82
Gabon	3.48	2.17	2.21	3.89	5.00	4.12
Togo	3.45	4.00	0.79	3.33	5.00	4.12
Cameroon	3.41	1.17	4.29	2.78	5.00	3.82
Gambia	3.38	2.17	4.29	2.22	5.00	3.24
Angola	3.32	1.33	3.21	4.44	4.38	3.24
Swaziland	3.26	0.92	2.86	2.78	5.63	4.12
Rwanda	3.25	0.83	4.64	1.67	5.00	4.12
Côte d'Ivoire	3.08	0.00	1.79	4.44	5.63	3.53
Congo-Brazzaville	2.89	1.25	2.86	3.33	3.75	3.24
Guinea	2.79	3.50	0.43	3.33	3.75	3.24
Djibouti	2.68	0.83	1.79	2.22	5.63	2.94
Zimbabwe	2.68	0.00	1.29	3.89	5.00	3.24
Sudan	2.38	0.00	1.79	3.33	5.00	1.76
Eritrea	2.34	0.00	2.86	1.11	6.25	1.47
Dem. Rep. Congo	2.15	2.58	1.07	2.22	3.13	1.76
Guinea-Bissau	1.99	2.08	0.00	2.78	1.88	3.24
C.A.R.	1.82	1.75	1.07	1.11	2.50	2.65
Equatorial Guinea	1.77	0.00	0.79	2.22	4.38	1.47
Chad	1.62	0.00	0.00	1.11	3.75	3.24

The EIU surveys, while centering on the same indicators of democracy as Freedom House, generally embrace a concept of democracy that is "thicker" than both the more minimalist and more overarching Freedom House conceptions in that they survey the extent of actual political participation and the extent of democratic political culture that Afrobarometer gauges in much greater depth.[19]

The EIU surveys present a trajectory of recent progress on democratic liberties that differs somewhat from those of Freedom House over approximately the same period. EIU finds modest democratic progress for sub-Saharan African countries, whereas Freedom House notes a decline. EIU records modest progress in electoral performance and in the observance of civil liberties. It found substantial progress in degrees of political participation, but a modest decline in governmental performance.

The EIU's finding of flawed overall slippage in political culture from 2006 to 2011 suggests that citizen perceptions of democratic performance, if perhaps

2006					
Total	A	B	C	D	E
3.90	3.00	3.21	4.44	5.63	3.24
2.72	0.50	3.21	2.22	5.63	2.06
1.75	0.00	0.79	0.56	5.63	1.76
3.27	0.92	3.21	2.78	5.63	3.82
4.39	4.00	4.64	4.44	5.63	3.24
2.41	0.50	2.14	1.11	5.63	2.65
2.93	1.75	2.86	2.22	3.13	4.71
3.82	3.00	3.57	2.22	5.00	5.29
3.38	1.25	2.86	3.33	5.63	3.82
3.19	1.42	2.86	2.22	5.63	3.82
2.00	2.08	0.07	3.33	1.88	2.65
2.37	2.50	1.43	0.56	5.00	2.35
2.62	0.17	0.79	3.89	5.63	2.65
2.90	2.25	2.36	1.67	5.00	3.24
2.31	0.00	2.14	1.11	6.25	2.06
2.76	4.58	0.36	2.78	3.75	2.35
2.02	1.00	0.79	2.22	3.75	2.35
1.61	0.42	1.43	1.67	1.88	2.65
2.09	0.00	2.86	1.11	5.00	1.47
1.65	0.00	0.00	0.00	5.00	3.24

A=electoral process and
  pluralism
B=govt. functioning
C=political participation
D=culture
E=liberties

not directly a cause of democratic retreat, is nonetheless a significant negative factor in slowing democratic momentum and endangering democratic sustainability. The political culture questions in the EIU survey derive in several cases, where possible, from the World Values surveys.[20] They probe citizen appraisal of democracy in general and of the government in addition to offering specific assessments of political parties and military and technocratic rule. Also included are questions gauging citizen interest in politics, attentiveness to the news, and willingness to participate in lawful demonstrations. Citizens were queried on their views on the capacity of democratic governments to preserve order and to manage the economy. Only Mauritius maintained a democratic political culture in both years, while six remained in the flawed category: Cape Verde, South Africa, Botswana, and Zambia, plus one hybrid, Uganda, and, remarkably, thoroughly autocratic Eritrea. Overall, only three countries moved into a higher category, from autocratic to hybrid: overall hybrids Niger and

Sierra Leone and autocratic Swaziland. In EIU's estimation, fourteen countries sank into a lower political culture category, most notably overall flawed democratic Namibia from fully democratic to hybrid, in addition to eight from flawed to hybrid and five from hybrid to autocratic.[21]

In sum, the three major surveys concentrating on the status of democratic liberties in sub-Saharan Africa suggest that a few countries have remained fully or nearly fully democratic, notwithstanding recent overall declines in upholding some rights, detracting from overall gains in observance of liberties over the two decades of sub-Saharan Africa's Third Wave democratic era. Though Freedom House has recorded a decline in the number of electoral democracies from twenty-two to eighteen since 2005, at the same time the surveys imply a consensus that overall democratic progress has been generally sustained in twelve countries: the four island countries of Sao Tome, Mauritius, Seychelles, and Cape Verde; the five southern African countries of South Africa, Botswana, Namibia, Malawi, and Lesotho; and the west African countries of Ghana, Benin, and Mali.

Freedom House data suggest declines in the upholding of liberties were concentrated among the already hybrid and nondemocratic countries rather than among the pacesetters. Where Freedom House found across-the-board overall regression in the upholding of political rights and civil liberties since 2005, CIRI recorded specific declines over the same period in rights to physical integrity, as well as empowerment rights corresponding to Freedom House data on civil liberties. CIRI found recent gains in women's rights, and noted a significant general deficiency in judicial independence, tallying with Freedom House observance of weakness in the rule of law. While EIU surveys detect a more mixed picture concerning recent trends on upholding basic rights, the organization did find a fairly precipitous decline in democratic political culture, pointing to a possibly important factor in slowing democratization momentum in recent years.

Democratic Governance

A centrally requisite element in strengthening democratic governance in sub-Saharan African countries has been constitutionalizing restraints on the exercise of executive power to end a long era of arbitrary, corrupt, and repressive executive behavior prevalent over the first decades of the region's independence era, in many respects a carryover from patterns of colonial rule. Popular manifestations of that project have been demands and demonstrations in support of limiting elected presidents to two five-year terms, campaigns that have been successful in many but not all countries in the first decades of the region's independence era.

The most widely cited index on these points has been Polity IV, which has targeted progress in constitutionalizing executive authority.[22] Its surveys have assessed countries in terms of the extent to which presidential power is subject to restraints and competition for the office is open and in fact competitive. More generally, Polity IV surveys have taken into account the extent to which political authority is subject to constitutional guidelines and political competition is generally orderly and rule governed. The Polity IV surveys have covered most of the world's states not only since the organization's inception in the mid-1990s but retrospectively back to 1800.[23] The Polity surveys probe both remaining elements of authoritarian governance and those that are democratic, each according to a scale of 0 to 10, with the authoritarian score subtracted from the democratic score. Polity's authors consider to be democratic countries that record scores of +6 or better; those that score –6 or lower are certifiable autocracies; and those with scores in between are considered ambiguous polities or *anocracies*.[24]

Table 5.7. Polity IV: African Executive Restraints, Openness, Access

	2010	Norm	2005	Norm	2000	Norm	1995	Norm	1990	Norm
Mauritius	10	0.84	10	0.85	10	0.87	10	0.89	10	0.90
South Africa	9	0.80	9	0.80	9	0.83	9	0.85	5	0.72
Comoros	9	0.80	6	0.65	–1	0.28			4	0.68
Kenya	8	0.75	8	0.76	–2	0.23	–5	0.12	–7	0.15
Ghana	8	0.75	8	0.76	2	0.45	–1	0.29	–7	0.15
Lesotho	8	0.75	8	0.76			8	0.81	–7	0.15
Botswana	8	0.75	8	0.76	8	0.79	7	0.77	7	0.81
Senegal	7	0.70	8	0.76	8	0.79	–1	0.29	–1	0.41
Zambia	7	0.70	5	0.59	1	0.39	6	0.72	–9	0.10
Mali	7	0.70	7	0.71	6	0.69	7	0.77	–7	0.15
Benin	7	0.70	6	0.65	6	0.69	6	0.72		
Sierra Leone	7	0.70	5	0.59			–7	0.07	–7	0.15
Burundi	6	0.64	6	0.65	–1	0.28			–7	0.15
Malawi	6	0.64	6	0.65	6	0.69	6	0.72	–9	0.10
Guinea-Bissau	6	0.64	6	0.65	5	0.63	5	0.66	–8	0.12
Namibia	6	0.64	6	0.65	6	0.69	6	0.72	6	0.77
Liberia	6	0.64			0	0.33				
Mozambique	5	0.58	5	0.59	5	0.63	5	0.66	–7	0.15
Guinea	5	0.58	–1	0.24	–1	0.28	–1	0.29	–7	0.15
Congo-Kinshasa	5	0.58							–8	0.12
Nigeria	4	0.51	4	0.53	4	0.57	–6	0.09	–5	0.22
Gabon	3	0.45	–4	0.12	–4	0.15	–4	0.15		

continues

Table 5.7. Polity IV: African Executive Restraints, Openness, Access *continued*

	2010	Norm	2005	Norm	2000	Norm	1995	Norm	1990	Norm
Niger	3	0.45	6	0.65	5	0.63	8	0.81	−7	0.15
Djibouti	2	0.39	2	0.41	2	0.45	−7	0.07	−8	0.12
Zimbabwe	1	0.33	−4	0.12	−3	0.19	−6	0.09	−6	0.19
Ethiopia	1	0.33	1	0.35	1	0.39	1	0.41	−8	0.12
Madagascar	0	0.27	7	0.71	7	0.74	9	0.85	−6	0.19
Burkina Faso	0	0.27	0	0.29	−3	0.19	−5	0.12	−7	0.15
Uganda	−1	0.22	−1	0.24	−4	0.15	−4	0.15	−7	0.15
Tanzania	−1	0.22	−1	0.24	−1	0.28	−1	0.29	−6	0.19
C.A.R.	−1	0.22	−1	0.24	5	0.63	5	0.66	−7	0.15
Angola	−2	0.17	−2	0.20	−3	0.19			−7	0.15
Togo	−2	0.17	−4	0.12	−2	0.23	−2	0.24	−7	0.15
Sudan	−2	0.17	−4	0.12	−7	0.07	−7	0.07	−7	0.15
Chad	−2	0.17	−2	0.20	−2	0.23	−4	0.15	−7	0.15
Mauritania	−2	0.17	−5	0.09	−6	0.09	−6	0.09	−7	0.15
Rwanda	−4	0.10	−3	0.15	−4	0.15	−6	0.09	−7	0.15
Cameroon	−4	0.10	−4	0.12	−4	0.15	−4	0.15	−8	0.12
Congo-Brazzaville	−4	0.10	−4	0.12	−6	0.09	5	0.66	−8	0.12
Gambia	−5	0.08	−5	0.09	−5	0.12	−7	0.07	8	0.84
Equatorial Guinea	−5	0.08	−5	0.09	−5	0.12	−5	0.12	−7	0.15
Eritrea	−7	0.04	−7	0.05	−6	0.09	−6	0.09		
Swaziland	−9	0.02	−9	0.03	−9	0.03	−9	0.04	−10	0.08
Somalia		0.27							−7	0.15
Ivory Coast		0.27			4		−6	0.09	−7	0.15
Africa Average	2.3		1.6		0.5		0.2		−4.7	
World Average	3.8		3.5		2.8		2.4		0.6	
Dem States	17		16		9		19		4	
Anocracies	24		22		27		10		5	
Autocracies	2		2		5		10		32	
State Collapse	2		5		4		6		3	

As Table 5.7 indicates, Polity IV has recorded a steady increase in the number of sub-Saharan democracies since 1990. Only Mauritius, Botswana, and Namibia qualified in 1990, the number rising to nine in 2000, seventeen in 2005, and eighteen in 2010. The countries found to be most democratic in their protection of liberties are also regarded as democracies in the Polity IV surveys, although the three island countries of Seychelles, Sao Tome, and Cape Verde are not included in the surveys. Between 2005 and 2010, Sierra

Leone, Liberia, and Zambia joined the list following the conclusion of the civil wars in the former two countries. In that same period, Niger and Madagascar dropped off the list. Several countries that qualify as democracies according to the Polity IV surveys have not appeared on those lists in other surveys: Kenya, Comoros, Guinea-Bissau, and Burundi. Kenya's new constitution, approved in August 2010, places significant limits on presidential authority although implementing legislation has been passed and executed only slowly and still incompletely as of this writing.

The World Bank Institute (WBI) "Governance Matters" surveys have undertaken annual (since 2002) comprehensive surveys of governance, probing the areas of voice and accountability, state stability, governmental effectiveness, regulatory quality, rule of law, and corruption control (Tables 5.8A and 5.8B).[25] WBI incorporates the findings of a great many surveys, including the ones considered in this chapter, in arriving at normed assessments in each of these categories for all countries. The tables outline trajectories in each category when the WBI surveys began in 1996; 2005, given the concerns about recent trends; and 2010.

Overall, the tables indicate that sub-Saharan African countries have continued to rank low by worldwide standards with averages in the vicinity of the 30th percentile. The data suggest only modest changes over time, including slight improvements in voice and accountability, state stability, and regulatory quality counterbalanced by similar slight erosion in the other three categories. Taking all six categories into account, the tables suggest four groups of sub-Saharan African countries: those that have made straight-line progressions or regressions from 1996 to 2010 and those for whom 2005 represented either a dip or a high point en route to 2010 scores above or below the 1996 starting point. Dividing the countries into quadrants, only the lowest quadrant averaged net declines in overall governance quality over the fifteen years of the surveys. Overall sub-Saharan African performance in the WBI surveys has been relatively strongest in the areas of state stability, voice and accountability, and corruption control, while governmental effectiveness, regulatory quality, and rule of law observance consistency trailed these three categories.

Eight of the twelve countries scoring highest in the preceding surveys also led in the 2010 WBI surveys, seven with overall scores above average worldwide, with Lesotho just under 50 percent and Mali, Malawi, and Sao Tome scoring lower although all within the top half of sub-Saharan African countries. Ten of the twelve countries leading in upholding basic liberties in the preceding surveys top the WBI surveys of voice and accountability, with Malawi and Lesotho coming in very near the top as well. As in the Freedom House surveys, net regression in the top quadrant was very low, averaging less than a point, albeit helped along by Ghana's large increase counterbalancing declines for seven of those countries.

Table 5.8A. World Bank Institute: African Governance Measures

	Totals			Voice			State Stability			Government Effectiveness		
	2010	2005	1996	2010	2005	1996	2010	2005	1996	2010	2005	1996
Mauritius	72.6	73.0	69.1	69.7	73.6	73.6	65.6	81.3	76.4	75.6	70.2	63.4
Botswana	70.1	73.6	72.8	59.7	65.9	74.5	78.3	82.2	77.9	67.5	71.7	68.3
Cape Verde	65.4	59.7	61.0	72.5	63.9	71.6	76.4	67.3	80.3	53.6	55.1	
Namibia	61.5	58.2	67.6	57.8	58.7	63.0	71.7	65.4	70.2	59.3	56.6	69.3
South Africa	59.4	63.2	62.9	65.4	70.2	74.0	44.3	41.3	27.4	65.1	72.2	79.0
Seychelles	57.3	58.2	72.9	53.6	52.9	53.4	75.0	80.8	82.2	62.2	58.5	75.6
Ghana	55.8	50.7	43.0	63.0	57.7	38.0	47.6	52.4	38.0	55.5	47.8	53.2
Lesotho	47.4	44.4	42.9	41.2	43.8	29.8	63.2	49.5	50.0	42.1	43.9	52.2
Rwanda	45.2	19.6	8.9	10.9	10.6	6.3	41.5	21.2	3.4	54.1	20.5	11.2
Mozambique	43.5	38.3	37.6	45.0	50.0	39.9	57.1	48.6	42.8	38.8	36.6	52.7
Malawi	43.1	36.4	38.8	43.6	32.2	42.8	49.5	47.6	29.8	41.1	27.3	33.7
Burkina	42.6	40.1	33.4	39.3	34.1	25.0	40.6	44.7	33.7	33.0	32.7	14.1
Benin	40.5	37.6	48.6	55.9	53.4	56.3	56.1	56.7	82.2	35.4	35.1	39.5
Tanzania	40.2	36.6	28.3	46.4	38.9	26.0	45.8	27.9	22.1	37.8	38.5	24.9
Sao Tome	38.8	37.2	52.7	54.5	55.8	51.4	52.4	66.8	82.2	28.7	26.8	39.5
Zambia	38.8	30.2	28.6	38.9	32.7	37.0	63.7	47.1	40.4	23.4	17.1	13.7
Senegal	36.8	49.5	46.3	36.0	54.3	55.3	33.0	40.4	23.1	37.3	47.3	57.1
Mali	36	44.7	35.8	55.0	59.6	48.6	34.9	53.4	53.4	19.1	27.8	9.3
Swaziland	35.1	24.7	36.3	12.8	8.2	11.5	42.9	36.1	43.3	36.4	13.7	27.8
Gambia	34	35.7	36.0	16.1	22.1	13.0	48.6	55.8	59.1	29.7	29.3	29.8
Uganda	32.5	29.2	28.8	33.6	30.8	19.7	15.6	8.2	7.7	34.4	32.2	24.9
Djibouti	31.4	23.4	24.3	14.2	16.8	17.3	55.7	26.0	31.7	15.3	23.4	17.1
Gabon	30.6	37.5	38.9	21.3	23.1	40.9	53.3	55.3	45.2	20.1	22.4	42.9
Kenya	28.9	27.5	27.3	39.8	41.8	32.7	13.7	13.5	20.2	35.9	25.4	43.4
Niger	28.5	31.8	15.8	29.9	40.9	3.4	14.6	31.7	41.3	27.8	24.4	8.3

continues

Table 5.8A. World Bank Institute: African Governance Measures *continued*

	Totals			Voice			State Stability			Government Effectiveness		
	2010	2005	1996	2010	2005	1996	2010	2005	1996	2010	2005	1996
Madagascar	28.4	47.0	39.1	28.0	46.2	41.8	15.1	45.7	48.1	23.0	41.5	31.2
Sierra Leone	26.4	18.2	12.1	41.7	29.8	26.9	37.3	34.6	4.8	11.0	6.8	4.4
Liberia	24.7	13.3	2.6	40.3	36.5	8.2	29.7	10.1	1.0	8.1	6.3	2.0
Ethiopia	22.7	16.8	13.0	11.4	13.5	14.4	5.2	6.3	16.8	42.6	20.0	6.3
Mauritania	21.1	37.4	45.3	23.2	21.2	33.2	12.3	37.0	54.3	17.2	44.4	52.2
Togo	20.1	13.2	26.4	19.9	10.1	16.8	38.2	7.7	28.8	5.7	3.9	22.0
Cameroon	20	19.8	13.2	16.6	18.3	19.2	26.9	39.4	15.9	18.7	19.0	14.6
Comoros	18.7	19.1	22.8	34.6	29.3	27.9	30.7	39.9	60.1	1.0	1.5	2.9
Guinea-Bissau	15.9	17.6	10.0	23.7	37.0	13.9	23.6	28.8	6.7	13.4	5.4	4.4
Angola	15.7	10.9	7.7	14.7	11.5	4.8	36.8	20.2	2.9	12.4	11.2	20.0
Congo-Brazzaville	15.7	11.7	10.2	18.0	15.9	16.3	35.4	16.3	9.1	8.6	8.3	8.3
Nigeria	15.2	15.6	12.1	27.0	23.6	4.3	3.8	5.8	12.0	10.5	22.0	15.1
Burundi	12.7	13.9	4.0	21.8	28.4	5.3	7.5	6.7	2.4	12.9	8.8	2.9
Eq. Guinea	12.6	9.2	13.8	3.3	4.8	7.2	53.8	30.8	35.6	1.9	4.4	13.2
Eritrea	12.5	19.7	27.1	0.5	1.0	7.7	19.8	24.5	19.2	6.2	16.1	11.2
Côte d'Ivoire	11.4	8.0	41.5	15.6	7.7	31.7	7.1	1.0	44.7	7.2	7.3	54.6
C.A.R.	11.1	9.9	11.2	15.2	24.0	20.2	3.3	9.6	12.5	5.3	2.9	5.4
Guinea	10.6	13.7	16.6	22.7	12.0	10.6	4.7	15.4	13.0	11.5	15.1	8.3
Chad	7.4	8.3	17.9	9.5	9.1	15.9	8.0	11.1	16.3	4.3	7.8	27.8
Zimbabwe	5.1	6.1	32.2	7.6	5.3	28.8	13.2	11.5	27.9	3.8	10.2	47.8
Sudan	4.9	4.1	5.5	4.3	4.3	2.4	0.9	2.4	1.4	6.7	4.9	12.2
Congo-Kinshasa	3.6	3.5	1.9	9.0	6.3	3.8	2.8	1.4	0.0	1.4	2.4	3.4
Somalia	0.5	0.6	0.5	2.4	1.9	0.0	0.0	0.5	0.5	0.0	0.0	0.5
Africa Avg.	30.3	29.1	30.1	31.0	31.0	28.5	34.5	33.5	33.3	26.3	25.6	28.1

Table 5.8B. World Bank Institute: African Governance Measures

	Reg. Quality			Rule of Law			Corruption Control		
	2010	2005	1996	2010	2005	1996	2010	2005	1996
Mauritius	76.6	63.2	50.5	74.9	81.8	77.5	73.2	67.8	73.2
Botswana	67.5	70.1	75.0	67.8	68.4	66.5	79.9	83.4	74.6
Cape Verde	51.2	45.6	26.5	64.0	60.3	65.6	74.6	65.9	
Namibia	54.5	55.9	64.7	61.6	52.2	61.2	64.1	60.5	77.1
South Africa	62.7	69.1	65.2	57.8	56.0	53.1	60.8	70.2	78.5
Seychelles	32.1	44.6	62.3	55.9	53.1	81.3	65.1	59.0	82.4
Ghana	54.1	52.0	35.3	54.0	49.8	44.5	60.3	44.4	48.8
Lesotho	28.7	26.5	35.8	46.4	46.9	54.1	62.7	55.6	35.6
Rwanda	47.8	18.6	7.4	46.0	20.1	4.8	70.8	26.3	20.0
Mozambique	40.7	25.5	27.0	37.0	31.6	23.4	42.6	37.6	40.0
Malawi	31.6	37.7	39.2	50.7	46.4	38.3	42.1	27.3	48.8
Burkina	50.2	38.7	41.2	48.3	36.8	22.0	44.0	53.7	64.4
Benin	41.6	27.0	43.6	28.0	35.9	50.2	25.8	17.6	20.0
Tanzania	37.3	40.2	33.3	36.5	43.1	48.3	37.3	30.7	15.1
Sao Tome	23.9	20.1	25.0	29.9	33.5	57.9	43.5	20.0	60.0
Zambia	34.9	24.5	33.8	38.4	36.4	31.6	33.5	23.4	15.1
Senegal	43.1	47.5	44.1	41.7	52.6	49.3	29.7	55.1	48.8
Mali	36.4	35.3	29.4	40.3	48.8	35.4	30.1	43.4	38.5
Swaziland	28.2	29.4	42.6	37.9	21.5	32.5	52.6	39.0	60.0
Gambia	38.8	32.4	19.6	36.0	45.0	56.0	34.9	29.3	38.5
Uganda	48.3	49.0	58.8	42.2	34.0	33.0	20.6	21.0	28.8
Djibouti	25.4	23.5	18.6	28.9	20.6	25.4	48.8	30.2	35.6
Gabon	29.2	48.0	54.4	35.5	38.8	34.0	24.4	37.1	16.1
Kenya	48.8	46.1	36.3	16.6	21.1	16.3	18.7	17.1	15.1
Niger	34.4	38.2	14.2	33.2	27.3	15.8	31.1	28.3	11.7

continues

Table 5.8B. World Bank Institute: African Governance Measures *continued*

	Reg. Quality			Rule of Law			Corruption Control		
	2010	2005	1996	2010	2005	1996	2010	2005	1996
Madagascar	30.6	46.6	17.2	23.7	44.0	32.1	49.8	58.0	63.9
Sierra Leone	24.9	14.7	4.9	18.0	10.5	5.3	25.4	12.7	26.3
Liberia	16.7	4.9	2.0	17.1	8.1	0.5	36.4	14.1	2.0
Ethiopia	21.1	13.7	8.8	27.5	23.0	23.0	28.2	24.4	8.8
Mauritania	22.5	43.1	27.9	22.3	32.5	44.0	29.2	46.3	60.0
Togo	20.1	21.1	34.3	19.0	14.4	29.7	17.7	22.0	26.8
Cameroon	25.8	20.6	14.7	15.2	11.0	7.2	16.7	10.7	7.3
Comoros	5.7	4.4	13.7	13.7	18.2	12.0	26.3	21.5	20.0
Guinea-Bissau	14.4	13.2	22.5	5.7	9.1	1.0	14.4	12.2	11.7
Angola	17.2	10.3	7.8	9.0	5.7	3.3	3.8	6.3	7.3
Congo-Brazzaville	8.1	9.8	10.3	12.3	5.3	6.7	11.5	14.6	10.2
Nigeria	23.0	23.0	22.1	10.9	7.7	10.0	15.8	11.7	8.8
Burundi	11.5	8.3	4.4	10.0	12.4	4.3	12.4	18.5	4.9
Eq. Guinea	6.7	7.4	5.9	8.5	7.2	14.8	1.4	0.5	6.3
Eritrea	1.4	2.5	13.7	8.1	24.4	40.7	39.2	49.8	70.2
Côte d'Ivoire	19.6	19.1	29.9	9.5	4.3	24.4	9.6	8.8	63.4
C.A.R.	12.4	8.8	20.6	6.6	4.8	3.8	23.9	9.3	4.9
Guinea	13.9	15.7	24.5	2.8	8.6	6.7	8.1	15.1	36.6
Chad	13.4	11.8	9.3	3.8	6.7	18.2	5.3	3.4	20.0
Zimbabwe	2.4	0.5	19.1	0.9	1.4	25.8	2.4	7.8	43.9
Sudan	7.2	7.8	8.3	6.2	2.9	3.3	4.3	2.4	5.4
Congo-Kinshasa	3.3	3.4	2.9	2.4	3.8	1.4	2.9	3.9	0.0
Somalia	0.5	1.0	0.0	0.0	0.0	0.0	0.0	0.0	2.0
Africa Avg.	29.0	27.5	27.3	28.4	27.7	29.1	32.4	29.5	33.1

Measuring governmental quality, absent its democratic voice and accountability element, seven of the same twelve countries recorded scores above worldwide averages, with Lesotho very close behind and Mali, Sao Tome, and Malawi registering notably lower. Again, the top dozen countries all recorded overall governance gains, with losses distributed fairly evenly across the other three quadrants.

Finally, the Mo Ibrahim Foundation assessed governance quality for all African countries, including those of North Africa, since 2000.[26] The Mo Ibrahim Index (MOI) differs from all the others in its more extensive combining of political and socioeconomic indicators. It assesses country progress annually on a scale of 0 to 100 in four broad areas: safety and rule of law, participation and human rights, sustainable economic development, and human development opportunity.

Each broad category includes two levels of subcategories, all assessed on a 0 to 100 scale. Subsectors of safety and the rule of law include measures of judicial independence and process, quality of power transfers, status of property rights, public-sector accountability and transparency, corruption control, measures of freedom from persecution and violent crime, personal safety, national security, and status of cross-border tensions and army involvement in conflict. Participation and human rights subsectors include measures of electoral quality, ability of elected governments to actually govern, observance of human rights conventions, workers' rights, freedom of speech and expression, freedom of the press, and freedom of association. It also measures gender equality, including the status of women in the workforce, in rural areas, in parliament, in primary and secondary education, and violence-against-women laws. MOI implicitly defines sustainable development in terms of the quality of public management (including budget management and debt management indices), quality of the business environment, infrastructure measures, connectivity indices, and the status of rural economies (including access to land, water, markets, and quality of dialogue between rural peoples and government). Human development subsectors include access to health and education facilities, labor and social protection facilities, improved water and sanitation, environmental sustainability measures, educational access, and disease protection regimes.

Table 5.9 portrays a contrast between, on the one hand, steady progress over the first eleven years of the new millennium in both sustainable economic development and human development opportunity and, on the other hand, roughly unchanged scores on participation and human rights and clear decline in the safety rule-of-law area, especially since 2006.[27] The evidence that marked socioeconomic progress has not been accompanied by corresponding progress, indeed some regression in the condition of African polities since 2005 can be interpreted in either or both of two ways: socioeconomic development processes are being pursued with indifference to their implications for the polity and/or lack of momentum or sense of empowerment not only to realize sustainable economic development and channel to human development purposes but to deploy it in pursuit of constructive political ends.

The MOI data for all sub-Saharan African countries (Tables 5.10A and 5.10B) indicate declines in overall scores averaging 0.8 points. They indicate marginal gains in three of seven basic political development subcategories: accountability, national security, and gender equality. They show average declines of about three points in the areas of rule of law, observance of civil rights, and freedom to participate politically. A sharp decline of 7.9 points occurred in the area of personal safety.

The data demonstrate that the strongest performers in the seven political performance categories were generally the same countries leading in the other indices. They also indicate that the declines were on average the least in this group (0.9 points), followed closely by the countries in the second quadrant (1.5 points). The bulk of the declines were concentrated in the least democratic countries, those in the third and fourth quadrants. Countries in the first three quadrants in terms of overall political performance averaged gains of about 4.5 points in sustainable development and about 5.5 points in human development opportunities. Countries in the lowest quadrant of political performance averaged notably smaller gains of about 0.09 in sustainable development and 3.7 points in human development opportunity.

Table 5.9. Mo Ibrahim Index: Sub-Saharan Africa Political Economy

	Safety & Rule of Law	Participation & Human Rights	Sustainable Economic Development	Human Development Opportunity	Overall Score
2010	52.8	46.6	45.9	53.8	49.8
2009	52.6	46.3	45.2	53.6	49.4
2008	54.3	47.1	44.3	52.4	49.5
2007	54.4	49.1	43.6	51.4	49.6
2006	54.8	48.9	43.2	49.8	49.2
2005	54.8	47.9	42.3	48.8	48.4
2004	54.6	47.2	41.3	47.4	47.7
2003	54.3	46.1	41.2	47.0	47.1
2002	54.9	47.1	41.0	46.2	47.3
2001	54.2	46.8	41.0	45.8	46.9
2000	53.5	46.5	40.6	44.9	46.4
2010/2000	−0.7	0.1	5.3	8.9	3.4
2010/2005	−2.0	−1.3	3.6	5.0	1.4

Table 5.10A. 2010 Mo Ibrahim Index: Progress Toward Democratic Stateness

	2010				
	Total	Rule of Law	Accountability	Personal Safety	National Security
Mauritius	83.1	94.0	81.7	80.0	100.0
Cape Verde	82.9	87.9	81.7	76.6	100.0
Botswana	78.7	96.6	86.1	65.0	100.0
Seychelles	73.3	74.1	67.9	70.0	99.7
Namibia	73.1	81.0	75.6	62.5	94.8
Ghana	70.7	84.7	60.9	52.5	89.6
South Africa	70.5	84.9	71.6	25.0	95.0
Lesotho	67.9	66.0	65.3	55.0	90.0
Benin	65.6	63.8	47.8	58.8	95.0
Sao Tome	64.1	55.6	45.3	68.8	89.9
Malawi	62.2	64.3	45.6	53.8	95.0
Tanzania	60.3	55.3	47.4	48.8	90.0
Mozambique	60.0	59.4	44.5	51.3	90.0
Mali	59.5	61.6	51.1	56.3	79.9
Senegal	59.0	58.1	42.2	56.3	78.8
Zambia	58.7	61.9	46.8	45.0	95.0
Burkina Faso	58.0	52.9	45.8	58.8	80.0
Sierra Leone	56.2	49.7	39.8	55.0	89.0
Uganda	54.8	65.5	47.7	46.3	71.7
Comoros	52.7	31.1	36.1	65.0	84.7
Togo	50.4	51.9	37.9	51.3	85.8
Gabon	50.2	54.2	32.5	52.5	94.9
Kenya	50.1	48.7	34.0	31.3	78.0
Liberia	50.0	28.6	47.5	47.5	64.1
Burundi	47.8	48.3	35.3	33.8	66.5
Mauritania	47.2	39.9	34.7	41.3	72.6
Swaziland	47.0	62.5	58.7	40.0	85.0
Djibouti	46.5	34.2	43.9	61.3	84.7
Niger	46.5	38.9	45.4	46.3	69.8
Gambia	45.6	37.0	24.6	40.0	84.3
Rwanda	44.7	42.5	58.9	40.0	53.6
Madagascar	44.0	20.7	45.1	26.3	85.0
Congo-Brazzaville	40.9	31.8	24.3	40.0	76.5
C.A.R.	31.1	35.6	25.6	30.0	23.3
Chad	30.9	34.4	22.2	23.8	62.8
Côte d'Ivoire	30.9	11.5	32.7	22.5	59.0
Eritrea	29.2	6.2	38.2	45.0	54.4
Zimbabwe	27.6	26.6	15.1	16.3	54.8
Sudan	21.5	17.5	19.6	16.3	30.5
Somalia	8.3	0.0	2.9	3.1	13.3
Africa Avg.	50.1	47.9	42.5	43.5	77.3

2010				
Participation	Rights	Gender	Sustainable Economy	Human Development
79.5	81.4	65.0	78.9	86.8
82.7	85.9	65.7	68.0	83.3
74.6	58.8	69.8	67.9	81.9
75.0	52.2	74.2	62.9	85.9
66.9	68.7	61.9	62.6	72.0
72.0	75.1	60.2	53.4	69.6
75.2	67.4	74.5	63.5	77.3
60.9	62.1	76.1	54.6	61.2
77.6	67.8	48.7	52.4	56.2
72.6	65.2	51.0	37.9	68.0
57.3	60.2	59.5	48.3	54.2
57.9	51.5	71.0	57.6	54.2
61.5	56.0	57.6	50.9	47.9
65.0	66.7	35.9	46.9	49.6
58.9	56.4	62.5	53.1	58.8
55.8	60.9	45.7	50.7	61.0
50.2	59.9	58.2	58.6	46.5
60.2	56.4	43.5	43.0	37.9
46.2	45.3	61.1	52.5	58.8
68.5	40.6	42.7	29.3	55.6
38.0	50.5	37.5	36.0	47.7
29.2	43.8	44.2	41.5	63.8
49.5	46.5	62.9	50.0	59.5
78.5	45.8	37.7	34.0	46.7
49.2	40.1	61.3	40.3	44.1
38.9	37.9	65.2	47.9	46.8
9.5	26.5	47.1	49.8	66.4
29.8	24.7	47.2	47.1	57.9
50.5	44.4	29.9	44.6	40.4
40.1	33.7	59.6	52.1	64.1
16.8	27.7	73.7	56.9	61.7
33.7	41.7	55.5	50.1	50.3
32.7	35.7	45.1	40.5	48.1
35.1	36.3	31.9	35.8	31.4
7.8	31.6	33.9	33.0	29.0
20.2	32.3	38.4	38.8	44.8
2.9	7.1	50.5	29.5	53.6
19.4	20.5	40.8	24.5	44.2
13.3	14.8	38.3	40.0	49.2
7.1	8.7	23.0	3.6	10.1
44.5	44.2	51.0	45.9	53.8

Table 5.10B. 2005 Mo Ibrahim Index: Progress Toward Democratic Stateness

	Total	Rule of Law	Accountability	Personal Safety	National Security
Mauritius	81.3	93.4	75.2	76.3	95.0
Cape Verde	84.7	90.0	84.4	89.1	100.0
Botswana	80.9	96.6	87.3	71.3	95.0
Seychelles	71.5	61.6	52.0	87.5	99.8
Namibia	77.0	90.7	71.9	55.0	94.7
Ghana	69.4	74.9	57.1	60.0	94.6
South Africa	74.5	91.0	78.9	35.0	90.0
Lesotho	69.2	67.2	65.7	55.0	90.0
Benin	66.3	65.3	49.9	73.8	95.0
Sao Tome	65.8	61.8	36.8	81.3	94.9
Malawi	61.3	68.8	38.9	61.3	95.0
Tanzania	61.5	55.8	43.0	48.8	95.0
Mozambique	65.6	60.7	48.1	66.3	95.0
Mali	60.8	59.8	52.7	61.3	75.0
Senegal	66.6	66.1	54.2	53.8	82.9
Zambia	59.2	68.2	44.8	50.0	95.0
Burkina Faso	61.9	58.9	50.2	73.8	90.0
Sierra Leone	44.9	28.4	24.2	47.5	60.9
Uganda	52.2	70.2	49.7	43.8	49.1
Comoros	54.4	40.0	35.1	68.8	84.9
Togo	36.7	26.1	29.1	38.8	80.5
Gabon	48.9	47.0	34.3	51.3	90.0
Kenya	57.3	54.7	42.2	32.5	81.7
Liberia	32.8	14.4	19.4	38.8	45.6
Burundi	48.9	62.1	35.9	50.0	43.5
Mauritania	53.6	62.3	52.2	38.8	79.5
Swaziland	48.6	63.7	51.9	47.5	85.0
Djibouti	49.0	42.6	32.5	68.8	89.7
Niger	53.5	57.6	46.2	55.0	65.0
Gambia	56.1	45.5	46.6	70.0	84.4
Rwanda	49.0	40.6	53.6	56.3	61.6
Madagascar	65.4	62.7	56.8	52.5	95.0
Congo-Brazzaville	37.5	30.7	24.6	41.3	50.2
Cameroon	43.4	42.1	31.1	38.8	84.7
Angola	35.5	32.7	11.1	42.5	72.2
Nigeria	41.1	44.7	25.2	15.0	84.5
Ethiopia	43.5	46.8	42.8	42.5	55.4
Guinea	44.6	37.3	35.2	52.5	76.9
Guinea-Bissau	47.5	31.3	18.7	43.8	79.6
Eq. Guinea	32.3	32.1	12.7	42.5	84.6

Participation	Rights	Gender	Sustainable Economy	Human Development
88.4	82.8	57.9	67.1	83.3
86.7	82.7	59.8	57.0	78.6
83.1	60.5	72.6	67.4	77.4
63.3	61.8	74.7	61.6	84.5
86.9	72.0	68.0	55.8	69.2
68.1	71.6	59.7	50.8	61.5
91.9	70.2	64.8	59.5	73.5
69.0	73.1	64.2	55.1	54.3
64.2	72.3	43.6	49.7	48.6
70.2	68.7	47.1	42.9	63.3
53.6	54.5	56.8	41.0	46.6
65.2	48.2	74.3	51.6	46.4
63.4	65.7	60.3	50.2	43.4
74.0	70.5	32.3	45.9	42.0
82.5	66.6	60.0	51.1	52.5
43.8	62.5	50.1	45.6	52.0
52.4	55.8	52.5	51.0	41.9
61.7	53.9	37.8	29.0	34.1
44.8	44.8	63.0	55.6	50.9
52.6	52.5	46.6	29.2	57.6
17.0	33.4	31.8	30.5	43.4
35.9	41.8	41.9	34.6	59.8
76.2	49.5	64.1	49.0	54.0
31.8	47.6	32.0	20.4	34.9
40.8	49.5	60.8	34.1	37.8
34.3	47.7	60.1	44.1	48.5
9.5	34.9	47.4	41.7	58.2
29.8	30.8	48.7	46.9	53.4
68.7	54.8	26.9	37.4	31.7
51.0	37.2	58.0	46.3	58.3
27.4	30.5	72.7	50.9	51.0
75.4	61.4	53.9	51.5	51.4
27.4	45.0	43.3	39.1	42.0
33.5	33.0	40.5	42.4	47.2
12.9	27.5	49.3	29.9	28.1
47.3	36.2	34.7	36.4	42.1
36.7	31.1	49.4	55.5	45.6
24.9	35.2	50.4	34.2	41.9
86.9	43.2	28.8	24.6	34.3
6.2	16.0	32.2	32.3	44.5

continues

Table 5.10B. 2005 Mo Ibrahim Index: Progress Toward Democratic Stateness *continued*

	Total	Rule of Law	Accountability	Personal Safety	National Security
Congo-Kinshasa	27.9	27.8	24.5	23.8	47.6
C.A.R.	32.0	28.4	21.5	42.5	43.3
Chad	36.8	37.6	30.1	52.5	55.8
Côte d'Ivoire	32.9	17.5	25.0	35.0	56.5
Eritrea	37.4	29.3	51.5	62.5	44.9
Zimbabwe	30.8	29.0	21.3	15.0	60.5
Sudan	23.0	15.0	27.3	21.3	30.8
Somalia	14.5	0.0	6.9	25.0	25.8
Africa Avg.	50.9	50.6	41.9	51.2	75.6

CONCLUSION

Table 5.11 aggregates the numerical evidence that roughly a dozen countries appear to be democratizing at rates at or above worldwide averages and substantially above average for sub-Saharan Africa as a whole. However, the fundamental empirical question this chapter posed at the outset was, and is, to what extent and in what ways African countries are on track not only to become democratic states, but also to take ownership of democracy in such ways as to shape improving rates of economic development and revolutionary communications technologies to the ends of strengthening democracy itself and improving the lives of ordinary citizens.

In broad terms, the conclusions of the foregoing analysis are:

1. All but the least democratic countries of sub-Saharan Africa have made some progress since 2005 in increasing opportunities for human development consistent with the acknowledged prerequisites and norms of working definitions of democratic stateness;
2. The data indicate both some regression in democratic performance, concentrated among all but a dozen of the best democratic performances to date, and at best limited momentum among all sub-Saharan African countries to make further substantial strides in democratization; and
3. Therefore, the extent to which African countries appear on track to take ownership of democracy by shaping strengthened economic development and technological opportunities to democratic political and socioeconomic ends anticipated by working theories of democratization appears to be at best indeterminate.

Participation	Rights	Gender	Sustainable Economy	Human Development
6.0	30.6	34.9	26.3	31.7
23.1	35.7	29.2	21.5	27.7
13.3	34.1	34.1	34.6	24.5
27.5	31.8	36.7	41.4	41.0
7.3	10.5	55.8	35.9	52.1
23.9	17.2	49.0	23.6	45.4
16.5	13.1	36.9	44.2	43.1
3.6	16.4	23.7	2.2	6.7
47.1	47.2	49.4	42.3	48.8

The evidence that sub-Saharan African countries have deployed recent markedly improved levels of economic development to strengthening human development opportunity consistent with prerequisites and objectives of working conceptualizations of democracy is supplied primarily by the Mo Ibrahim Index. But Polity IV, MOI, and World Bank Institute indices show that while a few African countries have exhibited relatively strong democratic governance required to uphold democratic liberties and political accountability, the overall picture is one of at best very limited momentum toward strengthened democratic governance, and in some areas marked decline. A notable area of declining democratic governance is in the rule of law, upon which the maintenance of civil order and upholding democratic liberties depends critically. Freedom House, CIRI, and EIU indices record a corresponding pattern of relatively strong performance in upholding democratic liberties by about a dozen countries, counterbalancing general declines concentrated among all but the strongest performers.

Clearly, the larger point appears to be weak to absent momentum both to significantly advance further democratization and to shape new patterns of economic growth and technological change to democratic ends consistent with working conceptions of democratic requirements, prerequisites, and aspirations. At the same time, those working conceptions of the democratic state emphasize the roles of citizens primarily as voters and possessors of basic liberties essential to that process. In so doing, they tend to implicitly understate the roles of citizens *between* elections in advancing democracy and reforming and strengthening the state, notwithstanding that citizen as well as leader engagement is essential to building momentum for democratic progress and citizen socioeconomic advancement.

Table 5.11. Sub-Saharan Democratic Progress

	FH	CIRI	EIU	POLITY	WBI	MOI	TOTAL
Mauritius	0.90	0.82	0.804	0.84	0.726	0.831	0.820
Cape Verde	0.90	0.85	0.792		0.654	0.829	0.805
Botswana	0.75	0.74	0.763	0.75	0.701	0.789	0.749
South Africa	0.82	0.56	0.779	0.80	0.594	0.705	0.710
Ghana	0.84	0.60	0.602	0.75	0.580	0.707	0.680
Namibia	0.76	0.70	0.624	0.64	0.615	0.731	0.678
Sao Tome	0.80	0.82			0.388	0.641	0.662
Lesotho	0.69	0.74	0.633	0.75	0.474	0.679	0.661
Seychelles	0.67	0.65			0.573	0.733	0.657
Benin	0.81	0.45	0.606	0.70	0.405	0.656	0.605
Mali	0.72	0.60	0.636	0.70	0.360	0.595	0.602
Malawi	0.57	0.70	0.584	0.64	0.431	0.622	0.591
Zambia	0.63	0.40	0.619	0.70	0.388	0.587	0.554
Senegal	0.71	0.31	0.551	0.70	0.368	0.590	0.538
Mozambique	0.59	0.45	0.490	0.58	0.435	0.600	0.524
Sierra Leone	0.67	0.45	0.451	0.70	0.264	0.562	0.516
Liberia	0.60	0.56	0.507	0.64	0.247	0.500	0.509
Comoros	0.55	0.60	0.352	0.80	0.187	0.527	0.503
Tanzania	0.64	0.40	0.564	0.22	0.402	0.603	0.472
Kenya	0.57	0.23	0.471	0.75	0.289	0.501	0.469
Burkina Faso	0.51	0.65	0.359	0.27	0.426	0.580	0.466
Niger	0.56	0.56	0.416	0.45	0.285	0.465	0.456
Gabon	0.34	0.51	0.348	0.45	0.306	0.502	0.409
Guinea-Bissau	0.45	0.51	0.199	0.64	0.159	0.379	0.390
Djibouti	0.29	0.60	0.268	0.39	0.314	0.465	0.388
Burundi	0.35	0.27	0.401	0.64	0.127	0.478	0.378
Uganda	0.42	0.13	0.513	0.22	0.325	0.548	0.359
Nigeria	0.49	0.07	0.383	0.51	0.152	0.407	0.335
Guinea	0.34	0.31	0.279	0.58	0.106	0.390	0.334
Mauritania	0.33	0.36	0.417	0.17	0.211	0.472	0.327
Madagascar	0.39	0.16	0.393	0.27	0.284	0.440	0.323
Gambia	0.24	0.45	0.338	0.08	0.340	0.456	0.317
Rwanda	0.25	0.31	0.325	0.10	0.452	0.447	0.314
Togo	0.44	0.19	0.345	0.17	0.201	0.504	0.308
Congo-Brazzaville	0.29	0.56	0.289	0.10	0.157	0.409	0.301
Swaziland	0.21	0.27	0.326	0.02	0.351	0.470	0.275
Ethiopia	0.19	0.11	0.379	0.33	0.227	0.406	0.274
Angola	0.29	0.27	0.332	0.17	0.157	0.408	0.271
Dem.Rep.Congo	0.20	0.07	0.215	0.58	0.036	0.312	0.236
C.A.R.	0.39	0.19	0.182	0.22	0.111	0.311	0.234

continues

Table 5.11. Sub-Saharan Democratic Progress *continued*

	FH	CIRI	EIU	POLITY	WBI	MOI	TOTAL
Côte d'Ivoire	0.24	0.19	0.308		0.114	0.309	0.232
Cameroon	0.23	0.11	0.341	0.10	0.200	0.408	0.232
Chad	0.21	0.27	0.162	0.17	0.074	0.309	0.199
Zimbabwe	0.20	0.04	0.268	0.33	0.051	0.276	0.194
Eq. Guinea	0.08	0.23	0.177	0.08	0.126	0.328	0.170
Sudan	0.10	0.13	0.238	0.17	0.049	0.220	0.150
Eritrea	0.06	0.03	0.234	0.04	0.125	0.290	0.130
Somalia	0.01				0.005	0.080	0.033
Africa Averages	0.46	0.40	0.428	0.43	0.303	0.501	0.424

NOTES

1. The term originates with Samuel Huntington in one of the first seminal works on current democratization: *The Third Wave: Democratization in the Late Twentieth Century* (Norman: University of Oklahoma Press, 1991). Huntington contended that the first two waves followed each of the world wars.

2. BRICS economies are Brazil, Russia, India, China, and now South Africa.

3. Crawford Young, *The African Colonial State in Comparative Perspective* (New Haven, CT: Yale University Press, 1994).

4. Under the leadership of Robert McNamara, the World Bank spearheaded a transformation of development priorities, followed by similar initiatives by the United States in what was known as the congressionally sponsored New Directions Mandate, and other bilateral donors. The focus was on the requirements of poor majorities, falling behind in developing countries, for direct assistance in support of land reform, appropriate technology, local participatory development, nonformal education, and other similar initiatives.

5. The new donor approach was heralded and set forth by a 1981 report by Elliot Berg titled "Accelerated Development in Sub-Saharan Africa." A seminal study by Robert Bates, *Markets and States in Sub-Saharan Africa: The Political Basis of Agricultural Policies* (Berkeley: University of California Press, 1981), was influential in pinpointing the corrupting influence of government policymaking on agricultural development, and in reasserting the primacy of agricultural development in overall development. Meanwhile, the academic study of politics took a contrary tack in reasserting the foundational importance of state autonomy. Theda Skocpol's *States and Social Revolutions: A Comparative Study of France, Russia, and China* (New York: Cambridge University Press, 1979) was influential in establishing this new approach.

6. A telling commentary on this trend was Nelson Kasfir, *The Shrinking Political Arena: Participation and Ethnicity in African Politics* (Berkeley: University of California Press, 1976).

7. Thomas Callaghy and John Ravenhill, eds., *Hemmed In: Responses to Africa's Economic Decline* (New York: Columbia University Press, 1993).

8. Ibid.

9. John Ferejohn, Jack N. Rakove, and Jonathan Riley, eds., *Constitutional Culture and Democratic Rule* (New York: Cambridge University Press, 2001).

10. A seventh key set of indices are those of Afrobarometer (www.afrobarometer .org) that have involved sample surveys of citizen perceptions of democracy and economic development in four rounds of surveys since 2000. Those surveys deserve consideration in this chapter, but to do so would lengthen the chapter unacceptably.

In addition to working papers to be found on the site, principal investigators Michael Bratton, Robert Mattes, and E. Gyimah Boadi address the findings of the first two rounds of surveys in *Public Opinion, Democracy, and Market Reform in Africa* (New York: Cambridge University Press, 2004).

11. In the interest of full disclosure, the author was an adviser to Freedom House on its sub-Saharan African estimates for several years.

12. www.freedomhouse.org.

13. Steven Radelet conveys a misleading picture of democratization in sub-Saharan Africa in his *Emerging Africa: How Seventeen Countries Are Leading the Way* (Baltimore, MD: Center for Global Development, 2010). Radelet chooses to treat countries as democracies that are actually hybrids, by treating countries receiving Freedom House scores of 4 or better as democracies, while Freedom House regards only countries receiving scores of 1 or 2 as democracies.

14. Freedom House has included Somaliland with independent countries in recent years. Neither South Sudan nor Eritrea was an independent country in 1990.

15. Freedom House has published these scores on its website since 2005.

16. South Sudan is excluded from the comparison, as it wasn't a country in 2005, and Somaliland is excluded for the additional reason that its independence has not yet been recognized.

17. http://ciri.binghamton.edu.

18. Economist Intelligence Unit, *Democracy Index 2011: Democracy Under Stress,* www.eiu.com. EIU's 2006 data are drawn from its report of that year.

19. www.afrobarometer.org.

20. www.worldvaluessurvey.org.

21. From flawed to hybrid: overall flawed Lesotho and Benin, overall hybrids Kenya, Burundi, Liberia, and Mozambique, and overall autocratic Ethiopia. Five overall autocracies slipped from hybrid to autocratic in political culture: Nigeria, Burkina Faso, Comoros, Congo-Brazzaville, and Equatorial Guinea.

22. www.systemicpeace.org/polity/polity4.htm.

23. Inexplicably the three island states of Seychelles, Sao Tome, and Cape Verde are not included in the surveys, while Comoros and Mauritius are.

24. Radelet, *Emerging Africa,* further offers misleading appraisals of the status of democratization in sub-Saharan Africa by treating as democracies countries that

Polity IV scores as 0 or better, where Polity's authors recommend that only countries receiving scores of more than 6 be so regarded.

25. http://info.worldbank.org/governance/wgi/index.asp.

26. www.moibrahimfoundation.org/en/section/the-ibrahim-index.

27. The MOI scores for the five North African countries of Algeria, Egypt, Libya, Morocco, and Tunisia have been excluded from the calculations in Tables 5.9, 5.10A, and 5.10B so as to retain the focus on sub-Saharan Africa and maintain comparability with the tables presenting the other indices.

six

In Pursuit of Authority
Civil Society and Rights-Based Discourses in Africa

AILI MARI TRIPP

One of the most important transformations globally in the 1990s and especially after 2000 has been the merger of development and human rights discourses to form new rights-based approaches (RBAs). There has been a convergence of thinking among UN agencies, international financial institutions, nongovernmental organizations (NGOs), international NGOs, such as Oxfam, Amnesty International, and CARE International, and social movements in Africa involved in a wide range of concerns from human rights to the environment, women's rights, and development.

This chapter examines the rise of RBAs within Africa and their global and local dimensions. It discusses the significance of the new interest in these approaches, as well as some of their critiques and limitations. The chapter explores a few examples of the kinds of legalistic and rights-based struggles that have animated the civil society landscape since the 1990s: presidential term limits, NGO regulatory legislation, struggles for media autonomy, environmental concerns, women's rights, and, in particular, challenges to customary laws and practices. The new emphasis on RBAs has not only catalyzed new forces demanding rights, it has also set various civil society groups on a collision course by animating contradictory claims.

In recent years, debates over civil society in Africa have questioned the meaning and roles of civil society in sub-Saharan Africa and other non-European contexts. Some have questioned how well the concept travels. Others have dismissed civil society as a weak donor-dependent sector that excludes much of society. Some authors have been critical of the liberal discourse that has emphasized how civil society is good for democratization and development. They have argued that civil society in Africa is fraught with ethnic divisions, patronage, corruption, donor dependence, and its elite nature, thus making it a problematic source for political transformation (Dicklitch 1998; Kasfir 1998; Kelsall 2002; Gibbon and Bangura 1992; Mercer 2003). Others have argued that NGOs are unlikely to have much impact on political reform because governments have become adept at constraining and dividing civil society. NGOs themselves are faulted for not having developed a notion of citizenship that would link state and society to promote democratization (Fowler 1993, 1995). And finally, some see donor funding of NGOs as responsible for depoliticizing NGOs, depriving them of legitimacy and autonomy, and diverting them from concerns that have to do with institution building and advocacy (Edwards and Hulme 1995).

From an anthropological perspective, Jean and John Comaroff (1999) have been critical of the way in which the idea of civil society has focused on Western-oriented intellectuals, lawyers, businesspeople, and Christian leaders, portraying them as untainted by identity politics, parochial loyalties, or intrusive governments. This understanding of civil society has erased that part of society that does not fall within a liberal notion of civil society. Rather than creating a homogenized universal civil society, they argue, globalization has instead fragmented society. Their critique is a useful one, especially since there certainly are discourses, codes of conduct, collective rituals, and ways of interacting with the state that do not fall within the rights-based approaches discussed in this chapter. It would be absurd to claim that RBAs are the only conceptual framework at play in Africa. However, this chapter highlights how the RBAs are becoming increasingly important not only as a result of globalizing influences, but also because of the way they have resonated with important political battles and dynamics on the ground.

THE SPREAD OF RIGHTS-BASED APPROACHES

Rights-based approaches came to be adopted by UN agencies, bilateral donors, and even international financial institutions involved in the development enterprise. They were inspired by the Senegalese jurist and legal scholar Kéba Mbaye's notion of development as a human right (Manzo 2003, 439)* as well as

---

*Mbaye wrote The Realities of the Black World and Human Rights; Family Law in Black Africa and Madagascar; and Human Rights in Africa. Mbaye served as vice president of the International Court of Justice; president of the International Commission of Jurists (1977–1985), and one of its commissioners from 1972–1987. He also served on the International Olympic Committee (1973–2002).

work on entitlements and human capabilities by Amartya Sen (1999) and Martha Nussbaum (2000). The adoption of the 1986 UN Declaration on the Right to Development was a watershed for UN agencies in linking rights and development conceptually and programmatically. The United States was the only country in the General Assembly that did not vote to approve the declaration, with eight other countries also abstaining. Agencies like the UN Development Programme and the UN Children's Fund (UNICEF) started using human rights measures as benchmarks to evaluate progress toward their objectives. In 2000 the British Department for International Development became one of the first to adopt such a rights-based approach (Manzo 2003, 437–439). African discourses on rights explored in this paper both informed and were informed by these changing international norms and debates around rights.

Thus, the new RBAs represented a nexus of international development and human rights concerns, bringing liberal thinking about rights together with African and other global realities, rooted in economic and social concerns. The marriage between these diverse approaches, as this chapter shows, is not without problems or tensions.

This expansion of rights-based approaches took place with the end of the Cold War, with the reconnecting of the two strands of human rights that had been enshrined in the 1948 Universal Declaration of Human Rights as indivisible, inalienable, and universal: civil and political rights *and* economic, social, and cultural rights pertaining to food, water, health, education, housing, and employment. In 1966 these two sets were recognized in two treaties: the International Covenant on Civil and Political Rights and the International Covenant on Economic, Social, and Cultural Rights. Western countries focused on civil and political rights, while the Soviet bloc and many developing countries emphasized economic and social rights. By the 1990s, the ideological barriers that had led to these distinctions had been removed, with the spread of democracy and political liberalization in Latin America, Eastern Europe, and parts of the former Soviet Union, Asia, and Africa (Manzo 2003, 446)

Civil society organizations were among the main forces in Africa pushing for political liberalization and democratization in the 1990s. While officially espousing the credo of democratization, many government leaders, in fact, resisted reforms and sought to limit political and civil freedoms, lift presidential term limits, undermine opposition parties, and create monopolies of power through various legal and extralegal means. This was in part because most countries in Africa shifted to being hybrid regimes (somewhere along the semi-democratic and semi-authoritarian spectrum) and did not fully embrace civil rights and political liberties. They did so only partially or in ambiguous ways. In 1985, 70 percent of countries were authoritarian, with only 23 percent hybrids. This started changing in the late 1980s and early 1990s, followed by some regression in some countries. Today most countries in sub-Saharan Africa are hybrids (47 percent), while 35 percent are authoritarian and 18 percent democracies, based on Freedom House rankings. Africa has more hybrids than any other part of the world, and while on the one hand political space has opened tentatively in most parts of the continent, the ambiguous nature of hybrids also creates ongoing challenges for civil society organizations.

The language of rights became ubiquitous as political liberalization was advanced in Africa. Rights-based approaches were adopted by a wide range of movements: of and for the disabled, women, children, landless, pastoralists, and many other marginalized groups; social movements of environmentalists, anti-poverty and land-grabbing groups, and human rights and other such activists; lawyers fighting to maintain the independence of the judiciary; church leaders fighting poverty and debt; pastoralists pursuing land rights; media workers defending press freedom; and NGO activists seeking to preserve their autonomy. The language of rights was also appropriated by traditional authorities in South Africa seeking to protect customary rights, Maasai organizations in Kenya and Tanzania who have reinvented themselves as "indigenous peoples" to preserve their cultural rights; religious leaders hoping to advance the uniqueness of their religious practices and beliefs; and others promoting monarchism or the authority of chiefs, clan elders, and other traditional leaders.

The discourses on rights in Africa draw on a variety of sources of authority depending on the context. They rely upon international treaties, conventions, and declarations; on regional and subregional treaties and agreements, such as the African Union Charter on Human and People's Rights; and on the African Union Protocol on Rights of Women. They also draw on national legislation and national constitutions. Since 1990, thirty-eight African constitutions have been rewritten and eight have had major revisions. Many of the changes have to do with rights, basic individual rights and liberties, the rights of traditional authorities, the protection of customary rights, issues of land rights, and the rights of women.

Many of these discourses on rights are not new. In Africa the struggles for independence and national liberation were framed in terms of demands for the right to self-rule, self-determination, and the right to citizenship. They formed the basis for struggles against colonial injustice (Cornwall and Nyamu-Musembi 2006). Later they were encompassed in the UN's New International Economic Order in the 1970s and popular notions of sustainable development/ "economics as if people mattered"/alternative technologies (Schumacher 1973) and later "people-centered development" (Korten 1995). By 1998, UN Secretary-General Kofi Annan had vowed to mainstream human rights through all UN agencies, and the World Bank had recognized the promotion and protection of human rights as one of its goals (Manzo 2003, 439).

What we are seeing today are multiple debates around rights, drawing on different sources of authority. Many of these approaches are incompatible and clash with one another, as we see in some of the debates between women's rights and cultural or group rights. Also advocates of similar approaches do not always see eye to eye when it comes to framing their objectives or in the tactics and strategies they adopt.

The RBAs represent a paradigmatic shift in thinking from seeing development as a need to development as a right. Development assistance, thus, has an obligation to help people fulfill their individual entitlements. Development as a right can be measured by adherence to international human rights treaties and the extent to which states promote their citizens' economic and social rights, such as food, shelter, education, and health care. This shift in thinking has also challenged the neoliberal market-based views of development and growth that became prevalent in the 1980s and is a response to the failures of that approach (Manzo 2003, 438). It has allowed the use of human rights treaties to hold accountable not only governments but also wealthy nations (Nelson and Dorsey 2003).

The approach has fostered new synergies between development, environmental, and human rights organizations, resulting in broad coalitions that link economic and social rights with more individually oriented civil and political rights. African NGOs, such as Nobel Prize winner Wangari Maathai's Greenbelt Movement in Kenya, pioneered the links between development, democracy, the environment, and human rights and already were making these connections in the 1980s. It is such movements as the Greenbelt Movement that have helped shape more general thinking along these lines globally. They have also helped dispel the onetime popular notion that human rights and women's rights were foreign neocolonial imports. As homegrown democrats, human rights activists, and feminists emerged, this type of effort to discredit these movements as representing foreign values became more difficult to justify and sustain.

Campaigns like the one led by World Vision, Amnesty International, and other INGOs targeting corporations in Africa have produced the Clean Diamonds campaign to restrict the extent to which military and political leaders have access to diamond export profits, which have been seen as fueling conflict and massive human rights violations in the context of civil war. Some have challenged the privatization of public goods, adopting a human rights approach to access to water, for example, the Ghana National Coalition Against the Privatisation of Water. Other organizations link human rights to health concerns, such as the campaign for access to essential medicines or the many organizations working on HIV/AIDS issues (Nelson and Dorsey 2003).

One sees a clear convergence of global discourses and local concerns in the fervent adoption of RBAs in postconflict countries, where the presence of international peacekeepers and UN agencies such as the UN Development Fund, UNESCO, UNICEF, UNIFEM, and others are especially visible and influential. In a postconflict country like Liberia, the rights discourses around human rights, and in particular the rights of the disabled, children, and women, are pervasive in the newspapers, radio, and on posters and fliers. While women's rights activists, for example, admit that they were first exposed to these discourses through regional or international conferences or through their interaction with these UN agencies or international NGOs, they insist that their interest in taking up these issues arose out of their own conditions that they have lived through, during, and after the years of civil war. In other words, these rights discourses would not resonate if there were not a basis for them within society. Women's organizations, regardless of whether they receive support from donors, draw on discourses of rights in carrying out their work to address problems women confront as a result of the war, especially pertaining to violence against women.

CRITIQUES OF RIGHTS-BASED APPROACHES

Rights-based approaches have not been adopted uncritically, even by their advocates. There are multiple, and often, competing discourses around approaches to rights. Many of the most active debates are within civil society itself. The language of rights generally draws from Western liberal rights frameworks, which incorporate notions of legal pluralism. However, not all rights are compatible, for example, religious freedom and cultural rights for ethnic groups frequently clash with women's rights and children's rights. These rights are all protected within various UN treaties, yet they cannot always be easily harmonized.

Some regard the lack of state capacity and willingness to enforce rights as a challenge to the utility of holding out the promise of justice if the rights themselves cannot be realized. Rights advocates in Africa have sought both to limit the state's reach when it has tried to restrict or control freedom of the media, of association, and of religion, and to get the state to become a source of rights and protector of rights, which has often proved challenging. Over the years, declarations like the 1966 International Covenant on Economic, Social, and Cultural Rights and the 1986 UN Declaration on the Right to Development and declarations on the right to food have added to the state's mandate the obligation to promote positive rights. Whether the state can realistically deliver is a very different matter and one that has caused considerable debate. However, in all societies the promise of rights remains aspirational and all states fall short of promises. Having a state aspiration gives society a measure by which to hold states accountable.

People's differential access in exercising their rights due to resource inequality and power differentials creates additional challenges. Expensive lawyers, lack of access to legal aid services, illiteracy or lack of education, use of bribes by wealthier litigants, and other such factors can affect the ability of more marginalized sectors of society to bring their claims to court.

Another concern has to do with the state's slowness in passing laws to protect individuals from violations of their rights by other nonstate actors, for example, violence against women and children in the home. This exposes the limits of legal and state-based frameworks. Moreover, extralegal action taken by authoritarian or semi-authoritarian states and the lack of judicial independence creates a situation where the legal system's credibility and utility are in question.

Because legal pluralism is prevalent in Africa, statutory law is often overridden by customary law either by design or by default, leaving women with weak protection of their property rights. They may be subject to discrimination in the area of personal law in countries such as Benin, Lesotho, Kenya, Niger, Swaziland, Zambia, and Zimbabwe. As Celestine Nyamu-Musembi has pointed out, the granting of land titles and reform of property rights does little to empower women if they do not have the means with which to exercise those rights. By the same token, the legal recognition of customary systems of land tenure in new land legislation in countries like Ghana (1999) and Tanzania (1999) does not necessarily ensure women's access to land (Nyamu-Musembi 2006, 1205).

Informal or customary legal institutions are often under the control of local male elders and political leaders, who may be more easily swayed by popular sentiments, bribes, and friendships in ways that may not serve justice. How laws are framed, and the normative contexts within which they emerge and exist, can also place limits on people's capacity to exercise their rights. They may, as Joe Oloka-Onyango (n.d.) has pointed out in the Ugandan local courts, be driven by archaic and exclusionist ideas about justice, without reference to the law or due process. Adjudicators may lack adequate training; they may act outside of their legal jurisdiction, arbitrarily and capriciously, and without reference to broader concerns regarding the status of women and individual rights.

In Uganda, for example, Lynn Khadiagala (2001) found that although Kigezi women could take their disputes to locally elected courts of the local councils, they tended to prefer the magistrate courts that were stationed at the county and subcounty level. Women preferred these courts because they were often cheaper than local councils, where officials often extracted excessive un-official payments. Moreover, women often perceived the local council courts to be biased against them.

Not all proponents of rights share the same objectives, frameworks, and strategies, and they may even work at cross purposes within the same general movement. These are all limitations of RBAs that need to be accounted for, while recognizing the emergence of these new sources of authority.

Finally, some, for example, Peter Uvin (2002), have characterized the World Bank's motives in promoting RBAs as a somewhat cynical attempt to benefit from the moral authority and political appeal of the human rights discourse. For him, the development community is in constant need of regaining the high moral ground to fend off criticism and mobilize resources. The develop-ment community has for this reason hitched itself to the human rights band-wagon. Thus, HIPC, PRSP, and the Millennium Development Goals remain programs of economic liberalization under the guise of addressing poverty and human rights. According to critics such as Uvin and Tsikata, the World Bank, meanwhile, draws on the language of rights, while promoting the priva-tization of essential services, such as water and national banks (Tsikata n.d.). The privatization of land, which is couched in the language of rights, has opened up new possibilities for massive land grabs by foreign companies in various parts of Africa. These developments suggest that it is important to think about *whose* rights are being protected. The creation of a rights-based regime may open up rights for one group while closing off rights to non-elites and those without access to state patronage.

RIGHTS-BASED STRUGGLES

Rights-based struggles, appealing to a variety of sources of authority, have emerged around a host of issues. Movements to limit presidential terms were often based in legalistic appeals to constitutionalism. Women's rights move-ments around land concerns, environmental movements, and struggles for NGO autonomy and media freedom frequently have drawn on international conventions as well as legislative and constitutional bases. What follows are a few examples of the kinds of rights-based struggles that have animated the civil society landscape since the 1990s. They are based on an understand-ing of the indivisibility of rights, in which environmental or land rights are seen as inherently human rights, and in which the rule of law, constitutional-ism, and the defense of political and civil liberties are essential to economic development.

Right to a Democratic State:
Movements for Presidential Term Limits

One type of political right relates to the need for a democratic state with an executive who is reined in by the legislature and judiciary. There were only a few instances in the pre-multiparty period when presidents stepped down voluntarily. One could count them on one hand: General Olusegun Obasanjo in Nigeria (1979), Ahmadou Ahidjo in Cameroon (1982), Julius Nyerere in Tanzania (1985), and Léopold Senghor in Senegal (1980)—and usually only after they had held office for over twenty years. With the introduction of multipartyism, civilian rule, and the rewriting of constitutions in the 1990s, presidents were limited to two terms in many countries. Today twenty-three countries in Africa have such limits. The era of presidents-for-life seemed to be over with a few exceptions, for example, Guinea's Lansana Conte and Omar Bongo of Gabon. However, it did not take long for presidents to begin tinkering with the term limits these new constitutions imposed.

The practice of prolonging the presidential term began in Namibia in 1998 when the country's constitution was amended to allow Sam Nujoma to have a third term. Term limits were also scrapped in Algeria, Burkina Faso, Chad, Djibouti, Gabon, Guinea, Togo, Tunisia, and Uganda despite opposition by legislatures and civil society. A few other heads of state toyed with the idea of extending their terms but ultimately stepped down, for example, Benin's Mathieu Kerekou, Kenya's Daniel Arap Moi, Mozambique's Joaquim Chissano, Botswana's Festus Mogae, and Ghana's Jerry Rawlings. Senegalese President Wade got the Constitutional Court to permit him to run for a third term, amid resistance from opposition parties and street protests, but he lost the second round of elections in 2012 to Macky Sall. He won praise from the international community when he conceded victory and graciously congratulated his opponent on his victory.

However, former Nigerian president Obasanjo's attempt to run for a third term in 2007, using a constitutional amendment bill, was blocked by the Senate Chamber and subsequently by the House of Representatives. Similarly, attempts in Malawi and Zambia to extend presidential terms were vigorously thwarted by civil society. In Malawi, where Hastings Banda had once declared himself president for life, civil society organizations and coalitions, including the Forum for the Defence of the Constitution, mobilized to resist efforts by President Bakili Muzuli to abolish term limits. In 2002, parliament voted down a bill that would abolish term limits.

Prodemocracy advocates press for term limits and adherence to the constitution to avoid the past authoritarian practices, in which leaders would monopolize power for extended periods of time, creating a zero-sum situation for other aspirants to power. In other cases, proponents of term limits may have specific grievances against a head of state and wish to see a process in place that would allow for a change in leadership.

The Law Association of Zambia in conjunction with key church coalitions, women's organizations, NGOs, and opposition parties successfully resisted President Frederick Chiluba's bid for a third term in 2001. Lawyers spearheaded the opposition, drawing on liberal principles of individual liberty, inalienable rights, and human equality to make their case. According to Jeremy Gould (2005), their appeals were based on a liberal legal conception of rights and liberties. It was not so much a political discourse as a legalistic one, drawing on the notion of the rule of law. A coalition of opponents of extending presidential term limits met in the Oasis Restaurant in 2001 and drafted what came to be known as the Oasis Declaration, laying out the basis on which term limits could not be extended. The declaration is heavily laden with references to the constitution and is what Gould has called a specifically *lawyerly* imagining of the state, and a specifically *legalist* mode of authority, politics, and political morality.

According to Gould, the three most outspoken societal groups in Zambia around term limits included first human rights and women's organizations and other advocacy groups. A second group included the churches (Catholic, Protestant, and Evangelical) with the Catholics in the forefront. The third and final group was the Law Association, which came in slightly later in 2001 to challenge the legal and ethical implications of extending term limits. Similar patterns of activism and actors can be found in other countries as well, although the independent media might also be considered a contributing factor in these developments and was extremely important in, for example, Nigeria.

In almost all cases, the movements to limit presidential terms came from societal coalitions. However, they required legislative support, which indicates not only changing relationships between society and the legislature, but also the strengthening of legislatures. The imposition of term limits suggests a growing sense of responsiveness of the legislature to popular pressures. Even in Uganda, where term limits were lifted in 2005, a coalition of parliamentarians from both the ruling party and the opposition, together with nonpartisan church leaders and other civil society actors—began forcefully pushing for the reinstatement of presidential term limits in 2012. While it would be an overstatement to suggest that there are close working relationships between civil society actors and parliamentarians, legislators are paying greater attention to what civil society actors are thinking and advocating. In the past under single-party rule, parliaments were rubber stamps and not worthy of study.

This is rapidly changing, as there is a fair bit of independence of the legislatures in Namibia, Mauritius, Ghana, Benin, Botswana, Lesotho, Liberia, Senegal, Mozambique, South Africa, and Tanzania.

Similarly, judiciaries are also beginning to assert greater independence and are seeking support from lawyers and their associations. Today, lawyers and judges increasingly come to the defense of judicial independence in the face of the most flagrant violations by the executive. In November 2005 in Uganda, the key opposition leader Kizza Besigye of the Forum for Democratic Change was arrested on charges of treason and rape. The day he was to be brought to the High Court to be released on bail, a Black Mamba armed security squad had been deployed at the court to rearrest him in an extralegal action by the president's office. This prompted protests from the High Court judges, the Chief Justice Odoki (who had been the head of the Constitutional Commission), the inspector general of government, leaders of the Uganda Law Society, the government's Human Rights Commission, and hundreds of lawyers, who condemned the siege of the courts as undermining the rule of law. Over three hundred lawyers went on strike to protest military interference in the independence of the judiciary. This would have been unthinkable even a few years earlier. There are increasingly other such examples of the assertion of judicial independence in Africa.

NGO Regulatory Legislation

Because so many NGOs began to explicitly link human rights to developmental concerns, they became increasingly suspect in many countries, leading governments in the mid-2000s to revive stalled efforts started in the 1990s to pass legislation regulating NGOs. In the late 1980s and 1990s NGOs increasingly found themselves fighting for the right to autonomy while opposing governmental legislative efforts to create agencies to monitor and control NGO activities in Tanzania, Botswana, Ghana, Kenya, Malawi, Zambia, Zimbabwe, Uganda, and other countries (Gyimah-Boadi 1998, 22; Ndegwa 1996; Bratton 1989, 577).

Human rights, women's, lawyers', environmental, and other groups opposed efforts to pass such regulatory NGO bills. While NGOs generally recognize the need to have an administrative and regulatory framework for NGOs, they have resisted what they consider heavy-handed infringement on their freedom to operate, even in countries calling themselves democracies. Bills regulating NGOs were drafted without sufficient transparency and without consulting NGOs, or by consulting only ones closest to the government. In the case of Uganda, an NGO regulatory bill was hurriedly pushed through parliament without adequate time for consultation with NGOs.

NGOs fear that these regulatory bodies will suppress civil society organizations that are deemed too political, especially if they adopt positions that challenge or differ from the government's stance, regardless of how benign the issue. In most of these struggles NGOs have complained that the legislation assumed they were acting as opposition political parties, when in fact NGOs considered themselves nonpartisan, hence excluded from restrictions on political parties. Developmental NGOs especially resent the assumption that they are seen as political. And while there are occasions when NGOs ally themselves with political parties to accomplish specific objectives, this does not warrant identifying them as political parties and therefore subject to the same restrictions parties face. While some NGOs are suppressed because of their agendas (e.g., the 2012 banning of thirty-eight NGOs in Uganda because they allegedly were promoting homosexuality), more often they are regulated wholesale because of their potential for antigovernmentalism as a result of their advocacy.

Because of government suspicions of the political nature of NGOs, especially those involved in advocacy, NGOs themselves are hesitant to attach the term "political" to their activities. Nevertheless, as Hamida Harrison of Ghana argues that for women activists, being political is unavoidable, given the nature of advocacy around women's rights:

> NGOs are supposed to be politically neutral, non-partisan and so on. And I think that many NGOs are afraid of the word "political," many of them actually say, "we are not political," while we in the women's movement are saying, "This is politics." The minute you start talking about power and resources and so on, it is politics. This is something that makes people within the NGO setting very uncomfortable. (Mama 2005, 129)

The NGO stance of claiming to be apolitical is understandable given the way these organizations are often treated. The 2003 Tanzanian NGO Act provides for criminal sanctions against NGOs that do not register with the government. It requires NGOs to align their activities with government plans and bans national NGO networks and coalitions. Tanzanian NGOs have strongly resisted these provisions, arguing that they contravene the Tanzanian constitution, the UN Declaration on Human Rights, and the International Covenant on Civil and Political Rights.

Past experiences with the deregistration of NGOs in countries such as Zambia and Uganda for questionable reasons caused many organizations to worry. In a more extreme case, Zimbabwe's 2005 NGO Act banned NGOs from receiving foreign funding for governance programs. In 2009, the Ethiopian government adopted a law restricting NGOs that receive over 10 percent of their financing from foreign sources from engaging in human rights and advocacy activities. Eritrea does not permit any independent civil society organizations to operate, and the independent media has been closed down since 2001. NGOs appealed to the government on rights-based grounds. Bob Muchabaiwa, of the National Association of Non-Governmental Organisations, petitioned President Robert Mugabe not to sign the bill into law. Reflecting the RBA that links development to human rights, the petition read: "Your Excellency, we appeal to you not to give assent to the NGO Bill because of its devastating effects on ordinary citizens, the economy and the country. . . . All the work that NGOs do is human rights work whether it is access to water, land, information, education, treatment or promoting the rights of people with disabilities or living with HIV and AIDS."* While Zimbabwe may have taken extreme measures, most NGO regulatory bodies cite the need to oversee foreign funding as one of their major functions.

Other NGO activists have appealed on constitutional grounds regarding NGO regulatory legislation. In some countries they were able to stall the process for many years. In Zambia it took nine years before the bill was passed. In Uganda, NGOs tried to preempt heavy-handed legislative restrictions on NGOs. Despite strong protests from NGOs and donor countries, parliament passed a restrictive Non-Governmental Organisations Registration Bill in 2006. For five years NGOs resisted the bill. They opposed the domination of the NGO board by government officials and security agents; the bill's stipulation that NGOs must register annually; and the board's powers to deregister an NGO for violating any law. They felt this gave the board too much control that could be used for political purposes and undermined associational autonomy.

As leader of the NGO coalition Development Network of Indigenous Voluntary Organisations, Jassy Kwesiga (2001) reflected on one of the core concerns of NGO activists in Uganda but also throughout Africa: "As for denial of registration on the basis of incompatibility with Government policy, plans and public interest, what if the NGOs are expressing the will of the people that may be at odds with Government policy and Government definition of public interest? History in Uganda and elsewhere is full of many state inspired undemocratic misfortunes in the name of public interest." Rather, state and society need to respect the "independence, rights and obligations of the other."

Regulation in order to suppress advocacy that challenges government policy is incompatible with democracy and is a holdover from the past thinking and practice of one-party states. Attempts to characterize normal NGO advocacy or watchdog activities as antigovernmental and subject to controls has been resisted, as have efforts to curtail the autonomy of civil society more

---

*"Mugabe Urged to Ditch NGOs Bill," *Zimbabwe Standard*, April 3, 2005.

generally. Placing security personnel on NGO regulatory boards, for example, suggests that NGOs might pose a security risk of some kind.

Civil society activists are pointing to alternative ways of thinking about state-society relations. Many feel there needs to be more mutual trust built between governments and NGOs with the understanding that a healthy democracy is built on productive synergies between the state and civil society. There needs to be room for societal activities that can help shape government policy through pressure and advocacy; can serve as a check on corruption; and can promote transparency. Civil society can also be an important resource for government, providing information, research, data, and other forms of knowledge to support activities of government. It can also provide powerful societal backing for policies and mobilize people to voluntarily participate in initiatives and campaigns.

The Ministry of Youth and Sports in Liberia, to take one example, works closely with youth and student organizations throughout the country, who have enthusiastically and actively lobbied the government around key issues, including corruption, transparency, and accountability, particularly in the education sector (e.g., grade buying). They play a watchdog role, monitoring the implementation of the 2011 education law and also other issues such as policy regarding petroleum resources and their use. These types of productive synergies are possible only if they can be built in an atmosphere of trust and cooperation. The Liberia National Student Union complained to President Ellen Johnson-Sirleaf directly when her appointee for national youth adviser was not from the student movement and had come from out of the country. The president was sympathetic to their concerns and appointed another liaison of whom they approved.

Since Johnson-Sirleaf took over as president of Liberia in 2006, the human rights situation has improved dramatically; the press operates more or less freely with some important exceptions, as do NGOs and political parties; and a zero-tolerance policy for corruption is enforced. The legislature and judiciary enjoy a level of independence rarely seen in Africa. NGOs have the confidence to operate freely because they know their advocacy will not be seen as antigovernmental and they in turn do their best to support government when there is a need to assist.

Struggles for Media Autonomy

As with NGOs, conflicts over media autonomy and freedom of the press have emerged over legislation to regulate media workers. These struggles have often placed media workers at the forefront of the civil-society struggles for autonomy from government control and freedom of expression. Media workers in Angola, Botswana, Chad, Kenya, Gambia, Nigeria, South Africa, Uganda, and Zambia have debated existing or proposed bills regulating the media in the past two years. Some of the worst infringements of the freedom of the press have occurred in Zimbabwe, where the independent media has been effectively silenced with the vigorous application of such legislation, including the Access to Information and Protection of Privacy Act and the Public Order and Security Act. But even in democratic South Africa, government legislation in the form of a Film and Publication Amendment Bill was proposed in 2006 that would require newspaper editors to submit their entire paper to regulators prior to publication, seriously curtailing press freedom.

In the early 1990s, as winds of political liberalization swept Africa and the media began to assert itself, various governments began to introduce new legislation to create regulatory councils to control media workers and their associations. The proposed legislation galvanized media workers to protect their professional interests as well as their freedom of speech (Lingo and Lobe 2001; Odhiambo 2001; Alabi 2001).

In Kenya, for example, the Mass Media Commission Bill (1995) and Press Council Bill (1995) were successfully put on the back burner by media organizations. The bills sought to regulate and discipline journalists and media workers and to oversee their registration. The legislation was widely rejected on the grounds that it restricted the freedom of speech. As M'inoti and Maina (1996) wrote: "Both bills propose to regulate speech as if it were some nuisance, a noxious thing or some other unlawful conduct. . . . The inarticulate premise in both bills is that the mass media and the craft of journalism are essentially venal and hence the need for a great deal of benevolent vigilance from the government." However, the continued battles over media bills throughout Africa suggest that African governments have yet to relinquish their attempts to restrict media freedom.

Women's Rights Movements

The 1990s saw the emergence of new women's movements, which served as catalysts for many of the new constitutional and legal challenges in women's rights that we are seeing today in Africa. These movements had new priorities, new leaders, and new sources of funding independent of state patronage networks, which older women's organizations had depended on to a greater extent in the past.

Women's rights organizations have drawn on international and pan-African treaties to advance their rights, especially the Convention on the Elimination of All Forms of Discrimination Against Women. Many of the post-1990 policies draw on the Platform for Action that emerged from the 1995 UN Beijing Conference on Women that encouraged women to seek equal gender representation in political and other institutions including legislatures, executives, judiciaries, nongovernmental associations, religious institutions, and other bodies.

At the pan-African level, women's organizations rely on such treaties as the African Union Protocol on Women's Rights to lobby about a new generation of policies seeking to protect women's bodily integrity through legislation around female genital cutting, domestic violence, and other such concerns, and to address women's rights to a livelihood through access to land, property, credit, inputs, and other resources.

Women's rights activists have been advocating increases in their representation in legislatures through regional organizations like ECOWAS and the Southern African Development Community (SADC). In 2005, SADC set a goal for its member countries to attain 50 percent female representation in their legislatures by the year 2015. In 1987 it set a goal of 30 percent female-held legislative seats by 2005. As a result of regional pressures, in 2012 non-SADC countries in Africa had on average 16 percent legislative seats held by women, while SADC countries had 24 percent.

Other women's rights issues have generated similar regional attention. In 2005, an African Parliamentary Conference held in Dakar, Senegal, focused on female genital cutting, and speakers and members of twenty African national assemblies unanimously adopted a declaration calling for an end to the practice, arguing that "culture is not immutable and that it is subject to perpetual change, adaptations and reforms" (African Parliamentary Conference 2005). They pledged to work with civil society, traditional chiefs and religious leaders, women's and youth movements, and governments to adopt strategies to end the practice, drawing on a human rights framework by taking into consideration the education, health, development, and poverty dimensions of the problem.

Some of the pressures to end the practice are quite extraordinary. A group of distinguished Islamic scholars met at Al-Azhar University in Cairo and issued a statement calling female genital mutilation "a deplorable, inherited custom, which is practiced in some societies and is copied by some Muslims in several countries."* They concluded that "there are no written grounds for this custom in the Qur'an with regard to an authentic tradition of the Prophet" and acknowledged that "female genital circumcision practiced today harms women

---

*Available at www.target-human-rights.com/HP-00_aktuelles/alAzharKonferenz/index .php?p=beschluss&lang=en, accessed December 16, 2006.

psychologically and physically." They insisted that the practice be stopped and called for the practice to be criminalized.

Since the 1990s, women's organizations have been pushing and often succeeding in getting constitutional reforms and legislative changes to protect their rights in ways that override customary laws and practices that violate women's rights, discriminate against women, or violate bill of rights provisions regarding gender equality.

These are profound challenges. They are, in effect, attempts to legitimize new legal-based sources of authority for rights governing relations between men and women, family relations, and women themselves. In the past, even when laws existed to regulate marriage, inheritance, custody, and other such practices, customary laws and practices coexisted and generally took precedence when it came to family and clan concerns. Today, women's movements are challenging these norms through constitutional and legislative changes in ways we have not seen in the past.

They have been actively chipping away at discriminatory customary laws through changes in family law/codes, land laws, and other such issues. They are also pushing through key legislation pertaining to women's bodily integrity involving violence against women and female genital cutting. These represent a new generation of policy measures to address women's status, distinct from the earlier legislation around marriage and inheritance, maternity leave, employment practices, and the taxation of women.

Since the 1990s, new constitutions in countries such as Namibia (1990), Ethiopia (1995), Malawi (1994), Uganda (1995), South Africa (1996), Rwanda (2003), Burundi (2005), and Swaziland (2006) have included nondiscrimination or equality provisions, prohibiting customary practices if they undermined women's dignity, welfare, or status. These were new developments in African constitution-making and can be contrasted with constitutions passed prior to 1990, in which customary law generally was not subject to any gender-related restrictions. Women's movements played an important role in ensuring that these clauses were included.

In terms of legislative changes, one of the most important has been the involvement of women's movements in changing land laws to strengthen women's property rights. One of the most dramatic changes in land tenure reform today is that for the first time since the precolonial period, states are giving legal recognition to existing African customary tenure regimes, which are being treated as legitimate land tenure systems on par with the freehold/leasehold systems, rather than being seen as systems to be eradicated or phased out. Unregistered customary tenure, which is the main system of land rights in Africa, is being recognized in the new policies. Ironically, at the very time that these gains are being won in the name of the rural poor, the pastoralists, women, and the landless, African women have mounted new movements to eradicate customary land tenure practices and fight for women's rights to inherit, purchase, and own land in their own name.

Feminist lawyers working with these movements have argued that customary law in the present-day context has been used to selectively preserve practices that subordinate women. Rather than seeing customary land practices as a basis on which to improve women's access to land, they are advocating for rights-based systems that improve women's ability to buy, own, sell, and obtain titles on land.

Bases of customary ownership have been eroded since the time of colonialism, making women's access to land significantly more precarious as the protections traditionally ensured by the clan system have been peeled away.

In recent years, with increased commercialization of land and problems of land scarcity, local leaders have felt mounting pressures to protect the clan system, and in so doing have placed even greater constraints on women's access to land. However, the clan system they seek to preserve often no longer affords women the supports it is once said to have guaranteed. For this reason women, both rural and urban, have responded to the renewed interest in protecting customary laws and practices through collective strategies, which in many countries have included movements to ensure women's access to and ownership of land. Women have also adopted individual strategies of purchasing land and taking their land disputes to court.

For example, in Uganda, women of all classes have been purchasing and selling land throughout the country. Several studies by Makerere Institute for Social Research, carried out in 1995 and 2000 in Lira, Mpigi, Mbale, Kamuli, Mbarara, Nebbi, Mubende, and Kabarole districts, show that between 15 percent and 20 percent of women own land in these districts throughout Uganda. A study of Mukono in 2002 showed that 45 percent of women owned land. Women's main concern in all these studies was difficulty in accessing land, which means that relying on their husbands was not a reliable strategy (Sebina-Zziwa, Kibombo, et al. 2002). Purchasing land has, in effect, become a way of circumventing the traditional authorities.

Women have been active in a variety of land alliances and coalitions throughout Africa, many of which have arisen in response to legislative and constitutional changes in tenure laws. New land laws were enacted in Uganda, Tanzania, Zanzibar, Mozambique, Zambia, Eritrea, Namibia, and South Africa in the 1990s. Rwanda, Malawi, Lesotho, Zimbabwe, Swaziland, and Kenya are drafting a land bill. Women have been at the forefront of such organizations as the Uganda Land Alliance, the National Land Forum in Tanzania, the Zambia National Land Alliance, National Land Committee in South Africa, Kenya Land Alliance, Rwanda Land Alliance, and the Namibian NGO Federation

(NANGOF)—all of which have fought for the land rights of women, pastoralists, the landless, and other marginalized people. Regional networks, such as Landnet in East Africa, have also formed to network between countries. At the same time, key women's organizations have been active around land issues in all these countries and have often played a leading role in forming the broader land alliances. At the regional level in eastern and southern Africa, Women in Law and Development in Africa (WiLDAF) has been active since the early 1990s on land and other issues, as has Women and Law in Southern Africa (WLSA) in seven southern African countries (Tripp 2004).

The new movements have been galvanized by mounting land pressures and the placement of constraints on women, who generally do not have sufficient access to or control over land. While the focus of the women's movements has been on customary land practices, they have also been concerned with the negative effects of the privatization of land and land grabbing as governments have increasingly sought foreign investment through tourism, mining, and other businesses. Women have joined forces with pastoralists, who have often found themselves shut out of vast grazing lands in many parts of East Africa, Botswana, and Namibia as a result of large land sales orchestrated by government officials (Palmer 1998).

The movements have taken up a variety of concerns. For example:

- Ugandan women's rights advocates have long fought to expand women's land rights. After facing numerous setbacks, advocates from Law and Advocacy for Women in Uganda finally got the Constitutional Court to strike down key provisions of the Succession Act regarding women's right to inherit property. The law did not allow women to inherit property of a deceased person including their husband's and was found to be discriminatory and unconstitutional.* It provided only for male intestacy, assuming that women who died intestate had nothing to bequeath; it allowed for 15 percent of the estate to go to the widow and 100 percent to the widower; provided for the appointment of a guardian of the children even though the widow could be appointed as guardian. This leaves parliament to enact laws to replace these provisions.
- Women's organizations were active in Tanzania, where they won the right to acquire, hold, use, and deal with land in the Land Act 1999 and Village Land Act 1999. These laws also ensure that women are represented in land administration and adjudication bodies. The Land Act overrides customary law if it denies women their right to use, transfer, or own land. Women's rights of co-occupancy are also protected.

---

*"Implication of the Ruling on Adultery." *New Vision* (Uganda), April 8, 2007.

- Women's organizations played a leading role in the passage of Mozambique's new land law in 1997. They were active in and led the Land Forum, a coalition of 200 organizations that participated in discussions leading up to the passage of the land bill. The law not only protects customary tenure arrangements, but also includes provisions that allow women to own land and protections that give them greater access to and control over land. Women still face enormous resource and social constraints in accessing land, but with this legislation many of the legal constraints have been removed.

Environmental Movements

Since 2000 environmental NGOs and others have responded to a series of environmental challenges on a scale not seen in the 1990s.

- When the Ugandan government considered a request by the Mehta Group's Sugar Cooperation of Uganda Ltd. to take over 7,100 hectares of Mabira forest to expand its sugarcane plantation and double sugar production, a broad coalition of NGOs protested the move.* They forced the cabinet to halt the proposed giveaway of the forest until a policy was developed to determine the use of such land. Mabira is the largest natural forest in the country and serves as a significant water catchment area for Lake Victoria. A broad range of environmental, religious, developmental, and human rights groups protested the move, arguing that it was a breach of the constitution to degazette the forest reserve.
- In Sudan a movement led by the Hamdab Dam Affected People aims to stop the construction of a Chinese-built Merowe dam that will displace several communities of 60,000 people and archaeological sites in proximity to the Nile within an area of 175 by 4 kilometers. The project is intended to double Sudan's power production.
- Protests broke out in Côte d'Ivoire with the news that a tanker ship of the Dutch Trafigura Beheer BV company had dumped around 528,000 liters of liquid chemical waste in Abidjan in 2006, causing 77,000 Abidjan residents to seek medical treatment. At least ten were known to have died from the

---

*These included the Uganda Joint Christian Council, National Foundation for Democracy and Human Rights in Uganda, Uganda Land Alliance, Environmental Action Network, Advocates Coalition for Environment and Development, Uganda Forestry Association, the Advocacy Coalition for Development and Environment, Greenwatch, the Environmental Action Network, Environmental Alert, and the Anti-Corruption Coalition.

chemical dumping. The Ivorian Human Rights League (Lidho) and officials of toxic-waste-victim associations sought compensation from the company. They have been pressing for and exploring changes in international legislation and monitoring mechanisms to avoid another such environmental catastrophe in Africa.

- In one of the better publicized struggles—especially after the execution of the environmental activist Ken Saro-Wiwa in 1995—the Movement for the Survival of the Ogoni People (MOSOP) has been seeking redress for environmental degradation as a result of oil drilling in the Niger delta by multinational oil companies, such as Royal Dutch Shell and Exxon Mobil. Over the past fifty years, over 1.5 million tons of crude oil has been spilled in the area, threatening rare species of birds and animals, and threatening the livelihood and health of 20 million residents. The Niger delta has been identified as among the five most polluted spots in the world. This has in turn fueled violence in the region.
- Kimarer-Sugutek Rights Group and others have protested pollution by Kenya Fluorspar Company as calcium fluoride was found to have been transported by the Kerio River into the gorges of the Kerio Valley, Rift Valley Province, making the water undrinkable for humans and animals.
- Earthlife Namibia, the National Society for Human Rights, and the German Oeko Institute raised concerns in 2005 about the uranium mining project carried out by the Langer Heinrich Uranium Mine. They were concerned about the polluting of ground- and surface-water sources, the emission of radioactive dust, and the ecological impact on plants and animals in the environmentally vulnerable Namib-Naukluft Park.

These are just a few of the many environmental movements that have sprung up across the continent and have resulted in linkages between various rights-based organizations.

CLASH OF RIGHTS

The new emphasis on RBAs has not only catalyzed new forces demanding rights, but it also has set various civil society groups on a collision course by animating contradictory claims. With the new 1996 constitution in South Africa, alliances such as the Women's National Coalition were able to lobby for and obtain key provisions ensuring the protection of women's rights. They gained greater representation at higher levels of government and in the legislature. Many women thought that with the end of apartheid and with the new constitution they would be free of discriminatory customary practices.

However, the constitution not only guaranteed women's rights, but it also provided for rights of traditional authorities, who are now threatening women's bid for a new allocation of resources, especially of land. Both women and traditional authorities draw on the 1996 constitution to make claims for their rights, but in ways that potentially clash. One finds in other parts of Africa similar conflicts between those claiming rights to religious and cultural freedom and women's rights advocates in other countries over issues like the Family Codes, polygamy, child marriage, and female genital cutting.

The political opening and democratization of South Africa not only provided space for women's mobilization, but it also energized the traditional authorities. In the case of chieftancies in southern Africa, to take one example, the weakness or inaccessibility of the state or local government has led populations to seek more accessible traditional authorities. After 1994 a strong lobby of chiefs emerged, seeking legal recognition and protection. Rather than disappearing, traditional authorities (clan formations, elder councils like the *kgotla* in Botswana, the monarchical parliament in Buganda, hometown associations, women's and men's councils in eastern Nigeria, etc.) have become invigorated with political liberalization throughout Africa. These institutions exist side by side and interact with modern parliaments and local governments.

In Nigeria there are tensions between advocates for children's rights who want to raise the age of marriage under the Child Rights Act of 2003 and the Supreme Council for Sharia in Nigeria that appeals to Islamic law for its authority. Federal laws passed at the national level are required to be passed within the state Houses of Assembly. By 2007, ten state assemblies had adopted the act. The Islamic Supreme Council says that if the act is passed by state assemblies it will destroy the very basis and essence of the *shar'ia* and Muslim culture. The controversial sections of the act include provisions that make it illegal for parents to marry off their daughter if she is younger than eighteen and to consummate a marriage with a child under eighteen years of age. Proponents of the law see the age limit as a way of ensuring that girls complete their schooling, which has implications for women's economic status and for development in the country more generally. The law also gives both boys and girls equal inheritance rights.

In other contexts, the conflicts are not only between forces supporting or resisting women's or other such rights, there are tensions between those who share a common agenda. At the end of military rule in 1999, women's groups in Nigeria found themselves with competing notions of rights and competing bases for appealing for women's rights. Some groups saw women's empowerment in terms of promoting family welfare, while feminists (e.g., Women in Nigeria) saw women's rights advancement linked to equality and opposition to discrimination. For some Islamic women's groups empowerment was tied to educating people and building women's awareness of their rights under the *shar'ia*. Still other Muslim women's organizations wanted to improve the rights of women and girls by appealing to Islamic law itself. The Federation of Muslim Women's Associations of Nigeria (FOMWAN) sees Islamic family law as historically constituted with well-defined notions of rights that can be reformed, but they can be reformed only within the Islamic legal system (Toyo 2006).

CONCLUSIONS

Rights-based approaches have acquired new salience in much of Africa with the convergence of local and global discourses around human rights, including the rights of children, women, and the disabled, and environmental, economic, and other rights. Certainly these are not the only discourses within society, but they are increasingly prevalent within civil society and have become an important frame for debates with the state in carving out greater autonomy for NGOs and the media, in limiting executive power, and in struggles for greater judicial and legislative independence. Emerging out of these debates are new norms and conceptions of state-society synergies and ways in which state and society can productively interact to advance both development and human rights broadly defined.

As we move into an era where RBAs increasingly prevail, it is also worth paying attention to the many and often competing definitions and sources of authority for rights and the politics of how rights come to be defined, for what purposes civil society employs these notions and to what end. While there may be agreement on the adoption of RBAs there are clearly different understandings of what they mean. Semi-authoritarian and authoritarian states have relied on legislative and constitutional sources of authority to rein in and control civil society and the media, while civil society has sought protection and autonomy using the same instruments. Land and other property laws have been embraced to protect the rights of marginalized groups while unleashing the forces of the market, creating forces that work at odds and establishing possible collision courses. New democratizing constitutions have invigorated not only women's and children's rights activists but also traditional authorities and religious activists who worked at cross purposes when it came to issues like women's land rights and personal law, for example, child marriage and polygamy.

It is thus necessary to look not only at the rise of rights-based approaches, but also at the reasons and ways in which rights discourses are being appropriated by different societal actors and the competing claims between them.

REFERENCES

African Parliamentary Conference on Violence Against Women, "Abandoning Female Genital Mutilation: The Role of Parliaments," Final Declaration, Dakar, Senegal, 2005, www.ipu.org/splz-e/dakar05/declaration.pdf.

Alabi, N. (2001). Western African Regional Perspectives, Summary Review., Windhoek, The Windhoek Seminar: "Ten Years On: Assessment, Challenges and Prospects," May 3–5.

Bratton, M. (1989). "The Politics of Government-NGO Relations in Africa." *World Development* 17(4).

Comaroff, J., and Comaroff, J., eds. (1999). *Civil Society and the Political Imagination in Africa*. Chicago and London: University of Chicago Press.

Cornwall, A., and C. Nyamu-Musembi. (2006). "Putting the 'Rights-Based Approach' to Development into Perspective." *Third World Quarterly* 27(7): 1415–1437.

Dicklitch, S. (1998). *The Elusive Promise of NGOs in Africa. Lessons from Uganda*. London: Macmillan.

Edwards, M., and D. Hulme, eds. (1995). *Beyond the Magic Bullet: NGO Performance and Accountability in the Post–Cold War World*. London: Earthscan; and West Hartford, CT: Kumarian Press.

Fowler, A. (1993). NGOs as Agents of Democratization: An African Perspective." *Journal of International Development* 5(3): 325–339.

———. (1995). "Assessing NGO Performance: Difficulties, Dilemmas, and a Way Ahead." In M. Edwards and D. Hulme, eds. *Beyond the Magic Bullet: NGO Performance and Accountability in the Post–Cold War World*. London: Earthscan and West Hartford, CT: Kumarian Press.

Gibbon, P., and Y. Bangura. (1992). "Adjustment, Authoritarianism. and Democracy: An Introduction to Some Conceptual and Empirical Issues." In P. Gibbon, Y. Bangura, and A. Ofstad, eds. *Authoritarianism, Democracy, and Adjustment: The Politics of Economic Reform in Africa*. Uppsala, Sweden: Nordiska Afrikainstitutet, pp. 7–38.

Gould, J. (2005). "Strong Bar, Weak State? Lawyers, Liberalism and State Formation in Zambia." Unpublished paper, University of Helsinki.

Gyimah-Boadi, E. (1998). "The Rebirth of African Liberalism." *Journal of Democracy* 9(2): 18–31.

Kasfir, Nelson ed. (1998). *Civil Society and Democracy in Africa: Critial Perspectives*. Portland, OR, and Ilford, UK: Frank Cass Publishers, pp. 84–107.

Kelsall, T. (2002). "Donors, NGOs, and the State: Governance and 'Civil Society' in Tanzania." In O. Barrow and M. Jennings, eds. *The Charitable Impulse: NGOs and Development in East and North East Africa*. Oxford: James Currey, pp. 131–148.

Khadiagala, L. S. (2001). "The Failure of Popular Justice in Uganda: Local Councils and Women's Property Rights." *Development and Change* 32: 55–76.

Korten, D. (1995). *When Corporations Rule the World.* West Hartford, CT: Kumarian Press.

Kwesiga, J. (2001). "NGOs Call for Change." *Monitor* (Kampala), March 6.

Lingo, C., and S. K. Lobe. (2001). Central African Regional Perspectives, Summary Review. Windhoek, The Windhoek Seminar: "Ten Years On: Assessment, Challenges, and Prospects," May 3–5.

Mama, A. (2005). "The Ghanaian Women's Manifesto Movement: Amina Mama speaks with Dzodzi Tsikata, Rose Mensah-Kutin, and Hamida Harrison." *Feminist Africa* (4): 124–138.

Manzo, K. (2003). "Africa in the Rise of Rights-Based Development." *Geoforum* 34: 437–456.

Mercer, C. (2003). "Performing Partnership: Civil Society and the Illusions of Good Governance in Tanzania." *Political Geography* 22 (7): 741–763.

M'inoti, K., and W. Maina. (1996). "The Press Council of Kenya Bill and the Kenya Mass Media Commission Bill: A Critical and Comparative Review." *Nairobi Law Monthly* 60: 15–17.

Ndegwa, S. (1996). *The Two Faces of Civil Society: NGOs and Politics in Africa.* West Hartford, CT: Kumarian Press.

Nelson, P. J., and E. Dorsey. (2003). "At the Nexus of Human Rights and Development: New Methods and Strategies of Global NGOs." *World Development* 31(12): 2013–2026.

Nussbaum, M. (2000). *Women and Human Development: The Capabilities Approach.* Cambridge: Cambridge University Press.

Nyamu-Musembi, C. (2006). "Ruling Out Gender Equality? The Post–Cold War Rule of Law Agenda in Sub-Saharan Africa." *Third World Quarterly* 27(7): 1193–1207.

Odhiambo, L. O. (2001). Eastern African Regional Perspectives, Summary Review. Windhoek, The Windhoek Seminar: "Ten Years On: Assessment, Challenges and Prospects." May 3–5.

Oloka-Onyango, J. (n.d.). "'Popular Justice,' Resistance Committee Courts, and the Judicial Process in Uganda (1988–1992)." Unpublished paper.

Palmer, R. (1998). "Oxfam GB's Land Advocacy Work in Tanzania and Uganda: The End of an Era?" Oxford, Oxfam.

Schumacher, E. F. (1973). *Small Is Beautiful: Economics as if People Mattered.* Point Roberts, WA, and Vancouver, BC: Hartley & Marks Publishers, 1999.

Sebina-Zziwa, A., R. Kibombo, et al. (2002). *Patterns and Trends of Women's Participation in Land Markets in Uganda.* 8th International Interdisciplinary Congress on Women, Kampala, Uganda, Makerere Institute of Social Research, Makerere University.

Sen, Amartya K. (1999). *Development as Freedom.* Oxford: Oxford University Press.

Toyo, N. (2006). "Revisiting Equality as a Right: The Minimum Age of Marriage Clause in the Nigerian Child Rights Act, 2003." *Third World Quarterly* 27(7): 1299–1312.

Tripp, A. M. (2004). "Women's Movements, Customary Law, and Land Rights in Africa: The Case of Uganda." *African Studies Quarterly* 7(4).

Tsikata, Dzodzi. (n.d.). "The Rights-Based Approach to Development: Potential for Change or More of the Same?" Working Paper, Center for Developmental Practice.

Uvin, P. (2002). "On High Moral Ground: The Incorporation of Human Rights by the Development Enterprise." *PRAXIS: The Fletcher Journal of Development Studies* 17.

seven

The International Factor in African Warfare

Will Reno

Generalizing about recent wars and their global connections in a continent as diverse as Africa is a tricky business. The 1998–2000 Ethiopian–Eritrean border war looked like a classic interstate war, with trenches and front lines, field artillery and coordinated ground-air attacks as armies fought over the delineation of an international boundary. Around the same time, wars in Congo and Somalia involved the collapse of state authority as ethnic militias, criminal gangs, religious ideologues, elements of old national armies, and armies of intervening states engaged in complex struggles. These wars have taken on new roles in global politics, too. After the September 11, 2011, attacks on New York and Washington, external actors began to view Somalia's conflict through the lens of counterterrorism. Congo's war appeared in international media as a humanitarian crisis. Some saw Sudan's counterinsurgency campaign in Darfur in the mid-2000s as an act of genocide and as Sudan's failure to fulfill a sovereign mandate to protect citizens.

Amid these diverse outcomes, distinct patterns emerge in the character of warfare in Africa—patterns rooted in changes in Africa's place in the international system. Most wars in Africa include "symmetrical irregular warfare" and the collapse of formal state institutions.[1] Large national armies play limited roles and diverse armed groups dominate the scene as they pursue varied goals and agendas in often interlocking conflicts. Fighters use cheap, portable weapons. Few of these groups offer extensive political programs, and even if they do, they do not offer to reform and strengthen state institutions like rebels did in earlier decades. Civilians in war zones are likely to suffer from chronic insecurity amid the collapse of effective central state authority, and many become refugees or internally displaced and encounter an international system of humanitarian aid and crisis management.

Most wars in Africa since 2000 have been fought across regions rather than solely within states, and thus are inherently international wars. In 2012, for example, local issues drove conflicts in Congo, South Sudan, Sudan Central African Republic, and Chad but also involved actors, relationships, and influences that spanned that region. Another regional complex appears in the Horn of Africa, with multiple armed groups inside Somalia's borders, some linked to ethnic kinsmen across borders and most pursuing global connections of some sort. Armed groups in northern Nigeria have links to conflicts in the Sahara and northern Sahel regions of West Africa, while the drug trafficking exacerbates political instability in several states in the region and has played a role in serious armed clashes in Guinea-Bissau.

This type of warfare in Africa defies conventional categories such as internal (civil) war and interstate war. It reflects the nature of political authority in parts of Africa where conflict is most prevalent. These are often Africa's largest states where formal state institutions are especially weak and regimes, instead, assert authority through political networks designed to control people's access to economic opportunities.[2] They manipulate the enforcement of their own laws to favor their political supporters and commercial partners and to manage external relations, giving some associates license to engage in predation, and in extreme cases, to seek out international criminals as collaborators. Resources such as international loans, proceeds from sales of resources on global markets, foreign aid, and diplomatic and material support for siding with powerful states in initiatives such as the US-led war on terrorism contribute to this store of political capital.

These "domestic" networks of political authority extend beyond the formal institutional and physical boundaries of states, and thus wars involving resources and political power connected to these networks take on global dimensions when measured against the grid of international boundaries. For example, when Tuareg rebels in Mali declared an independent state of Azawad in 2012, this appeared to be an internal affair. In fact, some rebel factions relied upon weapons that fighters who supported Libyan leader Muammar Gadhafi brought with them when their old patron was forced from power and they were driven from Libya. Similar networks linked Gadhafi to the government of Chad and to a rebel group across Chad's border in Sudan. Libyan money played important roles in electoral campaigns across the Sahel, and strategic Libyan investments provided leaders with the resources they needed to use commercial partnerships to build their political coalitions. Coups, violence, and political instability in Mali and other Sahel countries have much to do with local issues and actors, but events in Libya affected the timing and intensity of these events. This and other conflicts show how this political context complicates even the task of counting and categorizing wars in Africa. Is Mali's war in 2012 a separatist conflict or is it an extension of a war that took place in Libya, and how should one evaluate its relationship to political instability in Niger, or to fighting in Sudan's Darfur province that is linked to a branch of this wider network?

More generally, these wars are linked to the failure of twentieth-century state-building in the world's poorest countries. In the 1960s and 1970s, it made sense for leaders who faced fiscal constraints and domestic political threats to try to build as large a coalition of supporters as possible, at least until they were able to establish stronger state institutions. They used domestic resources and extracted as much as possible from the international community to sustain sprawling patronage networks. The scarcity of domestic resources hindered this project. But more important was the shift in international attitudes and approaches toward governance in these states that started in the 1980s and accelerated after 2000. Massive international interference into the details of governance and especially the growing depth and diversity of international intervention into issues related to the use of violence—care for refugees, direct contact with armed groups as political actors, and broad efforts to impose standards on myriad aspects of domestic governance—undermined this old twentieth-century strategy of building states on the basis of assembling coalitions of political clients, including through coercion.

A new framework is needed to understand contemporary warfare in Africa and its place in world politics. The next section of this chapter explains how the crisis of patronage politics in parts of Africa is linked to how states and their opponents use violence. The two sections that follow then examine how changes in the international environment, especially international intervention into the conduct of domestic politics in conflict zones, influence the conduct of warfare. In particular, since 2000 threats of international sanctions and calls to abide by protocols to protect civilians have changed the distribution of resources and calculations of actors in warfare. Many of these measures have strengthened the positions of armed groups and promote political fragmentation in parts of Africa where formal state institutions already are very weak. Other international factors such as US and European security aid to African states to combat terrorism have the reverse effect where state institutions already are fairly strong. International intrusion in these countries increases state capacities to monitor and regulate populations, providing these state actors in Africa's wars with new resources that they can use to enhance their positions. The final section considers the future of warfare in Africa in terms of these global political links.

WARFARE AND THE CRISIS OF PATRONAGE POLITICS

Despite more than two decades of sustained domestic and international pressure for reform, by various measures state institutions remain notably weak and regimes unstable across a wide range of African countries. Of the fifty-four member states of the African Union, only nine were rated as "free" in the 2012 Freedom House survey of political rights and civil liberties. Six were situated on the continent's main landmass (prior to the 2012 military coup in Mali), exactly as a decade before.[3] This dearth of democratic governance, despite widespread adoption of laws and institutions associated with it, highlights the subordination of this visible institutional apparatus of the state to a different kind of rule. Indexes that measure corruption show another side of the story. All but four sub-Saharan African countries occupy the lower half of the 2011 Transparency International perceptions of corruption index.[4] Corruption can signal personal enrichment, while also being compatible with the use of official positions and resources to channel favors to political supporters. Nine coups d'état occurred in seven sub-Saharan countries from 2000 to mid-2012 and numerous other attempts failed. When taken together, authoritarian rule, corruption, and coups d'état appear as the consequences of weak government administration and feeble political institutions across much of the continent. These also show the centrality of patronage politics and, in the cases of coups d'état, its unstable nature in some countries.

Systems of flexible informal connections centered on patron-client networks that link citizens to the leaders of regimes on the basis of personal affinities, ethnic kinship, and material rewards operate alongside weak formal institutions in many countries. Historically this alternative method of exercising authority has preserved a measure of political stability, if not economic prosperity, when a single leadership monopolizes the distribution of benefits to prevent others from mobilizing against them. As late as the 1980s it was still possible for notable scholars to propose that the president of Congo (then called Zaire) Mobutu Sese Seko was able to end large-scale political violence and turmoil through constructing a patronage system that was fairly inclusionary at an elite level. Mobutu's strategy reversed the collapse of authority and factional violence that affected Congo during its first five years of independence from 1960, and appeared to be one of the few ways to hold this vast country together.[5]

In this kind of authoritarian system, there is little official regard for laws or systematic guarantees of human rights or any ethic of public allocation of resources. The logic of this system prevents official support for private enterprise, lest those who do not owe their wealth to the ruler's favor use these resources to oppose him. There are no institutional channels for criticizing government or channels for opposition and no due process. This turns opposition in the direction of factional rivalries, which are more easily managed from statehouses. Those who oppose outright face the wrath of the regime, as targets of corruption investigations, purges, and in more sensitive or persistent cases, direct applications of violence. This fosters an image of the ruler's personal power and convinces most people of the futility of opposition. Loyalty to the ruler often follows a pragmatic calculation; better to benefit from the protection of the regime than to get nothing, or worse. This system of governance has been terrible for economies, sacrificing efficiency for political control. But as a measure of the capacity of this system of authority to manage opposition, in the late 1980s Jean-François Bayart wrote: "the salient feature of the last few decades south of the Sahara has been the absence of any collective agent capable or desirous of taking the lead in a social movement aspiring to a revolutionary alternative to the current grinding of the postcolonial state."[6] Most serious threats to these regimes come from within the elite coalition itself, with fundamental consequences for the character of warfare in Africa and its global connections.

While African governments hardly operated in solitude, during the first decades of African independence, the international community paid more than lip service to the principles in Article 2 of the Charter of the United Nations that all states enjoy equality in their sovereignty and as such, governments are protected from external intervention into their domestic affairs. Certainly Cold War adversaries and old colonial powers were prolific in their interference in the domestic politics of African states. They did not, however, challenge the basic logic of patronage-based systems of political control, and in notable instances acted to protect this logic so long as it served their interests. In a notable example, in 1982 the World Bank, the International Monetary Fund, private banks, and other creditors hired the German banker Erwin Blumenthal to investigate Zaire's official-level corruption. Blumenthal wrote in his report that it is "alarmingly clear that the corruptive system in Zaire with all of its wicked and ugly manifestations, its mismanagement and fraud will destroy all endeavors of international institutions, or friendly governments, and of commercial banks towards recovery and rehabilitation of Zaire's economy."[7] US pressure ended creditor efforts to impose conditions on this debtor country. This country's real value was as a Cold War ally providing a rear base for antigovernment rebels attacking Angola's Marxist government. Violations of human rights did not attract a great deal of international interference in internal affairs either. In 1977, the government of Uganda's President Idi Amin sat on the UN's Commission on Human Rights at the same time that his security forces were killing as many as a hundred thousand of his country's citizens. There was, as one scholar lamented, a sovereign "right to genocide" as massacres and other gross human rights abuses were considered domestic affairs.[8]

The end of the Cold War stripped these regimes of their protection from external scrutiny of their internal affairs and brought instead demands that they modify their behavior. World Bank reports stressed that political reform would be added to economic reform as conditions for continued access to foreign loans. From a reformer's perspective, it made sense to target the core logic of patronage politics, such as the leader's personal control over the distribution of resources, the manipulation of laws to favor political supporters and their enterprises, and the suppression of economic efficiency and accumulation outside of these political connections. In sum, attacking patronage politics would liberate citizens to be productive and enterprising. These reforms also were supposed to foster the formation of a class of independent holders of wealth who would organize behind campaigns to adopt better economic policies, and also to pressure for more open and democratic governance.

Officials in Africa's most corrupt and authoritarian political systems discovered in the 1990s that their ties to international actors were changing in an inconsistent manner that mixed periods of active scrutiny and pressure with a more general withdrawal. European and US officials announced that they would support human rights and democratic governance, but this failed to translate into steady backing for reforms. There was satisfaction in many quarters overseas as African protesters pressed for political change, but most Western governments shared the view of their old Soviet adversaries that "involvement in sub-Saharan Africa represented an unacceptable drain on Soviet resources . . . and by an increasing conviction that its manifold problems were peripheral to Soviet interests."[9] This withdrawal had a dramatic impact on the fortunes of the continent's most violent regimes. Between 1980 and 1985, Liberia's government received about $500 million in combined US economic and military aid, which then dried up as the US Congress grew concerned about human rights violations.[10] The government of Congo (Zaire) received about $2 billion in US aid from the mid-1960s to the end of the 1980s, but this, too, slowed to a trickle as Congo's strategic importance evaporated. By 1988, US aid to Somalia's dictator, totaling about $750 million over the previous decade, was ended as the US Congress investigated government massacres of about 50,000 citizens.[11]

Patronage-based political networks of the three top African recipients of US aid in the 1980s—Congo, Liberia, and Somalia—collapsed after financial aid was cut off. Congo's ruler was able to delay the collapse for several years, but the sharp decline in external resources directly under their personal control fatally weakened the authority that these rulers exercised over their clients. These rulers lost the capacity to manage factional struggles as key elite members of these networks struck out on their own, a tendency that is noted in the fondness of authoritarian rulers from Mobutu to Gaddafi for predictions that the collapse of the political system and violence will follow their departures from the political scene. In wars in the 1990s in each of these countries, most of the leaders of the main armed groups previously held significant positions in prewar political networks. These ambitious individuals no longer had a compelling reason to profess loyalty to their country's leaders and were free to build their own political networks in their pursuits of power. They could make better deals for themselves extracting resources from whatever part of these old networks that they could control, often in collaboration with the same business partners who had played key roles in helping prewar rulers gain access patronage resources.

The focus of these new armed groups on the appropriation of pieces of these patronage networks, including the external commercial connections that were vital to sustaining prewar networks, shaped how outsiders viewed these struggles. Some scholars describe this as "greed-driven" warfare.[12] While material gain appeared to play a major role in the purposes of fighting, the real objective of these wartime commanders was to control the resources of old patronage networks and to use them to assemble new versions of this kind of political authority. Capturing state power was still important, as the possession of sovereignty widened the scope of available resources. "Greed" in this context was at least as much about political authority as it was about personal enrichment, particularly as during the late 1980s and 1990s the resources of illicit trades in diamonds, timber, and other resources replaced Cold War–era foreign aid, loans, and other external transfers to states as the blood that animated this kind of system.

The recession of external support for patronage-based regimes in Africa in the 1990s undermined the central control of patronage networks in other ways, too. This weakening of central control boosted the relative power of those, whether from inside the ruling coalition or outside it, who were able to find ways to arm themselves to make their own bids for power. The US retreat from Somalia in 1993 and the decision of UN Security Council members to refrain from intervention in Rwanda's genocide in 1994 underlined this shift away from support for centralized networks. Many regimes found new ways to survive. Angola's rulers proved adept at extending and adapting political networks to include nongovernmental organizations to absorb the energies of educated urban citizens and to solicit donations from foreign businesses to channel to regime supporters.[13] This regime responded to international pressures from the 1990s for greater openness to global markets and foreign investors in its oil industry with joint ventures designed to enhance not only local but also international competition for the head of state's personal favor. These arrangements incorporate a complex web of foreign businesses, local entrepreneurs and fixers, and favored political cliques into this president-centric political network, absorbing their capacities to access sources of credits and to lobby foreign officials on the regime's behalf.[14]

Personal rule also survived in many places against international and domestic pressures for democratic governance. In a pattern repeated in many other countries, Cameroon's incumbent President Paul Biya faced a competitive election in 1992, his first since coming to power in 1982. He won with about 40 percent of the vote, prevailing only because the opposition was split among two main contenders and through using security forces against opponents and voting irregularities. The 1997 election was quite different, with Biya winning over 92 percent of the vote against a field of six other candidates. Though he won only 71 percent of the vote in 2007, the rest was split among fifteen other candidates.[15] In sum, pressures for democratic reform in the 1990s led to the formal adoption of multiparty elections in every African state except Libya. Yet by mid-2012 this continent counted seven heads of state who had managed elections well enough to remain in office for at least a quarter of a century.

Not all of these political networks survived in centralized form and the bulk of warfare in Africa from the 1990s was connected in significant ways to the fragmentation of these networks that followed changes in the international relations of African states. This signaled the failure of the patronage route to state-building, and unleashed former clients to seek their own external connections—criminal gangs, humanitarian agencies, Diaspora groups—to sustain their own patronage systems. Competition among regimes and political factions in neighboring states contributed to the internationalization of these conflicts surrounding the breakdown of centralized patronage networks. This happened in Congo when Rwanda and Uganda intervened in the mid-1990s to support various rebel groups. In the case of the Ugandans, their army officers had a tendency to conduct business on their own account with rebel commanders, a development that alarmed superiors.[16] Congo's faction leader Jean-Pierre Bemba, son of Mobutu's chief business partner and brother to the wife of one of Mobutu's sons, organized his *Mouvement de Libération du Congo* with help from Uganda's army, which also brought Sudan People's Liberation Army fighters across the border to fight against Chadian troops that had been lent to Congo's President Kabila and to keep another group of rebels at bay. Then in 2002, Central African Republic's President Ange-Félix Patassé called upon Bemba (and Libyan troops) to come to his aid to defeat a coup attempt. On Bemba's part, this alliance helped to keep Patassé in his own camp as other politicians from the Mobutu era were trying to woo the Central African Republic's president to support them instead.[17] The successful coup of François Bozizé in 2003 upended these arrangements and instead brought Bozizé's Chadian network to the capital, highlighting the extent to which political networks in this region had become so intermingled across international borders and reached beyond bureaucratic institutions to incorporate commercial groups and various militias.[18]

This general shift illustrates a broader trend toward the equalization of the internal capabilities and the external relations of armed groups, whether affiliated with the state or not, that further blurs distinctions between civil wars and international wars and reinforces conditions that produced the symmetrical irregular warfare as the prevalent mode of warfare in Africa. The international pressures promoting these trends intensified after the September 11, 2001, attacks on New York and Washington and underwent another significant shift. The primary consequence of these attacks was even more intense international scrutiny into the internal affairs of those who ran states and nonstate armed groups in Africa, along with a greater propensity to intervene. The nature of these interventions, and in particular the capacities of actors in Africa to influence and benefit from them, plays a critical role in shaping the nature of state-building in Africa, and thus also in the nature of warfare.

WARFARE, WORLD POLITICS, AND TWENTY-FIRST-CENTURY STATE-BUILDING

US and European interest in the internal politics of African states rapidly intensified after the September 11 attacks. The simultaneous suicide bomb attacks in August 1998 on US embassies in Nairobi and Dar es Salaam that killed more than 220 people and wounded over 4,000 had already demonstrated the danger to US interests that could emerge in areas where government institutions and thus surveillance capacities were weak. In 2002 US President George W. Bush highlighted the link between weak state institutions in Africa and threats to US security, noting that "with our European allies we must help strengthen Africa's fragile states, help build indigenous capability to secure porous borders, and help build up the law enforcement and intelligence infrastructure to deny safe haven to terrorists."[19] What were once viewed simply as internal affairs and disincentives for engagement, such as the lack of capacity or political unwillingness to exercise direct control over territory, to discipline subordinates, and to exercise a monopoly over the exercise of coercion, now were of considerable concern to outsiders and, the American president warned, grounds for intervention if they were not addressed. In sum, critical outsiders now insisted that domestic governance came with responsibilities to govern in particular ways and that sovereignty was no shield against external interference to correct deviations from standards.

This shift in thinking and policy has generated substantial consequences for regimes that govern through patronage networks, particularly when these networks rely on partnerships with illicit commercial operations and allow local actors to exercise violence against civilians on behalf of the regime. In Liberia, for example, UN experts who investigated Liberian President Charles Taylor's violations of an arms embargo detailed his business associations with arms traffickers and other private businessmen, alleging that he used these connections to provide funding and weapons to Sierra Leone's rebels to conduct a reign of terror in an eleven-year war in which 50,000 people died. The report also noted the extensive use of private bank accounts to conceal revenues and expenditures, suggesting that Liberia's government at the time had intimate ties to illicit networks that supplied Taylor's regime with weapons and funds to buy off key clients, support allied armed groups, and operate security forces.[20] Moreover, a journalist alleged that Liberia's illicit networks were linked to terrorist financiers from the Middle East.[21]

The recognition of these forms of governance as security threats essentially criminalized regimes that rely extensively upon patronage networks to govern, especially if these networks are implicated in violence against civilians and include illicit commercial transactions. Personalist regimes like Taylor's in Liberia now encountered serious international pressures in the form of sanctions and embargoes if they were seen as promoting conflicts inside their own territories or in other countries into which their networks stretched. This negative attention constricting the autonomy of sovereign actors affects how struggles between factions play out. In particular, the intensified scrutiny can make these actors easier targets for their opponents. In Guinea-Bissau, for example, tensions between army officers involved in drug trafficking and the prime minister led to a military coup on April 12, 2012. The prime minister had begun to reform the military and had built his own network with support from an Angolan security and training mission that also appeared to be linked to Angolan government efforts to gain favorable treatment in commercial deals.[22] His efforts to target alleged drug trafficking may have bought the prime minister greater international tolerance for his use of these methods. Once the coup leaders were in power, however, the Economic Community of West African

States (ECOWAS),with UN backing, proposed a regional military intervention geared toward the removal of the coup leaders and threatened to impose sanctions targeted against individual leaders and possible referral to the International Criminal Court (ICC) for prosecution.[23]

Regime engagement with illicit commercial networks as part of their strategies of governance is not a new phenomenon in Africa,[24] but the willingness of other states to intervene in the internal affairs of these states to halt this and other newly prohibited practices is a new development. Prior to the situation in Guinea-Bissau, UN sanctions and US pressure forced Liberia's President Taylor to leave office in 2003 and eventually led him to appear before a tribunal in 2006. He was sentenced in 2012 for his role in atrocities committed during Sierra Leone's war, to which he was linked through clandestine political and commercial ties to Sierra Leone's rebels.

The prosecution of Taylor and threats to prosecute other leaders involved in wars in Africa show that powerful international actors will withdraw their recognition of the sovereignty of leaders who stray from an increasingly complex set of norms. This reinforces the license of outsiders to pressure and intervene in affairs of internal governance in these countries, provided that these countries are too weak to press back against these sanctions. This right to intervene is accepted among many African governments, at least in principle, and is codified in the African Union's 2003 African Charter on Democracy, Elections, and Governance.[25] This has led to applications of sanctions and diplomatic pressure against regimes from other African governments, such as against Senegal for harboring former Chadian president Hissene Habré. During the 1980s, Habré's regime killed thousands of political opponents and members of their communities as part of his strategy for regime survival as it faced numerous armed factions that eventually led to his overthrow in 1990. During the 1980s, the United States and France supported Habré as a counterbalance to Libyan influence and gave him aid and diplomatic support. External support, along with his violent strategy, enabled Habré to maintain a modicum of control over an otherwise highly fragmented set of political networks. Once out of power, by 2005 Habré faced an indictment in Belgium for crimes against humanity and other violations. ECOWAS requested that he be tried before a special tribunal, and in 2012 he remained under house arrest in Senegal.

Though this obligation to govern in a particular way puts new pressures on those who rule through patronage-based networks, particularly if this produces human rights violations and political instability in neighboring countries, some regimes have discovered that external interference offers resources that can be used to strengthen executive control over political networks. This usually requires that a basic level of control already be in place and that the regime play some role in the strategic aims of powerful non-African states that will help shield the regime from external scrutiny. This relationship can develop in the context of wars in Africa and represents an important global connection in these wars.

Numerous US policy initiates aimed at strengthening state institutions in Africa are useful to rulers who seek to shield their domestic affairs from critical scrutiny. This requires that these rulers accept another set of external demands to conform to a standard set of practices—in this case, in the realm of security. In effect, warfare, or at least the anxiety of outsiders to counter security threats, can be turned into a political resource for these regimes. The Combined Joint Task Force–Horn of Africa (CJTF-HOA) deployed 1,800 US soldiers to Djibouti and became part of the newly established US Africa Command (AFRICOM) in 2007. AFRICOM operations, along with programs like the Pan-Sahel Initiative, bring civilian agencies customarily involved in development activities into partnerships with the military to train police and military personnel in African countries and to work with state agencies in these countries to implement reform programs. CJTF-HOA describes these operations "as part of a comprehensive whole-of-government approach . . . aimed at increasing our African partner nations' capacity to maintain a stable environment, with an effective government that provides a degree of economic and social advancement to its citizens."[26] The UK's Africa Conflict Prevention Pool preceded this policy and provided a model, having been established in April 2001, to coordinate the activities of a variety of African and foreign "partner" civilian government agencies and nongovernment organizations to operate alongside military forces to change local security environments in what are referred to as "complex operations."

Drawing upon ideas about fighting irregular and counterinsurgency warfare, complex operations lay the basis for preemptive counterinsurgency in African host states. This approach identifies the need that governments hold territory to deny access to rebels. Controlling local populations is a precondition to achieving this goal. This means using foreign and domestic civilian agencies, humanitarian organizations, and a variety of nongovernment organizations and civic groups to extend services to local populations so that they will depend upon the state rather than rebels for protection and will provide information about rebel infiltration to preserve this beneficial relationship with the state. As US Secretary of State Colin Powell noted in 2001, "NGOs are such a force multiplier for us, such an important part of our combat team." Though officials subsequently downplayed this statement, the idea that it expressed is central to the concept of complex operations that leverage the knowledge and operations of many organizations to increase the capacities of governments to behave like bureaucratic states.

Even though complex operations envision a step-by-step state-building enterprise on a continental scale, these externally designed policies are compatible with the underlying logic of patronage-based authority. Even better for the ruler, these policies strengthen the ruler's position to coerce members of a political coalition to demonstrate obedience to his authority. The strengthened security and surveillance capabilities of the state mean that the ruler need not offer so much in the way of patronage in return for this support. The improved capacity to detect dissent, and in some cases, the labeling of discontent and opposition as terrorism or support for radicalism means that some recalcitrant opposition communities simply can be cut out of political bargains. Foreign aid to state agencies also helps to concentrate the allocation of resources into the hands of the ruler, particularly if the regime is able to turn elections into a facade of competition and to keep legislators politically weak and subservient. These resources and the appearance of visible external backing enhance the role of the ruler's personal discretion in political decisions. This creates the appearance of political stability that may seem to be the product of foreign-supported state-building projects. Stability also can be the product of more centralized control over patronage and a ruler's increased capacity to dictate the terms of membership in a political coalition centered on control of the state.

Uganda provides a particularly good example where the internationalization of war fighting in Africa intersects with domestic patronage strategies. Yoweri Museveni has occupied Uganda's presidency since 1986, building a core coalition of security forces and key political associates while exercising careful personal control over the flow of resources. Domestic and international pressure that led to multiparty electoral competition after 2005 posed a threat to this control. The introduction of real competition for supporters provided subordinate members of this network and ambitious political outsiders with incentives to challenge the president. This raised the price of cooptation back into the political network since elections empowered some people to launch efforts to build their own political networks. This causes what Joel Barkan calls "inflationary patronage," which forced the president to distribute money in campaigns to coopt viable opposition candidates, buy the support of communities, and maintain the loyalty of his associates, tasks that observers estimate cost up to $300 million in an election year.[27]

This external and domestic pressure for political reforms, which continues in Uganda, contributes to undermining the stability of a centralized political network through weakening the president's hold over clients. Electoral violence in Kenya, Côte d'Ivoire, and elsewhere highlights how competition in the context of patronage-based politics can contribute to political fragmentation, often in a violent fashion—another link between African wars and world politics. The problem for external and domestic proponents of political reform is that, while democratic governance may offer better prospects for long-term political stability and economic efficiency, it risks provoking the collapse of state authority where the logic of politics centers on patronage. Even Kenya, thought of as a relatively stable African state before the 2007 elections, could suffer more than a thousand deaths in electoral violence in early 2008 in clashes of armed gangs aligned with politicians. Advocates of reform therefore have to consider carefully the paradox of their positions; caught as they are between a desire to fundamentally change these political systems to conform to what they see as global norms, while relying upon what they see as the problems of governance to provide short-term political stability. External actors are also caught in this bind since the stability of patronage networks, even if they are implicated in illicit commerce and human rights abuses, is central to their concerns about security threats.

This paradox is visible to the public. A US embassy official noted, "Many Ugandans believe President Museveni will never hold top officials . . . accountable for corruption, and Uganda's continued failure to seriously investigate and prosecute allegations of corruption involving senior government officials seemingly supports such conclusions."[28] Increased repression of those without political leverage resulted in human rights abuses that attracted more external condemnations.[29] These strategies—lamentable though logical in the context of patronage politics—led to reductions in what had been $600 million in World Bank annual budget support, a serious blow to a government that relied upon aid for about half of its budget expenditures.

Uganda's government found salvation in African warfare's role in world politics. The US government recognizes Uganda as a key ally in ensuring support for the Transitional Federal Government in Somalia, the creation of internationally mediated negotiations to counter the Islamic Courts Union in southern Somalia and the establishment of the African Union Mission in Somalia (AMISOM) to provide military protection to the new government. Uganda has supported AMISOM since its organization in 2007, fielding more than 5,000 infantry near Mogadishu. This willingness to serve in a multilateral African expeditionary force to fight Islamist enemies of the UN-backed provisional government led to a reversal of the cutoff of US military aid. Aid had been halted in 2000 over Ugandan military abuses of civilians and involvement in illicit commercial operations in Congo. But since 2007, US military assistance has averaged about $200 million a year, supplemented with significant UK aid. The US State Department also oversees contracts with private operators for logistical support to Uganda's military.

Foreign training programs have played an important role in helping to create a core of professional military officers, a key element of developing state institutions that are capable of providing order and asserting the state's authority over the country's territory (and fighting in Somalia). Military training also is compatible with tightening executive control over armed forces. Uganda's military includes armored units, such as the Presidential Guard Brigades that remain under the personal control of the president and his son, who also has received US military training.[30] This distribution of tasks in Uganda's military enables a fairly effective institutional enclave to attract eternal resources to contribute to the president's personal authority while remaining flexible enough to adapt to new tasks to attract more external support.

Uganda's political authorities also benefit from global condemnation of the Lord's Resistance Army's use of child soldiers and commission of atrocities against civilians in northern Uganda and elsewhere in the region, and US aid to Uganda's military to capture or kill the LRA's leaders. The LRA first appeared on the US State Department's list of terrorist organizations in 2001, partly in response to pressure from advocacy groups. Aid to northern Uganda coordinated through State Department, Defense Department, USAID, and intelligence services has provided logistical and intelligence support to Uganda People's Defence Force and helped to build infrastructure and services for which Uganda's government could take local credit. The United States provided about $168 million in aid to northern Uganda in 2009 and about $165 million in 2010.[31] Conflict thus plays an important role in generating overall State Department and USAID assistance to Uganda that totaled about $400 million in 2009 and over $450 million in 2010.[32]

In October 2011, about one hundred US soldiers arrived in Uganda to assist in the fight against the LRA. This presence, along with US trainers in Senior Command and Staff Colleges, provided a visible display of US support for Ugandan authorities. In sum, Uganda's president benefits from external support to build institutions in ways that do not interfere with his personal role as a distributor of patronage and economic opportunity. His country's strategic interventions in wars elsewhere on the continent help to deflect international criticism of his domestic political strategies, particularly the failure to fully implement political reforms. US and European engagement with other governments for counterterrorism activities provides regimes with long-serving presidents, such as Burkina Faso's Blaise Compaoré (in office since 1987) with modest amounts of military aid, specialized training for soldiers, and more important, the image of protection of a powerful external patron that prioritizes security and stability and is less likely to be critical of regime strategies for governance.[33]

WARFARE, WORLD POLITICS, AND
TWENTY-FIRST-CENTURY STATE COLLAPSE

Countries like Uganda show how regimes that control centralized networks of supporters and use only limited applications of violence against critics and opponents are able to manipulate external aid designed to strengthen the institutional capacities of their states. Regimes struggling to control fragmented patronage networks, however, are much more disadvantaged in Africa's new place in global politics. External scrutiny of their desperate efforts to manage unwieldy coalitions and armed opponents directly undermines their basic survival strategies. Sudan (and newly independent South Sudan), Central African Republic, Congo, Chad, Niger, and Mauritania, but also some small countries like Guinea-Bissau and Comoros, have substantial histories of political instability and violent factional conflict. For decades, rulers have struggled to prevent fragmentation of these coalitions, using a combination of patronage (supported with considerable external financial assistance), considerable palace intrigue, and episodes of considerable violence against opponents and their home communities. Politics in these countries bears more resemblance to the shifting alliances of strongmen and conflict-ridden center-periphery relations of great unwieldy empires than it does to the ideal model of governance in contemporary states. Thus some of the conflicts that scholars code as Africa's civil wars are in fact conflicts within this kind of political system, as authorities in regions that regard themselves as equals to the president call upon ethnic kinsmen and other networks that stretch across international borders.

Global efforts to limit the sovereign capacities of these rulers to manage their patronage systems as these rulers see fit can promote further fragmentation and political disorder. Unlike Uganda's President Museveni, rulers like Sudan's President Omar Bashir who cannot convince outsiders that they are essential allies against terrorism face severe limits on external financial assistance to their treasuries, at least from US and European sources. As noted above in cases such as Guinea-Bissau, these rulers face sanctions and embargoes, further weakening their appeal to subordinates and regional power brokers that they can act as effective patrons. Bashir, for example, faces an arrest warrant issued by the ICC in 2010 on counts of war crimes, crimes against humanity, and genocide after his government's bloody repression of a rebellion in Darfur.

Alex de Waal points to Darfur's conflict as an example of just such a "political marketplace" in Sudan where local strongmen discovered that international condemnation of the head of the political network enhanced their own power. They can leverage international negotiations as platforms for their otherwise insignificant rebel forces. They attack government forces strategically to raise the price of their cooptation into a weakened patron's network. This international intervention into conflicts, argues de Waal, enables these armed local actors to negotiate deals instead with foreign critics of their government, multilateral peacekeeping forces, and global commercial networks.[34] Within Darfur's political marketplace, the ICC arrest warrants issued in 2007 for Ali Khushayb and Ahmed Mohammed Haroun for war crimes and crimes against humanity, committed while leaders of government-supported militias, further damaged the president's capacity to buy off his opponents, and showed that using violence against them instead would further isolate the regime from the international community.

The International Commission of Inquiry into Darfur, set up by the UN Security Council, in January 2005 concluded that Sudan's government was fighting a counterinsurgency campaign in Darfur, historically a customary right of governments, albeit not one that allows for wanton abuses of human rights.[35] In 2004, however, US Secretary of State Colin Powell stated that "genocide has been committed in Darfur and that the government of Sudan and the Jingaweit bear responsibility."[36] This twenty-first-century response was quite different from the relatively muted responses in the 1990s as the Angolan government's counterinsurgency campaigns resulted in loss of life that exceeded the toll in Darfur.

Internationally backed negotiations involving all parties to conflicts equip commanders of local armed groups and power brokers to drive hard bargains in negotiations with heads of patronage networks. For example, Somali participants in peace negotiations—stretching over many years—allegedly found that they could buy preferential treatment in negotiations.[37] The costs of their consent in the formal and informal elements of these negotiations rose in tandem with their capacities to display visible measures of autonomy from their superiors in political networks. The best way to do this was to continue to be active in armed conflicts. This dynamic imposes costs on these actors, too, since subordinates within their own groups have incentives to break away and establish their own militias to gain entrée into negotiations and a possible settlement. The 2006 Darfur Agreement included only three rebel groups, while negotiations a year later involved over a dozen groups, many of which split into multiple factions. Though this fragmentation in part reflected the Sudanese regime's efforts to make deals with their opponents to undermine their capacities to cooperate, negotiations may have offered these targets of cooptation other options and thus the means to bid up their price. Negotiations can offer more direct benefits, too. Even Uganda's LRA, noted above as a target of US-trained Ugandan soldiers, in 2007 demanded $2 million from donors as their fee to participate in negotiations.[38]

Payments to members of armed groups for internationally sponsored disarmament and postconflict reconstruction in the context of already fragmented patronage networks can channel resources into the hands of local commanders rather than national governments. These local power brokers then strengthen their own political networks. International support for policies of decentralization and grassroots civic action can provide institutional support for this fragmentation of political networks. These arrangements may turn out to be peaceful, as some of these networks focus more on commercial activities and civic matters. But in countries where presidents historically have had a hard time maintaining political coalitions and controlling the flow of patronage resources, these local power brokers instead may bargain more vigorously and demand a higher price for their support.

Not all rulers of contentious patronage networks fail to adapt to contemporary conditions. Chad's President Déby probably would not be in power in 2012 were it not for his decision to break his agreement with the World Bank consortium over the use of oil revenues. Eighty percent of these revenues were supposed to be used for economic development and poverty reduction, 10 percent for a sovereign fund, 5 percent for oil producing areas, and 5 percent for government revenues.[39] The deal fell apart in 2006 when Déby decided to run for reelection, right after a serious rebellion in the eastern part of the country that was connected to the conflict in Darfur. His decision to abrogate the agreement restored his position as the arbiter of a centralized patronage network, a status that he underlined with his use of oil revenues to purchase weapons. Even with this advantage, Déby was nearly overthrown in 2008 when rebel armies reached the capital.

The survival of Déby's regime in Chad highlights the importance to rulers of Africa's patronage-based political systems of leveraging their relations with external actors to ensure survival. Chad's army participates in the United States' Trans-Sahara Counter-Terrorism Initiative to monitor and block the movement of violent extremists across the Sahara. More important, however, is the continued flow of oil and the revenues that this export generates. These resources support the president's efforts to keep rebel groups factionalized and weak and convinced some leaders to change sides. Chad's president showed considerable skill negotiating a favorable position in the context of increased international scrutiny of the political strategies of African regimes, particularly when they are engaged in conflicts. His and other rulers' fates show how warfare can be either a resource or a curse in organizing patronage politics, a dynamic that sheds light on the future of the role of African wars in world politics.

WORLD POLITICS AND THE FUTURE OF AFRICAN WARS

It is not likely that international pressure on elements of the conduct of patronage politics in the world's weaker states—usually seen in terms of corruption and human rights violations—will abate. The increase in global connections only steps up the demands for common standards and uniformity of behavior. This is true across a wide array of tasks conventionally associated with bureaucratic states. Increasingly governments are called upon to certify that they are observing and protecting their borders, monitoring commercial transactions, watching for signs of extremism, and numerous other tasks. This is the continuation of a long-term process. Since the start of the colonial era, globalization has supported the universalization of states throughout Africa. In the past decade or two, global connections have resulted in the universal spread of very specific forms of governance, such as multiparty politics, limits on uses of violence, particularly against citizens, and at least nominal efforts to tackle corruption. Globalization has resulted in the infringement of the prerogatives of the sovereignty of African states. But this infringement has been part of a process of state construction and has reinforced the importance of states as a basic unit of politics in Africa as it has elsewhere.

The pages above show how this international engagement has expanded the resources available to some African states, while also expanding resources to some of their armed opponents. Though some state actors in Africa can manipulate and mitigate global pressures to behave in certain ways, these pressures are likely to produce some common effects on warfare in Africa's future that follow from this shift in relative capabilities of state and nonstate actors. First, wars have become halting affairs, punctuated with cycles of negotiation and fighting. International intervention stays the hands of state actors while keeping nonstate armed groups politically and militarily viable for longer than might otherwise be the case. This has reduced the intensity of wars, including a decrease in death tolls, even if it drags them out.

This shift in relative capabilities of actors marks contentious politics in other ways. The violent response of Guinea's government to the September 2009 protests of citizens against military rule, for example, resulted in the deaths of at least 150 people. Two decades earlier this would have been an unremarkable event in international terms, but probably would have been critical in Guinea's domestic politics for widening factional splits in that government and leading to much greater violence. Or it could have ended the challenge against this regime in a decisive and bloody manner. Instead, African Union, US, and European Union pressure on President Moussa Dadis Camara and several dozen others to step down led to elections in 2010 for a new civilian government. In contrast, government repression in the 1960s and 1970s in Guinea resulted in the murder of 50,000 people with little international comment.[40] This earlier event in a contemporary context would be viewed as regionally destabilizing and the potential start of a civil war. In sum, the principle that regimes are not allowed to systematically apply violence against citizens in the pursuit of political authority has reduced the incidence and intensity of warfare on the continent at the same time that it has reduced the capacities of regimes in Africa to manage splits and factional strife among members of their own elite. As this and other examples show, external intervention into the domestic politics of these states and their regimes can have some very positive benefits alongside effects that some might see as negative. In any event, this intervention has a major impact on the terms of state-building in Africa, whether for better or for worse.

This reduction of violence does not mean that all rulers in Africa will simply abandon patronage politics and will refrain from using coercion to strengthen their hands in political bargains with critics and challengers. But as noted above, the capacities of rulers to use global political changes to their benefit varies widely. Those that can manipulate external intrusion, such as Uganda's President Museveni, actually may choose to strengthen personalist aspects of rule at the expense of institutional development with considerable help from foreign patrons. Others such as Sudan's President Bashir face diminishing options. But even this president, without apparent strategic value to foreign powers, has some leverage. The threat of disorder that would be the consequence of fragmenting patronage networks causes international actors to think pragmatically: Do they wish to launch far more expensive and politically risky interventions in the event that a president loses his political grip and no rival is strong enough to replace him? In essence, the threat of political suicide, to be followed with state collapse—or more accurately, the collapse of a political network rather than state institutional collapse—turns out to be a political resource.

These political consequences of recent changes in Africa's place in world politics and its impact on the character of warfare produce a general portrait of illusory state-building at best in the more conflict-ridden and politically unstable parts of the continent. Though governments may hesitate to massacre their own citizens to degrees seen in previous decades, there is very little evidence that these changes are leading to greater democratic accountability in state relations with citizens. As the example of Uganda showed above, the domestic political consequence of these changes can include reinforcing the personalist, patronage-based elements of regime politics.

Ultimately, the context of patronage politics in many African countries and the turmoil that accompanies it highlight a tight link between African state-building, global politics, and African wars. Most of these wars arise out of contention within elite networks rather than challenges from rural farmers or the urban unemployed. They are products of the political systems out of which they emerge and rarely go far to reshape these political systems, even when accompanied by high levels of violence. Fundamental change in the character of warfare in Africa and in its links to global politics will have to await a fundamental change in the logic of politics and of state-building in Africa. That prospect is quite far off, particularly in Africa's largest countries, such as Somalia, Congo, Central African Republic, South Sudan, Sudan, Chad, Niger, and Mali, and in some of the chronically unstable countries, such as Guinea-Bissau. These are also the countries that see the bulk of conflict on this continent now and in the foreseeable future.

NOTES

1. Stathis Kalyvas and Laia Balcells, "International System and Technologies of Rebellion: How the End of the Cold War Shaped Internal Conflict," *American Political Science Review* 104, no. 3 (2010): 418.

2. This is an idea developed in part in Christopher Clapham, Jeffrey Herbst, and Greg Mills, eds., *Big African States: Angola, DRC, Ethiopia, South Africa, Sudan* (Johannesburg, South Africa: Witswatersrand University Press, 2006).

3. Freedom House, "2012 Freedom in the World" (Washington, DC: Freedom House, 2012), www.freedomhouse.org/report-types/freedom-world.

4. Transparency International, "2011 Corruption Perceptions Index" (Berlin: Transparency International, 2011), http://cpi.transparency.org/cpi2011.

5. Thomas Callaghy, *The State-Society Struggle: Zaire in Comparative Perspective* (New York: Columbia University Press, 1982).

6. Jean-François Bayart, *The State in Africa,* 2nd ed. (Cambridge, UK: Polity, 2009), p. 209.

7. Quoted in Thomas Callaghy, "The International Community and Zaire's Debt Crisis," in Georges Nzongola-Ntalaja, ed., *The Crisis in Zaire: Myths and Realities* (Trenton, NJ: Africa World Press, 1986), p. 226.

8. Leo Kuper, *Genocide: Its Political Uses in the Twentieth Century* (New Haven, CT: Yale University Press, 1982), pp. 161–184.

9. Christopher Andrew and Vasil Mitrokhin, *The World Was Going Our Way: The KGB and the Battle for the Third World* (New York: Basic Books, 2006), p. 469.

10. Bill Berkeley, *The Graves Are Not Yet Full: Race, Tribe, and Power in the Heart of Africa* (New York: Basic Books, 2001), p. 116.

11. US Congress, House of Representatives, Subcommittee on Africa, Reported Massacres and Indiscriminate Killings in Somalia (Washington, DC: Government Printing Office, 1989).

12. Most notably, Paul Collier and Anke Hoeffler, "Greed Versus Grievance in Civil War" (Washington, DC: World Bank Development Research Group, 2000), www-wds .worldbank.org/servlet/WDSContentServer/WDSP/IB/2000/06/17/000094946_000602 05420011/Rendered/PDF/multi_page.pdf.

13. Christine Messiant, "The Eduardo Dos Santos Foundation: or, How Angola's Regime Is Taking Over Civil Society," *African Affairs* 100, no. 399 (2001): 287–309.

14. Ricardo Soares de Oliveira, "Business Success, Angola-Style: Postcolonial Politics and the Rise of SONANGOL," *Journal of Modern African Studies* 45, no. 4 (2007): 595–619.

15. http://africanelections.tripod.com/cm.html.

16. UNSC reports and Republic of Uganda, *Judicial Commission of Inquiry into Allegations into Illegal Exploitation of Natural Resources and Other forms of Wealth into the Democratic Republic of Congo—Final Report* [Porter Commission Report] (Kampala, Uganda: UN Security Council, 2002).

17. Gérard Prunier, *From Genocide to Continental War: The "Congolese" Conflict and the Crisis of Contemporary Africa* (London: Hurst & Company, 2009), pp. 204–205, 290.

18. Andreas Mehier, "The Shaky Foundations, Adverse Circumstances, and Limited Achievements of Democratic Transition in the Central African Republic," in *The Fate of Africa's Democratic Experiments,* ed. Leonardo Villalón and Peter VonDoepp (Bloomington: Indiana University Press, 2005), pp. 147–148.

19. George W. Bush, *The National Security Strategy of the United States of America* (Washington, DC: White House, 2002), pp. 10–11.

20. *Report of the Panel of Experts Appointed Pursuant to Paragraph 4 of Security Council Resolution 1458 (2003), Concerning Liberia* (New York: UN, 2003).

21. Douglas Farah, *Blood from Stones: The Secret Financial Network of Terror* (New York: Broadway, 2004).

22. "Return of the Narco-State," *Africa Confidential* 53, no. 9 (April 27, 2012): 8.

23. UN Security Council, *Special Report of the Secretary-General on the Situation in Guinea-Bissau* (New York: United Nations, 2012), p. 7.

24. Jean-François Bayart, Stephen Ellis, and Béatrice Hibou, *The Criminalization of the State in Africa*, (Bloomington: Indiana University Press, 1999).

25. Article 23, available at www.africa-union.org/root/au/Documents/Treaties/text/Charter%20on%20Democracy.pdf, accessed June 1, 2012.

26. www.hoa.africom.mil/, accessed May 31, 2012.

27. Joel Barkan, *Uganda: Assessing Risks to Stability* (Washington, DC: Center for Strategic and International Studies, 2011), pp. 8–9.

28. US Embassy Kampala, "Uganda's All-You-Can-Eat Corruption Buffet," Wikileaks cable, January 5, 2010.

29. Human Rights Watch, *Open Secret: Illegal Detention and Torture by the Joint Anti-Terrorism Task Force in Uganda* (New York: Human Rights Watch, 2009).

30. The president's son wrote a book on military strategy: Muhoozi Kainerugaba, *Battle of the Ugandan Resistance: A Tradition of Maneuver* (Kampala, Uganda: Fountain Publishers, 2010).

31. Alexis Arieff and Lauren Ploch, *The Lord's Resistance Army: The U.S. Response* (Washington, DC: Congressional Research Service, 2011), p. 14.

32. Lauren Ploch, *Countering Terrorism in East Africa: The U.S. Response* (Washington, DC: Congressional Research Service, 2010), pp. 60.

33. Craig Whitlock, "U.S. Expands Secret Intelligence Operations in Africa," *Washington Post,* June 13, 2012, www.washingtonpost.com/world/national-security/us-expands -secret-intelligence-operations-in-africa/2012/06/13/gJQAHyvAbV_story.html?hpid =z2, accessed June 14, 2012.

34. Alex de Waal, "Dollarized," *London Review of Books* 32, no. 12 (June 24, 2010): 38–41.

35. *Report of the International Commission of Inquiry on Darfur to the United Nations Secretary General, Pursuant to Security Council Resolution 1564 of 18 September 2004* (New York: United Nations, 2005), p. 4.

36. BBC, "Powell Declares Genocide in Darfur," Sept 9, 2004, http://news.bbc.co.uk /2/hi/3641820.stm, accessed June 4, 2012.

37. Otsieno Namwaya, "Somalia: Untold Story in the Peace Talks," *The Standard,* May 28, 2006, http://allafrica.com/stories/200605300784.html, accessed June 18, 2012.

38. BBC News, "Uganda Rebels Want $2m for Talks," July 30, 2007.

39. Jane Guyer, "Briefing: The Chad–Cameroon Petroleum and Pipeline Development Project," *African Affairs* 101, no. 402 (2002): 109–115.

40. BBC, "'Mass Graves' Found in Guinea," Oct 22, 2002, http://news.bbc.co.uk /2/hi/africa/2349639.stm, accessed June 14, 2012.

eight

The Diplomacy of African Boundaries

I. William Zartman[1]

Four disparate but vicious conflicts have soiled Africa as the twenty-first century begins, all involving territorial or boundary questions in a continent that is otherwise territorially stable. The oldest, Western Sahara, currently in remission but since 1975 pitting Algeria and the Polisario Front against Morocco, entered a new phase in 2007 when the UN Security Council dropped the idea of a referendum for a negotiated solution and Morocco officially proposed the solution of autonomy. Two border wars, in 1998–2000 and 2011 and counting, declared and undeclared, respectively, followed state self-determination when Eritrea broke away from Ethiopia and South Sudan broke away from Sudan. Finally, an army mutiny freed the northern part of Mali to declare independence under the National Liberation Movement of Azawad, which was then pushed aside by various Islamist movements under the control of al-Qaeda in the Islamic Maghrib (AQIM) in 2012.

African boundaries and territorial allocations are artificial, we hear, and are the root of all evil. "Colonial partition had inserted the continent into a framework of purely artificial and often positively harmful frontiers," wrote Basil Davidson.[2] African academics and diplomats alike inveighed against the evil the colonizers wrought against the continent by cutting it up in 1895 and thereafter.

And yet most boundaries around the world are artificial, in that they separate people from one another. "Borders separate the me from the non-me," wrote the famous geographer Vidal, begging the question of how separate the two identities are. African anthropologies generally contribute to the misunderstanding by showing tribal areas as homogenous and bounded by a line, whereas their populations usually intermingle around the edges.[3] They ignore the fact that historically African states or political entities were generally population states rather than territorial states; the state was its people, rather than the reverse, and the units are often unsettled as to their territory. In fact, no one has ever indicated a "natural" set of lines to bound African states, or any other way to define African political entities physically.[4]

ARTIFICIALITY AND NATURALNESS

Although boundaries separate people, "natural frontiers" are usually thought of in terms of physical geography. Mountains, rivers, lakes, and deserts form the natural walls and moats that help define and defend the territorial state. Yet physical features are not stable boundary makers in and of themselves but rather in relation to the people they separate. When they cross areas of low population and thus divide fewer people, they contribute to stability. Rivers are uninhabited and may provide good defenses, but they are also the backbone of economic basins and populous regions, whereas mountains tend to decrease in population as they increase in altitude, offering both defense and stability. Caesar's crossing the Rubicon was a symbolic moment of decision, but Hannibal's crossing the Alps was an exceptional military feat.

Half of Africa's boundaries are formed by rivers (generally in the thalweg), most of them serving both as transportation arteries through their region and as circulation systems for their economic basins. Cross-river traffic tends to be heavier than downriver traffic. Only a small percentage of Africa's boundaries follow crest lines, because the continent's mountains tend to come in clusters rather than in folds; most of the "crests" that do provide the basis for Africa's boundaries are low watersheds or drainage divides rather than elevated ridges, marking no population gradients. About a fifth of the continent's boundaries run across relatively unpopulated deserts without visible topographic features where stable divisions are best provided by the most unnatural of boundaries: straight (geometric) lines.

Many of Africa's 110 boundaries run through sparse populations.[5] Half of the boundaries cross 100-kilometer-wide (60-mile-wide) border zones with a population density of less than 20 per square kilometer, and three-quarters of the African boundaries cross border zones with a density of less than 40. The 12 least-populated border zones, with densities of less than 1 person per square kilometer, run through desert areas mainly along geometric lines. Only 9—less than a tenth of Africa's boundaries—cross border zones with a density greater than 100, all of them in the Great Lakes region of central Africa, where at least

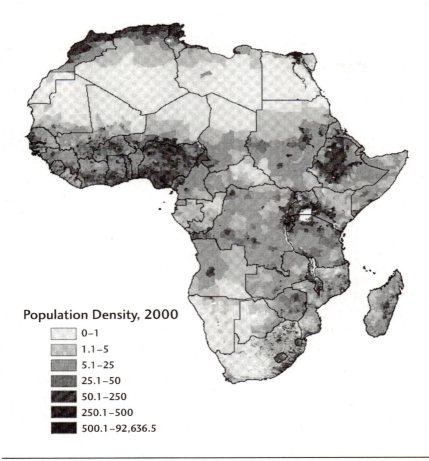

Population Density, 2000

- 0–1
- 1.1–5
- 5.1–25
- 25.1–50
- 50.1–250
- 250.1–500
- 500.1–92,636.5

Figure 8.1. African Population Density

three-quarters of the lines are determined by rivers and lakes, which unite as much as they divide. Thus, except for this last group, Africa's boundaries divide relatively sparsely inhabited areas.

AFRICANIZATION

But beyond its referents in physical and human geography, the debate over artificiality refers to another dimension, that of historic ownership. African boundaries were established by foreign occupiers, the colonial powers. To be naturalized, like citizens, they need to be Africanized, to be reestablished by the African states themselves. This process can be accomplished in two ways: by war and by diplomacy.

War has not worked to change boundaries in Africa; at best, its failure has served to Africanize inherited boundaries. African states have tried to change boundaries by military action many times: Morocco and Algeria, Ethiopia and Somalia, Mali and Upper Volta (now Burkina Faso), and Dahomey (now Benin) and Niger in the 1960s; Uganda and Tanzania, and again Ethiopia and Somalia, and Mali and Upper Volta in the late l970s; Nigeria and Cameroun, and Chad and Libya in the early 1980s, and Senegal and Mauritania, and again Mali and Burkina Faso, and Nigeria and Cameroun in the late 1980s; Nigeria and Cameroun again in the early 1990s; Eritrea and Ethiopia, and Egypt and Sudan in the late 1990s; and DRC and Uganda, Central African Republic and Cameroun, and Burundi and Rwanda in the first decade of the 2000s. None of these wars resulted in boundary changes, and not all of them have succeeded in naturalizing the inherited borders to both sides' satisfaction. There is a positive though costly aspect to military attempts in that failed efforts to change actually Africanize the boundary by confirming it as unchangeable!

Diplomacy has done better in Africanizing foreign-drawn boundaries. Continental efforts began with the Organization of African Unity (OAU) Charter in 1963, whose article III made territorial integrity a basic norm of inter-African relations. The norm was renewed more specifically in a resolution passed by the OAU at Cairo the following year, to leave no doubt that inherited, artificial boundaries were generically naturalized and legitimized. Only two countries— Morocco, which never had a southeastern border with Algeria, and Somalia, whose border treaty with Ethiopia was not only contested but lost—objected to this blanket legitimization, although some other countries agreed with silently crossed fingers, as the subsequent wars testify. The two initial actions provided a blanket multilateral Africanization of the inherited boundaries. Given this deliberate and conclusive effort by the founding members of the OAU, it was odd to hear African diplomats criticize their boundaries later on.

Some OAU members Africanized their boundaries bilaterally, by diplomatic agreements either sanctifying or rectifying the status quo. Before the founding of the OAU, in 1902 Egypt and Sudan, and in 1963 Mali and Mauritania, rectified their border to fit transhumant patterns; the former changes were finally resolved in 2008. Algeria and Morocco drew a common border for the first time in 1972; both states ratified the agreement in their fashion but bad blood still exists between the neighbors. Zaire and Zambia rectified uncertainties in their border in 1989 with small alterations to accommodate local populations. After a bloody war, an international boundary commission established a firm border between Eritrea and Ethiopia in 2003, to the dissatisfaction of the latter. The International Court of Justice (ICJ) confirmed the independence borders between Libya and Chad in 1994, between Cameroun and Nigeria in 2003, between Botswana and Namibia in 1999, and between Benin and Niger in 2005. A number of these cases—such as Benin-Niger over Lete island that appeared at Niger River low water—concerned islands (Darak between Nigeria and Cameroun, Kainasara and Tewa between Nigeria and Chad, Rukwanzi between DRC and Uganda, Singabezi between Zimbabwe and Zambia, Kasikili between Namibia and Botswana) or shifting rivers (as between Uganda and DRC, Zambia and DRC, and Senegal and Mauritania) on which the boundary had been hung, and sooner or later were resolved by diplomatic attention.

While most of these agreements went through their states' normal ratification processes, other means of accepting inherited or rectified boundaries include simple declarations by the head of state. Liberian President William Tubman accepted the hitherto-disputed frontier with Ivory Coast, even though it ran on the right (west) bank of the Cavally River to Liberia's disfavor, in a speech in 1961.[6] King Hassan II of Morocco ratified the new border agreement with Algeria by royal declaration, in the absence of a parliament to ratify, in 1973, and repeated in 1981.[7] Presidents Gowon and Olusegun Obasanjo of Nigeria accepted border agreements with Cameroun, unfavorable to Nigeria, in 1975 and 2003, and Guide Muammar Gadhafi accepted the ICJ ruling on the border with Chad, unfavorable to Libya, in 1994.

Rather than naturalize colonial boundaries by acceptance, some African states have proposed "African" criteria for new boundaries, generally without success. Idi Amin of Uganda started the war that overthrew him by claiming that the Kagera River was a more natural frontier with Tanzania than the colonial straight line; his African neighbor did not share his view and invaded. Morocco's historic claims over western Algeria, northern Mali, and Mauritania on the grounds of past conquest and religious allegiance have been withdrawn. Interestingly, in the ICJ case between Nigeria and Cameroun, while Cameroun argued the sanctity of the 1913 colonial treaties, Nigeria argued the prior sanctity of the domains of the kings and chiefs of Old Calabar, recognized in 1884 by a protectorate agreement with the queen of England; Nigeria ended up giving back the awarded territory.[8] The Mali-Mauritanian and Egyptian-Sudanese rectifications were made to bend straight-line borders to conform to customary grazing patterns.

The relation of secession and unification to boundaries is unclear. Obviously the appearance of a new state or the disappearance of an old one involves boundary changes, although these are usually considered territorial changes rather than changes to an established line. The OAU/AU doctrine of *uti possedetis* (boundary inviolability) has generally been interpreted to allow the unification of existing entities, such as in Tanzania (Tanganyika-Zanzibar); this is usually accomplished by a referendum, as advised by the ICJ in its 1974 opinion on the Western Sahara, although no referendum took place in Tanzania. As a prelude to independence, a number of referenda, notably in Togo, Cameroun, and Kenya, helped determine territorial allocation. Unification generally would pose little difficulty but there are no examples other than Tanzania, although the unification of Western Sahara with Morocco is still contested.

It is secession that continues to pose boundary/territorial challenges. The extension of *uti possedetis* is the doctrine of state—not national— self-determination, in which the referent or self of the self-determination is a previously existing (colonial) territory. Thus, two elements are involved in secession: a state (constitution of a colonially established unit) and determination (popular expression of the will for independence). Like anything in law, international or not, these precisions solve nothing at all; they merely kick the contest down the road. Thus, on the first (the state self), among prospective newcomers, Eritrea and Somaliland were both separate colonial units, the first now recognized and the second shunned by the international community; South Sudan and Biafra were both administrative distinctions within a single state but nothing more, the first now recognized by the international community and the second shunned. It's all politics, which uses law for its own purposes. On the second element (determination), all four of the territories mentioned fought for their independence; Eritrea and South Sudan duly held their referenda, Biafra did not, and Somaliland passed a popularly supported declaration of independence confirmed by a referendum in 2001. Azawad (northern Mali) has declared its independence, which was then hijacked by a number of Islamist groups, and Casamance has tired of its independence struggle; neither territory was a separate administrative unit before independence.

PROBLEMS AND PROSPECTS

And yet many border problems remain, with boundaries not yet fully Africanized by their states' acceptance. Three types of problems persist. In some cases, large pieces of territory are still contested. In others, small rectifications are needed to make user-friendly for contemporary populations the boundary that was often drawn in ignorance of the actual terrain or under conditions now changed. And in a still large number of cases, borders delimited on paper have not yet been demarcated on the ground.

Many of the territorial contests in the continent have faded into history, although they could be revived at any time that would fit a worsened state of relations between the countries concerned. Prime examples are the two major irredentist issues, the Moroccan and the Somali. The Western Sahara remains the major territorial issue of Africa in the twenty-first century, and despite the fact that "any African state can have a boundary issue if it wants one,"[9] there is no apparent basis for any other claim of importance. Morocco has recognized (even if not always officially pictured) its borders with all its neighbors but retains its claim over the Western Sahara, which it administers with UN recognition. The degree of conflict over the territory is directly related to the state of relations between Morocco and Algeria, and Algeria holds the key to resolving the conflict. The Somali Transitional Government has a hard time enforcing its writ beyond the boundaries of Mogadiscio and so cannot pursue its claims to the Ethiopian Ogaden, although a boundary has never been officially settled between the two countries; Somaliland, Puntland, and the al-Shabab-held territories elude its grasp. The likelihood in even the middle term of a irredentist claim's being pursued is slim in the absence of a strong, coherent Somali state and a unifying external enemy.

Other transborder irredenta are less active, despite the role of ethnic disputes in African states' domestic politics. Rwandan irredentist claims on undefined parts of northeast Congo were internationally decried when intimated by Rwandan President Pasteur Bizimungu in 1996 and have not resurfaced, officially; the Nigerian claim over the Bakassi Peninsula of Cameroun, several times withdrawn, could always be revived. Ugandan claims over the Kagera salient of Tanzania and the western region of Kenya vanished when Idi Amin was overthrown in 1979. In the longer run, slivers and enclaves like Gambia, Cabinda, Lesotho, Swaziland, and even Djibouti may rejoin the neighbors of which they are "naturally" a part, but there is no such pressure at present.[10] The era of large territorial claims in Africa, the aftermath of decolonization, appears to be slowly passing as states realize the difficulties of expansion and become more comfortable in their skins.

However, the cultivation of distinct national identities—often the only thing that distinguishes neighbors from each other—makes national property lines the subject of conflict. Large national identities can be aroused by small border incidents, even along clearly demarcated lines, and border incidents can be triggered by sharpened national identities. When Mauritania expelled some of its Senegalese-like citizens—the Hapular—along the Senegal River boundary in 1995, Senegalese attacked Mauritania traders with whom they had always worked peacefully in Dakar 200 kilometers (125 miles) away. When Morocco and Algeria tout their historic distinctions from each other, skirmishes and incidents break out along a border a century and a half old. Africa's bloodiest interstate war broke out in 1998 when Eritrea and Ethiopia, in search of mutually exclusive identities after their recent "friendly" divorce, discovered that their boundary was undemarcated. In Mali, land of paradoxes in 2012, the army mutinied because it was not given the means to defeat the Tuareg National Liberation Movement of Azawad, whereupon the movement declared independence for northern Mali. Somaliland, declared independent in 1992, has been proceeding with relative stability despite its non-recognition, and Puntland maintains its autonomy. The territorial state and the identitarian nation make an explosive mix.

Raw materials are often cited as a cause of competing border claims, although they are weak as a justifying reason. A desire to control their own resources was certainly an element in the secessionist efforts of Biafrans, Casamançais, Western Sahrawis, Southern Sudanese, and Cabindans, and a desire to share more equitably in others' resources was—paradoxically—in part behind the rebellion of the Tuareg. A relatively new category of boundary disputes, however, concerns maritime boundaries across offshore oil fields, as between Guinea and Guinea-Bissau, Nigeria and Cameroun, Ivory Coast and Ghana, and Tunisia and Libya, generally susceptible to resolution by the ICJ.

In sum, the issue of irredenta, secession, and territorial disputes is minimal in Africa, with the notable exceptions of different types (Western Sahara, Azawad, Somaliland) standing out because of their rarity. The near-absence of irredenta can be explained by the uselessness and illegitimacy of claims compared to the cost: It's not worth it. Similarly, as the Tuareg are discovering, secession too is costly and illegitimate; the first country to break the *uti possedetis* norm, South Sudan, shows that it takes over a half century to do so (as noted, both Eritrea, which took three decades of war, and Somaliland are not exceptions to the rule). It is hard to make a conclusive choice between two causes, but the norm of stringent illegitimacy of territorial changes in Africa is a powerful deterrent.[11]

The second type of problem, the major issue in current African border relations, concerns border rectifications. Many African boundaries can stand a good second look after years of use to make sure they are user-friendly. There are several reasons why minor rectifications are needed. First is the ignorance of the original boundary makers. Numerous are the cited terrain features that simply do not exist; equally numerous are those of multiple or otherwise ambiguous existence. For example, the Mali-Mauritanian border follows the Wadou "River" at one point, and one can well imagine the colonial administrator asking his interpreter the name of the watercourse in question, with the response, "*C'est le wadou, M'sieur.*" However, *wadou* means "intermittent river" (*wadi*) and the area is crisscrossed by such but only when it rains; finding the right *wadou* poses a challenge.

As Lord Salisbury said at the signing of the Anglo-French Convention of 1890 on the boundary between present-day Nigeria and Niger,

> We have been engaged in drawing lines upon maps where no white man's foot ever trod; we have been giving away mountains and rivers and lakes to each other, only hindered by the small impediment that we never knew exactly where the mountains and rivers and lakes were.[12]

Second, imprecise and transient features are often chosen as boundary indicators. Rocks, promontories, even trees, and other features prominent at the time give way to wear and weather, so as to be no longer visible. Human geographic features fall into this category as well; transhumant patterns for grazing and watering that are often used as a basis for African boundaries can change over time, as a consequence of climatic, topographic, and demographic changes. These were the elements used to define the Ethiopian-Somali boundary, such as it is, and their transience is notable. Indeed even boundary markers established for demarcation need maintenance and renewal with time. Third, even correctly identified and well-established geographic features often change. Rivers change their course, islands emerge and submerge, and mountain crests wear away, wandering into neighboring states' territory as humans have tried to define it.[13] When after three years of study the ICJ in 1999 decided that an island in the Chobe River toward the end of the Caprivi Strip, not far from the Botswana-Namibia-Zambia-Zimbabwe quadripoint, was the Sedudu south of the thalweg in Botswana and not the Kasikili north of the thalweg in Namibia, it left in doubt the nationality for five more intermittent islands in the Chobe.[14]

Finally, human settlements, movements, and activities introduce a new element not taken into account a century ago. New villages and towns spring up and grow, new roads are traced between them, new bridges and ferries cross rivers, and new activities from airports to mines spring up and require more new roads to connect them. Where state control is weak in border regions, they often find themselves incorporated into trade networks and even currency zones of their neighbors, in disregard of established borders. In sum, areas formerly comfortably separated by boundaries now find them an increased nuisance. The importance of roads in the context needs to be highlighted: Many African boundaries were drawn to follow preexisting roads, keeping transportation flows on one side of a border, as seen notably in the border between Algeria and Libya. These are not only imprecise and transient features, similar to geographic landmarks already noted, but they also reflect changing patterns of human relations, both in their course and in the larger socioeconomic areas through which they pass.

In sum, for reasons of imprecision at the outset and of change since then, borders need to be revisited, reviewed, and revised as necessary. The basis for such reviews is the colonially inherited border. The work is done by bilateral boundary commissions, as have been established among a number of countries. However, many African borders remain unvisited, often in very inhospitable terrain and often in the midst of very incompatible relations between the two border states. Without being revisited, the borders can be an ingredient in already bad relations or a pretext for worsened ones. Thus, the work of border commissions and border rectifications is part of normal diplomacy conducted between states with positive relations.

Borders can be made acceptable to the divided populations by focused efforts to involve frontier populations on both sides of the line in local efforts to make that division livable. In many areas, people of the same ethnic group, conducting trade and social relations across the border, find themselves to be margins of peace even when interstate relations back in the capitals are hostile. Borderland populations have learned how to live together across the artificial line that separates them. As a result, their traditional relations can be used to soften conflict and improve relations. Often this is not the case, as borderlanders take up and add to the hostilities of their capitals. But in other cases, either on their own or with the help of peacebuilding programs, borderland populations can soften the rigidity of the line and the hostility of official relations, as in such varied places as Kenyan-Somali, Ghanaian-Ivorian, and Togolese-Beninois borderlands.[15]

The third type of problem deals very specifically with the absence of *physical border demarcation* on the ground, even if the line has been established in documents for delimitation.[16] Three decades ago, with the northern two-thirds of Africa independent, four out of every ten African boundaries were defined on paper but not demarcated on the ground. Most of the undemarcated borders separated states previously under the same former colonial ruler, where demarcation had been considered unnecessary. Since then, some of these lines have been marked while relations between the neighbors were good, in order to reduce the danger of future conflict. For example, Algeria has made the establishment of border markers with its neighbors an article of its policy for normalized relations.[17]

However, recent eruptions of border wars between Eritrea and Ethiopia and between Sudan and South Sudan highlight the fragility of borders in the special case of secession or state separation. Unless borders are demarcated before secession, the split is certain to bring about a border war. Territory and lines are not the problem; it always lies deeper in the bitterness of secession, but the bitterness is triggered into action by border disputes. The cause of the

Eritrea-Ethiopia war lay deep in the psyche of the two countries' leaders; the issue in the inter-Sudanese war, undeclared but active, was oil, among other things.

Demarcation makes borders visible, but it is only half the process. Rigid borders can be as much a cause of incidents and bad relations as uncertain borders, particularly in more densely populated or heavily traveled areas. Even in the absence of conflicts over borders, conflicts across borders are likely to occur and need to be prevented from escalating.[18] Border regimes need to be established to render the clear borders permeable under controlled conditions and to forestall incidents that are certain to occur in the normal course of life along the borders. By establishing clearly marked yet permeable borders, African governments can reduce the likelihood of boundary disputes and also the chance that low-level human activity across borders will provoke high-level conflict between states. Good fences—with gates—make good neighbors.

The rest of Africa could do well to follow the example of Algeria, Nigeria, and Congo (among others), and establish border commissions to rectify and demarcate boundaries during times of stable relations. It is in this area that the dynamics of boundary relations in the twenty-first century in Africa lie, and not in the search for new types of boundaries or the pursuit of territorial conflicts. That is the message that emerges from this team of specialists from inside and outside the continent.

CONCLUSION

Africa is territorially quite stable, despite persistent claims to the contrary. This stability can be attributed largely to the authority of the *uti possedetis* norm that the African states are willing to enforce diplomatically. Only in rare cases is it worth the cost and trouble to break the norm. But the norm cannot cover all ambiguities, which come above all from undemarcated boundaries. More broadly, they come most often either from large issues, such as secession, or small issues, such as inconvenient turns. The former run to high politics, as the four twenty-first-century cases testify. The latter are easily resolved by normal diplomacy and study of human effects. The most important measure to take to reduce conflict is to demarcate the borders at times when conflict is low, and particularly when secession is in process but before it is finally consummated. The challenge is to make these lines as user-friendly as possible. In the process, African states are learning to live within their skins and are getting used to the fit, so that with the experience of living with newness, irredenta and territorial ambitions are fading into history.

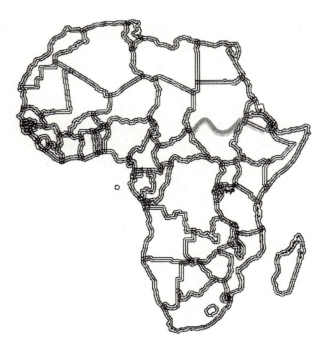

Figure 8.2. African Boundaries: 50 km Bands

Source: Center for International Earth Science Information Network, "Population along African Borders," draft data set, Palisades, NY, May 2003.

NOTES

1. I am grateful to Kwaku Nuameh for his fine research assistance, and to Mark Levy and Bryan Frederick for furnishing important statistics.

2. Basil Davidson, *The Black Man's Burden: Africa and the Curse of the Nation-State* (New York: Three Rivers Press, 1992).

3. For example, George Peter Murdock, *Africa: Its Peoples and Their Cultural History* (New York: McGraw-Hill, 1959).

4. Not even Jeffrey Herbst, Marina Ottaway, and Greg Mills, "Africa's Big States: Toward a New Realism," Carnegie Endowment Policy Outlook, February 2004. One of the rare attempts to indicate "natural" African states merely aggregates the fifty states into seventeen larger ones, by changing the boundaries between them; Richard Mukisa, "Toward a Peaceful Resolution of Africa's Colonial Boundaries," *Africa Today* 34, no. 1 (1997): 7–32.

5. Center for International Earth Science Information Network, "Population Along African Borders," draft data set, Palisades, NY, May 2003.

6. *Fraternité* (Abidjan), December 1, 1961.

7. I. William Zartman, *Ripe for Resolution* (New York: Oxford University Press, 1989), p. 76.

8. Timothy Daniel, "Trans-boundary Co-operation and Territorial Dispute Resolution: The Experience of Nigeria," paper presented to a State Department conference on African boundaries, May 28, 2002, p. 20.

9. I. William Zartman, *International Relations of the New Africa* (Englewood Cliffs, NJ: Prentice-Hall, 1969), p. 79.

10. The Front for the Liberation of the Enclave of Cabinda, which operated with support from Kinshasa, has lost its steam with improved relations between Congo and Angola.

11. Bryan Frederick, *Territorial Disputes,* PhD diss., SAIS–Johns Hopkins University, 2012.

12. Quoted in J. C. Anne, *The International Boundaries of Nigeria 1885–1960: The Framework of an Emergent African Nation* (London: Bristol, 1970), p. 3.

13. For an adventurous tale, see James Workman, "'Drawing a Line' in the Water Breeds African Border Disputes," *ICWA Letters* JGW-14 (April 2003).

14. James Workman, "Curse of the Thalweg: Islands in the Stream," *ICWA Letters* JGW-14 (Hanover, NH: Institute for Current World Affairs, 2003).

15. Judith Vorrath, "On the Margin of Statehood? State-Society Relations in African Borderlands," in *Understanding Life in the Borderlands: Boundaries in Depth and in Motion,* ed. I. William Zartman (Athens: University of Georgia Press, 2010), pp. 85–104; Henry Kam Kah, "Regulatory Societies, Peacebuilding, and Maintenance in the Cross River Region of Niogeri and Cameroon," in I. William Zartman, ed., *African Conflict and Peacebuilding Review* 1, no. 2 (special issue; Fall 2011): 30–73; Alexander Ramsbotham and I. William Zartman, eds., *Building Peace Across Borders,* Accord 22 (special issue; 2011); PACT, *Peace in East and Central Africa II (Peace II) Program,* annual report (Washington, DC: USAID, 2011).

16. I. William Zartman, "Bordering on War," *Foreign Policy* 124 (May–June 2001): 66–67.

17. Algeria demarcated its borders with Mali, Niger, and Tunisia in 1983 and with Mauritania in 1985, and defined its border with Libya in agreements signed in August 2001.

18. Kjell Åke Nordquist, "Drawing Lines: Boundary Disputes," in *Preventive Negotiations,* ed. I. William Zartman (Lanham, MD: Rowman & Littlefield, 2001); Ajamu Olayiwola Owolabi, "Nigeria and Cameroun: Boundary Disputes and the Problem of Border Security," *African Notes* 15, no. 1/2 (1991): 39–47.

nine

The Changing Role of the AU Commission in Inter-African Relations

The Case of APSA and AGA

Ulf Engel[1]

INTRODUCTION

During the past decade intergovernmental relations in Africa have undergone rapid and far-reaching change. With the transformation of the Organization of African Unity (OAU) into the African Union (AU) in the period 1999–2002, new norms, institutions, and players have arisen. This has had two consequences: first, competing ideas toward the political and economic integration of Africa have gained ground and partly yielded tangible results. And second, relations between the African Union and AU member states and between the AU and the so-called Regional Economic Communities (RECs), but also between the AU and its non-African international environment, are changing. At the center of this change is the African Union Commission (AUC), which in the transformation from "unity" to "union" has replaced the rather weak OAU General Secretariat.[2] Inter alia, the Commission's mandate is to represent the Union; initiate proposals for consideration by other organs; implement the decisions taken by other organs; organize and manage the meetings of the Union; act as the custodian of the "Constitutive Act," its protocols, and the treaties, legal instruments, and decisions adopted by the Union; coordinate and monitor the implementation of AU decisions; work out draft common AU positions;

and coordinate the actions of member states in international negotiations. It is also tasked with ensuring the promotion of peace, democracy, security, and stability; providing operational support to the Peace and Security Council (PSC); and coordinating and harmonizing the programs and policies of the Union with those of the RECs.[3] Under its two chairpersons—former Malian president Alpha Oumar Konaré (2003–2008) and former Gabonese foreign minister Jean Ping (2008–2012)—the Commission has become a player in its own right, with an increasingly distinctive policy agenda. Partly the rise of the Commission has been attributed to the impact of "Africrats"—the continental organization's bureaucrats—in the process of the institutionalization of the African Union.[4] But more important, this new role has to be understood in the context of a fierce though not always explicit debate among AU member states over the institutional design and ultimate nature of the African Union and the continent's political and economic integration, which often resemble the debates that led to the foundation of the OAU on May 25, 1963.[5]

This transformation was taken one step further when the African Union, at a special session of its 12th Assembly of Heads of State and Government, held on February 1, 2009, in Addis Ababa, Ethiopia, adopted a plan to gradually develop the AU Commission into an AU Authority, a kind of Union Government, with the ultimate aim of establishing the "United States of Africa" sometime in the future.[6] In particular the AU Assembly agreed that the Authority would "have the power to coordinate and advocate for the common policies of the African Union in four key pillars of peace and security; integration, cooperation and development; [and] shared values and institution and capacity building." To provide the background for the changing role of the Commission in inter-African relations, the next section will reconstruct the debate on the Union Government and the United States of Africa. This will be followed by a shorter analysis of two main areas of AUC activity: In the third section of this chapter the implementation of the African Peace and Security Architecture (APSA) will be looked at, and in the fourth section the realization of the centerpiece of the "shared value" topoi—the so-called African Governance Architecture (AGA), which deals with the democracy, good governance, and human rights agenda of the Union—will be scrutinized. Finally, conclusions will be offered with regard to the extent to which the African Union on its way to greater political and economic integration over the past decade has developed forms of communitarization (*Vergemeinschaftung*) of these particular policy fields and the role of the AUC in this. The implications of these developments will be discussed with regard to their impact on changing inter-African relations, but also relations with non-African players.

FROM AU COMMISSION TO AU AUTHORITY

As part of the transformation from OAU to African Union, member states confirmed the principles that already had guided intra-OAU relations: national sovereignty, noninterference in internal affairs, territorial integrity, and equality of member states. Yet, important for the normative foundations of inter-African relations, and clearly reflecting the experience of the genocide in Rwanda in 1994, they also added the right of the Union "to intervene in any Member State pursuant by a decision of the Assembly in respect of grave circumstances."[7] After an amendment to the original Constitutive Act, adopted by the 2nd ordinary session of the AU Assembly held July 10–12, 2003, in Maputo, Mozambique, grave circumstances include "war crimes, genocide and crimes against humanity as well as a serious threat to legitimate order to restore peace and security to the Member State of the Union, upon the recommendation of the Peace and Security Council."[8] In the academic debate, this change from the principle of noninterference to at least non-indifference usually is attributed to a shift in interests among AU member states from what is labeled as regime security to human security, and the related rise of the international norm of a "responsibility to protect" (R2P) that treats sovereignty not just as a right of states, but as a responsibility (including the right of other states to interfere whenever this responsibility is not exercised).[9]

However, the major caesura in changing inter-African relations indeed has been the above-mentioned decision to transform the AU Commission into an AU Authority. With the purpose of reforming and refining the existing governance structure of the AU "as a tool for accelerating political and economic integration of the continent" and promoting pan-Africanism, the AU Assembly in February 2009 decided not only that the new AU Authority would have the above-mentioned power to coordinate and advocate for the common policies of the African Union in key areas; according to this plan, the Authority would also assume responsibility for "continent-wide poverty reduction; free movement of persons, goods and services; interregional and continental infrastructure (road networks, bridges, railways, ports, energy and communications, etc.); global warming, desertification and coastal erosion; epidemics and pandemics, such as HIV/AIDS; research/university centers of excellence; international trade negotiations; peace and security; transnational crime (terrorism, drugs, arms trafficking, legal positions and frameworks)."[10] RECs were seen as integral parts of the African Union. The officially recognized eight partner RECs of the African Union are the Community of Sahel-Saharan States (CENSAD), the Common Market for Eastern and Southern Africa (COMESA), the East African Community (EAC), the Economic Community of Central African States (ECCAS), the Economic Community of West African States (ECOWAS), the Intergovernmental Authority on Development (IGAD) based at the Horn of Africa, the Southern African Development Community (SADC), and the Arab Maghreb Union (UMA). While it was foreseen that the AU Authority would coordinate the activities of the RECs "in its areas of competence," in a concept of shared responsibilities the necessity was stressed that the Authority had to cede some programs and activities to RECs "where the RECs have comparative advantage."[11] Implementation of the AU Authority was planned in three phases: During phase I, "Operationalization," from February 2009 to January 2010 current commissioners would be appointed secretaries; in phase II, "Consolidation," from February 2010 to January 2012 institutions would be strengthened; and in phase III a "Constitutional Conference" would set the basic framework for the United States of Africa (to commence in 2016 and to be concluded in 2017).[12]

This transformation was heavily pushed for by Libya's military dictator, Muammar Gadhafi (1942–2011). As part of his strategy to (re)gain international recognition, but also playing to his megalomaniac ego, he employed a specific pan-African tradition that reinvoked debates about a United States of Africa and an African High Command (as originally proposed by Ghana's first president, Kwame Nkrumah).[13] When Gadhafi hosted the 4th extraordinary OAU summit in Sirte, Libya, on September 8–9, 1999, to the surprise of the participants he proposed to create the United States of Africa.[14] Opposing a suggested merger of the OAU with the not-yet-existing African Economic Community (AEC) within a gradual process of institutional change, shortly afterward the presidents of Chad, Ghana, Liberia, Mali, Malawi, Senegal, and Sudan came out in support of Gadhafi.[15]

In January 2005, again Libya proposed to establish continental ministerial posts in various areas, including defense, foreign affairs, transport and communications, and foreign trade.[16] The 4th AU Assembly, held January 30–31, 2005, in Abuja, Nigeria, decided to set up a committee of seven heads of state under the leadership of President Yoweri Museveni of Uganda to examine the proposal in all its ramifications.[17] Based on the committee's report, the 5th AU Assembly, held July 4–5, 2005, in Sirte, without referring to any timelines, only affirmed that "the ultimate goal of the union is fully political and economic integration leading to the United States of Africa."[18] The summit also decided to establish another committee of heads of state and government chaired by Nigerian President Olusegun Obasanjo, who at that time was AU chairperson, and composed of the presidents of Algeria, Kenya, Senegal, Gabon, Lesotho, and Uganda.

This committee collected opinions of RECs, experts, and members of civil society, and came up with recommendations that basically slowed down Gadhafi's quest for a speedy establishment of the United States of Africa. On November 12–13, 2005, the committee organized a conference in Abuja on "Africa and the Challenges of the Changing Global Order: Desirability of a Union Government." It concluded that the necessity for an eventual Union Government was not in doubt and "that it must be a union of the African people and not merely a union of states and governments," but it should also be based on shared values. The committee also found that "basic internal contradictions at the national level must be reviewed and resolved," that a "principle of gradual incrementalism" should be followed, and that the RECs "must be made more effective as the building block[s]" for the continental framework.[19] The following 6th AU Assembly, held January 23–24, 2006, in Khartoum, Sudan, noncommittally reaffirmed "that the ultimate goal of the African Union is the full political and economic integration of the continent leading to the United States of Africa" and requested the committee to canvass all opinions on this matter, including the contribution of "the Brother Leader," and to submit a consolidated document with a road map for consideration by the Assembly at its next ordinary session in July 2006.[20] This report describes the Union Government as "a political transitory arrangement towards the United States of Africa" and suggests sixteen strategic areas of focus in which the Union Government would "concentrate exclusively or concurrently with Union Members on the 'Community Domain.'" The Commission, the report continues, "should accordingly be assigned the executive authority and responsibility to effectively implement the related activities." And with regard to the requested road map, the Obasanjo report suggests an ambitious concrete schedule with an initial phase for the establishment of the Union Government (2006–2009), its consolidation (2009–2012), and finally the establishment of the United States of Africa by 2015.[21] The 7th AU Assembly, held July 1–2, 2006, in Banjul, Gambia, took note of the report and called on the Executive Council to organize a special meeting to discuss its implications.[22]

The differences among AU member states on the question of the United States of Africa were openly expressed at the 9th extraordinary session of the Executive Council, held November 17–18, 2006, in Addis Ababa.[23] Apart from a discussion on procedural questions—what exactly had the Council been entrusted with?—some member states insisted that, while in general not opposed to the idea of a Union Government, the "AU should remain a union of sovereign states based on regional groupings." Another group of states did not want to repeat the debates preceding the inception of the OAU in 1963 and "urged to speed up the process of integration with the timeframe as proposed in the study." And a third, apparently smaller group, "even expressed full support for the recommendations contained in both the base document and the implementation modalities and called for their adoption." Hence the Council concluded that all member states "accept the United States of Africa as a common and desirable goal"; however, "differences exist over the modalities and

timeframe for achieving this goal and the appropriate pace for integration."
With regard to existing institutions, member states agreed on the need for an
audit review of the state of the Union as well as the necessity to strengthen the
Commission.[24] Ultimately this audit, which was conducted in 2008, set in
motion a process that changed the immediate priorities within the Union
Government debate toward the concrete working of the Commission and the
Union's other organs (see below).

Against this background the 10th AU Assembly, held January 29–30, 2007,
in Addis Ababa, took note of the Executive Council's report and decided to
devote the 9th ordinary session of the Assembly to be held July 1–3, 2007, in
Accra, Ghana, to the theme "Grand Debate on the Union Government."[25] It
also endorsed a Council proposal to hold a retreat of ministers of foreign affairs to reflect on the state of the Union, followed by an extraordinary session
of the Executive Council. In preparation for this debate, the Commission
launched a website, "Public Consultation on the Grand Debate on an African
Union Government."[26] In Accra AU member states expressed their minimal
consensus in a Declaration on the Union Government of Africa.[27] The United
States of Africa with a Union Government is described as "the ultimate objective of the African Union." Yet another committee was established, inter alia
to identify "the contents of the Union Government concept and its relations
with national governments" as well as the "domains of competence and the
impact of the establishment of the Union Government on the sovereignty of
member states." The committee was furthermore asked to define the relationship between the Union Government and the RECs, and to present a road
map and time frames for establishing the Union Government. On the basis of
the Accra Declaration and the committee's subsequent report, the 11th AU
Assembly, which met June 30 to July 1, 2008, in Sharm El-Sheikh, Egypt, endorsed the committee's recommendations and requested that the Commission work out the modalities and details of implementation.[28] As a result of
these consultative processes, the special session of the 12th AU Assembly was
then able to adopt the above-mentioned decision on the transformation of
the AU Commission to the AU Authority and the related time plan for the introduction of the United States of Africa by 2017.

Apart from the obvious role of Gadhafi, who was appointed to a one-year
term as AU chairman at the summit in Libya, who are the main actors and what
are their stated and nonstated interests in this debate? With regard to the 1999–
2002 phase of the debate, Thomas Tieku juxtaposes Libya vis-à-vis South Africa
and Nigeria. Highlighting President Thabo Mbeki's alleged interest in "the promotion of neo-liberalism in Africa," Tieku suggests that Mbeki forged a coalition with President Olusegun Obasanjo, who aimed at the integration of the
Conference on Security, Stability, Development, and Cooperation in Africa

(CSSDCA), which he spearheaded during the so-called Kampala process, into the new African Union.[29] For the Union Government debate of 2005–2009, Tieku basically suggests a similar divide.[30] This view has become a conventional wisdom according to which the conflict within the Union is one between so-called maximalists and minimalists, and in substance is about the pace and content of continental integration.[31] Recently this interpretation has been challenged by Witt, who argues that the conflict rather is about "the normative basis of political authority." Divergent positions in the debate are conceptualized "as either the need for decision-making positions at the continental level to prevent 'foreign domination,' the necessity of multiple levels of accountability and a people-centred orientation of continental politics, or as the need for the enhancement of managerial capacities of functional states."[32] Accordingly she detects three competing frames: (1) the idea of a "defense union" whose proponents, mainly Libya, perceive current globalization processes as a hostile environment, who insist on the territorial integrity of states, argue the need for decision-making positions, and call for continental defense and foreign policy mechanisms; (2) the notion of a "people's union" with an emphasis on outcome-orientation of continental politics, participation, multiple arenas of decision-making, and a community of values, which basically has been advocated by South Africa and Ghana, but also the AU Commission, the Pan-African Parliament, and others; and (3) finally a "manager-states' union" in which states are confronted with problems of interdependency and are the (only) drivers of continental politics. This position mainly has been supported by Nigeria, Uganda, Senegal, Egypt, and Ethiopia. So the controversy is less about how much sovereignty member states are willing to give up, "but rather [about] those normative grounds the constitution of political order ought to be justified upon and balanced against."[33] In the end, South Africa and Nigeria brought together their respective coalition partners to thwart Gadhafi's plans. The post-Sirte summit fate of the Union Government debate clearly confirms this.

In the months that followed the 12th AU Assembly legal issues dominated, initially with regard to the question of whether the Constitutive Act had to be amended to allow for the planned transformation. Thus the Assembly mandated the council to look into these and related matters.[34] It also discussed which policy fields the AU Authority should coordinate, but could not reach a consensus on this. And again, just like in 1999 at the Sirte summit, Gadhafi tried to catch his colleagues off-guard. At the 13th AU Assembly, held July 1–3, 2009, in Tripoli, Libya, on short notice he filed a proposal to establish an African Defense Council as part of the AU Authority. Although the summit's participants concurred, some obviously quite reluctantly, on all other questions the AU Assembly simply tasked the Commission with reporting on implementation progress, through the Council, to the summit to be held one year later.[35]

In response to this report the 15th AU Assembly, which met July 25–27, 2010, in Kampala, Uganda, requested that the Commission convene a follow-up meeting of government experts and another meeting of ministers of justice/ attorneys general of AU member states to consider the legal instruments neces- sary for the envisaged transformation. While the legal debate continued, fur- ther attempts of Gadhafi to reopen the debate and renegotiate the decision on transforming the Commission into an Authority were rejected.[36] Eventually the legal debate started slowing down the process of policy implementation. The 16th AU Assembly, held January 30–31, 2011, in Addis Ababa, requested that the Commission convene another meeting of experts, by then the fourth of its kind.[37] And finally, the so-called Arab Spring, the popular uprisings in North Africa and parts of the Arab peninsula took center stage. With Gadhafi under siege by the bombardment of the NATO-led coalition, the next summit only deferred consideration of the issue to the next summit, at which the ques- tion was once more deferred to the following summit.[38] And at this 19th AU Assembly, held July 15–16, 2012, in Addis Ababa, the matter was not even raised any longer (behind the scenes the last two summits in fact had been dominated by competition for the position of AUC chairperson).

Thus, implementation of the 2009 decision on the Union Government and the United States of Africa has been severely delayed—in fact the future of the whole transformation of the AU Commission into the AU Authority seems to be in limbo. Yet at the same time, as a result of the ongoing debate as well as the emphasis on consensus decisions and a resulting gradualism, the role of the AU Commission has been substantially strengthened, in terms of the legitimacy it enjoys among AU member states, but also in terms of resources and power to initiate and carry out policies on behalf of its members. However, Bossuyt cau- tions, at least under Chairperson Konaré, "limited successes were achieved in convincing Member States to provide coherent mandates to the AUC as well as sufficient levels of power and resources for effective action. The capacity to change the AUC 'from within' also proved difficult."[39] In this respect the audit of the Union that was conducted in the second half of 2007 by a High-Level Panel chaired by Nigerian professor Adebayo Adedeji, a former UN under-secretary general and executive secretary of the UN Economic Commission for Africa (UNECA), indeed revealed some major weaknesses. With regard to the Com- mission the Panel found that there was "lack of clarity in the set-up of its leader- ship," that its activities were "spread too widely for it to be effective in playing the role envisaged for it," and that its general management "needs to be im- proved."[40] The Panel highlighted severe deficits in leadership, management cul- ture, accounting, and recruiting at the AUC. In particular the lack of strategic debate and "silo mentalities" in the different AUC departments were singled out. Relations with the Permanent Representatives Committee of member states' ambassadors to the Union were based on misunderstandings of respective roles, and the division of labor between the Commission and the RECs needed to be articulated. But the Panel also noted that "the Commission has played an active role in drafting treaties, common policy frameworks and positions," and that the "initiation and formulation of Treaties and common positions and standards is one of the Commission's major successes."[41] In this respect in particular the role of the Commission in peacekeeping in Darfur, Sudan, in the negotiations between Sudan and what eventually became South Sudan, and with regard to the 2007 African Charter on Democracy, Elections, and Governance (see below) is mentioned. The work of the Commission, the Panel concludes, "is now informing the priorities of Africa's external partners."[42]

PEACE AND SECURITY

After the AU Assembly's 2009 decision to gradually develop the AU Commission into the AU Authority, the Commission immediately integrated the named "common domains," "broad intervention areas," or "strategic pillars" into its "Strategic Plan 2009–2012," the third such plan to guide its activities since 2004.[43] With regard to peace and security it planned to fully operationalize the African Peace and Security Architecture (APSA), which apart from the PSC comprises the African Standby Force (ASF), the Panel of the Wise, the Continental Early Warning System (CEWS), and the Peace Fund.[44] Currently implementation of APSA is behind schedule. Instead of meeting the overambitious 2010 target, nowadays internal planning rather is looking at 2014/2015 as the time when the APSA will be fully implemented. But thanks to road maps, implementation of the ASF and CEWS is fairly advanced.[45] Furthermore, the Commission aimed at facilitating the development of a program on conflict prevention, management, and resolution, promoting the Common African Defense and Security Policy (CADSP) as well as programs on postconflict reconstruction and development (PCRD). In addition, the "Strategic Plan" foresees activities to achieve "continental security and stability"—including the promotion of the development and stabilization of security, political, and economic systems; continental social and environmental management systems; and policies on combating transnational organized crime.

Still far from any substantial communitarization of policies or a noticeable delegation of sovereignty to the Commission by member states, but close to a policy coordination and harmonization role, it increasingly has become the locus of managing the Union's peace and security activities. Thus, the Commission organizes and sets the agenda of PSC meetings; it also drafts all major PSC communiqués and decisions as well as related summit documents. Since its first meeting on March 16, 2004, the PSC has held almost 330 meetings (on average three per month), addressing all major conflicts on the continent, including, for instance, the 2010 postelection crisis in Côte d'Ivoire or the 2011 Arab Spring,[46] but also numerous postconflict scenarios (among them Burundi, the Central African Republic, Comoros, the Democratic Republic of Congo, Liberia, and Sierra Leone, where the Commission renders support to the Union's field missions). The Commission also serves as the logistical backbone of AU peacekeeping missions, most important the 2006-approved AU Mission in Somalia (AMISOM), which supports the Transitional Federal Government against the al-Shabaab militia from Mogadishu and for the most part is made up of troops from Uganda, Burundi, and Kenya. It also backs up what by now is a hybrid UN/AU Mission in Darfur (UNAMID), which started operating in 2004 as AMIS.[47] As indicated by the AU High-Level Panel, the Commission indeed has become the most important African voice for international partners, as demonstrated by regular joint consultative meetings between the Commission on the one hand and the United Nations or the European Union on the other (or the PSC and the UN Security Council and the EU Political and Security Committee, respectively).[48] The Panel of the Wise, which was only launched on December 18, 2007, is striving hard to find its role. After not having been involved in the mediation of postelection violent conflicts in Kenya and Zimbabwe in 2007/2008, in 2012 the Panel, for instance, became actively involved in mediating the electoral crisis in Senegal, where the incumbent tried to get a third, unconstitutional term. As in many other cases, the unfolding division of labor between the Commission and the relevant REC, in this case ECOWAS, was a work in progress. The Panel also convened meetings to strengthen political governance for peace and security (April 27–29 in Tunis) and to develop relations with similar regional mechanisms (June 4–5 in Ouagadougou).[49] On CEWS the Commission signed a Memorandum of Understanding with the RECs in January 2008 to fulfill its policy coordination and harmonization role and started regular quarterly technical meetings.[50] Finally, assisted by donors, the Commission is also managing the Peace Fund, although external finance for the Union's peace and security operations and other related activities still stands at up to 95 percent of expenditure, which clearly raises questions of ownership, dependency, and commitment of member states.

In relation to external actors, the Commission has tried to develop further the principle of "African solutions for African problems," but had to concede a major setback with the developments unfolding in Libya in 2011 when a NATO-led alliance intervened on the basis of a UN mandate to enforce a no-flight zone. While the African Union as a whole struggled hard to make up its mind about the nature of the conflict in Libya and adequate responses (existing policy scripts simply did not foresee revolutions), it lost precious time and was soon outmaneuvered by NATO, which obviously harbored plans towards regime change.[51] The Union's plan for conflict resolution was neglected, and its mediation efforts, spearheaded by an Ad Hoc High-Level Committee chaired by South African President Jacob Zuma, were sidelined. In a report presented to an extraordinary summit of the AU Assembly, held April 25–26, 2011, in Addis Ababa, an obviously highly frustrated AUC chairperson therefore deplored "the reluctance of members of the international community to fully acknowledge the AU role in the promotion of peace in the continent and their selective application of the principle of ownership." He claimed that any partnership on conflict resolution should be "fully based on Africa's leadership," because "without such leadership, there will be no ownership and sustainability; because we understand the problems far better than even the closest partners; because we know which solutions will work, and how we can get there; and because, fundamentally, these problems are ours, and our peoples will live with their consequences."[52]

AFRICAN GOVERNANCE

With regard to the community domain of "shared values" the "Strategic Plan 2009–2012" lists a number of benchmarks, including the promotion of good governance, democracy, and human rights as well as the ratification and entry into force of all outstanding legal instruments adopted by the AU Assembly.[53] Indeed, at face value, African heads of state and government have committed themselves to an impressive set of principles on human rights, democracy, and good governance. These values are enshrined in the OAU "Decision on the Rights of Political Participation" (1999) and also in the "Declaration on the Principles Governing Democratic Elections in Africa" (2002).[54] They are also reflected in the "Declaration on Democracy, Political, Economic and Corporate Governance" of the New Partnership for Africa's Development (NEPAD) of 2002. This set of values was reiterated in January 2011 through the adoption of a "Declaration on the Theme of the Summit: 'Towards Greater Unity and Integration through Shared Values'" by the AU Assembly.[55]

However, despite all progress since the "second wind of change" and democratic transitions all over the African continent since the 1990s, over the past decade Africa has witnessed a decrease in the quality of democracy. Comparing Freedom House reports for 2005 and 2012, one will find that the status ("free," "partly free," "not free") of seven countries was downgraded; and twenty-three countries had scores for political rights and/or civil liberties (on a scale from 1 to 7) that were less in the 2012 report than in the 2005 report.[56] There are basically three developments responsible for this regression: (1) coups d'état, (2) election-related violence, and (3) revisions of constitutional provisions that change the rules of the game in favor of the incumbent. Between 2003 and the beginning of the Arab Spring there were nine successful coups d'état; in 2012 two more coups happened in Mali and Guinea-Bissau. In addition, fourteen countries entered into prolonged crisis over presidential third-term debates.[57]

Mainly driven by the AU Commission, the Union has responded to these developments by developing new norms for inter-African relations and a related policy script on what it termed "unconstitutional changes of government" (UCG).[58] Originally based on OAU summit decisions of 1999 and 2000 not to accept any such changes and a related "Framework for an OAU Response to Unconstitutional Changes of Government" (also known as the Lomé Declaration),[59] these changes were defined to include (1) military coups d'état against democratically elected governments; (2) interventions by mercenaries to replace such governments; (3) replacements of democratically elected governments by armed dissident groups and rebel movements; and (4) refusals by incumbent governments to relinquish power to the winning party after free, fair, and regular elections.[60] A later attempt to add cases of presidential third-term manipulation to the definition failed. When adopting the African Charter on Democracy, Elections, and Governance (see below), the 8th AU Assembly on January 30, 2007, only agreed to consider "any amendment or revision of the constitution or legal instruments which is an infringement on the principles of democratic change of government" as the fifth constitutive element of unconstitutional changes of government.[61] The Lomé Declaration and the African Charter also outline a detailed policy script on how to deal in practice with unconstitutional changes of government. Condemnation of the UCG by the AUC chairperson was to be followed by a PSC meeting. The perpetrators of the UCG were to be suspended from participating in Union activities for a six-month period until constitutional order was restored. In the meantime the AUC chairperson would engage in fact-finding, seeking the contribution of African leaders and personalities, and enlist collaboration of the relevant REC. If needed, sanctions would be imposed against the perpetrators by the AU Assembly.[62] Through additional decisions taken at the 12th and 13th AU Assemblies in 2009, the Union fine-tuned its policy stance and UCG response options.[63]

In remarkable contrast to the 1990s and early 2000s, the African Union now also proactively started addressing cases of UCG, starting with Mauritania (2008), Guinea (2009), Madagascar (2009), and Niger (2010).[64] In these cases the Commission became the key actor in engaging AU member states and coordinating international mediation efforts, mainly through International Contact Groups (ICGs). Some best practice was established in cooperation with international partners, such as the United Nations and in particular the European Union (for instance, in the case of Mauritania).[65] The AUC chairperson played an active diplomatic and decision-making role.[66] With regard to the integration of APSA and the Union's governance agenda, collaboration between the Commission and the RECs became extremely important, in particular with regard to ECOWAS and SADC.[67] However, in some cases it could not prevent other international actors—the United States and France in the case of Guinea in 2009–2010, France and South Africa in the case of Madagascar in 2010—from hijacking its mediation efforts or interfering in its strategy. Commission efforts to enhance the effectiveness of the policy on UCG therefore included consulting with member states and international partners to enforce AU decisions more effectively, enhancing information gathering, refining the sanctions regime, establishing a review mechanism on the state of democracy in member states, and redefining the role of the Panel of the Wise with regard to elections and unconstitutional changes of government. On balance, the Commission managed to help restore constitutional order in Mauritania, Niger, and Guinea, but so far is struggling with the situation in Madagascar. Crucial remaining issues include the division of labor between the Union and the RECs, the role of African mediators who often act too idiosyncratically, divisions within RECs, a lack of professionalism of mediation, the role of the Panel of the Wise, and—most important—the root causes of conflict in these cases.

The ratification process of the African Charter demonstrated how difficult the African policy environment is for the Commission. The African Charter summarizes the African Governance Agenda (AGA); it is based on universal values and principles of democracy and respect for human rights. It promotes adherence to the principles of the rule of law, constitutional order, regular free and fair elections, independence of the judiciary, and so on. The African Charter was adopted on January 30, 2007, but it was only just before the January 2012 summit in Addis Ababa that the necessary number of fifteen ratifications was deposited so that the charter could enter into force on February 16, 2012—five years after its adoption. Member states who deposited early were Mauritania (2008) as well as Ethiopia and Sierra Leone (2009). The others joined in fairly late: Burkina Faso, Ghana, Lesotho, and Rwanda in 2010; Chad, Guinea, Niger, South Africa, and Zambia in 2011; and finally, Cameroon, Guinea-Bissau, and Nigeria in 2012. Member states that to date still refuse to sign the African Charter include Algeria, Angola, Botswana, Cape Verde, Egypt, Eritrea, Libya, Madagascar, Malawi, Seychelles, Somalia, Tanzania, Tunisia, and Zimbabwe.[68]

The slow process of ratification of the African Charter clearly demonstrates the growing divide between AU member states when it comes to issues of democracy, good governance, and human rights. Although the reasons for ratification/non-ratification of the charter are all very case-specific and defy easy interpretation (e.g., Ethiopia and Rwanda have ratified; Botswana has not), it seems evident that the Commission is unable to enlist the support of all member states for its democracy and good governance agenda. While African regimes may not be able to avoid signing up for principles they don't share—because of peer and international pressure—a considerable number of AU member states are not willing to implement related instruments.

Against this background the developments in North Africa in 2011 had an important impact also on inter-African relations as they created the discursive background for a renewed attempt to forward the agenda of the AU Commission. Based on documents prepared by the Commission, the PSC, at a meeting held at ministerial level on April 26, 2011, in Addis Ababa, expressed "its conviction that the uprisings in North Africa should be used as an opportunity for Member States to renew their commitment to the AU democratic and governance agenda, give added momentum to efforts deployed in this respect and implement the political and socio-economic reforms which are called for in every particular national situation."[69] In his report to the extraordinary summit, held May 25–26, 2011, in Addis Ababa, the AUC chairperson constructs the uprisings in Tunisia and Egypt as a catching-up process of North Africa with developments elsewhere in Africa in the 1990s; the grievances that have driven the revolts are described as universal. Stressing the need to strengthen African efforts "to address the root causes of conflicts in a holistic and systematic manner," the chairperson then calls on member states to implement existing instruments in the areas of human rights, the rule of law, democracy, elections, and good governance, and for those who have not yet done so, "speedily to sign and/or ratify those instruments and fully implement their provisions."[70] It remains to be seen how the Commission will continue this policy under its new chairperson, former South African foreign minister Nkosazana Dlamini-Zuma, who was elected chair on July 16, 2012.

CONCLUSIONS

The debate about African political and economic integration that revolved around the issues of Union Government and the United States of Africa has brought new dynamics into inter-African relations. Driven by Libya's leader Gadhafi, the debate has forced alliances of different AU member states to develop their own visions about the future of African institutions and find ways of implementation. In a constant process of renegotiating Africa's integration, the role of and policy space for the AU Commission has changed, too. Still short of any real communitarization of particular policy fields as foreseen for the AU Authority, in practice the Union has given substantial powers to the AU Commission. Conversely, the Commission has carefully cultivated these prerogatives and expanded its room to maneuver vis-à-vis AU member states as well as RECs. The examples of the African peace and security and the governance architectures have demonstrated that the Commission has become an important continental and international actor in its own right and today serves as a reference point for member states, RECs, and international partners alike. And it has contributed substantially to making inter-African relations more complex. Africa's interstate relations are increasingly complemented by inter-region relations. Although in terms of management, policy coordination, and harmonization the Union and in particular the AU Commission are still far from what they are meant to be, they have emerged as the centerpiece of Africa's "new regionalisms."[71]

NOTES

1. Research on this chapter was partly enabled by a fellowship at the Wallenberg Research Centre of the Stellenbosch Institute for Advanced Study (STIAS). The support is gratefully acknowledged.

2. African Union, *Constitutive Act of the African Union* (Lomé: African Union, 2000), §20.

3. African Union, *Statutes of the Commission of the African Union* [ASS/AU/2(I)–d] (Durban: African Union, 2002); as amended by AU Assembly, *Decision on the Proposed Amendments to the Rules of Procedure of the Assembly of the Union, the Executive Council and the Permanent Representatives' Committee, and the Statutes of the Commission* [Assembly/AU/Dec.146 (VIII)] (Addis Ababa: African Union, 2007).

4. Thomas K. Tieku, "The Evolution of the African Union Commission and Africrats," in *The Ashgate Research Companion to Regionalisms*, ed. Timothy M. Shaw, J. Andrew Grant, and Scarlett Cornelissen (Farnham, UK: Ashgate, 2011).

5. Although, as van Walraven concludes, "the real bone of contention was the issue of non-African influences and presence on the continent." See Klaas van Walraven, *Dreams of Power: The Role of the Organization of African Unity in the Politics of Africa, 1963–1993* (Aldershot, UK: Ashgate, 1996), p. 378.

6. AU Assembly, *Special Session of the 12th Ordinary Session of the Assembly. Report on the Outcome of the Special Session on Follow Up to the Sharm El Sheikh Assembly Decision AU/Dec.206 (XI) on the Union Government* [Sp/Assembly/AU/Draft/Rpt(1)] (Addis Ababa: African Union, 2009).

7. African Union, *Constitutive Act*, §4(h).

8. AU Assembly, *Decision on the Amendments to the Constitutive Act* [Assembly/AU/Dec.26 (II)] (Addis Ababa: African Union, 2003). For a discussion see Evarist Baimu and Kathryn Sturman, "Amendment to the African Union's Right to Intervene: A Shift from Human Security to Regime Security?" *African Security Review* 12, no. 2 (2003): p. 39.

9. Cf. Ben Kioko, "The Right of Intervention Under the African Union's Constitutive Act: From Non-Interference to Non-Intervention," *International Review of the Red Cross*

85, no. 852 (2003): 807–824; Paul D. Williams, "From Non-Intervention to Non-Indifference: The Origins and Development of the African Union's Security Culture," *African Affairs* 106, no. 423 (2007): 253–279; Musifiky Mwanasali, "From Non-Interference to Non-Indifference: The Emerging Doctrine of Conflict Prevention in Africa," in *The African Union and Its Institutions,* ed. John Akokpari et al. (Cape Town and Auckland Park: Centre for Conflict Resolution and Fanele, 2008); and Tim Murithi, "The African Union's Transition from Non-Intervention to Non-Indifference: An Ad Hoc Approach to the Responsibility to Protect?" *Internationale Politik und Gesellschaft* 1 (2009): 90–106. See also Eboe Hutchful, "From Military Security to Human Security," in *The African Union and Its Institutions,* ed. John Akokpari, Angela Ndinga-Muvumba, and Tim Murithi (Auckland, Cape Town: Jacana Media and Centre for Conflict Resolution, 2008); and Ademola Abass, "African Peace and Security and Protection of Human Security," in *Protecting Human Security in Africa,* ed. Ademola Abass (New York: Oxford University Press, 2010). For the international policy debate on R2P, see International Commission on Intervention and State Sovereignty, *The Responsibility to Protect: Report by the International Commission on Intervention and State Sovereignty* (Ottawa: International Development Research Centre. 2001); and United Nations, *A More Secure World: Our Shared Responsibility. Report of the Secretary-General's High-Level Panel on Threats, Challenges and Change* (New York: United Nations, 2004). On Africa see Tim Murithi, "The Responsibility to Protect as Enshrined in Article 4 of the Constitutive Act of the African Union," *African Security Review* 16, no. 3 (2007): 14–24.

10. AU Assembly, *Special Session of the 12th Ordinary Session of the Assembly. Report on the Outcome,* §7.

11. Ibid., §21.

12. Ibid., §24.

13. Cf. Asteris Hulerias, "Qhadafi's Comeback: Libya and Sub-Saharan Africa in the 1990s," *African Affairs* 100, no. 399 (2001): 5–25; and Isabelle Werenfels, *Qadhafi's Libya: Infinitely Stable and Reform-Resistant?* (Berlin: Stiftung Wissenschaft und Politik Research Papers 5, 2008). See also T. A. Imoghibe, "An African High Command: The Search for a Feasible Strategy of Continental Defence," *African Affairs* 79, no. 315 (1980): 241–254.

14. OAU, *Draft of the Establishment of a State of the United States of Africa. Libyan Proposal to the Sirte Summit* (Addis Ababa: OAU, 1999).

15. Kassim M. Khamis, *Promoting the African Union* (Washington, DC: Lilian Barber Press, 2008), p. 91. The AEC was planned since June 3, 1991, with the aim of creating an African free trade area, a continental customs union, an African Common Market, as well as a Pan-African Monetary Union and a single African currency.

16. AU Assembly, *Items Proposed by the Great Libyan Arab Jamahiriya* [Assembly/AU/5 (IV) Add. 3–5] (Abuja: African Union, 2005).

17. AU Assembly, *Decision on the Proposals of the Great Socialist People's Libyan Arab Jamahiriya,* Assembly/AU/Dec.69 (IV)] (Addis Ababa: African Union, 2005).

18. AU Assembly, *Decision on the Report of the Committee of Seven Heads of States chaired by the President of the Republic of Uganda, on the Proposal of the Great Socialist*

People's Libyan Arab Jamahiriya [Assembly/AU/DEC.90 (V)] (Addis Ababa: African Union, 2005). Other members of this committee included Botswana, Chad, Ethiopia, Niger, Senegal, and Tunisia.

19. AU Committee of Heads of State and Government, *Africa & the Challenges of the Changing Global Order: Desirability of a Union Government. Conclusions and Recommendations. 12–13 November 2005, Banquet Hall, State House, Abuja* (Abuja: mimeo, 2005).

20. AU Assembly, *Decision on the Report of the Committee of Seven Heads of State and Government, Chaired by President Olusegun Obasanjo of the Federal Republic on Nigeria* [Assembly/AU/Dec.99 (VI)] (Addis Ababa: African Union, 2006).

21. AU Committee of Heads of State and Government, *A Study on an African Union Government: Towards the United States of Africa, July 2006* (Addis Ababa: African Union, 2006), §§ 15, 41, 115, and 118. The report has been submitted as document Assembly/AU/2 (VII) to the summit.

22. AU Assembly, *Décision sur le Gouvernement de l'Union* [Assembly/AU/Dec.123 (VII)] (Addis Ababa: African Union, 2006).

23. AU Executive Council, *Report of the 9th Extraordinary Session of the Executive Council* [Ext/EX.CL/RPT(IX)] (Addis Ababa: African Union, 2006), in particular §§14–16.

24. Cf. AUC Chairperson, *Report of the Chairperson on the Strengthening of the African Union Commission. Towards a Union Government* [EX.CL/328 (X)] (Addis Ababa: African Union, 2007).

25. AU Assembly, *Decision on the Report of the 9th Extraordinary Session of the Executive Council on the Proposals for the Union Government* [Assembly/AU/Dec.156 (VIII)] (Addis Ababa: African Union, 2007).

26. www.africa-union.org/ConceptNote.htm, accessed August 14, 2012.

27. AU Assembly, *Accra Declaration on the Union Government of Africa* (quoted from www.dfa.gov.za/docs/2007/ghan_decl0706.htm; accessed August 14, 2012).

28. AU Assembly, *Decision on the Report of the Committee of Twelve Heads of State and Government on the Union Government* [Assembly/AU/Dec.206 (XI)] (Addis Ababa: African Union, 2008).

29. Cf. Thomas K. Tieku, "Explaining the Clash and Accommodation of Interests of Major Actors in the Creation of the African Union," *African Affairs* 103, no. 411 (2004): 254f.

30. Cf. Tim Murithi, ed., *Towards a Union Government for Africa: Challenges and Opportunities* (Pretoria: Institute for Security Studies, 2008).

31. See, for instance, Delphine Lecoutre, "Vers un gouvernement de l'Union africaine? Gradualisme et status quo v. immédiatisme," *Politique Etrangère* 73, no. 3 (2008): 629–640.

32. Here and in the following Antonia Witt, "The African Union and Contested Norms," paper presented to the 2nd Annual Graduate Conference "Norms in Conflict," Cluster of Excellence "Normative Orders," Goethe University Frankfurt, December 3–5, 2010 (mimeo), p. 10.

33. Antonia Witt, "The African Union and Contested Political Order(s)," in *Towards an African Peace and Security Regime. Continental Embeddedness, Transnational Linkages, Strategic Relevance*, ed. João Gomes Porto and Ulf Engel (Farnham, UK: Ashgate, 2012), p. 24f.

34. AU Assembly, *Decision on the Special Session of the Assembly on the Union Government* [Assembly/AU/Dec.233 (XII)] (Addis Ababa: African Union, 2009). See also AU Executive Council, *Conclusions of the 12th Extraordinary Session of the Executive Council* [EXT/EX.CL.Concl. (XII)] (Addis Ababa: African Union, 2009).

35. AU Assembly, *Decision on the Establishment of an African Defence Council* [Assembly/AU/Dec.258 (XIII)] (Addis Ababa: African Union, 2009). Later, for instance, Botswana's Vice President Mompati Merafhe, who attended the summit on behalf of his president, openly criticized Gadhafi for rushing through proposals without proper debate. See Witt, "The African Union and Contested Norms," p. 13. See also AU Assembly, *Decision on the Transformation of the African Union Commission into the African Union Authority* [Assembly/AU/Dec. 263 (XIII)] (Addis Ababa: African Union, 2009).

36. AU Assembly, *Decision on the Transformation of the African Union Commission Into the African Union Authority* [Assembly/AU/Dec.298 (XV)] (Addis Ababa: African Union, 2010); and *Decision on the "Reconsideration of Decision Assembly/AU/Dec.263 (XIII) on the Transformation of the African Union Commission into the African Union Authority"* [Assembly/AU/Dec.329 (XV)] (Addis Ababa: African Union, 2010).

37. AU Assembly, *Decision on the Transformation of the African Union Commission into the African Union Authority* [Assembly/AU/Dec.341 (XVI)] (Addis Ababa: African Union, 2011)

38. AU Assembly, *Decision on The Transformation of the African Union Commission into the African Union Authority* [Assembly/AU/Dec.372 (XVII)] (Addis Ababa: African Union, 2011); and *Decision on the Transformation of the African Union Commission into the African Union Authority* [Assembly/AU/Dec.415 (XVIII)] (Addis Ababa: African Union, 2011).

39. Jean Bossuyt, "The Ongoing Institutional Reform of the AU: Exploring Avenues to Operationalize the African Union Authority," in *Building the African Union: An Assessment of Past Progress and Future Prospects for the African Union's Institutional Architecture*, ed. Geert Laporte and James Mackie (Maastricht: European Centre for Development Policy Management, 2010), p. 71.

40. AU High-Level Panel, *Audit of the African Union*, December 18, 2007 (Addis Ababa: African Union, 2008), p. xxiii; on the commission see also pp. 42–77.

41. Ibid., p. 66f.

42. Ibid., p. 76.

43. AU Assembly, *Special Session of the 12th Ordinary Session of the Assembly. Report on the Outcome*; and AU Commission, *AUC Strategic Plan 2009–2012* [EX.CL/501 (XV) Rev. 2, May 19, 2009] (Addis Ababa: African Union, 2009).

44. Cf. African Union, *Protocol Relating to the Establishment of the Peace and Security Council* (Durban: African Union, 2002). See Ulf Engel and João Gomes Porto,

eds., *The New Peace and Security Architecture of the African Union* (Farnham, UK: Ashgate, 2010).

45. Cf. Louis M. Fisher et al., *Moving Africa Forward: African Peace and Security Architecture (APSA). 2010 Assessment* (Addis Ababa: African Union, 2010).

46. Cf. AUC Chairperson, *Report of the Chairperson of the Commission on the Situation in Cote d'Ivoire* [PSC/PR/2 (CCLXXIII)] (Addis Ababa: African Union, 2011); and *Report of the Chairperson of the Commission on the Situation in Tunisia* [PSC/PR/Comm.2 (CCLVII)] (Addis Ababa: African Union, 2011). See also AU PSC, *Report of the Peace and Security Council on Its Activities and the State of Peace and Security in Africa* [Assembly/AU/6 (XIX)] (Addis Ababa: African Union, 2012), §2.

47. Cf. AUC Chairperson, *Report of the Chairperson of the Commission on the Situation in Somalia* [PSC/PR/2 (CCXCIII)] (Addis Ababa: African Union, 2011); and *Report of the Chairperson of the Commission on the Implementation Phase Two of the Mandate of the AU Mission in Somalia* (AMISOM) [PSC/PR/ (CCCII)] (Addis Ababa: African Union, 2011). See also Tim Murithi, "The African Union's Evolving Role in Peace Operations: The African Union Mission in Burundi, the African Union Mission in Sudan and the African Union Mission in Somalia," *African Security Review* 17, no. 1 (2008): 70–82; and Paul D. Williams, "The African Union's Peace Operations: A Comparative Analysis," *African Security* 2, no. 2–3 (2009): 97–118.

48. AUC Chairperson, *Report of the Chairperson of the Commission on the Partnership Between the AU and the UN on Peace and Security (AU-UN)* [PSC/PR/2 (CCCVII)] (Addis Ababa: African Union, 2012).

49. AU PSC, *Report of the Peace and Security Council on its Activities,* §§ 40–46. See also AU Panel of the Wise, *Election-Related Disputes and Political Violence. Strengthening the Role of the African Union in Preventing, Managing, and Resolving Conflict* (New York: International Peace Institute, 2010).

50. African Union, *Memorandum of Understanding on Cooperation in the Area of Peace and Security Between the African Union, the Regional Economic Communities and the Coordinating Mechanisms of the Regional Standby Brigades of Eastern and Northern Africa* (mimeo) (Addis Ababa: African Union, 2008).

51. See AU PSC, *Declaration of the Ministerial Meeting of the Peace and Security Council on the State of Peace and Security in Africa* [PSC/PR/BR.1 (CCLXXV)] (Addis Ababa: African Union, 2011); AUC Chairperson, *Report of the Chairperson of the Commission on the Activities of the AU High-Level Ad Hoc Committee on the Situation in Libya* [PSC/PR/2 (CCLXXV)] (Addis Ababa: African Union, 2011); and *Report of the Chairperson of the Commission on the Situation in Libya and on the Efforts of the African Union for a Political Solution to the Libyan Crisis* [PSC/AHG/3 (CCXCI)] (Addis Ababa: African Union, 2011). See also Gerrie Swart, "A Right to Intervene . . . A Reluctance to Protect? Probing the African Union's Response to and Failed Intervention in the Libyan Crisis," in *New Mediation Practices in African Conflicts,* ed. Ulf Engel (Leipzig: Leipziger Universitätsverlag, 2012).

52. AUC Chairperson, *Report of the Chairperson of the Commission on Current Challenges to Peace and Security on the Continent and AU's Efforts. Enhancing Africa's*

Leadership, Promoting African Solutions [EXT/ASSEMBLY/AU/2.(01.2011)] (Addis Ababa: African Union, 2011), §48.

53. AU Commission, *AUC Strategic Plan 2009–2012.*

54. OAU, *Decision on the Rights of Political Participation* [AHG/Dec.141 (XXXV)] (Addis Ababa: OAU, 1999); and *OAU Declaration on the Principles Governing Democratic Elections in Africa* [AHG/Decl.1 (XXXVIII)] (Addis Ababa: OAU, 2002).

55. OAU, *NEPAD Declaration on Democracy, Political, Economic and Corporate Governance* [AHG/235 (XXXVIII), Annex I] (Durban: OAU, 2002); and AU Assembly, *Declaration on the Theme of the Summit: "Towards Greater Unity and Integration through Shared Values"* [Assembly/AU/Decl.1 (XVI)] (Addis Ababa: African Union, 2011).

56. See Freedom House, "Freedom in the World" reports for 2005 and 2012, www.freedomhouse.org/template.cfm?page=1, accessed August 14, 2012. On electoral violence see J. Shola Omotola, "Explaining Electoral Violence in Africa's 'New' Democracies," *African Journal of Conflict Resolution* 10, no. 3 (2010): 51–73; and Thad Dunning, "Fighting and Voting: Violent Conflict and Electoral Politics," *Journal of Conflict Resolution* 55, no. 3 (2011): 327–339; on coups cf. Naison Ngoma, "Coups and Coup Attempts in Africa: Is There a Missing Link?" *African Security Review* 13, no. 3 (2004): 85–94; and Francis N. Ikome, *Good Coups and Bad Coups: The Limits of the AU's Injunction on Unconstitutional Changes of Government* (Johannesburg: Institute for Global Dialogue, 2007); and on third-term conflicts see Bruce Baker, "Outstaying One's Welcome: The Presidential Third-Term Debate in Africa," *Contemporary Politics* 8, no. 4 (2002): 385–401; and Daniel Vencovsky, "Presidential Term Limits in Africa," *Conflict Trends* 2 (2007): 15–21. This is in contrast to considerable gains made in the democratization of African states elsewhere. See, for instance, Daniel N. Posner and Daniel J. Young, "The Institutionalization of Political Power in Africa," *Journal of Democracy* 18, no. 3 (2007): 126–140; and Emmanuel Gyimah-Boadi, "Africa: The Quality of Political Reform," in *Democratic Reform in Africa: The Quality of Progress,* ed. Emmanuel Gyimah-Boadi (Boulder, CO, and London: Lynne Rienner Publishers, 2005).

57. Compiled on the basis of *Africa Research Bulletin. Political, Social and Cultural Series* (Wiley Online Library).

58. See Issaka K. Souaré, *The AU and the Challenge of Unconstitutional Changes of Government in Africa* (Pretoria: Institute for Security Studies, 2009); and Kathryn Sturman, *Unconstitutional Changes of Government: The Democrat's Dilemma in Africa* (Johannesburg: South African Institute of International Affairs, 2011).

59. OAU AHG, *Decision on Unconstitutional Changes in Government* [AHG/Dec. 142 (XXXV)] (Addis Ababa: OAU, 1999); *Decision on Unconstitutional Changes of Government in Africa* [AHG/Dec.150 (XXXVI)] (Addis Ababa: OAU, 2000); and *Declaration on the Framework for an OAU Response to Unconstitutional Changes of Government* [AHG/Decl.5 (XXXVI)] (Addis Ababa: OAU, 2000).

60. OAU AHG, *Declaration on the Framework,* p. 3.

61. AU Assembly, *African Charter on Democracy, Elections and Governance* [Assembly/AU/Dec.147 (VIII)] (Addis Ababa: African Union, 2007), §23(5).

62. AU Assembly, *African Charter,* §25, based on OAU AHG, *Decision on Unconstitutional Changes of Government in Africa.*

63. AU Assembly, *Decision on the Resurgence of the Scourge of Coups d'État in Africa* [Assembly/AU/Dec.220 (XII)] (Addis Ababa: African Union, 2009); and *Decision on the Prevention on Unconstitutional Changes of Government and Strengthening the Capacity of the African Union to Manage Such Situations* [Assembly/AU/Dec.253 (XIII)] (Addis Ababa: African Union, 2009).

64. For a detailed discussion see Ulf Engel, "The African Union and Mediation in Cases of Unconstitutional Changes of Government, 2008–2011," in Engel, ed., *New Mediation Practices.*

65. Antonia Witt, "A Constructive Engagement? The European Union's Contributions to Mediating Coups d'État in Africa," in Engel, ed., *New Mediation Practices.*

66. See, in particular, AUC Chairperson, *Interim Report of the Chairperson of the Commission on the Prevention of Unconstitutional Changes of Government Through Appropriate Measures and Strengthening the Capacity of the African Union to Manage Such Situations* [Assembly/AU/7 (XIII) (mimeo, draft)]; (Addis Ababa: African Union, 2009); and *Report of the Chairperson of the Commission to the PSC on the Prevention of Unconstitutional Changes of Government and Strengthening the Capacities of the African Union to Manage Such Situations* [Assembly/AU/4 (XIV)] (Addis Ababa: African Union, 2010).

67. Cf. Babatunde T. Afolabi, "ECOWAS and Conflict Mediation in West Africa," in Engel, ed., *New Mediation Practices;* and Helmut Orbon, "SADC and Conflict Mediation in Southern Africa," in Engel, ed., *New Mediation Practices.*

68. African Union, *List of Countries Which Have Signed, Ratified/Acceded to the African Charter on Democracy, Elections and Governance* (Addis Ababa: African Union, January 17, 2012), /www.au.int/en/sites/default/files/Charter%20on%20Democracy%20and%20Governance.pdf, accessed February 15, 2012. Cf. Ibrahima Kane, "The Implementation of the African Charter on Democracy, Elections and Governance," *African Security Review* 17, no. 4 (2008): 44–63.

69. AU PSC, *Declaration of the Ministerial Meeting of the Peace and Security Council on the State of Peace and Security in Africa* [PSC/MIN/BR.1 (CCLXXV)] (Addis Ababa: African Union, 2011), §3.

70. AUC Chairperson, *Report of the Chairperson of the Commission on Current Challenges to Peace and Security,* §§5–6 and 46–47, respectively.

71. As to the concept, see Björn Hettne, "Globalization and the New Regionalism: The Second Great Transformation," in *Globalism and the New Regionalism,* ed. Björn Hettne, András Inotai, and Osvaldo Sunkel (London: Macmillan, 1999); Fredrik Söderbaum and Timothy M. Shaw, eds., *Theories of New Regionalism: A Palgrave Reader* (London and New York: Palgrave Macmillan, 2003); and Timothy M. Shaw, J. Andrew Grant, and Scarlett Cornelissen, eds., *The Ashgate Research Companion to Regionalisms* (Farnham, UK: Ashgate, 2011).

PART IV

GLOBAL ENGAGEMENT

The preceding sections have centered on the complexities African countries have confronted, both individually and collectively, in strengthening and reforming their states in a profoundly changing world order in which both economic power and political influence, if not military power, have become much more widely diffused than during the four decades of bipolar Cold War confrontation. In this evolving world order, Africa has acquired markedly increased significance both for newly recognized opportunities for economic investment and, increasingly, for broadening significance in global counterterrorism campaigns interacting with homegrown religious, cultural, and political insurgency.

This concluding section centers on two of the most profound crises of state failure: civil war in Sudan resulting in the emergence of Africa's newest state, and the crisis in the Great Lakes in which weak and failed states deepened each other's failure. It focuses on rapidly expanding Chinese investment and aid in Africa, in the context of deepened economic engagement by other G-20 powers, notably Brazil, India, and Saudi Arabia. Finally, it explores two different and, perhaps in some respects, contrasting perspectives on strengthening and reforming weak states in a world order in which international regimes upholding democracy and human rights have acquired increasing prominence and commitment in the nearly quarter century since the end of the Cold War.

Ambassador Francis M. Deng's chapter on "Responsible Sovereignty" addresses the fundamental principle of the evolving international regimes. The principle that all states respect one another's untrammeled sovereignty derives from the 1648 Treaty of Westphalia ending the Thirty Years' War and is a founding principle of the UN Charter. The evolving principle of responsible sovereignty holds that state sovereignty is conditioned on protecting the well-being of their constituent populations, specifically their basic human rights and their entitlement to democracy. Responsible sovereignty at least implies *collective, multilateral* authority and a responsibility to uphold the principle against the recalcitrant, failed, and failing states whose tragic circumstances gave rise to the evolving principle.

The other chapters of this section point to the fundamental challenges to realizing the principle of responsible sovereignty. Manning's and Berg's chapter suggests powerfully that for all the skills and resources multilateral actors bring to civil war and failed-state crises, bilateral actors may also supply indispensable resources and skills in persuading the contestants in these crises to accept the adoption costs involved in making peace. As they acknowledge, however, some recalcitrant regimes may still be strong enough to effectively resist these multilateral and bilateral ministrations, for example, in Rwanda. Of course, bilateral actors have their own agendas, not necessarily in sync with multiple efforts to secure responsible sovereignty.

Ambassador Princeton N. Lyman's chapter examines the danger-fraught issues of oil revenues, citizenship, boundaries, and many others, left to the two Sudans to work out after the independence of South Sudan in July 2011, rather than before, as was envisaged under the Comprehensive Peace Agreement, that continues to render peace elusive. While efforts of third parties to *facilitate* the approach to common ground, issue by issue, have been the prevalent modalities, the alternative of *mediation* remains potentially available entailing the formulation of a comprehensive set of solutions. But, as Ambassador Lyman observes, a potentially elusive "totally unified international position" would be essential to its success.

Filip Reyntjens's chapter on the Great Lakes crisis details the depth of the state failure of Congo and the weakness of its neighbors, the profitability of war, the unchallenged impunity, and the embroiling of new and long-standing local conflicts that makes this crisis so intractable. He is at pains to advise that while the worst of the interconnected conflicts have been tamped down for the present, the possibility of their reemergence remains real. Without saying so, this warning makes clear how limited has been the capacity of the international community to address these underlying causes of prolonged conflict to effect responsible and capable sovereignty to protect the peoples of the region from further tragedy.

Finally, Ian Taylor's chapter on China in Africa demonstrates in depth another fundamental barrier to the exercise of responsible sovereignty in sub-Saharan Africa. The greatly expanded levels of investment, trade, and aid to Africa from China and other G-20 powers have been important in generating strong positive rates of growth in Africa in the first years of the twenty-first century. In this they have belatedly fulfilled an "implicit bargain" communicated when the international financial institutions imposed structural adjustment on African countries in the 1980s: that public and private investment would follow African adherence to IFI conditionalities. Eventually African countries have begun to adhere, and G-20 countries in addition to those of the West have responded.

Taylor highlights two serious dangers inherent in the expanded Chinese investment. First, African countries may find it difficult to resist falling into a new form of dependency, given the apparent lack of Chinese conditionalities, just as their belated reforms under IFI oversight have begun to free them from that very dependence. Second, G-20 countries other than those of the West may also be less inclined to insist that African countries adhere to the norms of transparency, human rights, and democracy underlying responsible sovereignty and the responsibility to protect.

ten

Bilateral vs. Multilateral Peacebuilding in Africa

Carrie Manning and Louis-Alexandre Berg

INTRODUCTION

This chapter explores the role of bilateral donors in postconflict peacebuilding processes. We argue that the success or failure of complex, multidimensional peace operations is too often assumed to hinge on the UN mission itself. However, bilateral donors have also played a critical role in securing successful outcomes and perhaps also in contributing to the failure of peace missions, though this has not been extensively examined. Of particular interest is how bilateral aid interventions may affect both the capacity and the political will of domestic political actors by offering credible commitments to reduce the costs to local actors of embracing postwar democratic politics.

Peacebuilding is an inherently political process, not a technocratic one. While peace agreements and UN mandates often explicitly call for the UN peace mission and other external actors to oversee *political* reforms or transformations, there is an implicit assumption that these actors will not be getting their hands dirty by engaging in the kind of political horse trading, cajoling, threatening, and deal making that characterizes political interaction in such settings. Instead, international technocrats are to apply rules, along with rewards and punishments for following or deviating from these rules.

This view overlooks the fact that domestic political actors are in fact *actors,* who may or may not be disposed to follow the rules. In effective peace operations, UN mission leaders and the representatives of major donors rely not on the willingness of domestic actors to recognize their authority and obey the rules, but on their own ability to alter the costs to local actors of embracing the peace agreement, which includes not only laying down arms but also surrendering to the uncertainties of democratic politics. To alter these costs, external actors must have a credible capacity to impose costs and confer benefits, in the eyes of domestic actors. We argue that UN peace operations on their own are unlikely to have such credibility.

This chapter proceeds as follows. The next section introduces the notion of adoption costs. Adoption costs refer to the cost-benefit calculation of local elites about the risks and gains to be had from cooperating rather than defecting on the commitments required by the peace agreement. We then outline the expected characteristics of effective guarantors, based on a reading of the comparative literature on postconflict peacebuilding. While bilateral donors can never replace UN peace missions, we argue that they complement these missions in indispensable ways. In the following section, we explore the conditions under which bilateral actors are likely to serve as effective guarantors, highlighting the impact of relationships among domestic political elites. We use the cases of Mozambique, Liberia, and Rwanda to illustrate the contribution of bilateral donors toward securing sustainable peace under different conditions. In Mozambique and Liberia, the role of bilateral donors was critical, despite the common tendency to attribute success in each case primarily to the UN mission. In Rwanda, by contrast, strong domestic political actors had little need of external support to overcome political rivals. While they still relied on international aid, donors were often unable or unwilling to truly condition aid funds on performance or to influence policy.

We make two main claims. First, we find that the UN is most effective when it is backed up by the leading bilateral donor. A division of labor, in which the UN and bilateral actors assume responsibility for separate tasks, does not seem to be as effective as when both the UN and the major bilateral donor provide complementary forms of support for the same tasks. Second, both the relationship between the major bilateral donor and domestic elites, *and* the relationships among competing domestic actors, affect adoption costs in important ways. Although bilateral actors are often better placed than multilateral actors to establish effective relationships with domestic elites, in some cases the nature of domestic political relationships limits the influence of even the most credible external actors on peacebuilding outcomes.

One caveat is in order before proceeding further. This paper deals only with cases where there is an actual peace agreement, and we are concerned with what happens after that agreement is signed. We do not examine the role of external actors in the process of getting belligerents to the negotiating table in the first place. We examine the period after a UN peace operation has been deployed to the country in question, not how the decision about whether and how to intervene in a given country is made.

ADOPTION COSTS AND PEACEBUILDER LEVERAGE

Effective guarantors lower adoption costs for actors who will benefit from the terms of the settlement, but who lack confidence that the rules will be enforced. They can also allay the concerns of those who face risks to their physical, political, or economic security if they embrace the terms of the settlement. Effective guarantors lower the cost of moving from war to peace by ensuring the benefits of peace and minimizing its dangers for the weaker party.

In assessing adoption costs, we look at the impact of the peace settlement on domestic actors' physical, political, and economic security, following the work of Hartzell and others.[1] We are interested not just in the end of conflict, but in the set of institutional reforms required to fulfill the terms of the postwar political settlement that is part of the peace process. This often includes restructuring security forces and establishing or strengthening democratic institutions, anticorruption measures, and human rights protections. These reforms imply potential costs for domestic political actors.

For rebels, laying down arms and moving into civilian life implies surrendering their security to the very government authorities they have been battling with lethal force. For their part, governments seek to create conditions to guarantee that rebel soldiers are effectively disarmed and demobilized, or integrated into the state's security sector. Many if not most peace agreements contain provisions for disarmament, demobilization, and restructuring of security forces. Even with such assurances, domestic actors' assessment of risk will depend both on who is to oversee these processes as well as the balance of forces between rebels and government.

In addition to physical security, governments and rebels may be concerned with their access to political and economic power. As Eva Bertram points out, "Peace building is nothing less than the reallocation of political power; it is not a neutral act."[2] Zartman, among others, highlights the importance of political inclusion as a foundation for peace: "Insurgents must be assured of getting a real role in a new political system, with guarantees of protecting that role, so that the agreement becomes not just the end of the war but the beginning of a new partnership that does not let the old neglect and discrimination happen again."[3] For incumbent factions, embracing more inclusive, democratic politics brings considerable risk that they might lose the means to maintain their political authority. Political actors may also face an economic price for adopting the postwar political settlement. For example, where rebels have used lootable natural resources to finance their war, the end of war will also mean an end to unfettered access to these resources. UNITA faced this dilemma in Angola in 1997 and found the adoption costs of peace too high. Similarly, where governments have used the war as cover for the diversion of resources away from development and into private bank accounts, peace comes with costs.

Hartzell and Hoddie argue that institutions for political and economic power sharing might effectively substitute for external guarantors.[4] But brand-new institutions are unlikely to constrain the behavior of powerful actors in the short term. Belligerents often seek to build provisions into the peace agreement that guarantee them some measure of access to political and economic power. Credible external guarantors, alongside provisions that make it hard for one side to exclude the other from access to political or economic participation, are more likely to lower adoption costs for domestic elites.

Adoption costs depend both on domestic political actors' assessments of how the terms of the peace settlement will affect them, *if enforced,* and on their assessment of the ability of external actors to enforce those terms. For this reason, the identity of the external interveners matters. But one size does not fit all. No category of external actor will be effective in all cases. There will be cases in which domestic political actors face such high adoption costs that external actors can do little or nothing to allay them. Nevertheless, we argue that under certain circumstances that we explore below, bilateral donors can be critical to the success of the peace settlement.

Effective Guarantors

What makes an effective guarantor? An effective guarantor is one with sufficient resources, capacity, and credibility to induce the cooperation by relevant domestic actors that is necessary to implement a peace agreement. In the post–Cold War period, "implementing the peace agreement" usually includes establishing formally democratic political systems as well as establishing physical security. Since some of these measures are costly for domestic actors to adopt, effective guarantors employ a range of negative and positive incentives to get the job done. These include, most importantly, reducing uncertainty regarding physical, political, or economic security of former belligerents; offering tangible benefits or costs, monetary, or in-kind support; or threatening sanctions or the use of force. As Fortna points out, such interventions support peacekeeping by "raising the costs of war and the benefits of peace."[5] External actors play a similar role throughout the peacebuilding process as political actors weigh the costs of implementing the terms of a peace agreement and democratic reforms.[6]

Merely providing resources and troops is not sufficient to guaranteeing the peace. Especially when adoption costs are high, external actors use their resources to "cajole" reluctant leaders and engage in a process of "continuous bargaining" over the implementation of the peace agreement.[7] The leverage of external actors depends not only on the amount of resources they provide, but on their ability to bargain effectively, to promote a consistent agenda, to monitor behavior on the ground, and to use that information to respond flexibly to changing conditions.[8] Even where adoption costs are lower, domestic leaders' ability to fulfill the terms of the peace agreement may depend on receiving the external backing necessary to implement costly measures and guarantee their political survival. Domestic actors are interested not only in their prospects for the present and immediate future, but for the more distant future as well. The ability of external actors to credibly commit to future support—and withhold resources in case of noncompliance—may affect their calculations over whether to embrace the terms of the postwar democratic political settlement.

In the extensive literature seeking to explain effective peacebuilding efforts, there is broad agreement that to be effective, peacebuilders should:

1. be flexible and responsive to changing circumstances on the ground;
2. be able to identify spoilers and deal effectively with them;
3. understand the incentive structures facing key domestic actors (including understanding root and immediate causes of tension and conflict, capacity constraints, political challenges, and economic opportunities);[9] and
4. be able to coordinate with other external actors to "speak with one voice."[10]

These "lessons learned" suggest that the UN is at a distinct disadvantage as an effective external guarantor in postconflict peacebuilding, or at least that it could be helpfully supplemented by other external actors.

First, UN peace missions are recently created, ad hoc amalgamations. Domestic political actors have no basis on which to assess the credibility of the UN mission in their country at the start of that mission. Instead, domestic actors must take their cues from bilateral actors who are known to them. The behavior of major donors with an established presence in the country may be far more consequential to the success or failure of peace missions than has been acknowledged thus far. In other words, the behavior of established bilateral donors provides important signals to domestic political actors about the risks and benefits of implementing the peace agreement.

Bilateral donors are likely to have greater local knowledge, more flexibility, and the ability to impose conditionality on discrete components of the peace process that are not within reach of the UN mission, with its heavy bureaucracy and broad mandate. Bilateral donors interacting directly with domestic elites in the peace implementation process may also present higher audience costs to elites considering defection from the agreement. Walter points out that powerful states might dilute their influence in this respect when they participate in multilateral missions, because choosing to act under a UN umbrella could signal weak rather than strong commitment to enforcing the peace agreement (since they are not willing to take direct bilateral action).[11] On the other hand, bilateral actors working in complement to the UN mission can help compensate for the UN's inability to impose audience costs on its own.

There is an important temporal dimension as well. Credibility may come from long-standing relationships in which donors have demonstrated to domestic elites their ability to deliver the goods. Bilateral actors may play important roles in providing ancillary support to create the background conditions necessary to induce cooperation by domestic elites. This is often done behind the scenes, before and during peace talks themselves. Bilateral donors may have long-standing relationships with one or another of the belligerents, which enhances their ability to act at least as "partial" guarantors for one side. Other comparative advantages of bilateral actors may not come into play until the longer term—as guarantors of economic support, providers of technical and financial aid for necessary administrative reforms, and long-term monitors of the democratic process, at election times as well as between elections. Domestic political actors might be willing to discount their immediate interests to win approval from international actors, if they believe that support from these actors will be crucial and forthcoming in the future. Such reciprocity is not likely from a relatively short-lived UN mission, but may well be expected from a bilateral donor with established roots and interests in the country.

Bilateral donors are not ultimately responsible for the overall outcome of the peace implementation mission. They may therefore be better able to apply pressure or supply positive incentives to improve compliance on specific aspects of the process that the UN may feel obliged to overlook because of pressure to achieve the overall goal on schedule, an unwillingness to ruffle the feathers of the government, or a lack of human or financial resources to attend to these nuances.

This perspective calls into question the assumption that impartial actors make the best guarantors. It also undermines the idea that ad hoc peace missions cobbled together from multilateral contributions or "coalitions of the willing" make effective guarantors of peace agreements. It suggests instead that bilateral donors play not just a supporting role but a potentially determining role in shaping the attitudes and behavior of domestic elites in post-conflict settings. This suggests a need for a better understanding of the role bilateral actors have played in successful or unsuccessful peace operations.

Importantly, money or financial leverage is not the only or even necessarily the most important issue. It is not simply the amount of aid provided by a donor during the process, but the relationships and local knowledge of major donors or "development partners" that may play a pivotal role in the outcome of peace operations.

Second, peacebuilding is not a two-sided interaction with a unitary external actor—the UN mission—on one hand and "domestic actors" on the other. Postconflict settings are very complex environments, in which the multitude of external actors resembles Migdal's description of countries with strong societies and weak states. In Migdal's formulation, weak states compete with myriad rival sources of social authority to make the authoritative rules that will dictate citizens' behavior. In the peacebuilding context, the UN peace mission and various bilateral actors share a common broad goal (peace) but have divergent short-term objectives and offer different costs and benefits for domestic actors doing business with them. Various external actors may offer peace through development, or peace through democracy, or peace without strings. They may offer security guarantees or not, financial incentives or not, reputational enhancement or not. Domestic actors can choose to accept what each of these external actors is offering (or not). The offers are not always consistent with one another, and may work at cross purposes. Virtually every study of postconflict peacebuilding, whether focused on bilateral donors or the UN, bemoans the lack of coordination and cooperation among external actors.

Thus domestic political actors may know relatively little about the resources and capacities of most external actors seeking to contribute to postconflict peacebuilding, particularly UN missions. Each UN mission has a different mandate, different leadership, and participation from different countries with different capacities. Even if the contingents and mandate of a mission are known in advance, it is not safe to make sweeping assumptions about how fully and how effectively the mandate will be implemented.

In addition, the multiplicity of external actors may tempt domestic political elites to play these actors off one another to maximize gains for themselves. Domestic political elites can bid up the price of cooperation on a particular agenda item, take advantage of information asymmetry among external actors about what is happening in a particular geographic or issue area, or exploit preexisting relationships they may have with particular donors to achieve more favorable terms of participation.

This picture of external peacebuilders as a diverse array of "free agents," creating a buffet of opportunities for domestic political actors to modify the terms of their participation in the postwar settlement, is in stark contrast to much of the literature, which presents peacebuilding as a two-sided affair with the UN on one side of the table and domestic elites on the other.

Domestic Politics and External Influence

The arguments laid out so far suggest that the ability of external actors to serve as effective guarantors of peacebuilding processes depends on their capabilities for achieving unified and coherent approaches. The domestic side of the equation also affects the potential for peacebuilder leverage. Domestic political actors, whose cooperation is critical to the successful implementation of reforms, are embedded in political and economic networks that affect the risks and benefits of a given set of reforms. Even after a peace agreement is signed, political actors struggle to achieve authority and to survive politically. The strength of their networks and the relationships among them affect the adoption costs of implementing the terms of the peace agreement, as well as the value of external resources and guarantees. Relationships among domestic factions also affect their ability to maneuver around external actors, or to manipulate information asymmetries or multiple donors to achieve their results. The relationships within the postconflict country thus shape the opportunities for leverage by external actors. The influence of external actors depends, in turn, on their ability to navigate and respond to these domestic relationships.

Under what conditions, then, can external actors serve as credible guarantors and affect the behavior of domestic political elites in ways that support peacebuilding? When and how do they lower adoption costs in practice? First, relationships between external actors and domestic political elites create or diminish leverage. A recent comparative study of nine cases of postconflict peacebuilding finds that aid per se has a limited impact on democratic outcomes.[12] Instead, aid relationships work on outcomes in more complex and nuanced ways, most importantly, by creating the potential for donors to exercise conditionality, and by facilitating trust between domestic elites and external actors that is necessary for peacebuilder leverage. Most important, these positive effects come through the relationships that donors who contribute to and participate in peacebuilding missions have established with domestic elites over long years of aid provision.

The relationships that exist between donors and domestic political actors and among donors themselves at the onset of the intervention are important because they affect mutual confidence between peacebuilders and domestic political actors, and hence add to or subtract from the credibility of donors as external guarantors; the ability of donors to coordinate with one another; and the degree to which donors have local knowledge about political, social, cultural, and other conditions that could affect the peacebuilding process. A history of consistent support for the government from a given group of donors during the humanitarian crisis brought on by war, for example, can give that donor group credibility with domestic political actors. Trust in external peacebuilders lowers elite adoption costs by reducing perceived threats posed by the democratic political settlement and enhancing confidence among domestic leaders that external actors will follow through with their commitments.

Where donors have a history of working together in a country before or during the war, they can more easily overcome the coordination and cooperation challenges that plague many peace missions. Donor cooperation in a humanitarian emergency can provide a precedent and even an institutional template (such as donor working groups) for cooperation during the peace process. Coherence among donors reduces the ability of local actors to "divide and conquer" external actors during the peacebuilding process to evade provisions they dislike. And it increases donor ability to implement conditionality, thereby increasing peacebuilder leverage.[13] Local knowledge and connections forged from long experience in a country also increase external actors' ability to implement conditionality effectively. In short, the degree to which peacebuilders leverage the resources available to them (and indeed their ability to mobilize resources from their own governments) depends to a considerable extent on preexisting relationships between donors and domestic elites, and on relationships forged or modified throughout the peacebuilding process.

On the other side of the equation, relationships between domestic elites also affect adoption costs and the ability of external actors to serve as effective guarantors. In a study of the impact of external assistance on postconflict institution-building, Berg finds that external resources are most influential when political elites are weakest domestically, leaving them reliant on external support for their domestic political survival.[14] Domestic actors facing fragmented political coalitions or who lack control over a reliable source of revenue are more likely to depend on external support to manage political challenges and consolidate their authority. Conversely, leaders with a more cohesive political base or control over a concentrated revenue source face higher adoption costs in the potential loss of control over resources or state institutions, and lower benefits of external assistance relative to domestic sources of support. Relationships among domestic elites not only determine adoption costs, they also affect the value of external assistance to domestic leaders, and thereby shape the opportunities for influence available to external actors.

Within the context of domestic political struggles, the credibility of external actors and the confidence of domestic leaders that they will fulfill their commitments affect their calculation of the benefits of external assistance. For leaders of factions that are relatively weak, externally provided funds, legitimacy, informational advantages, and physical protection can compensate for the limitations on their authority that come with democratic reforms and help them neutralize challenges from rival factions. Peacebuilders with a history of providing assistance, deep relationships, and the ability to reliably commit to long-term support are more likely to inspire the necessary confidence and to help them respond to domestic political challenges. The flexibility of bilateral actors also enhances their credibility that they will withhold support if domestic leaders fail to uphold their commitments.

Even the most credible external actors may not always achieve the leverage necessary to influence local actors, however. Leaders of factions that are embedded in powerful and cohesive domestic networks may lose more from adopting reforms that undermine their source of authority, and gain less from external support. These leaders are less likely to develop effective relationships with external actors or to respond to external pressure for reforms that threaten their interests. External actors therefore find fewer opportunities for leverage where the postconflict political context is dominated by more cohesive factions.

Over time, however, external actors may also disrupt local networks, or shift the balance of power among competing factions. Where opportunities for external leverage are limited, such changes may open new opportunities by weakening powerful networks. On the other hand, changes in domestic networks that reinforce a party's domestic power base or reduce the reliance on external support may reduce external influence. For external actors, achieving and maintaining leverage requires detailed knowledge of the changing local context and the ability to respond in ways that reinforce opportunities for influence.

Given the complexities of postconflict politics, serving as effective guarantors requires the ability to develop deep knowledge of local political and economic networks, respond credibly and flexibly to changing conditions, and maintain effective relationships with domestic elites that help them minimize domestic adoption costs. Bilateral actors are more likely than the UN to achieve these capabilities. Nonetheless, the reality of local politics often limits the potential for even the most credible and coherent external actors to influence core aspects of the peacebuilding process. The next three sections flesh out the argument made here by examining three important cases in sub-Saharan Africa: Mozambique, Liberia, and Rwanda.

BILATERAL DONORS AND PEACEBUILDING IN MOZAMBIQUE

The Mozambican case provides examples in which bilateral actors played a critical role in ensuring the peace by successfully deploying their extensive local knowledge and the political capital gained from long experience in the country and from the understanding of a longer-term commitment from aid donors in an aid-dependent country.[15] Major donors provided domestic elites with demonstrations of their ability to enforce the peace using a range of strategies that were beyond the reach of the UN mission alone.

In postwar Mozambique, donors successfully used a variety of modalities for providing aid conditioned on (and designed to give direct support to) advances in the peace process. After the 1992 signing of the General Peace Agreement (GPA) between the government of Mozambique and the rebel group Renamo, the peace process was formally overseen by UNOMOZ (United Nations Observation Mission in Mozambique), and the UN operation has received much of the credit for the success of the peace process there. While UNOMOZ was crucial in overseeing the cease-fire and providing the overarching formal framework within which the peace process was carried out, the success of this process largely depended upon flexible and responsive interventions on the part of bilateral donors, who filled in critical gaps left by UNOMOZ. These donors had significant country experience, local standing with domestic actors, and resources independent of those allocated for the UN peace operation. They also had a stake in the outcome of the peace process that was tied to their longer-term interests as donors in Mozambique. These factors permitted donors to employ effective conditionality on discrete aspects of the peace process.

Peace conditionality, "the use of aid as a lever to persuade conflicting parties to make peace, to implement peace accords, and to consolidate peace," was employed in Mozambique on two levels.[16] First, a large infusion of aid was committed by the country's major donors upon signing of the peace agreement in Rome in 1992. This commitment of aid was based on the expectation that the government of Mozambique and Renamo would move forward to implement the commitments each had made in Rome.

However, as the peace process unfolded, donors involved themselves in the details of the implementation process in ways that enabled them to exercise an implicit conditionality over specific measures. The broad quid pro quo of money for progress in the peace process developed into the use of more narrowly targeted peace conditionality to overcome specific obstacles over the course of the implementation process. UNOMOZ as an institution was limited both by its mandate and by resource constraints, and strictly limited its involvement or the sharing of its equipment and other resources for other parts of the electoral process for which it was not specifically tasked (its priorities were electoral observation and administration).[17] Bilateral donors stepped in at many points during the implementation and electoral processes to offer support where UNOMOZ could not. These bilateral actors not only achieved an unaccustomed degree of coordination among themselves with respect to important goals and activities in support of the political transition; they also succeeded in limiting the government's ability to "divide and conquer" the donor community by allowing donors to speak with one voice on the most important issues of implementation. The fact that Aldo Ajello, as special representative of the secretary-general (SRSG), so visibly supported these efforts by bilateral donors was crucial.

In addition, donors sometimes conditioned their own donations on the participation of a critical mass of other donors, to ensure that their own contributions would not go toward a fatally underfunded project. In these ways, donors not only selectively exerted leverage over leaders of the warring parties, but also over UNOMOZ and one another, shaping and reshaping key aspects of the process along the way.

Thus, the specific peace conditionalities that helped produce a successful transition from war to peace in Mozambique were not planned in advance of the peace operation, but developed by donors in response to specific challenges that arose over the course of implementing the peace agreement. When problems arose in the implementation of the agreement, donors stepped in, singly or in groups, to provide good offices, inject additional resources, and remind both sides of their commitments.

Donors' history of engagement in Mozambique provided the necessary backdrop for the application of microlevel conditionality in support of the peace process. By the time of the peace process, the major donors were known quantities to the government and Renamo. The like-minded donors had been intimately involved with supporting the state since independence. The United States, Italy, the World Bank, and other donors provided significant support later on, but were established actors well before the war ended. This is not to say that relations between these donors and the government or Renamo were uniformly warm. Nevertheless, major donors had established a track record with the government by the time of the peace agreement, and their priorities and proclivities were clear. This was a very different government-donor relationship than the conditional sets of relationships that often emerged elsewhere in the 1990s.

Extended experience in the country gave donors the local knowledge necessary to sense what kinds of positive and negative inducements were most likely to work. Conditionality could be fine-tuned through consideration of the context. Moreover, donors had significant experience working with one another in Mozambique in the context of the humanitarian emergency during the civil war. This experience, their shared understanding of the political, social, and economic contexts, and the absence of complicating factors like lucrative natural resources or strategic political or economic importance made donors more willing and able to cooperate with one another.

Mozambique's experience supports the arguments of scholars who find that peace conditionality is likely to work best where conditions imposed are specific, flexible, and well matched to the problem, where donors share common goals and are able to create coordination mechanisms, and where short-term conditions are part of a longer-term relationship and set of goals. Thus, while donors used aid to overcome specific sticking points, these punctual interventions were clearly part of a set of longer-term goals that donors would continue to support for many years after the formal transition. These included macroeconomic stabilization, not least to provide a favorable investment climate for foreign investors, strengthening the management of public finance and the overall capacity of the Mozambican state to provide basic services, and democratic governance. In the years after the transitional general elections in 1994, donors have continued to support Renamo financially, to provide support for election implementation and monitoring, and to play an active part in monitoring and conditioning their aid, on the requirement that both the government and Renamo remain committed to maintaining peace and moving forward with democratization.

The Mozambican case reinforces many of the findings from the literature on the role of third-party guarantors in securing negotiated peace settlements. Specifically, it provides insight into the complex interactions that underpin effective leverage for outside actors during the peace implementation process. For example, a number of scholars find that belligerents in both interstate and civil wars are influenced by "audience costs."[18] Fortna argues that "the international community has a strong effect on belligerents' decisions about war and peace. States worry about international audience costs."[19] Audience costs are the opportunity costs of breaching the agreement, and are higher when international actors are able to monitor implementation closely and respond with rewards or punishment as appropriate. The effectiveness of audience costs is often diminished in UN operations because UN peace operations tend to be multifaceted, with responsibility for overseeing the cease-fire, elections, human rights, and more. Fortna finds in her study of interstate war that "the effects of international audience costs are often limited, either by the UN's desire to maintain neutrality or by great powers turning a blind eye for strategic reasons."[20]

The same often holds true in post–civil war peacekeeping. Typically, leaders of peace operations are forced to prioritize between, say, timely elections or compliance on the cease-fire, and accountability on human rights. Efforts to take a firm stand on one particular issue may face opposition by powerful members of the Security Council, or compromise the mission's ability to carry out another dimension of its mandate. The literature suggests that while third parties *can* affect the behavior of belligerents in positive ways, the terms of their involvement tend to limit their effectiveness in this regard.

In Mozambique, this problem was avoided because of the intensive, direct involvement of bilateral donors in areas that were technically covered by the

UN mandate, and because of the active cooperation of the SRSG with bilateral donors. Nevertheless, the structure and multifaceted nature of the mission gave UNOMOZ itself little effective leverage in some of these areas. The UN had formal authority to oversee demobilization and elections; bilateral donors had the resources, knowledge, and practical capacity to make it work. Bilateral donors supplemented UN funding for elections, party transformation, and disarmament, demobilization, and reintegration (DDR), and played a direct role in monitoring these aspects of the agreement. Even if the UN itself was forced to turn a blind eye to violations of agreements on one or more of these dimensions in exchange for success on another, or to ignore government transgressions to continue to operate, bilateral donors—working with the SRSG's blessing—had the ability to impose direct conditionality, and they did so.

When the parties engaged in excessive foot-dragging on key measures of electoral law during the multiparty conference, donors withdrew funding for the conference facilities. When Renamo pulled out of the elections on the eve of voting, donors promised to investigate Renamo's concerns. When donors feared demobilized soldiers would become a source of instability in the countryside after their severance pay ran out, they designed and funded a program to extend their benefits.[21] None of this would have been possible for the UN peace mission alone, whose multifaceted mandate made it incapable of taking calculated risks in one area, out of fear that this might compromise its role in others. The direct involvement of bilateral actors allowed the international community as a whole to fine-tune its role as a credible guarantor of the peace agreement.

BILATERAL AND MULTILATERAL DONORS IN LIBERIA

The case of Liberia after 2003 provides further evidence for the role played by bilateral actors in supporting a peace process beyond what was possible by the United Nations and other multilateral actors. While the United Nations was formally responsible for implementing certain elements of the peace agreement, it relied heavily on bilateral actors for financial support and political backing. At crucial times during the process, bilateral actors used their long-standing reputation with local actors, their local knowledge, and their ability to make credible threats to enforce key terms of the peace agreement. Bilateral actors also helped reduce the adoption costs of democratic reforms by developing the confidence of Liberian leaders and helping them to overcome domestic political challenges.

The complementary roles of bilateral actors were recognized in the Comprehensive Peace Agreement, which ended the conflict in 2003. The agreement requested the assistance of the United Nations, the African Union, and the Economic Community of West African States (ECOWAS) to implement key provisions such as maintaining security, demobilizing combatants, organizing elections, and strengthening state institutions. The agreement also recognized the role of bilateral actors, and called specifically on Liberia's largest bilateral donor, the United States, to "play a lead role" in organizing the restructuring of the armed forces of Liberia.[22] Even where multilateral actors were designated to play the primary role, bilateral actors provided most of the funding, either by contributing to funds managed by the United Nations or through direct bilateral assistance programs. Bilateral actors also provided logistical and material support to enable multilateral actions. For example, the United States and Nigeria provided the logistics and the personnel to deploy the ECOWAS force that stabilized Monrovia at the end of the conflict, and provided ongoing support to the UNMIL peacekeeping force. Bilateral actors played active roles in organizing many of the core peacebuilding processes, and in providing the political backing, coordination, or moral support when obstacles arose.

Bilateral actors helped to advance implementation of the peace agreement by helping to overcome opposition or disagreements at key moments. Many of the terms of the peace agreement were costly for Liberian political actors, in threatening their political influence or access to resources. The intervention of bilateral actors with promises to provide or withhold funding or other forms of support enabled them to work through these challenges. Even when the UN was nominally in the lead, it often called upon bilateral actors to help. For example, the United Nations Civilian Police Mission (UNPOL) component of UNMIL was designated in the peace agreement to play the lead role in restructuring and training the Liberian National Police.[23] Early on in the process, UN officials ran into opposition to their plan to vet and retrain every police officer, which they saw as essential to building a credible force. The leaders of the main warring factions preferred to reserve places for their fighters, while top police officials opposed being subjected to investigation and retraining. After difficult negotiations, the issue was resolved after the US ambassador conditioned the provision of bilateral resources on the acceptance of the UN's terms for the police restructuring process. US officials also helped reassure individual leaders that they would provide them with political backing and financial assistance to carry out these difficult decisions.

Organizational and political constraints within UNMIL forced it to rely repeatedly on the United States and other bilateral actors to overcome roadblocks in the peacebuilding process. The Liberian case confirms the findings from the literature on the importance of coherent action for effective peacebuilding, as well as the difficulty of the United Nations in this area. Achieving leverage through conditionality requires sufficient unity to achieve coherent goals and positions, as well as the ability to gather information, share it internally, and use it to respond to specific issues. The UN mission in Liberia, which included the UNMIL peacekeeping force along with numerous UN agencies joined by loose coordination structures, had trouble achieving coherent positions and managing information internally. Within UNMIL, short rotations of personnel from different countries, backgrounds, skill sets, and leadership styles often inhibited the development of relationships with Liberian counterparts that are necessary for deeper local knowledge and responsiveness to changing conditions. Especially in areas like police development, which required both detailed knowledge and a coherent, long-term approach, the diversity of backgrounds and operational approaches impeded the development of unified doctrine or policies. When UNMIL did achieve clear positions, it often struggled to enforce them since it could not threaten to withhold assistance or impose audience costs without soliciting the support of its member states.

Instead, the UN often relied on bilateral actors who were involved in these processes on the ground. Bilateral actors were better positioned to develop the credibility, local knowledge, and flexibility necessary to apply conditions to address specific issues. The United States in particular had a long history of close ties with Liberia, starting from Liberia's establishment with US government support in the early 1800s, and continuing with US financial and political backing through the 1980s.[24] The United States had played a central role in negotiating the Comprehensive Peace Agreement. The US ambassador had developed personal credibility by remaining in Monrovia during the worst episodes of fighting in 2003 after many other international officials departed, and by sheltering thousands of Liberians in the US embassy compound. Liberian and US officials communicated frequently and developed close personal relationships. These close connections allowed US officials to develop a deeper understanding of local constraints, and to respond to specific challenges as they arose. In the case of the police, for example, American UNPOL advisers would report obstacles to US embassy officials, who could raise them during their frequent conversations with senior Liberian officials. As the largest bilateral donor, the United States could achieve significant impact by threatening to withhold its resources or backing to individual leaders or programs.

Other bilateral actors also played an important role. For instance, the United Kingdom had developed a reputation for credible intervention in neighboring Sierra Leone, other European countries provided expertise or funding for particular issues, and regional players like Nigeria and Ghana offered crucial pieces of assistance or reassurance to unblock stalled negotiations or help advance reforms. Coordination was most effective when the lead bilateral donor used its dominant role to set the policy agenda and bring other donors along.

The role of bilateral actors in Liberia extended beyond supporting specific reform efforts to serving as credible guarantors of the peacebuilding process. This role was rooted in the political context within Liberia. The leaders of the National Transitional Government of Liberia (NTGL) and the government of Ellen Johnson-Sirleaf, elected in 2005, relied heavily on external backing to manage the political challenges within the country. Within the NTGL, which was made up of representatives from the three main warring factions—the Liberians United for Reconciliation and Democracy, the Movement for Democracy in Liberia, and remnants of the Charles Taylor government—eighteen political parties, and numerous special interest groups, no faction or leader was powerful enough to consolidate its authority. Some, like the members of the former government, were under physical threat and many relied heavily on external support. The Johnson-Sirleaf administration was also politically vulnerable. With a combined total of only twelve out of ninety-four seats in the two houses of the legislature and saddled with over $3.5 billion in national debt, the new president depended on the support of several powerful warlords and faction leaders to maintain a political coalition and bring revenue into the state coffers. Faced with this fragmented political environment, political leaders would depend heavily on external support to bolster their internal political legitimacy and to secure desperately needed funds.

External support helped these relatively weak leaders to overcome the substantial costs of implementing the terms of the peace agreement and adopting reforms. For example, restructuring the police and military challenged the interests of rival politicians from the warring factions who hoped to retain influence over those forces, while governance and anticorruption measures undermined access to financial resources for members of the transitional government and legislature. Leaders confronting opposition to these reforms needed the active support of external actors, both to finance the reforms and to provide political backing— and sometimes physical protection. The willingness of Liberian leaders to adopt these difficult reforms depended in large part on their confidence that external actors would provide the necessary support. The credibility of external actors in the eyes of local leaders was therefore crucial in shaping decisions.

Their relationships with Liberian leaders and their responsiveness to the rapidly changing political environment helped bilateral actors establish their credibility. The role of the US government as dominant funder and sponsor of the peace process—its funding amounted to over $1 billion in the first decade after the conflict—raised its visibility in the process and provided its officials with unlimited access. US embassy officials met frequently with leaders of all of the main factions within the NTGL and used their ability to provide or withhold resources and political support to secure their cooperation on a wide range of issues, from disarmament and security-sector reform to elections and governance. During her first term as president, Johnson-Sirleaf visited the White House five times and addressed a joint session of the US Congress. Frequent communication facilitated trust among Liberian and US officials, and enabled US officials to respond to changing conditions, and to promise assistance or threaten to withhold it when obstacles arose. The UNMIL mission, meanwhile, was hampered by a short-term mandate, changing leadership and constraints imposed by member states, which undermined its credibility as a long-term partner. In some areas where the US and bilateral actors were less involved in taking an active role, Liberian leaders were less able to rely on their support, and the implementation of reforms suffered as a result.

The most sensitive areas of peacebuilding were handled through the active intervention of bilateral actors. For example, the United States took the lead on restructuring the military, committing over $250 million to the process in the first five years.[25] After a series of negotiations, US and Liberian officials signed a bilateral agreement that formalized a US commitment to fund and Liberian agreement to restructure the force. The commitment of US financial and political support enabled Liberian leaders to make politically controversial decisions, including disbanding the entire armed forces and starting a new recruitment from scratch.[26] The United States funded and managed a comprehensive vetting and recruitment process that involved teams of investigators deployed around the country to overcome informational constraints, and enforced strict recruitment standards. The involvement of US officials in recruitment decisions shielded Liberian officials from pressure by political factions to secure places for their supporters in the new force. On the other hand, in the absence of meaningful involvement by multilateral actors, the dominant role of the United States has engendered criticism and undermined the legitimacy of the reforms among some segments of Liberian society.[27]

Similarly, US and European officials were instrumental in creating the Governance and Economic Management Assistance Programme. The program aimed to reduce rampant corruption by placing foreign financial experts within Liberian government agencies with the authority to approve or disapprove expenditures. Viewed as a threat to Liberia's sovereignty, and opposed by factions that were benefitting from looting government resources, the plan was nonetheless adopted by NTGL Chairman Gyude Bryant after concerted pressure by bilateral donors. The United States, European Union, and several bilateral donors threatened to withhold the considerable funds they had promised for reconstruction and security-sector reform, and to hold Bryant personally responsible for the loss of outside funding.[28] In this case, multilateral support from ECOWAS and the UN, and technical oversight by the World Bank and the IMF, provided broader legitimacy for the program.

The Liberian case thus reveals the complementary roles played by multilateral and bilateral actors in the peacebuilding process. The presence of multilateral peacekeeping forces organized by the United Nations, ECOWAS, and the African Union were essential to building confidence among previously warring factions, providing the legitimacy for external involvement, and mobilizing personnel and resources. Bilateral actors were better placed than the United Nations to help Liberian elites overcome the adoption costs of reform based on their long-standing relationship, local knowledge, flexibility, and responsiveness to changing conditions. In turn, the broad legitimacy of the UN and other multilateral actors enabled bilateral actors to act forcefully and unequivocally. While peacebuilders were not successful in all areas of peacebuilding in Liberia, in the many successful instances, bilateral and multilateral actors acted in complementary roles.

RWANDA

Rwanda is a case with strong incumbent domestic political leaders facing a weak and fragmented opposition. Our theory predicts that such leaders will be less likely to embrace reforms that might undermine their physical, economic, or political security. In addition, several factors weakened the potential for donor leverage. Rwanda revised its constitution to accommodate multiparty politics in 1991, and for some observers the democratization process and the outbreak of civil war are inextricably linked. Multiple attempts to reach a negotiated peace in 1992 and 1993 included provision for the formation of a unity government, and democracy was enshrined in the August 1993 Arusha Accords. A UN observation mission (UNAMIR) was established in October 1993. However, after renewed fighting and the genocide that ensued between April and June 1994, UNAMIR was dramatically downsized. Though attempts were made to bolster the UN force with UNAMIR II in May 1994, the only real international muscle deployed after the onset of genocide came in the form of Operation Turquoise, a French-led mission authorized by the UN with a Chapter VII mandate, which began in June 1994. The fighting ended in military victory for the Rwandan Patriotic Front (RPF).[29] There was no new ceasefire or peace agreement, though a broad-based national unity government was installed in July 1994.

Donors with the longest presence in Rwanda before the war, such as France, enjoyed little influence with the new regime. France's ties with the Habyarimana regime, which the RPF replaced, as well as the RPF's historic ties to anglophone Africa, undermined francophone influence. The United

States and the UK have since forged strong political and security ties with the RPF government, but these ties have yielded comparatively little influence over the regime in the wake of the genocide. Compared to Mozambique, where relatively strong leaders faced both a fear that resources would be withdrawn for noncooperation and an opposition with the potential to spoil the peace settlement, the case of Rwanda highlights the limits of external leverage, especially where domestic opposition to the regime is weak. In Rwanda, the costs to domestic political actors of adopting democracy were relatively high, while the costs of failing to do so were low. Following the 1994 genocide, the government faced few political opponents or other veto players within Rwanda. Instead, it faced armed extremists and political opponents based outside the country. The former in particular helped the government to limit democratic and human rights reform without risking loss of external support.

Though Rwanda's leaders were heavily dependent on external aid and diplomatic support, they were able to resist external pressure for reform without losing support. Victory on the battlefield gave the Rwandan Patriotic Front little incentive to compromise, and the genocide gave credence to that government's claims that democratization could endanger the country's security. Moreover, the international community's failure to act effectively in the face of the genocide undermined the credibility of bilateral actors as well as the UN.[30] This included those with long-standing relationships in the country. The government effectively resisted donor pressures to democratize, publicly rebuking donors who pushed too hard for political reform.[31] Aid flows were not significantly affected by this resistance—in short, bilateral donors failed to apply conditionality, despite their experience with the country and its leaders that might have permitted them to do so effectively.

Bilateral donors had begun pressing for democratic reforms in Rwanda as early as 1990. According to Uvin, the United States played a leading role in this push, reducing aid in 1992 in the face of human rights violations.[32] However, US humanitarian aid increased the next year. In 1993, the United States and several European donors threatened to cut aid in response to a negative UN human rights report, but did not in fact reduce aid allocations. According to some observers, donors feared that exerting too much pressure would endanger the Arusha peace agreement. After the genocide, France, Belgium, Switzerland, and Germany sought to pressure the government on refugee return and transitional justice. Though the government paid lip service to these goals, progress was limited. As Hayman points out, "As far as the RPF was concerned, by its failure to prevent or stop the genocide and its provision of aid to camps where the guilty were fed alongside the innocent—in quantities which dwarfed aid to Rwanda itself—the international community had lost its 'right to criticize' the new regime."[33]

Conditionality was ineffective both because donors did not consistently apply it, and because domestic political leaders had the necessary political and economic resources to resist external pressure related to both the timing and the content of postconflict reforms. Hayman notes that "since 1994, external actors have been constrained by collective guilt over the genocide which limits their leverage over the regime, and by differences amongst them in terms of strategic and developmental objectives as well as their individual relations with the new regime."[34] Moreover, there is a history of division among donor countries in their attitude toward the government of Rwanda. During the first five years after the conflict, donors were almost divided into two opposing camps: those who were positive about the new regime (often new donors who had a limited history of bilateral relations with the country, such as the Netherlands, Sweden, and the UK) and those who were negative about the new regime (those with longer histories in the country, including ties to the former regime, such as France and Belgium). Positions became less polarized as time passed, but aid in the early years after the conflict was affected by the different stances of donors. The government was able to rely on certain friends, and could afford to ignore demands made by other donors.[35]

For example, the run-up to Rwanda's 2003 legislative and presidential elections, the first since the genocide, saw the first real application of conditions to aid directly related to democracy. A clampdown on opposition parties and voices, as well as human rights abuses, led several donors to withhold or threaten to withhold aid, including the European Commission, the United Kingdom, and the Netherlands. The UK halted aid to the media sector when the government did not liberalize the airwaves, and the Netherlands did not disburse their aid to the elections; the European Commission released the money but only after the elections had taken place. The action taken by the Netherlands was ultimately undermined by other donors' releasing funds and coming out in support of the government.

As Hayman points out, since 1994 "RPF has controlled political space and only allowed a gradual, and controlled, democratic process to develop on their terms and in such a way as to not threaten their power or national stability and security."[36]

CONCLUSION

Peacebuilding after civil war involves deeply political interactions among domestic and external actors. In deciding how to approach the terms of the postwar settlement, domestic leaders weigh the costs and benefits of specific provisions of the agreement, while external actors seek to alter these costs and benefits to promote particular outcomes. The empirical evidence presented here suggests that the impact of external aid on peacebuilding outcomes is mediated by the relationships between donors and domestic elites, and the degree to which donors are able to respond to political realities within the country to mitigate the costs of adopting reforms.

This chapter suggests two generalizable conclusions. First, leverage from aid depends on the *relationships* that aid provision creates over time among donors who fund and/or implement key aspects of peacebuilding and local actors whose support is crucial for their implementation. The relationships that exist between donors and domestic political actors at the onset of the intervention are important because they affect mutual confidence between peacebuilders and domestic political actors, and hence add to or subtract from the credibility of donors as external guarantors. These relationships evolve in response to the political conditions within the postconflict country, as changing political relationships affect domestic actors' receptiveness to external support.

Second, aid increases leverage where it is structured in such a way that it enables donors to respond flexibly to unforeseen challenges in the peace process, and it is most effective when individual donors are able to tie their own contributions to actions required of domestic political actors to move the peacebuilding process forward. Donors with resources and the organizational wherewithal to make timely interventions using those resources have more leverage than those who do not. Aid is *not* effective in increasing leverage or mitigating the adoption costs of democracy when donors are unable or unwilling to apply conditionality; when they lack a clear commitment to democracy over other concerns; when they lack the coherence necessary to act decisively and predictably; and when they lack the local knowledge and connections necessary to take advantage of opportunities to gain leverage.

We used these insights to argue that bilateral donors may enjoy structural advantages over UN missions in implementing postconflict political and other institutional reform. In addition, a comparison of these three cases allows us to refine the theory as initially advanced. First, we asserted that bilateral actors can serve as more credible guarantors of postconflict political settlements. The structural factors that enhance their coherence, flexibility, and responsiveness relative to multilateral actors enable them to more credibly lower the adoption costs of these settlements for domestic political actors. We found that the most effective instances of peacebuilding arise when bilateral actors complement multilateral assistance through credible and flexible commitments of support. Second, bilateral actors are not always effective in this role. Their ability to lower the relative cost of adopting particular aspects of the peace agreements depends not only on the resources and modalities of intervention, but also on domestic political networks and the balance of power among these actors. We asserted at the outset of this chapter that domestic political networks were important because they affect adoption costs and the value of external assistance. Weaker leaders are more likely to accept outside help to bolster their domestic positions, while leaders who are already strong may have less to gain from external support, and more to lose from the establishment of democratic political institutions, implementation of comprehensive security sector reform, or anticorruption efforts. The leverage of even the most credible bilateral actors depends on the extent to which their assistance helps leaders overcome the domestic political challenges that raise the costs of accepting such reforms.

In Liberia, weak leaders accepted reforms because external support lowered their adoption costs by providing politically useful funding, legitimacy, and information that helped overcome domestic political challenges. Although the UN was in the lead on many aspects of peacebuilding, it often turned to the United States and other bilateral actors to reinforce its stance with credible commitments of support or threats to withhold it. On the other hand, bilateral actors benefited from the broader legitimacy provided by the UN and ECOWAS.

In Mozambique, incumbents in power at the onset of peace were by far the stronger party in terms of their ability to make the transition to competitive politics compared to Renamo. However, they were dependent on the international community for the resources necessary for postconflict economic rehabilitation, and they used their cooperation in the peace process to leverage more advantageous terms of support from bilateral donors and multilateral institutions like the World Bank. Despite the political advantages of the ruling party, the opposition Renamo was a potential spoiler that needed, and received, vital assurances and resources from major bilateral donors. The UN alone would have been unable to provide such guarantees for either party.

Finally, in Rwanda strong incumbents faced little domestic opposition after the war and genocide there. Instead, the government faced a credible security threat in the form of cross-border attacks by opposition forces that had gained refuge in eastern Democratic Republic of the Congo. These leaders had little need of external support to overcome domestic challenges, and on sensitive issues bilateral donors were unwilling to press hard to overcome the resistance of incumbents.

Thus in two of our three cases, Mozambique and Liberia, the ability of bilateral actors to credibly commit to provide or withhold resources, to develop trust with local actors, and to respond flexibly to their specific needs as determined by the context was crucial in ensuring that their assistance overcame local adoption costs. Multilateral actors did not have the same abilities, although they provided broader legitimacy that bilateral actors often lack. In Rwanda, even those abilities were not sufficient due to the domestic context.

The contribution of external actors to peacebuilding processes is far more complex—and far more political—than often described. Although external actors often help improve stability and support democratic reforms in fulfillment of peace agreements, their impact depends on political relationships both within and outside the recipient country. In this chapter, we have explored several characteristics of external actors and domestic politics that shape these relationships. How donors succeed in understanding and managing these dynamics is crucial to their impact on the political dimensions of peacebuilding.

NOTES

1. Caroline Hartzell and Matthew Hoddie, "Institutionalizing Peace: Power Sharing and Post–Civil War Conflict Management," *American Journal of Political Science* 47 (2003): 318–322.

2. Eva Bertram, "Reinventing Governments: The Promise and Perils of UN Peace Building," *Journal of Conflict Resolution* 39, no. 3 (1995).

3. I. William Zartman, *Elusive Peace: Negotiating an End to Civil Wars* (Washington, DC: Brookings Institution, 1995), p. 339.

4. Hartzell and Hoddie, "Institutionalizing Peace."

5. Virginia Page Fortna, *Does Peacekeeping Work? Shaping Belligerents' Choices After Civil War,* (Princeton, NJ: Princeton University Press, 2008), p. 86. See also Michael Doyle and Nicholas Sambanis, eds., *Making War and Building Peace: United Nations Peace Operations* (Princeton, NJ: Princeton University Press, 2006), p. 55.

6. Fortna, *Does Peacekeeping Work?*

7. Lise Morjé Howard, *UN Peacekeeping in Civil Wars* (Cambridge: Cambridge University Press, 2007). Christoph Zuercher and Jens Narten, "Peacebuilding Is Interaction: Explaining the Outcomes of Postwar Democratic Transitions," paper presented at APSA Annual Meeting in Toronto, Canada, 2009; Michael Barnett and Christoph Zuercher, "The Peacebuilder's Contract: How External Statebuilding Reinforces Weak Statehood," in *The Dilemmas of Statebuilding: Confronting the Contradictions of Postwar Peace Operations,* ed. Roland Paris and Timothy D. Sisk (London: Routledge, 2008).

8. Howard, *UN Peacekeeping in Civil Wars,* and Roland Paris, *At War's End: Building Peace After Civil Conflict* (Cambridge: Cambridge University Press, 2004).

9. Diana Cammack et al., "Donors and the 'Fragile States' Agenda: A Survey of Current Thinking and Practice," report submitted to the Japan International Cooperation Agency, March 2006.

10. Tetsuro Ijo, "Cooperation, Coordination, and Complementarity in International Peacemaking: The Tajikistan Experience," *International Peacekeeping* 12, no. 2 (Summer 2005): 189–204.

11. Barbara F. Walter, "Designing Transitions from Civil War: Demobilization, Democratization, and Commitments to Peace," *International Security* 24 (1999): 127–155.

12. Christoph Zürcher and Carrie Manning et al., *Costly Democracy: Peacebuilding and Democratization after War* (Stanford, CA: Stanford University Press, 2012).

13. For a full discussion of these effects in the Mozambique case, see Carrie Manning and Monica Malbrough, "Bilateral Donors and Aid Conditionality in Post-Conflict Peacebuilding: The Case of Mozambique," *Journal of Modern African Studies* (2010): 143–169.

14. Louis-Alexandre Berg, "Local Networks and the Limits of External Influence in Post-Conflict Security Sector Reform," paper presented at the 2012 Annual Meeting of the International Studies Association. This paper is part of a larger study on the impact of external assistance on post-conflict institution-building, focusing on Bosnia and Herzegovina, Liberia, Sierra Leone, and Timor-Leste.

15. This section draws on Manning and Malbrough, "Bilateral Donors and Aid Conditionality."

16. G. Frerks, *The Use of Peace Conditionality in Conflict and Post-Conflict Settings: A Conceptual Framework and a Checklist* (The Hague: Netherlands Institute of International Relations, 2006), p. 1.

17. N. Ball and S. Barnes, "Mozambique," in *Good Intentions: Pledges of Aid for Post-conflict Recovery,* ed. Shepard Forman and Stewart Patrick (Boulder, CO: Lynne Rienner, 2000), 159–203.

18. Doyle and Sambanis, *Making War and Building Peace*; Fortna, *Does Peacekeeping Work?*; Walter, "Designing Transitions from Civil War."

19. Fortna, *Does Peacekeeping Work?*, p. 213.

20. Ibid., p. 205.

21. Carrie Manning, *The Politics of Peace: Post-Conflict Democratization in Mozambique* (Westport, CT: Praeger, 2002).

22. Comprehensive Peace Agreement between the government of Liberia, the Liberians United for Reconciliation and Democracy, the Movement for Democracy in Liberia, and the Political Parties, Accra, Ghana, August 18, 2003, Article VII.

23. Berg, "Local Networks and the Limits of External Influence."

24. See Jeremy I. Levitt, *The Evolution of Deadly Conflict in Liberia* (Durham, NC: Carolina Academic Press, 2005), and Amos Sawyer, *Beyond Plunder: Toward Democratic Governance in Liberia* (Boulder, CO: Lynne Rienner, 2005).

25. For an overview of the Security Sector Reform Program, see Mark Malan, *Security Sector Reform in Liberia: Mixed Results from Humble Beginnings,* Strategic Studies Institute, US Army War College, March 2008.

26. Arrangement Between the Government of the United States of America and the National Transitional Government of Liberia Concerning Security Sector Reform in the Republic of Liberia, May 17, 2005.

27. Thomas Jaye, "Liberia: Parliamentary Oversight and Lessons Learned from Internationalized Security Sector Reform," Center on International Cooperation, New York University, available at www.cic.nyu.edu/peacebuilding/docs/Liberia_SSR.pdf, accessed on August 6, 2012.

28. Renata Dwan and Laura Bailey, "Liberia's Governance and Economic Management Assistance Program: A Joint Review by the Department of Peacekeeping Operations' Peacekeeping Best Practices Section and the World Bank's Fragile States Group," May 2006.

29. Chapter VII empowers the UN Security Council to take what actions may be needed to restore international peace and security in any given situation, including the use of force.

30. Rachel Hayman, "External Democracy Promotion in Post-Conflict Zones: Evidence from Case Studies: Rwanda," Free University Berlin, 2009. Available at http://aix1.uottawa.ca/~czurcher/czurcher/Transitions_files/Final%20Report%20Rwanda.pdf.

31. Ibid.

32. See, for example, Peter Uvin, *Aiding Violence: The Development Enterprise in Rwanda* (Bloomfield, CT: Kumarian Press, 1998).

33. Hayman, "External Democracy Promotion in Post-Conflict Zones," p. 39.

34. Ibid., p. 41.

35. Hayman, "External Democracy Promotion in Post-Conflict Zones."

36. Ibid., p. 43.

eleven

Sudan

A Fragile "Peace"

Princeton N. Lyman[1]

A year after the successful secession of South Sudan from Sudan, a much-heralded landmark in Sudan's troubled history, the peace between the two countries is fragile. At times over the past year, the two have clashed along the border and veered close to a return to major war. Why that has happened provides a lesson in the limitations of diplomacy and indeed of practicality amid an atmosphere of lingering anger—the lingering memories of societies too long at war.

The more than twenty years of the most recent civil war in Sudan ended in 2005 with the Comprehensive Peace Agreement (CPA). It provided for a six-year period of a government of national unity, a referendum in the South in 2011 to decide on continuing unity or independence, and if independence was chosen, a six-month period to prepare for separation. The "comprehensive" in the CPA was just that: the agreement was intended to accomplish much more than to end the war. It was supposed to bring about a political transformation in both North and South, that is, a broadening of political participation from the domination of one party in each part of the country. In the event of independence of the South, it provided a quite detailed road map for adjustment of relations between the two states, covering borders, the integrated oil sector, citizenship, assets and liabilities, aeronautical arrangements, trade, a referendum to determine the status of the disputed region of Abyei, and nearly every other aspect of relations between the two bordering countries. Thirteen countries and international organizations signed as witnesses promising a continuing international role. In 2010, to facilitate the process, the African Union created a High Level Implementation Panel (AUHIP), headed by former South African president Thabo Mbeki, to oversee the negotiations.

With all that planned preparation, in 2012 none of the major issues between them had yet been resolved. Indeed, so contentious were the negotiations over the oil sector they shared that earlier in the year South Sudan stopped all its production, risking its own economic survival as well as provoking even further conflict with Sudan. Almost no institutions exist between the two countries. The border is closed. Trade is blocked or illegal. Citizenship or residency rights of southerners in the North and northerners in the South are uncertain at best. The Abyei referendum never took place and the region was occupied by Sudan troops in 2011, demanding months of intense international effort to reverse it. There is no relationship between the two central banks, though currency and foreign exchange issues would demand such. In fact, almost any meeting between the two governments comes about when the AUHIP convokes one, and then in Ethiopia rather than in one of the two countries. Only two formal agreements of any significance have been signed between Sudan and South Sudan since the latter's independence. One is to reverse Sudan's military takeover and provide for Sudan and South Sudan jointly to manage Abyei until its status is resolved. The other is a complex but promising arrangement for border monitoring and security. Yet neither has been perfectly implemented. Abyei and the border remain dangerously contentious matters.

The political transformation the CPA promised also failed to happen. The culmination of that transformation was to be the elections in both North and South Sudan in 2010. Instead, the elections reinforced the existing incumbent control in both areas: the National Congress Party (NCP) in the North and the Sudan People's Liberation Movement (SPLM) in the South. This left the parties that had fought the war for more than a decade—the NCP came to power in 1989—to make the peace. This has a major impact on the ways in which the various issues are addressed, or rather not addressed.

It is not that international attention has flagged. In addition to the intensive efforts of the AUHIP, the UN Security Council regularly addresses the situation. A UN peacekeeping mission existed to assist the CPA through South Sudan's independence in July 2011. Three UN peacekeeping missions continue to operate: one in Sudan's Darfur region, UNAMID (joint UN–African Union); one in South Sudan, UNMISS; and one in Abyei, UNISFA. The United States has had a presidential envoy for Sudan (and now Sudan and South Sudan) since 2003. Many other countries, in addition to the EU and the UN—the UK, Norway, China, Russia, France, Sweden, India, South Africa, and others—have special envoys for Sudan/South Sudan. The Intergovernmental Authority for

Development, an East African organization, played a critical role in negotiating the CPA and continues to focus on the situation. Neighboring countries, especially Ethiopia, Kenya, Egypt, and Uganda, regularly engage on the situation.

International attention, however, has not focused only on the CPA. The rebellion in the Sudan region of Darfur that began in 2003 resulted in charges of war crimes and genocide against the Khartoum government. The International Criminal Court (ICC) has issued indictments on those charges against the president, the minister of defense, and the governor of the state of Southern Kordofan in Sudan. This has complicated the diplomacy around the CPA. The United States and most Western European governments will not have direct dealings with those indicted. In practice this means no direct contact with the president, who is the most important decision maker in Sudan, or with the influential minister of defense. In 2011, fighting broke out in the two Sudan states of Southern Kordofan and Blue Nile. Focus on that conflict, including a looming humanitarian disaster, has not only occupied much of the attention of the international community but also has further poisoned the relationship between Sudan and South Sudan. In April 2012, that conflict spilled over into the most serious border clashes between Sudan and South Sudan since 2005 and the most serious threat since then of a return to all-out war.

This chapter does not seek to analyze all these issues individually. Rather, it looks at why the CPA failed to lead to a more peaceful and cooperative outcome between the two states and how international involvement has both succeeded and failed to play an effective mediating role.

PUTTING OFF THE ISSUES

Virtually every analyst of the CPA had concluded that there were several issues that had to be resolved if there were to be a successful referendum in the South in January 2011, and surely if there were to be peaceful independence of South Sudan on July 9 of that year. An analysis by the United States Institute of Peace listed dozens of such issues, among which six or more were listed as critical, including oil, borders, and Abyei. Oil was considered critical because at independence South Sudan acquired 70 percent of the once–single country's oil production, but Sudan possessed the export facilities, including the pipelines leading to Port Sudan. Issues in the oil sector included ownership of assets, assistance to Sudan to absorb the loss of so much income, and commercial fees for South Sudan's exports. As one adviser to the AUHIP predicted as the negotiations dragged on, "Whatever else, by July 10, 2011, there has to be an agreement because the day after independence the oil has to continue to flow." Abyei was considered critical to resolve because it was a deeply emotional as well as political issue between the two countries and had been one of the most difficult to address in the CPA. Without resolution, the likelihood of resumed conflict loomed large. Agreement on borders was deemed critical because there were several disputed areas along the border, the need existed to protect the rights of migrating groups that traditionally crossed into the South during the rainy season, and arrangements were needed to facilitate trade on which both economies depend. None of these matters, experts argued, could be left to chance once South Sudan became independent. Or so everyone thought.

On July 9, 2011, with none of these matters resolved, South Sudan became independent, peacefully. Sudan's President Omar al-Bashir attended the ceremony, seated side by side with South Sudan President Salva Kiir, and spoke of harmonious relations between the two states in the future. On July 10 the oil did indeed continue to flow. But negotiations dragged on.

For those who had witnessed, participated, or kibitzed these negotiations over the past several years leading up to July 9 and even for a time thereafter, the process was slow, meandering, without urgency on the part of the parties or often without sufficient senior-level political attention. Watching the labyrinth of cluster groups, sub-cluster groups, lead panels, and other mechanisms established to address the issues over which the AUHIP labored, one joked that the one item on which the meetings could agree was a motion to adjourn, often offered within the first hour. Why should that have been so? Here are a few reasons:

- Both parties, ironically, felt that they would be in a more advantageous bargaining position after the referendum or even more so after South Sudan's independence. South Sudanese felt that once they gained their independence, Sudan would have to treat the South with more respect and recognize the new country's bargaining power. After July 9 in particular, South Sudan would own 70 percent of the oil, would have the right to defend its borders, would have all the other rights of an independent nation, and would have full international recognition and backing. However, Sudan— the North—believed that the responsibilities of independence, the ethnic fissures, the lack of skills, and the desperately poor economy in the South would quickly weaken, perhaps even overwhelm the SPLM, forcing it to rapid and more accommodating agreements. Frequently Sudan officials would tell Western diplomats, perceived to be the backers of southern independence, "You will regret this. You will soon see a failed state in the South."
- Before the referendum of January 9, when the South voted for separation, the negotiations had a stilted character. They had perforce to examine each issue on the basis of two possible outcomes, continued unity and southern independence. As southerners' preference for independence became ever clearer, while the Sudan government's advocacy of unity remained a politi-

cal tenet, the negotiations often only went through the motions until this anomaly could be set aside.

- There was a lack of comparable skills on each side, particularly in the more technical areas. This was demonstrable in the early oil negotiations, when the North's long experience and management capability were superior to those in the South. This led some of the AUHIP's technical advisers at the beginning to advocate continuing largely northern management structures of the sector for some time after independence, a prospect anathema to the South. Consequently, until the South gradually built up both indigenous and contractual expertise—not until well into 2011—there was a lot of political posturing but little progress in these talks.

- The two sides had fundamentally different negotiating strategies. South Sudan looked toward an eventual "grand bargain" in which it would trade concessions on oil and debt relief, and other things vital to Sudan, for obtaining Sudan's full transfer of Abyei to the South and acceptance of international arbitration of the several border disputes. For this reason, South Sudan negotiators insisted at every stage of the negotiations, when even the slightest of agreements was at hand, that "nothing is agreed until everything is agreed." Sudan, on the other hand, refused to acknowledge a trade-off of "oil for Abyei" or, for that matter, border agreements, and thus was less wedded to a grand bargain. It had political interests in Abyei, in particular its relations with the migrating Misseriya tribes, which weighed at least equal to its need for an oil agreement. Moreover, it had other priorities, particularly an agreement on debt relief, which Sudan saw as a test of South Sudan's commitment to the economic viability of both states and wanted South Sudan (and the Western nations) committed to it early and definitively. This difference in approach also reflected each side's appraisal of the other's strength. South Sudan believed that oil was at the center of Sudan's interests and Sudan would have to bargain away Abyei and other matters to get what it needed in that sector. Sudan felt that South Sudan was so dependent on oil for its own budget and weak in so many other areas, and indeed that it could be bullied or intimidated by force, that South Sudan would have to give in on oil and other matters, even Abyei, for its own survival.

- The role of the AUHIP has never been entirely clear. Note the title: Implementation Panel. While that could refer to implementing the CPA, with all that is encompassed in negotiation and mediation, it also implied there were or would be agreements by the parties under the CPA to be implemented. In fact, the panel has vacillated between being more a facilitator of negotiation than a mediator. There is a fundamental difference. The AUHIP has done extraordinary work as a facilitator of the negotiations, by shaping, managing, pushing forward, and indeed laying out agendas and forward-looking ideas

242 PRINCETON N. LYMAN

to the parties. Indeed without it there would have been almost no negotiations. But the panel has shied away from putting definitive (not multiple) recommendations on the table for the most contentious issues, as a mediator. This could be a realistic assessment of its political ability to drive the parties to accept such definitive outcomes. It also reflects President Mbeki's view, with which it is hard to disagree in principle, that it is the responsibility of the two states to resolve these issues and in particular that of the two presidents to resolve and compromise the most contentious ones. The AUHIP, in his view, must therefore be a facilitator, not a mediator. Nevertheless, as the parties fail to rise to this level of responsibility and in particular the two presidents fail, despite promises to the contrary, to resolve issues on which the two sides' negotiators are hopelessly divided, such as Abyei, criticism has arisen as to whether the panel has clung too long to this more modest role.

THE CHANGING INTERNATIONAL ROLE

People long familiar with the history of the CPA, and all the preceding agreements and processes that led up to it, often wax nostalgic for the mediation in those days. The process was long and arduous, which sometimes nostalgia forgets. But there was a forceful, broadly based international role that played both a facilitative and a mediating role in that process. The international oversight came from the Intergovernmental Authority for Development, the association of East African states. Kenya was the lead nation in the effort, having long been affected, and indirectly involved in the war through refugees coming across the border, and humanitarian programs like Operation Lifeline Sudan operating from its territory. All the East African states were, however, affected or involved one way or the other, as the war went on for so long. Kenya provided the chief negotiator, General Lazarus Sumbweiywo, a forceful, no-nonsense figure. There was also a Friends Group of other nations that played active political and supportive roles. For example, the Troika—the United States, the UK, and Norway—was especially active in both providing input and ideas and bringing political pressure to bear on the parties. In contrast to the protracted Abyei negotiations of today, people look back on US envoy John Danforth, who in 2005 put down a compromise protocol on Abyei on a virtually take-it-or-leave-it basis to break that major logjam in the CPA.

But the international scene is different today. The most important "game changer" was the outbreak of conflict in Sudan's province of Darfur in 2003 just as the CPA was moving toward final agreement. Darfur took over much of the international attention as charges of genocide, war crimes, and other depredations were laid against the government of Sudan. As the conflict continued, much of the international community's focus was on stopping the attacks on the rebels but in particular on helping civilians, gaining humanitarian access to the more than 2 million displaced people and to refugees, and negotiating the deployment of UNAMID. The same intensity of international effort on the CPA as in its early days did not return until mid-2010, when first the elections and then the January 9 referendum appeared in jeopardy.

But Darfur did more than shift international attention. It changed the relations between the West and the Sudanese government. In the negotiation leading up to the CPA, as Sudan officials are always ready to remind us, promises were made to the government that if it signed the CPA and fulfilled its conditions, rewards would flow. Of particular importance was the expectation that the United States would lift Sudan from the list of states sponsoring terrorism (SST). This would bring Sudan much more into the international community's orbit with economic opportunities and other benefits to follow. But ever since 2004, Darfur has become a permanent obstacle to providing Sudan with most if any such rewards. Not only did the US administration harden its stance, formally accusing the government of genocide in Darfur, but Congress also enacted numerous sanctions in several pieces of legislation, almost all linked to resolving the Darfur conflict. Those legislated sanctions remain today. They tie the United States' hands, preventing it from providing Sudan debt relief, development aid bilaterally, as they do also from the World Bank or the IMF. They prohibit American investment in Sudan and most trade with the United States; and they target Sudan's financial dealings and other operations. Most Western European governments have followed suit, if not in quite the same extensive way. Of special effect on any mediating role, the United States no longer will deal directly with Sudan's head of state and regularly demarches any state that invites him to visit instead, to honor the ICC indictment. Sanctions and isolation from the head of state diminishes the potential for direct mediation and the ways in which the United States can with confidence promise incentives and rewards to Sudan.

In 2010, the Obama administration did move to link at least the decision on SST more to implementation of the CPA than Darfur and similarly to lift some of the sanctions. In a letter to Senator John Kerry in November 2010, which the senator delivered to the Sudanese government, President Barack Obama offered, of course conditional on Sudan's meeting the terrorism conditions in the law, to lift the country's SST designation if by July 9 the result of the January referendum was recognized and the major CPA issues resolved. Darfur was not omitted in the letter, but the focus was on implementing the CPA. Once the January 9 referendum took place and was recognized by Khartoum, Obama began the six-month process under the law to determine whether Sudan was continuing to sponsor international terrorism. Some licenses were also approved for agricultural equipment, and the United States supported technical work by the World Bank on Sudan's debt problems that could lead to major debt relief. Alas, the timeline in the letter was linked to the expectation that the major CPA issues would have to be resolved by July 9, 2011. As described above, neither party was so committed to that timeline. While the administration was relatively flexible in extending the deadline, the lack of resolution of those issues still today has made that offer moot. As described below, President Obama made another offer on SST in November 2011.

A NEW POISON: CONFLICT IN THE TWO AREAS

Perhaps ever cursed, in 2011 Sudan experienced another crisis that has overtaken and deeply affected full implementation of the outstanding CPA issues and the prospects for normalization of relations with much of the international community. In Sudan's civil war significant numbers of people from the states of Southern Kordofan and Blue Nile (known as the Two Areas) fought alongside the SPLM of the South to claim their own political rights. Two divisions of the SPLM's army—the SPLA—were from those states, and much of the fighting occurred there. The CPA provided that those states remain inside Sudan, not go to South Sudan, but provided for a process of "popular consultation," which would allow the people in those states to bring their political grievances and demands to the central government, the process to be completed by July 9, 2011. The SPLA divisions from the Two Areas were supposed to be disarmed and integrated with the Sudan military and police, but it was largely if tacitly expected (though with protests from the Khartoum government) that this would take place in the context of the popular consultation process. Elections were to take place in each state before the popular consultations got fully under way. In Blue Nile an SPLM (after July 9, 2011, SPLM-N)[2] leader was elected governor and the popular consultations did begin. But the election in Southern Kordofan did not take place until May 2011, already making it impossible to meet the timeline for popular consultations there. Moreover, the election was hotly contested and when the NCP candidate was declared the winner, the SPLM candidate, a former SPLA general, refused to recognize the results and took refuge in the Nuba Mountains with his troops.

Clashes took place shortly afterward and the Sudanese government decided to disarm the two divisions by force. The result was a new full-scale rebellion. It spread quickly to Blue Nile, where the Sudanese government decided to sack the SPLM-N governor, who then also took command of rebel forces in that state. In June the AUHIP mediated an agreement that would have stopped the fighting and provided for parallel talks on political and security matters between the Sudanese government and the SPLM-N, but the agreement was aborted when President Bashir repudiated it. A subsequent attempt by Ethiopian Prime Minister Meles Zenawi to bring the two sides together similarly failed.

Like most conflicts in Sudan, in this new conflict it is not only the conflict itself that becomes of concern, but also the human rights violations that go with it. The Sudanese government has long relied on its airpower superiority through bombing and the use of auxiliary militia—the Popular Defense Forces—as principal methods for fighting its internal wars. The bombing has targeted civilians as much as or more than military targets (exacerbated because of the notorious inaccuracy of its Antonov bomber fleet, from which bombs are pushed out of its bay). The Popular Defense Forces are often associated with looting, raping, executions, and other human rights violations. Government intelligence officials and regular army members have also been accused of such crimes. Finally, by the Sudanese government's isolating the Two Areas from humanitarian assistance and displacing large numbers of people, charges of ethnic cleansing and genocide have arisen in this conflict, as they did in Darfur, though no formal investigations or charges have taken place. Thus this conflict has created a new rift with the international community that grows stronger each day as reports of looming starvation reach the outside world. Every effort to negotiate humanitarian access, including a joint proposal by the UN, African Union, and the League of Arab States—designed to address the government's suspicion of Western governments and NGOs—failed to obtain government approval.

To end this conflict before it had huge political and humanitarian consequences, President Obama made another offer to Sudan in November 2011. Recognizing that the provisions of the Kerry letter were overtaken by time and events, President Obama approved a new offer on SST. It would relate specifically and solely to ending the conflict in the Two Areas. If the government of Sudan would end the bombing in the Two Areas, open them up to humanitarian access, and begin political talks with the SPLM-N as a recognized political party, and assuming Sudan continued to abstain from sponsoring terrorism, the president would inform Congress of his intention to lift Sudan from the SST list. Under the law, Congress has forty-five days to respond to the president on the matter. The offer was relayed to Sudan by Deputy National Security Adviser Dennis McDonough and this author, with a deadline set for the end of December that year, to take into account the congressional calendar as well as the urgency of the situation. The government of Sudan did not formally respond, but made clear in the next several weeks that it was pursuing a military strategy and was not prepared to take up any of the provisions of the offer.

The conflict in the Two Areas thus continued and steadily poisoned the relations between Sudan and South Sudan. Sudan has argued from the beginning that it is South Sudan's support to the SPLA-N in the Two Areas that fuels the conflict. Moreover, it lays responsibility on South Sudan to disarm the two SPLA-N divisions there as it claims the CPA required. Sudan has therefore sought to cut off supply lines between South Sudan and the Two Areas, with bombing and ground clashes along the border. Over a year's time, these acts have bred anger, frustration, and counteraction from South Sudan. Tens of thousands of refugees from the fighting have also crossed into South Sudan. For its part South Sudan has stoutly denied that it provides support to its erstwhile comrades in the Two Areas, but its claim rings hollow. It would be more honest and more helpful to negotiating a settlement for South Sudan to articulate its real security interest in what happens in those two states.

Those interests are considerable. It is not only the historical and professional links between these two elements of the original SPLM/A, and the debt South Sudan owes to those in the Two Areas who fought with the South, though this is a significant factor within the government and army there. South Sudan has also long been concerned with Sudan-supported militia launched against it from the Two Areas, and to where they retreat for rest and resupply. South Sudan thus cannot accept this border region's being in full control of the ruling party in Sudan with no political role and thus security influence from its allies there. In short, it cannot allow the SPLA-N to be defeated. That does not mean it is intent on using the conflict in the Two Areas as a stepping stone to overthrow the Khartoum regime—a stated aim of the SPLM-N. South Sudan would welcome a political solution to the conflict.

The border clashes climaxed in April 2012 when after feints in that direction South Sudan forces occupied the Heglig region of Southern Kordofan. Though a disputed area between the two countries, Heglig provides 50 percent of the oil Sudan retained under the CPA. This was the first post-CPA attack by either country on a vital strategic resource of the other, and thus raised the conflict to a new level. In Sudan there were calls for jihad and overthrow of the SPLM regime in Juba. Seeing a risk of the two slipping into all-out war, the entire international community denounced the occupation of Heglig and demanded South Sudan withdraw. Much shuttle diplomacy, the impact of the strong international reaction, and a large-scale counterattack by Sudan convinced South Sudan to withdraw. The African Union Peace and Security Council (AUPSC) met in emergency session April 24 and mandated the two countries to cease hostilities, withdraw forces behind the border, and implement a previously agreed but never acted upon plan for demilitarizing the border and establishing a verification and monitoring system aided by the UN Interim Security Force for Abyei. The AUPSC communiqué also demanded the two countries settle all the major outstanding issues between them within ninety days. The UN Security Council followed suit on May 4, endorsing the AUPSC road map, and threatening sanctions if the two sides did not comply. The AUPSC also instructed that if the parties had not agreed to a resolution of these issues by then, the AUHIP should submit to the AUSC proposed resolutions of the issues. Thus the AUHIP was being asked to step up to a mediating role, more than it has wanted or sought.

OIL: THAT WHICH BINDS AND
THAT WHICH DIVIDES

As noted, this article does not seek to analyze all the issues that divide the two Sudans. Abyei, which remains an emotional land mine, deserves much space of its own and so is not addressed here.[3] But understanding the oil issue and how it has been treated provides insight not only into the issue itself, but also into some of the dynamics that affect all the negotiations.

Oil would seem to be a natural way to bring the parties together, of necessity if nothing else, as the sector is so divided yet intertwined between them and on which both depend so much. As already described, South Sudan at independence acquired 70 percent of the two countries' oil while Sudan contained the pipelines, port, processing facilities, and other infrastructure for exporting it, as well as the refinery on which both depend for product. Beyond the need for allocating ownership of facilities and commercial property, and making normal commercial arrangements, the CPA instructed South Sudan to provide some transitional financial arrangement (TFA) to ease Sudan's loss of so much of its revenue and budget resources (80 percent of its export earnings and 70 percent of its budget). Sudan would need time and the TFA to adjust its economy. For its part South Sudan since 2005 has derived 98 percent of its budget from oil and has little prospect of developing other comparable resources in the near future. A desperately poor country with almost no infrastructure and little indigenous food production, let alone industry, South Sudan cannot develop without assured income, and oil is its only source for now.

Negotiations over oil have stuck largely on the size and nature of the TFA. It is not only a matter of measuring the size of Sudan's "gap" from the loss of oil revenue (on which six months was wasted, in this author's view, on trying to use a totally impractical formula), nor the principle of compensation from South Sudan, nor even at the beginning an understanding of South Sudan's share of that gap to be filled. It is as much the emotional and political question of whether the TFA is something Sudan is owed, or as Bashir has sometimes put it, Sudan's right and even something Sudan "owns," or whether this is a gesture of assistance, of "aid," to Sudan for which South Sudan should not only be appreciated but compensated in resolution of other issues. South Sudan, for example, demanded that its development gap be computed along with Sudan's budget and foreign exchange gap to demonstrate what a great sacrifice it was for South Sudan to provide any such payment. South Sudan has long resisted any upfront TFA payment—the highest priority for Sudan—insisting at various times that Sudan's debts to South Sudan be subtracted first, or that Abyei and border issues be resolved first. In its defense, South Sudan argued that any such payment would be wildly unpopular in South Sudan when its own needs were so great, when memories of the war were still fresh, and indeed while Sudan was bombing its border. There would have to be a quid pro quo to make it palatable.

As 2011 drew to a close with no agreement, Sudan was feeling the pinch as foreign exchange reserves were dwindling, the reality of its economic situation becoming more apparent, an austerity budget being put in place, food prices rising, and grumbling growing in the population. Taking a leaf from some earlier ideas from consultants to the AUHIP, who thought the TFA might best be "hidden" in some combination of TFA and various transitional commercial fees, Sudan tried to get its payment through hiking the transit fee for South Sudan oil going through the pipelines. Sudan presented South Sudan with a bill charging $36 a barrel (retroactively to July 10) for the transit fee against South Sudan's argument that the fee should be less than $1. South Sudan refused to pay. In December Sudan retaliated. It blocked tankers from entering Port Sudan to pick up South Sudan oil, diverted some of that oil to its own storage tanks and to the refinery, and defiantly said it was only claiming what was rightfully its own. South Sudan protested and when it got no satisfaction, shut down all its oil production. The world was shocked. Now it seemed both parties were cutting off their noses to spite their faces, or more bluntly committing mutual economic suicide. Later South Sudan's attack on Heglig, which damaged some oil facilities important to South Sudan's exporting ability, seemed to reinforce this conclusion.

Looking deeper into these negotiations and the current standoff, one finds all the elements that divide the two countries on other issues and keeps peace so fragile. Deep distrust is one. Throughout the oil negotiations charges were made by South Sudan's negotiators that Sudan had systematically stolen South Sudan oil over many years (South Sudan produced a "bill" of over $5 billion Sudan owed to South Sudan, dwarfing the proposed TFA); that Chinese, Indian, and Malaysian oil companies had also done so in collusion with the North; and that Sudan was intent in its border clashes on seizing South Sudan's oil wells. After Sudan had blocked South Sudan's oil exports and diverted some of its oil, South Sudan demanded guarantees from the international community that if production was resumed, this would never happen again. On the other side, charges abounded about South Sudan's disingenuousness, either of never really intending to reach any agreement or of never planning to implement it. Using exorbitant transit fees to get compensation, argued the Sudanese government, was the only way to force South Sudan to meet its obligation. One of the most frequent charges each side makes is that the other side never lives up to its agreements.

Strategy is another. Despite the hardships South Sudan is undergoing without any income to speak of, South Sudan still believes its oil gives it the upper hand with Sudan. South Sudan is thus still hoping for the "grand bargain," the oil-for-Abyei-and-borders deal. Thus it vacillates between recognizing that only with an unconditional upfront payment will Sudan come to an agreement on the TFA and on the other hand the desire to condition such payment on an equally upfront quid pro quo. For its part, Sudan thinks it, too, is in the driver's seat. As in the period leading up to South Sudan's independence, Sudan believes that South Sudan needs oil revenue more than it does, that the South is a weak and divided society, and that the government there will crumble long before Sudan's does under the weight of economic distress. Moreover, if it cannot be led to an agreement favorable to Sudan, it can be browbeaten into one.

War memories, and all the resentments that linger, are yet another factor. In South Sudan, some wonder why they should make any agreements with a regime that they believe is led by a warmonger, that would always be seeking to destabilize South Sudan, indeed to recapture it, and that it was better to wait, however long, for a change in regime. In almost parallel fashion in Sudan, South Sudan is seen by many as bent on fomenting regime change in Khartoum through support of an alliance of groups (the SPLM-N and three Darfur groups that have come together under the umbrella of the Sudan Revolutionary Front). South Sudan's persistent denial of any support to the SPLM-N is also seen as a sign of both South Sudan's duplicity and its refusal to negotiate honestly on security matters. These sentiments on both sides continuously run up against the practical necessity of reaching agreement on so vital a matter as oil (or borders, or almost anything else) and always create a hesitation, a certain pulling back, as the parties reach the point where they have to make the final concessions to close a deal. In each country, there are those holding these views who would oppose, block if they can, any agreements within reach. These may well be the forces that undercut one of the most promising breakthroughs in the March 2012 negotiations.

In Addis Ababa in March the two parties were coming to the end of another fruitless round of negotiations under the auspices of the AUHIP. Oil was the main subject, but also the rights of southerners in Sudan and northerners in South Sudan, along with a rather innocuous agreement on how to proceed on border issues. Yet there had been some intense discussions on the sidelines of the negotiations about the impasse that these talks almost inevitably reach, whether the parties were prisoners of their own preconceptions, whether the practical needs of both sides could not lead them to a better outcome. They had each tabled papers on oil, papers that left them far apart. Sudan's negotiators had upped the gap from a previously agreed $7.4 billion to $10 billion (carefully cloaked in scenarios for dividing TFA and commercial fees, but each scenario reaching the same total for South Sudan to provide). South Sudan had submitted a heavily caveated proposal for a TFA, steps back from a more generous offer a few months before.

In a moment of candor, even an epiphany, the two agreed to put aside the papers (Thabo Mbeki formally withdrew them) and begin a "new approach." There was some frank talk about South Sudan's relations with the SPLM-N and other frank talk from Khartoum that broke down barriers between them. The "new approach" they then proposed began with accepting that Sudan needed $10 billion over three years to adjust its economy, not just $7.4 billion as previously proposed. But it was also agreed that South Sudan, in whatever combination of TFA and fees, could not be expected to cover more than a third. Once agreement along these lines was finalized, the two countries would work together to mobilize international support for at least another one-third of the gap, leaving Sudan to make internal adjustments to cover the rest. In this new atmosphere of trust and cooperation, the parties initialed the agreements on nationalities and borders and South Sudan agreed to invite President Bashir to a summit in Juba where this new approach would be formally inaugurated, the two initialed agreements signed, and directions given to the negotiators to reach an agreement on oil along the above lines. South Sudan's principal negotiator went afterward to Khartoum to deliver the summit invitation.

The Sudan negotiators, however, came home to a storm of criticism from certain Islamist personages and others within the NCP. The rights in the agreement they had initialed for southerners in Sudan were seen as giving rights to traitors, or at least giving something away for nothing. Having Bashir go to Juba was decried. A poignant story in the press described the chief negotiator defending, with tears in his eyes, his patriotism and the reasons for the positions he had taken to an angry mosque congregation. A few days later South Sudan forces responded to a border clash by marching into the Heglig area, and in an unscripted moment President Kiir proclaimed that Heglig had been taken (not true) and was "ours." Bashir suspended his plans for the summit. Two weeks later the SPLA responded again, this time taking over Heglig in fact and once again laying claim to it. Bashir denounced the SPLM government as "insects," called for jihad and said negotiations were over and that South Sudan only understood the gun. The "new approach" had died.

CONCLUSION: DIPLOMACY'S ROLE

International actors, whether facilitators, would-be mediators, or just concerned influential countries, have been torn between on the one hand addressing the outstanding issues piecemeal and on the other hand seeking a basic rapprochement between the two countries at the highest level that would eliminate the underlying distrust that blocks progress in all such specific negotiations. There certainly have been many attempts at the latter. The CPA itself heralded such mutual cooperation. In 2011, Sudan's recognition of the results of the South's referendum and President Bashir's fulsome participation and warm remarks at South Sudan's independence seemingly reconfirmed a new beginning had been reached between the longtime belligerents. The AUHIP has negotiated many agreements since that pledge: peaceful resolution of all issues, commitment to creating two viable states living in harmony, a non-aggression pact, renouncing support of rebel movements in each other's territory, and so on. These have had little effect, and often are broken within days of their signing. Some find the AUHIP's predilection for such agreements to be a diversion, a valueless fallback when more substantive agreements have not been reached, and which are misleadingly trumpeted as progress.

Yet it is hard to believe that agreement on how to manage the borders, to resolve the future status of Abyei, to stop the reality of mutual destabilization efforts, or to develop trustworthy arrangements for long-term oil sector collaboration—indeed any major issue that relies on trust and cooperation between the two countries—is possible without a fundamental change in the basic attitudes each maintains about the other. Thus there are frequent calls for a summit of the two presidents to reach an overall understanding that would guide negotiations on all these matters. But summits between them in the past have not achieved anything of the sort. The underlying distrust is not some kind of miscommunication, some unresolved tension that can be overcome through a dramatic embrace, or even stirring words. Each side has reason to mistrust the other. Each side does harbor thoughts of destabilizing if not overthrowing the other. Each side believes the other is inherently evil or inherently incompetent and thus not worthy of such trust and cooperation.

For that reason, the outsiders fall back at the same time to addressing the individual issues. With memories of how the United States and the USSR managed fifty years of the Cold War, with many of these same negative sentiments between them, while avoiding war and indeed making a number of practical agreements, there is hope that necessity will win out over darker sentiments between the two Sudans and allow for some agreements that help reduce both the tensions and the costs of continued impasse. The agreement on temporary joint administration of Abyei is one such achievement. Both countries managed to institute new currencies without undermining the other, as many feared would happen, though not through cooperation so much as mutual caution. Despite harrowing situations such as the recent occupation of Heglig and its aftermath, both sides have managed to keep any armed clashes within bounds and to avoid falling back into all-out war—again on the basis of practicality rather than any formal understanding between them—but still to their mutual credit. These facts give hope that agreements to at least control the border more effectively, to resume oil production that both sides so badly need, and agreement to protect the right of people of each country to reside in the other are worth pursing in their own right.

If that is the best way forward, to pursue individual agreements even while seeking to build overall understanding and trust between them over time, then one must return to the question of mediation versus facilitation. In the case of these two governments, the normal means of persuasion—pressure—are not very effective. Sudan has been under heavy sanctions for nearly two decades but has not changed its basic approach to its internal problems or followed clearly marked paths to reintegration with the world economy, even in the face of serious economic problems. The overhang of the ICC indictment surely limits the degree of full reconciliation with the West and thus the breadth of incentives that the West can offer. Changes are likely to occur only at the margin, for example, in withdrawing most but not all its troops from Abyei, in accepting only "in principle" the AUPSC communiqué and its mandates, and in hemming in UNAMID as much as possible while pursuing a limited peace plan in Darfur. South Sudan is much more sensitive to international opinion and is heavily dependent on international assistance. Thus, it quickly reversed its occupation of Heglig and shortly afterward withdrew its remaining forces from Abyei. But an oil agreement may be a bridge too far, if it means providing substantial financial assistance to Sudan and delaying its quest for a "grand bargain." South Sudan's SPLM leadership may well risk not only economic but political suicide in part because it is still thinking more like a liberation army—one that can go back to the bush and fight from there while the population fends for itself—rather than a government that has different responsibilities and different expectations from its people.

Thus, to bring the parties to even individual agreements may require new forms of international influence. The AUPSC communiqué and the follow-on UNSC resolution are important steps in this direction. Not only do they lay out a specific road map of negotiations, but they also imply international pressures on the parties if they do not comply. Sanctions, however, are too complicated in this situation and, as noted, Sudan already is under many. The key will be a totally unified international position that the solutions, brought if necessary by a mediator, will be adopted by the AU, the UN, and perhaps the League of Arab States. This means that neither party can turn to sympathetic friends to get out from under those solutions. Neither party will find an economic rescuer, even for the short term. At the same time, the consequences of the current impasses between the parties need to be further articulated, publicized, and made clear to civil society as much as to governments. If solutions are not found for the critical economic crisis each country faces, it will surely be the people who will suffer the most from further war.

Under these circumstances the potential for successful mediation is enhanced. Indeed only if backed by firm and united international opinion, by individual countries and regional and international organizations important to the parties, can the mediation have the political weight to force the parties to agreements they would not reach on their own. But finally, in this atmosphere, and only in this atmosphere, facilitation may in the end prove the winning course. Faced with the inevitable prospect of a mediated solution to some of these vital issues being enforced upon them, the parties may turn to each other, and with the aid of facilitators, the AUHIP now the authorized entity, decide better to reach solutions on their own, ones they prefer, than bow to what outsiders may make them do.

NOTES

1. The views expressed in this chapter are the personal ones of the author and do not necessarily represent those of the US government.

2. Following South Sudan's independence, the SPLM, which was a national party, reorganized itself with the SPLM in South Sudan, structuring itself as a new party separate from and with no operations in Sudan, while the cadres and members of the SPLM in Sudan designated themselves as the continuing and previously registered SPLM there. The commonly used designation for the Sudan party is thus SPLM-N, and for its two army divisions SPLA-N. The government of Sudan contests this arrangement, arguing that the SPLM-N is still but an extension of the SPLM in South Sudan, that it needs to register itself as a new party, and many in the government of Sudan believed it should change its name altogether to disassociate itself from a party in a now-foreign country. In the armed conflict that broke out in the Two Areas, the Sudanese government formally outlawed the SPLM-N for its stated aim to overthrow the Khartoum regime, arrested many of its members, and closed most of its offices throughout the country. SPLM-N leaders are the deposed governor of Blue Nile, Malaak Agar; the leader of the SPLA-N in (and former deputy governor of) Southern Kordofan, Abdulazziz Hilu; and former SPLM candidate for president of Sudan in 2010 Yasir Arman, all now in exile or under cover in the Two Areas.

3. In May 2011, after clashes with the South Sudan police, Sudan's army occupied Abyei, driving 100,000 Ngok Dinka from the area and sending the UN peacekeepers there cowering. Months of painstaking diplomacy, headed by the AUHIP but aided at a critical moment by US Secretary of State Hillary Clinton, produced an agreement whereby until its final status was agreed, Abyei would be jointly administered by the presidents of Sudan and South Sudan through the Abyei Joint Oversight Committee. A new UN peacekeeping force (UNISFA) was brought in, entirely Ethiopian, which has been both forceful in keeping the peace but also admirable in bringing the two contending communities—the Ngok Dinka and the Misseriya—together to allow for the first time in three years the annual nomadic migration. The oversight committee functions reasonably well, but disagreements between the parties has prevented formation of a civilian administration, the Sudanese army has not entirely withdrawn as required in the agreement, and the displaced have not yet been able to return. Nevertheless, the Abyei Joint Oversight Committee represents one of the only functioning agreements between the two countries and thanks to UNISFA and the forbearance of both sides, Abyei withstood being drawn into the recent clashes in neighboring Southern Kordofan. Its final status, however, remains far from settled.

twelve

War in the Great Lakes Region

F ILIP R EYNTJENS

INTRODUCTION

This chapter examines a two-decade period of instability, violence, war, and extreme human suffering in central Africa. Considered in the past as peripheral, landlocked, and politically and economically uninteresting, in the 1990s the African Great Lakes region found itself at the heart of a profound geopolitical recomposition with continental repercussions. Countries as varied as Namibia in the south, Libya in the north, Angola in the west, and Uganda in the east became entangled in wars that ignored international borders. However, the seeds of instability were sown from the beginning of the 1960s: the massive exile of the Rwandan Tutsi, who fled to neighboring countries during and after the revolution of 1959–1961, and the virtual exclusion of Tutsi from public life in Rwanda, the radicalization of Burundian Tutsi who monopolized power and wealth, and the insecure status of Kinyarwanda-speakers in the Kivu provinces—all these factors were to merge with others to create the conditions for war.

I argue that a unique and contingent combination of factors explains the occurrence of the war, its course, and its outcome.[1] While this combination of factors helps us to understand the past, it may also have some value for assessing the future. Indeed, as long as these factors persist, the risk of renewed war continues to exist. The factors studied here are (i) the weakness of the Zairean/Congolese[2] state; (ii) the territorial extension of neighboring countries' civil wars; (iii) the shifting regional alliances; (iv) the profitability of war; (v) the linking up of local stakes; and (vi) the impunity for major human rights violations.

The acute destabilization of the region started on October 1, 1990, when the Rwanda Patriotic Front (RPF) attacked Rwanda from Uganda with Ugandan support. After the collapse of the 1993 Arusha peace accord and following the genocide and massive war crimes and crimes against humanity, the RPF won a military victory and took power in July 1994. Over a million people died and over 2 million fled abroad, mainly to Zaire and Tanzania. Eight months earlier, the democratic transition had ended in disaster in Burundi: tens of thousands of people were killed, and the country embarked on a decade-long civil war. At the end of 1993, some 200,000 Burundian refugees inundated the Zairean Kivu provinces, followed in mid-1994 by 1.5 million Rwandans. This was the beginning of the dramatic extension of the neighboring conflicts, most prominently of the Rwandan civil war.

Given the complexity and abundance of events, a brief timeline of the war is proposed here.[3] After the genocide and the overthrow of the Rwandan Hutu-dominated regime in July 1994, 1.5 million Hutu refugees settled just across the border in Zaire. Among them were the former government army, the Forces Armées Rwandaises (FAR), and militia. They launched cross-border raids and increasingly became a serious security threat for the new regime, dominated by the mainly Tutsi RPF. First under the guise of the "Banyamulenge rebellion" and later the "AFDL [Alliance des Forces pour la Libération du Congo-Zaïre] rebellion," the Rwanda Patriotic Army (RPA) attacked and cleared the refugee camps during the autumn of 1996. Having security concerns similar to those of Rwanda, Uganda and Burundi joined from the beginning, later to be followed by a formidable regional coalition intent on toppling Mobutu. In May 1997, Laurent Kabila seized power in Kinshasa. During the latter half of 1997, relations between the new Congolese regime and its erstwhile Rwandan and Ugandan allies soured rapidly. In August 1998, Rwanda and Uganda again attacked, once more under the guise of a "rebel movement," the RCD (Rassemblement Congolais pour la Démocratie), which just like the AFDL was created in Kigali. The invading countries expected this to be a remake of the first war, only much faster this time. The reason for this failing to occur was a spectacular shift of alliances, when Angola and Zimbabwe sided with Kabila against their former allies Rwanda and Uganda. This intervention made up for the weakness of the Congolese army, thus ensuring military stalemate along a more or less stable frontline that cut the country in two.

Considerable pressure from the region led to the signing of the Lusaka Accord in July 1999.[4] However, Kabila blocked its implementation and only after his assassination and succession by his son Joseph in January 2001 was the peace process resumed. Again under great pressure, by South Africa in particular, and after cumbersome negotiations, the Congolese parties signed a "Global and All-Inclusive Accord" in December 2002.[5] It took another three and a half years to implement the accord, along a bumpy road replete with incidents, obstructions, negotiations, and renegotiations, and constantly threatened by the resumption of the war. An informal international trusteeship, supported by a large UN peacekeeping force and also by the international and Congolese civil society, imposed elections on very reluctant political players. These took place in July–October 2006, in an overall free and fair fashion, and were won by Joseph Kabila and his party, PPRD. Kabila was sworn in in December, both houses of parliament were installed in January 2007, and a new government was formed in early February, thus formally ending the transition.

STATE FAILURE

Well before the start of the war, Zaire had ceased to empirically perform a number of essential state functions, such as territorial control, public taxation, the provision of essential services, the monopoly of violence, and the rule of law. The gradual failure of the state preceded its collapse, and the first signs of a "shadow state"[6] were visible in the 1970s, after the "Zaireanization" measures allowed the transfer of large parts of the economy to political and military elites. This heralded the putting into place of a prebendary and neo-patrimonial exercise of power that profoundly corrupted official institutional norms and frameworks.[7]

Georges Nzongola-Ntalaja writes that "the major determinant of the present conflict and instability in the Great Lakes Region is the decay of the state and its instruments of rule in the Congo. For it is this decay that made it possible for Lilliputian states the size of Congo's smallest province, such as Uganda, or even that of a district, such as Rwanda, to take it upon themselves to impose rulers in Kinshasa and to invade, occupy and loot the territory of their giant neighbour."[8] Indeed, the void left by the state was filled by other, nonstate actors. Some of these—such as NGOs, churches, local civil society, or traditional structures—assumed some functions abandoned by the state, but other less benign players also seized the public space: warlords, (ethnic) militias, and "entrepreneurs of insecurity," both domestic and from neighboring countries.[9] This not only explains the extreme weakness in battle of the FAZ/FAC,[10] which mirrored the collapsed state, but also why a small country like Rwanda was able, without much of a fight, to establish extraordinary territorial, political, and economic control over its vast neighbor. What Achille Mbembe has called the "satellization" of entire provinces by (much) smaller but stronger states was accompanied by the emergence of new forms of privatized governance.[11]

In eastern DRC, most functions of sovereignty were thus privatized, as some examples show. In 1996 and 1998, the Zairean/Congolese government forces hardly engaged in combat; during the war that started in 1998, foreign and nonstate forces faced each other—the Angolan and Zimbabwean (and, at one point, Chadian and Namibian) armies, and Rwandan and Burundian rebel groups on Kabila's side, and on the other the Rwandan and Ugandan armies with their RCD and MLC (Mouvement de Libération du Congo) proxies. Territorial control, the provision of (in)security, and the management of populations were taken over by militia, rebel groups—both domestic and from neighbors Rwanda, Uganda, and Burundi—and the armies of neighboring countries (and even the former Rwandan government army).

A UN panel monitoring an arms embargo reported compelling data on the absence of the state in controlling cross-border traffic, including at ports and airports; indeed "irregular aircraft practices are the norm."[12] The state's fiscal function, too, which was limited anyway, was profoundly eroded. Import and export levies collected by militias, rebel groups, and Rwandan and Ugandan "elite networks" funded the wars and lined the pockets of individuals. Toll barriers (*péages*) were put up to extract resources from peasants taking their meager surplus products to markets, so the possession of a gun was a sufficient means to impose internal taxation. In North Kivu, travelers passing between the zones controlled by two opposing wings of the RCD[13] were required to declare goods and pay duties at the "border." There were fixed tariffs for pedestrians and vehicles, and traders were required to hand over some of their merchandise. In areas controlled by the RCD, there were annual taxes on vehicles and a panoply of charges for individual journeys, road "tolls," and "insurance."[14] The RCD taxed the coltan[15] trade, sold mining rights, and demanded license fees, nonrefundable deposits, various export taxes, and a "war effort tax."[16] The panel documented a number of other examples showing that borders and their control became prized assets for armed groups and their sponsors in Rwanda and Uganda, allowing them the necessary revenue to maintain and resupply troops.[17] It concluded that "as an institutionally weak state, the DRC significantly lacks control over both customs and immigration."[18]

TERRITORIAL EXTENSION OF CIVIL WARS

While the sources of instability in the Great Lakes region were, in essence, domestic, reflecting as they did the political conflicts in Rwanda, Burundi, the Kivu, and Zaire more generally, their repercussions were increasingly felt throughout the larger region. This regionalization of violence was reinforced by the geographic proximity of conflicts, by the game of alliances, and by population flows.

In the mid-1990s, the territory of Zaire was used by insurgent forces of several neighboring countries as a base for attack and retreat. They included the Allied Democratic Forces (ADF) from Uganda and several groups (CNDD-FDD and Palipehutu-FNL, in particular) from Burundi. From mid-1994, the most serious threat concerned Rwanda, after 1.5 million Hutu refugees fled into North and South Kivu after the genocide and the victory of the RPF. Rwanda was facing an increasing security threat since 1995,[19] particularly in the three western prefectures, affected by commando operations emanating, at least in part, from Zairean territory. During a speech in Tambwe on February 19, 1995, General Kagame set the tone: "I wholeheartedly hope that these attacks take place! Let them try! I do not hide it. Let them try" (translated from Kinyarwanda). Kagame candidly told journalist François Misser that "if another war must be waged, we shall fight in a different fashion, elsewhere. We are prepared. We are ready to fight any war and we shall contain it along the border with Zaire."[20] Officials from the United States and The Netherlands, two countries close to the Rwandan regime, confirmed that they had had to dissuade Kagame on several occasions from "breaking the abscess" of the Rwandan refugees in Zaire the hard way.[21] During a visit to the United States in August 1996, one month before the start of the "rebellion," Kagame told the Americans that he was about to intervene,[22] the more so since, according to some sources,[23] the ex-FAR were preparing a large-scale offensive against Rwanda from Goma and Bukavu. Faced with the obvious unwillingness or inability of the international community to tackle this problem, Kigali's patience had reached its limits.

In September 1996, under the guise of the "Banyamulenge rebellion" first and later hiding behind the back of a Congolese rebel group, the AFDL created in Kigali, the RPA cleared the refugee camps around Goma and Bukavu. Thousands of civilian refugees were killed in the initial attack, hundreds of thousands were forcibly returned to Rwanda, and hundreds of thousands more moved westward, where they became the victims of a phased extermination campaign by the RPA. Pourtier noted that "the strategic choice (of Kigali) to attack the camps clearly shows the fundamental objectives of a 'rebellion' that was no longer (a rebellion), because what really happened was the extension of the Rwandan civil war into Zairean territory."[24]

Faced with similar (though less vital) security concerns, Uganda and, to a lesser extent, Burundi participated in the war, thereby destabilizing the bases of their "own" rebel groups. By the end of 1996 Angola, another country facing a rebellion (UNITA) supported by Mobutu's cronies and operating in part from Zaire, realized that its security concerns had not been met by the situation created in eastern Zaire and decided to make a difference.[25] Luanda's position, which was to expand the ambitions of the rebellion to the whole of

Zaire, eventually prevailed.[26] Angola provided the crucial impetus through the Katangese Gendarmes, known as the "Tigres."[27] During two weeks in mid-February 1997, several battalions (2,000–3,000 "Tigres" men) were airlifted to Kigali, and taken from there by road to Goma and Bukavu. This operation was logistically supported by the Angolan army, obviously in close cooperation with Rwanda. The entry of the Gendarmes and, later during the war, of the Angolan army caused the "rebellion" to pick up speed. While it took four months (October 1996–January 1997) to occupy less than one-twentieth of the country, the remainder of Zaire was captured in the three months that followed the arrival of the "Tigres" (mid-February to mid-May 1997). The outcome of the war, namely regime change in Kinshasa, was the consequence of the merger of several civil wars that were intrinsically unlinked, but that came together against the background of a weak state in Zaire and of geographical proximity.

SHIFTING ALLIANCES

The players in what became a regional civil war reasoned in the logic of "the enemy of my enemy is my friend." The fact that Mobutu had made many enemies explains the emergence of the formidable regional alliance that eventually defeated him. But that such a circumstantial alliance is also very fragile was clear during the second phase of the war, from 1998, when yesterday's friends became today's enemies almost overnight. Indeed, coalitions shifted dramatically.

At the beginning of the resumption of the war in August 1998, Kabila was saved by Angola and Zimbabwe, who turned against their former allies Rwanda and Uganda. Angola was concerned about two developments. Former Mobutu generals Nzimbi and Baramoto had been seen in Kigali before the new war broke out, and some politicians of the Mobutu era openly joined the rebellion, as did some former FAZ units. Because of their support for UNITA in the past, these elements were considered archenemies in Luanda. Moreover, Angolan intelligence was aware that there were contacts between UNITA and the rebel leadership and their Rwandan and Ugandan sponsors. Indeed, elements of UNITA later fought alongside rebel forces, the MLC in particular. Given the likelihood of the resumption of the Angolan civil war (which indeed materialized a few months later), for Luanda the choice was clear: those supporting UNITA were the enemy, and their enemies merited support.

The motives behind the involvement of Zimbabwe were diverse. The DRC had an important war debt outstanding toward Zimbabwe, and the Zimbabweans were worried about repayment in the event of Kabila's being overthrown.[28] A second motive was also economic: Zimbabwean business interests had made efforts during the past year to penetrate the Congolese market and to invest in the mining sector, partly at the expense of South African ventures. Some of President Mugabe's business associates and high-ranking army officers stood to lose important assets if Kabila were defeated. Finally, the "old revolutionary" Mugabe saw the Congolese crisis as an opportunity to reassert some of his leadership in the region,[29] lost to Mandela's South Africa, and to short-circuit the new leaders of the "African Renaissance," such as Museveni and Kagame,[30] who were being promoted—notably by the Americans[31]—much to Mugabe's dismay.

Other realignments soon occurred. Thus the local *mai-mai* militias[32] in the East, which had been fighting Kabila even before he came to power, now aligned with him in the context of an "anti-Tutsi" coalition. Within the same logic, an even more spectacular shift brought the ex-FAR and former Interahamwe militia into Kabila's camp, although less than a year earlier, the Rwandan Hutu had suffered massive loss of life during and after the previous rebellion at the hands of Kabila's AFDL and his erstwhile Rwandan allies. FAR were brought in from neighboring countries, rearmed, retrained, and deployed on the northern and eastern fronts.[33] A UN report noted that "the changing alliances in and around the DRC have unexpectedly worked to the advantage of the former Rwandan government forces," because the ex-FAR and ex-Interahamwe "have now become a significant component of the international alliance against the Congolese rebels and their presumed sponsors, Rwanda and Uganda." The commission found it "profoundly shocking that this new relationship has conferred a form of legitimacy on the Interahamwe and the ex-FAR."[34] Likewise, the Burundian FDD's (Forces pour la Défense de la Démocratie) alliance with Kabila opened access to equipment, weapons, training, and bases, and even to a degree of respectability. They were headquartered in Lubumbashi, and troops recruited in Tanzanian refugee camps were transferred to the DRC.[35] Another shift in the East concerned Sudan, which had supported the Mobutu regime against Kabila's rebellion but now sided with Kabila against the new rebellion. The context here was the conflict between Khartoum and Kampala, as the latter supported the South Sudanese rebellion.

The frailty of the alliances again showed when conflict erupted between Rwanda and a major section of the Banyamulenge, who had earlier sought the protection of Kigali, while at the same time being used as a pretext for the Rwandan invasion in 1996. Already by the autumn of 1996, Banyamulenge leaders had realized that they were being instrumentalized by Rwanda and that, rather than protecting their community, their close association with Kigali further marginalized and threatened them. This feeling of being used increased further when, in October and December 1996, the RPA attempted to convince Banyamulenge leaders to resettle their entire community in Rwanda, an idea most of them rejected.[36] Disagreements with RPA commanders of the FAC over command positions and deployment of troops further exacerbated the tensions in the early months of 1998. When the second "rebellion" started in August 1998, the Banyamulenge were again faced with a crucial dilemma. On the one hand, they knew they were going to be instrumentalized once again by Rwanda and that this would worsen their relations with other groups, but on the other hand, they needed the physical security the RPA provided, including for their men in Kinshasa.

As the war progressed, it became increasingly clear that those Banyamulenge (like Ruberwa, Nyarugabo, and Bizima Karaha) who had joined the RCD were a minority, and that most Banyamulenge opposed the RCD and Rwanda. This rejection received both a political and a military translation. On the one hand, leaders such as Müller Ruhimbika and Joseph Mutambo created the Forces Républicaines et Fédéralistes (FRF) just after the beginning of the war. Operating from outside the territory occupied by the RCD/RPA, they vehemently opposed the RCD and the occupation by the Rwandan army.[37] On the other hand, the military response was the result of the growing distrust between Banyamulenge officers and the RPA. After repeated confrontations since early 1999, Munyamulenge commander Patrick Masunzu retreated to the South Kivu Haut Plateau in early 2002, and in the following months several battles were fought between the RPA and Masunzu's men. Masunzu even cooperated with *mai-mai,* and he eventually joined the government army, becoming a commander of the Forces Armées de la République Démocratique du Congo (FARDC).[38]

The most dramatic shift occurred between the former core allies Rwanda and Uganda. In the words of Charles Onyango-Obbo, chief editor of the Ugandan daily the *Monitor,* in August 1999 "the impossible happened":[39] the Rwandan and Ugandan armies fought a heavy battle in Kisangani, and more clashes followed later. In May and June 2000, the RPA and the UPDF again confronted each other in Kisangani; heavy weapons were used and some 400 civilians and 120 soldiers were killed. The rift had several causes. While Uganda wished to avoid repeating the mistake made in 1996–1997, when Kabila was parachuted into power without much Congolese ownership, Rwanda preferred a quick military solution and the installation of yet another figurehead in Kinshasa. Prunier noted that Kampala had no problem with an independent and efficient government in the DRC, a vision dramatically opposed to the view of Kigali that wanted to keep its Congolese proxies under control.[40] In addition, "entrepreneurs of insecurity" belonging to the elite networks in both countries were engaged in a competition to extract Congolese resources (see below).[41] Finally, Museveni resented the geopolitical ambitions of his small Rwandan neighbor and the lack of gratitude displayed by Kagame, who owed his accession to power to Uganda's support.

Just like the extension into the DRC of the Rwandan civil war, the conflict with Uganda was fought out on the soil of a weak neighbor and, in part, by proxy. Both countries supported rebel movements and (ethnic) militias in the context of an increasingly fragmented political-military landscape. They continuously traded accusations of supporting each other's rebel groups, which both sides indeed did. In March 2001, Rwanda was declared a "hostile nation" by the Ugandan government. Despite attempts at appeasement during the following months, on August 28, 2001, Museveni sent a long and bitter letter to UK Secretary of State for International Development Clare Short "about the deteriorating situation in the bilateral relations between Uganda and the government of Rwanda, led by President Kagame." As a consequence, Rwandan-Ugandan relations further deteriorated, and troops were massed on both sides of their common border. On November 6, 2001, Short summoned her two protégés to London to put an end to a situation that risked becoming a fiasco for the UK, just like the Ethiopian-Eritrean war of 1998–2000 had been for the United States. While relations did not become cordial, the threat of direct war subsided.

A dangerous escalation occurred again when, in early 2003, Rwanda started sending troops and supplies to the Ituri region in support of the Union des Patriotes Congolais (UPC), which until then had been supported by Uganda.[42] The attempt by the RCD-Goma and Rwanda to intervene in the Ituri conflict was seen by Kampala (which considered Ituri as its "backyard") as a lethal threat and again brought the two countries to the brink of direct war.[43] In the summer of 2003, both countries were forced out of Ituri as a result of a great deal of pressure by the international community,[44] while at the same time the political evolution in the DRC, where an agreement on political transition was arrived at and the war formally came to an end (see below), made it more difficult for them to be seen as overtly derailing the process. As Kigali and Kampala were held on a leash by the United States and the UK, the Congo offered less food for conflict between them, though relations were never again friendly.[45]

PROFITABILITY OF WAR

A UN panel[46] set up in 2001 published a number of increasingly detailed reports on the criminal practices of "elite networks," both Congolese and from neighboring countries, and identified elements common to all these networks. They consisted of a small core of political and military elites and businesspeople and, in the case of the occupied territories, rebel leaders and administrators. Members of these networks cooperated to generate revenue and, in the case of Rwanda, institutional financial gain. They derived this benefit from a variety of criminal activities, including theft, embezzlement and diversion of "public" funds, underevaluation of goods, smuggling, false invoicing, nonpayment of taxes, kickbacks to officials, and bribery. International "entrepreneurs of insecurity" (among them Viktor Bout) were closely involved in this criminal economy, as the local and regional actors drew support from the networks and "services" (such as air transport, illegal arms dealing, and international transactions of pillaged resources) of organized international criminal groups.[47]

The linkage between military engagement and illegal economic activities was a clear trend. Indeed pillaging was no longer an unfortunate side effect of war, but economic interests rather became its prime driving force. Christian Dietrich has drawn attention to the dangers inherent in what he calls "military commercialism," whereby a stronger state deploys the national military in a weaker neighboring country, supporting either the sovereign power (as did Zimbabwe) or insurgents (in the cases of Rwanda and Uganda), in exchange for access to profits.[48] Under these circumstances, economic criteria invade military decision-making, for example with regard to troop deployment and areas of operation.[49] In addition, if domestic resources are scarce or cannot be illicitly mobilized as a result of the scrutiny of the international community, cross-border predatory behavior, out of sight and/or hidden behind political and military concerns, provides an alternative resource. Finally, when control over resources has become a military objective in itself, this is a strong disincentive for troop withdrawal, simply because the "expeditionary corps" and those they support, whether rebels or governments, need each other. Put simply by Samset, "war facilitates excessive resource exploitation, and excessive exploitation spurs continued fighting."[50] As late as mid-2007, a panel monitoring the UN arms embargo confirmed that "the most profitable financing source for armed groups remains the exploitation, trade and transportation of natural resources. . . . All supply chains from areas controlled by armed groups are compromised."[51] Crawford Young notes that this "ability to sustain themselves through traffic in high value resources under their control" distinguishes contemporary insurgents from their predecessors.[52]

Nowhere is this as clear as in the case of Rwanda, a small and very poor country with few natural resources, but with an elite needing to maintain a lavish lifestyle and possessing a large and efficient army.[53] In 2000, the revenue collected by the RPA in the DRC from coltan alone was believed to be US$80–100 million, roughly the equivalent of official Rwandan defense expenditure (which stood at US$86 million).[54] In a similar vein, the UN panel found that in 1999–2000, "the RPA must have made at least US$250 million over a period of 18 months."[55] Stefaan Marysse calculated that in 1999, the total value added of diamond, gold, and coltan plundered in the DRC amounted to 6.1 percent of Rwanda's GDP,[56] and to 146 percent of its official military expenditure.[57] The Kigali economy, which is virtually disconnected from the Rwandan economy as a whole, was largely dependent on mineral and other extraction in the DRC (as well as on international aid). Pillaging the Congo not only allowed the Rwandan government to beef up the military budget in a way that was invisible to the donor community,[58] but also bought much-needed domestic elite loyalty. This is what Stephen Jackson calls the "economisation of conflict": a process whereby conflicts progressively reorient from their original goals (in the case of Rwanda: securing its borders) towards profit, and through which conflict actors capitalise increasingly on the economic opportunities that war opens up.[59]

The Rwandan military and civilian elites thus benefited directly from the conflict.[60] Indeed a UN panel noted a great deal of interaction among the military apparatus, the state (civil) bureaucracy, and the business community. It found that the RPA financed its war in the DRC in five ways: (i) direct commercial activities; (ii) benefits from shares it held in companies; (iii) direct payments from the RCD-Goma; (iv) taxes collected by the "Congo Desk" of the external military intelligence office ESO (External Security Organisation),[61] and other payments made by individuals for the protection the RPA provided for their businesses; and (v) direct uptake by soldiers from the land.[62] In sum, the Congolese funded their own occupation by neighboring countries' armies. Local coltan diggers were even forced out of the market in 2001–2002, when Rwanda used its own forced labor, among other things under the form of prisoners "imported" from Rwandan jails. After officially withdrawing its troops from the DRC in September 2002 as a result of discreet but intense international pressure, Rwanda therefore changed tactics by seeking alternative allies on the ground and sponsoring autonomist movements, in order to consolidate its long-term influence in eastern Congo and make the most out of the Kivu region.[63] In addition, even after its official withdrawal, Rwanda maintained a clandestine military presence in the DRC.[64]

The unpublished part of the UN panel's final report of October 2003 is particularly revealing in this respect.[65] At the request of the panel, this section was to remain confidential and not to be circulated beyond the members of the Security Council, as it "contains highly sensitive information on actors involved in exploiting the natural resources of the DRC, their role in perpetuating the conflict as well as details on the connection between illegal exploitation and illicit trade of small arms and light weapons."[66] The findings showed an ongoing presence of the Rwandan army in the DRC. It had, the panel found, continued shipping arms and ammunition to the Kivus and Ituri, provided training, exercised command, supported North Kivu Governor Serufuli's militia, and manipulated ex-FAR/Interahamwe by infiltrating RDF (Rwanda Defence Forces, the name of the RPA since 2002) officers into them. The panel considered the "Rwanda Network" "to be the most serious threat to the Congolese Government of National Unity. The main actor in this network is the Rwandan security apparatus, whose objective is to maintain Rwandan presence in, and control of, the Kivus and possibly Ituri."[67] Rwandan support for dissident forces went on throughout 2004, while the DRC was engaged in its delicate and fragile political transition. A later UN panel was concerned that "the territory of Rwanda continues to be used for recruitment, infiltration and destabilisation purposes,"[68] and it observed a "residual presence" of the RDF in North Kivu.[69]

Uganda, too, greatly benefited from its military/commercial presence in the DRC. Although, unlike Rwanda, it did not set up an extra-budgetary system to finance its activities there, the UN panel found that the "re-exportation economy" had a significant impact on the financing of the war, in three ways: by increasing the incomes of key businessmen, traders, and other dealers; by improving Uganda's balance of payments; and by bringing more money to the treasury through various taxes on goods, services, and international trade.[70] By way of example, Ugandan gold exports totaled US$90 million in 2000, while the country produced practically no gold.[71]

The logic of military commercialism could also be seen in the strategies developed by domestic armed groups. Thus the Walikale region west of Goma became a battleground between RCD rebels and *mai-mai*, both supposedly integrated into the FARDC, but who ceased to obey the FARDC Eighth Military Region commander, an RCD general who himself refused to obey orders from Kinshasa. In their fight for control over Walikale's cassiterite mines, these ex-*mai-mai* units cooperated with FDLR troops. Small aircraft based in Goma collected the cassiterite "caught" by the RCD for purchasing agents; once it arrived in Goma, shares were distributed to local military and political authorities before being transported across the border to Rwanda, where a smelting plant is located near Kigali, or exported to South Africa.[72]

Clearly, criminal or informal regional integration was very real, and it was certainly more effective than the often-called-for formal integration. Jeroen Cuvelier has shown how the support of Rwanda for the RCD heralded a growing cooperation between businesspeople, politicians, and high-ranking military on both sides of the border.[73] The establishment of SOMIGL (Société minière des grands lacs) and of the Congo Holding Company were instruments set up by the rebel group and Rwanda to get as much financial benefit as possible out of the international interest in Kivu's natural resources. Two Rwandan companies with close links to the RPF and the army, Rwanda Metals and Grands Lacs Metals, were key in organizing the Congolese commercial ventures of the Kigali regime. What is novel about what Ian Taylor suggests are "neo-imperialist" regional networks of violence and accumulation is that they are managing to develop their own links and ties to the international arena, often on their own terms.[74] The type of alliances and transboundary networks currently reconfiguring central Africa may well, in his view, offer a prophetic vision of what is in store for vulnerable and peripheral areas of the world.[75]

LOCAL DYNAMICS

The mega-conflict developed against the background of several local level conflicts. Problems related to identity in the Kivu region are ancient. Important migratory flows before, during, and after the colonial period, considerable demographic pressure, the uncertain status of (neo-)traditional authorities, the political and economic dynamism of the region, its peripheral situation in the Zairean context, and its partial incorporation in the East African space: these factors form the local background to events in eastern Zaire. The most visible and violent expression of this was the situation of the Banyarwanda, the Kinyarwanda speakers living in the Kivu. They consisted of several groups: the "natives," established since precolonial days; the "immigrants" and the "transplanted" of the colonial period;[76] the "infiltrators" and "clandestines" before and after independence (1960); and the Tutsi[77] and Hutu[78] refugees. This mixture gave birth to conflict in the 1960s during the so-called Kanyarwanda rebellion, when the Banyarwanda faced the threat of expulsion from the North Kivu region.[79] After a long period of calm under the regime of Mobutu, whose influential director of the political bureau, Barthélémy Bisengimana, was himself of Tutsi origin, the problem came to the fore again during the National Conference (1991–1992), when representatives of civil society of North and South Kivu raised the question of the "Zaireans of dual or doubtful citizenship," a coded expression referring to the Banyarwanda.

While the conflicts have older roots, this chapter picks up the story from early 1993 onward.[80] The events that started in North Kivu in March 1993 show how fluid ethnic categories are. Indeed, those who became the victims of a wave of violence waged by such "indigenous" ethnic groups as the Hunde, Nande, and Nyanga, supported by their respective militias (the *mai-mai* and the Bangilima), were the Banyarwanda, Hutu, and Tutsi alike. Only two years later, the Hutu and Tutsi confronted each other in "ethnic" strife.

There are various reasons for the violence that erupted in early 1993. First, the democratization process under way since 1990 opened up a new way of competing for power. As only nationals exercise political rights, citizenship became important, particularly in regions with a high proportion of Banyarwanda (in the extreme case of the zone of Masisi, they numbered 70 percent of the population). Second, in this relatively overpopulated part of Zaire, conflicts over land set groups against each other in two ways. On the one hand, two types of land use, agriculture and stock breeding, began competing with each other. On the other hand, two concepts of land tenure and access to land clashed with each other: land use by members of a group that holds corporate ownership (the customary law regime), as opposed to the concept of individual ownership of the modern law type, which allows for contractual transactions in land. A third source of conflict, not unrelated to the previous one, concerned the position of customary authorities. Groups that are immigrant or presented as such tend to try to free themselves from the authority of local chiefs, thus threatening their position and differentiating themselves from "indigenous" populations. This attitude of distancing was more frequently adopted by pastoral communities of Tutsi extraction. Under these circumstances, the denial of citizenship became a means for the political and economic exclusion of the Banyarwanda, and of the Tutsi in particular.

The conflict came to the fore again during the Zairean National Conference, and confrontations had already taken place in 1991 and 1992, particularly in the zones of Masisi and Rutshuru.[81] However, conflict spread dramatically in March 1993.[82] Violence started in Ntoto in the zone of Walikale, close to Masisi. There were large-scale killings of Hutu and Tutsi Banyarwanda, their houses were burned, and their cattle were stolen. During the following days, the violence extended to the zone of Masisi, where, however, the Banyarwanda were the majority group and had organized their defense. As the casualties show, a real war broke out with many deaths: "indigenous" and "immigrant" communities lost about 1,000 each; tens of thousands more were displaced. Each party accused the other: the Banyarwanda claimed that the "indigenous" wanted to chase and even massacre them, while according to the "indigenous," the Banyarwanda, and the Hutu in particular, intended to claim a territory they allegedly considered to be part of "Ancient Rwanda."

Two factors contributed to the pacification of North Kivu, at least for a short period. President Mobutu went to Goma, where he stayed for a month and met with most local players, and units of the Special Presidential Division (Division spéciale présidentielle—DSP) were deployed; their sheer presence brought apparent calm without a shot being fired. In the long run, "reflection days," organized in November 1993 and February 1994, consolidated the return to order. Together with NGOs, the local Catholic church of Mweso brought together representatives of territorial units, tradespeople, teachers, local NGOs, clergymen, officers of the DSP, leaders of cooperatives, customary chiefs, civil servants, and simple peasants—a total of eighty-eight local actors who were joined by thirty external "observers."

Only a few months after pacification, North Kivu was flooded by over 700,000 Rwandan Hutu refugees who fled the civil war in their country and the victorious RPF, accompanied and to some extent controlled by those responsible for the Rwandan genocide. Concentrated in five huge camps (Katale, Kahindo, Kibumba, Lac Vert, and Mugunga) on a limited area close to the Rwandan border, they completely upset the demographic situation, and therefore the politics of the region. At the beginning of the 1990s, approximately 425,000 Banyarwanda lived in the three zones (Masisi, Rutshuru, and Goma) where the refugees settled; out of a total population of about 1 million, this was about 40 percent.[83] Obviously, as a result of this massive injection of people, the Banyarwanda and the Rwandan refugees suddenly constituted the majority of the regional population. In addition, the Hutu (both the Rwandan refugees and the Zairean Hutu) had now become largely dominant in numbers, thus breaking the fragile balance put in place earlier in the year. The alliance of Hutu and Tutsi Banyarwanda broke up and, as in Rwanda, the two groups entered into violent conflict. The massive arrival of refugees also had other destabilizing effects: the environment was thoroughly disturbed by deforestation, poaching, and pressure on water supplies; the economy was destabilized by dollarization and the dramatic decrease of livestock; and basic infrastructure, already very weak before the crisis, was badly damaged.

However, large-scale violence did not start until November 1995. Probably unwillingly, the Zairean government contributed to the instability in August 1995 by announcing that the Rwandan refugees were to be expelled; they were given until December 31, 1995, to leave the country. As a result, many refugees left the camps and attempted to settle in the zones of Masisi and Rutshuru, where they inevitably clashed with the "natives" and Tutsi Banyarwanda, whose houses and land they threatened to occupy. On a more general political level, these attempts at occupation heightened the fears of many Zaireans that a "Hutu-land" was being put in place in North Kivu.[84] Incidents of uneven intensity in September and October 1995 were the prelude to a real war that started first in Masisi but rapidly spread to Rutshuru and Lubero.

Massacres by Hutu militias against the Hunde and Tutsi and by Hunde militia against the Tutsi and Hutu progressively created ethnically homogenous spaces. By March and April 1996, the zone of Masisi had been "ethnically cleansed": most local Tutsi fled to Rwanda, where about 18,000 refugees had arrived by the end of April. In March, the conflict extended to the zones of Rutshuru, Walikale, and Lubero, where the Bangilima, a Hunde militia, attacked the Banyarwanda. In May and June about 65,000 people were displaced in Rutshuru alone.

The spread of violence was enhanced by the ambiguous attitude of the local authorities, used to manipulating ethnicity for plutocratic purposes. Thus in May 1995, the governor of North Kivu, Christophe Moto Mupenda, stated during a public meeting before a Hunde audience in the town of Masisi that "hospitality has its limits" and that it was necessary "to strike and strike now against the immigrants." During the following year, two Goma-based radio stations fueled anti-Tutsi feelings, while megaphones were used to call on residents to chase the Tutsi out of town; Tutsi businessmen were arrested by local authorities without specific charges.[85] In November 1995, FAZ Chief of Staff General Eluki declared publicly that "the Hunde, Nyanga and Batembo are right to fight for the land of their ancestors and to chase the foreigners away from it."[86]

Séverine Autesserre has shown that the relationship between local and national or regional tensions was not merely top-down, and that issues usually presented as regional or national had significant local components, which fueled and reinforced the larger dimensions.[87] This reality was particularly strong in the region, as Hutu and Tutsi are found in Kivus, Rwanda, and Burundi, a situation that is conducive to cross-border alliances, solidarities, and strategies.

IMPUNITY

Although an important factor, the practice of impunity for persistent gross violations of human rights can only briefly be mentioned. The humanitarian consequences of the conflicts in the Great Lakes region over the past twenty years have been disastrous. Millions have died since 1990, of which over a million were the victims of direct violence. Generally speaking, those responsible for crimes against humanity, war crimes, and even genocide have remained unpunished. The only justice at work in the region has been victor's justice meted out to the authors of the genocide in Rwanda, MLC leader Jean-Pierre Bemba and a few Ituri warlords. However, the RPF, for instance, was not held accountable for the crimes it committed in Rwanda before, during, and after the genocide or for those perpetrated in Zaire/DRC, particularly at the end of 1996 and the beginning of 1997. While these crimes were well documented,[88] no prosecutions took place before the International Criminal Tribunal for Rwanda, before Rwandan or Congolese courts, or before courts in third countries on the basis of universal jurisdiction.[89]

This practice of victor's justice had a dual consequence. On the one hand, as impunity prevailed, it reassured criminals that they could commit new crimes without risk of judicial prosecution. For instance, it is likely that the RPA would not have massacred tens of thousands of civilian refugees in Zaire/DRC had those responsible for crimes committed in Rwanda in 1994 been prosecuted before the International Criminal Tribunal for Rwanda (ICTR). On the other hand, biased justice created frustration and resentment among the victims of these crimes, thus creating a fertile breeding ground for new violence. Many Rwandan Hutu and Congolese remember what the RPA did to them, and they may well take revenge if and when the occasion presents itself.

CONCLUSION

This chapter has addressed the combination of factors that allows one to understand why war occurred in the Great Lakes region, and why it unraveled the way it did. While this analysis has an explanatory function, it may also offer clues as to future developments. Indeed, if these factors are still present, one could conclude that a context favorable to new wars continues to prevail.

Although some steps have been made toward state reconstruction in the DRC, the state remains very fragile, particularly (but not exclusively) in the East, where earlier conflicts started. Territorial control is limited, private taxation continues, and the illegal exploitation and the smuggling of natural resources goes on.[90]

With regards to neighbors' civil wars, the one in Angola came to an end in 2002. The last remaining Burundian rebel movement, Palipehutu-FNL, laid down arms at the end of 2008 to become a political party under the name FNL. However, after the outcome of the 2010 elections was rejected by several opposition parties, some politicians, including chair of the FNL Agathon Rwasa, went underground. At the time of writing, a new rebellion seemed to be under way, with Burundian combatants operating in South Kivu, where they were joining forces with Congolese and Rwandan insurgent groups.[91] The Ugandan Allied Democratic Forces continue to operate on both sides of the Congo-Uganda border in the Ruwenzori region. The Lord's Resistance Army (LRA) is no longer active inside Uganda, but it operates in the DRC, though many of its fighters have relocated to the Central African Republic.[92] The porous region straddling the DRC, the Central African Republic, and South Sudan remains particularly open to insurgent activities. While peace seems to have returned in Rwanda, this is only apparent. Structural violence is widespread, and an authoritarian regime attempts to keep a lid on the volcano.[93] Dissident Tutsi who once occupied very high positions in the Rwandan political and military establishment entered into open opposition in 2010. They created a political structure, the Rwanda National Congress, and there are signs that they are preparing a military capacity intent on overthrowing Kagame (see below). The Hutu FDLR continue to be active in both South and North Kivu, and Rwanda supports the Tutsi CNDP, which, while officially incorporated into the FARDC, continues functioning as a militia.

In a situation of relative regional peace, alliances between states have become less prominent, but they continue to be concluded at more reduced scales. Thus the Rwandan RPF dissidents are suspected of having been in contact with armed movements in eastern DRC, such as the Nkunda wing of the CNDP and the FRF, and possibly with elements of the FDLR, while at the same time seeking support inside Rwanda.[94]

In the Kivu provinces in particular, the national army, several armed groups, and Uganda and Rwanda continue the exploitation of Congolese resources. Despite attempts to tag some materials and to raise awareness in the business community of due diligence guidelines, conflict around mineral and other wealth remains attractive. The UN panel of experts found that minerals continued to be transported through illegal border crossings between the two Kivus and Rwanda.[95]

Local tensions based on (ethnic) identity remain as intense as before, in Rwanda in particular, and cross-border alignments along these lines are still present. However, intra-Tutsi elite differences, as shown by the dissidence of the RNC and by the fact that many Tutsi Banyamulenge are opposed to the regime in Kigali, may alleviate the ethnic divide, though this may be replaced by other lethal alliances and the emergence of new violent strategies.

Finally, the issue of impunity has not been addressed seriously. For instance, the 2010 mapping report of the UN High Commission for Human Rights (see above) has not (yet) been acted upon. Despite an arrest warrant issued by the ICC against General Bosco Ntaganda for crimes committed in Ituri, he lives and moves about openly in Goma, where—in addition to being involved in illegal activities (see above)—he was involved in the murders of family members or former supporters of Laurent Nkunda, whom Ntaganda ousted from the leadership CNDP in January 2009 with the help of Rwanda, where Nkunda remains illegally detained. The Congolese government refused to execute the ICC arrest warrant "in the interest of maintaining peace," asserting that Ntaganda is needed to keep the former CNDP troops integrated in the Congolese army.

Clearly the conflict factors outlined in this chapter have not disappeared, although they have generally decreased in extent and intensity. Two of these factors need to be especially monitored. On the one hand, for both the development of the country and regional stability, state reconstruction in the DRC is essential. Given the colossal nature of this endeavor, putting Humpty Dumpty together again will need to start with the main functions of sovereignty: regaining control over the state's territory and reestablishing links with the population; rebuilding public fiscal capacity, with revenues collected and spent in a transparent, efficient, and honest fashion, and resources harnessed as public goods; and restoring legal security and the rule of law. On the other hand, the Rwandan regime must address the country's severe problems of political governance. Rwanda has been at the origin of two major regional wars, and it could be so again if current authoritarian practices are not amended.

NOTES

1. I use the term "war" in singular, because the two wars (the one in 1996–1997 was called the "war of liberation" by many Congolese, whereas the one from 1998 to 2003 was dubbed the "war of occupation") were in reality two episodes of one and the same conflict.

2. This text uses the name of the country at the time of the events that are analyzed: Zaire before May 1997, Congo or DRC after that date.

3. Appendix 12.1 summarizes the timeline. Appendix 12.2 offers an overview of the main actors. For a fuller treatment of the war, see G. Prunier, *Africa's World War: Congo, the Rwandan Genocide, and the Making of a Continental Catastrophe* (Oxford: Oxford University Press, 2009); F. Reyntjens, *The Great African War: Congo and Regional Geopolitics, 1996–2006* (New York: Cambridge University Press, 2009); and J. K. Stearns, *Dancing in the Glory of Monsters: The Collapse of the Congo and the Great War of Africa* (New York: PublicAffairs, 2011).

4. In addition to a cease-fire signed by Congo, Angola, Namibia, Rwanda, Uganda, and Zimbabwe, as well as by the Congolese rebel movements, the accord provided for an "open national dialogue" involving the government, the rebel groups, the unarmed opposition, and civil society. This was to lead to a new political dispensation.

5. The accord provided for a two- to three-year transitional period, during which the executive branch would be made up of a president and four vice presidents, and a government in which the rebel movements and the unarmed opposition would be represented. A bicameral parliament included the same entities as those represented in the government.

6. W. Reno, "Shadow States and the Political Economy of Civil Wars," in *Greed and Grievance: Economic Agendas in Civil Wars,* ed. M. Berdal and M. Malone (Boulder, CO: Lynne Rienner, 2000), pp. 43–63.

7. G. de Villers, "La guerre dans les évolutions du Congo-Kinshasa," *Afrique Contemporaine,* 215 (2005): 54.

8. G. Nzongola-Ntalaja, *The Congo from Leopold to Kabila: A People's History* (London and New York: Zed Books, 2002), p. 214.

9. The expression is from S. Perrot, "Entrepreneurs de l'insécurité: la face cachée de l'armée ougandaise," *Politique Africaine* 75 (1999): 60–71. It refers to rational makers of cost-benefit analyses, who realize that war, instability, and absence of the state are more profitable than peace, stability, and state reconstruction.

10. Forces Armées Zaïroises until May 1997, Forces Armées Congolaises between 1997 and 2003. The national army was renamed Forces Armées de la République Démocratique du Congo (FARDC) as a result of the agreement.

11. A. Mbembe, *On the Postcolony* (Princeton, NJ: Princeton University Press, 2001), pp. 92–93.

12. UN Security Council, *Report of the Group of Experts on the Democratic Republic of the Congo,* S/2004/551, July 15, 2004, para. 56.

13. In 1999, a wing known as the RCD-ML broke away in protest over Rwandan domination and placed itself under Uganda tutelage. The RCD-Goma remained a proxy for Rwanda.

14. Amnesty International, *Democratic Republic of Congo: Rwandese-Controlled East: Devastating Toll* (London: Amnesty International, June 19, 2001), pp. 16–18.

15. Coltan, short for "columbite-tantalite" and known industrially as tantalite, is a dull black metallic ore from which the elements niobium (formerly "columbium") and tantalum are extracted.

16. Ibid., p. 33.

17. UN Security Council, *Report of the Group of Experts*, para. 44.

18. Ibid., para. 31.

19. In *The Congo Wars: Conflict, Myth and Reality* (London and New York: Zed Books, 2007), pp. 15–16, Thomas Turner rightly points out that this threat applied to the regime, but not per se to Rwanda as a whole. Indeed, the majority of the population may well have considered those posing this threat to be its allies and potential liberators. Likewise, when Kigali argued that it needed to protect the Congolese Tutsi, this may well have reflected the feelings of many Rwandan Tutsi, but probably not those of many Hutu.

20. F. Misser, *Vers un nouveau Rwanda? Entretiens avec Paul Kagame* (Brussels, Belgium: Luc Pire, 1995), p. 121.

21. EU Special Representative for the Great Lakes Region Aldo Ajello has confirmed this information to this author.

22. According to the then–US ambassador to Kigali, Robert Gribbin, Kagame had already told him in March 1996 that "if Zaire continues to support the ex-FAR/*Interahamwe* against Rwanda, Rwanda in turn could find anti-Mobutu elements to support," adding that "if the international community could not help improve security in the region, the RPA might be compelled to act alone"; R. E. Gribbin, *In the Aftermath of Genocide: The U.S. Role in Rwanda* (New York: iUniverse, 2005), pp. 144–145.

23. The existence of this project was later confirmed by documents discovered in Mugunga camp in November 1996. Although these documents have never been published, some echoes can be found in extracts published in newspapers, for example, *Le Monde,*

November 19, 1996, and *Le Figaro,* November 20, 1996. It is surprising that neither the AFDL nor the RPA has kept these archives; on the contrary, they reportedly burned them (S. Boyle, "Rebels Repel Zaire Counter-Offensive," *Jane's Intelligence Review,* April 1, 1997). However, copies of a number of these papers are on file with this author.

24. R. Pourtier, "Congo-Zaïre-Congo: un itinéraire géopolitique au coeur de l'Afrique," *Hérodote* 86–87 (3rd–4th Term 1997): 27.

25. The more historical causes for the Angolan intervention in the war are addressed by T. Turner, "Angola's Role in the Congo War," in *The African Stakes of the Congo War,* ed. J. F. Clark (New York and Houndmills, UK: Palgrave Macmillan, 2002), pp. 77–81.

26. Thus, the Angolan weekly *Espresso* of May 3, 1997, affirmed that President Dos Santos insisted that Kabila should pursue his offensive to the end.

27. Having fled to Angola after the collapse of the Katangese secession in early 1963, a number of them were eventually integrated into the Angolan army, of which they (or rather their sons) became the 24th Regiment in 1994.

28. The exact amount, due mainly to the state-owned Zimbabwe Defence Industries, is unknown, but estimates range from US$40 million to US$200 million.

29. Zimbabwe happened to chair SADC's Organ on Politics, Defence, and Security. As Kabila's Congo had become a member of SADC, it benefited from a defense agreement providing for member states' assistance in case of an attack. However, South Africa and Botswana disagreed with the intervention in the DRC. Although presented as such by the coalition of the willing, it is doubtful whether the operation of Angola, Namibia, and Zimbabwe occurred under the SADC umbrella.

30. Other members of the club included Eritrea's Afewerki and Ethiopia's Meles Zenawi. All four eventually turned out to be just banal African dictators.

31. Addressing the Economic Commission for Africa in Addis Ababa on December 9, 1997, Secretary of State Madeleine Albright stated, without mentioning their names, that "Africa's best new leaders have brought a new spirit of hope and accomplishment to your countries—and that spirit is sweeping across the continent. . . . [Africa's new leaders] share a common vision of empowerment—for all their citizens, for their nations, and for their continent. . . . They are moving boldly to change the way their countries work—and the way we work with them."

32. Space prohibits a discussion of the *mai-mai* phenomenon. Suffice it to say that this is a generic term designating a wide array of local groups with very diverse organizational structures and ideologies, all claiming to protect the "indigenous" populations against exactions by "foreigners." A useful treatment can be found in K. Vlassenroot, "The Making of a New Order: Dynamics of Conflict and Dialectics of War in South Kivu (DR Congo)," PhD diss., University of Ghent, 2002, pp. 300–343. Vlassenroot insists that, while the *mai-mai* were also a resistance movement against foreign occupation, they can be understood only as an indigenous reaction to marginalization and exclusion. The theme of the *mai-mai* militias as an experience of more egalitarian forms of solidarity-based social organization, with violence as its main discursive mode, is developed in F. Van Acker and K. Vlassenroot, "Les 'maï-maï' et les fonctions

de la violence milicienne dans l'Est du Congo," *Politique Africaine* 84 (December 2001): 103–116.

33. It is important to restate that, contrary to Rwandan claims (thus "justifying" the invasion by the RPA), this occurred *after* the beginning of the war. In other words, the Rwandan invasion was not a consequence of the involvement of *génocidaires,* but rather its cause.

34. UN Security Council, *Final Report of the International Commission of Inquiry (Rwanda),* November 18, 1998, S/1998/1096, paras. 86–87.

35. International Crisis Group, *Scramble for the Congo: Anatomy of an Ugly War,* December 20, 2000, p. 19.

36. On this strange episode, see M. Ruhimbika, *Les Banyamulenge (Congo-Zaïre) entre deux guerres* (Paris: L'Harmattan, 2001), pp. 61–63, and K. Vlassenroot, "Citizenship, Identity Formation & Conflict in South Kivu: The Case of the Banyamulenge," *Review of African Political Economy* 29, no. 93–94 (2002): 510–511.

37. Ruhimbika explained that "we have founded the FRF as a reaction to the invasion of our country by Rwanda and to express our refusal of the instrumentalization of the Banyamulenge by Kigali" (*La Libre Belgique,* September 1, 2000).

38. More details on the parting of ways between the RCD/RPA and most Banyamulenge can be found in M. Ruhimbika, *Les Banyamulenge . . . , op. cit.,* pp. 80–109, and K. Vlassenroot, *The Making of a New Order . . . , op. cit.,* pp. 235–250. Vlassenroot notes that, as a consequence of their instrumentalization by Kigali, "the future of the Banyamulenge community risks becoming very grim" (*Ibid.,* p. 248).

39. *East African,* August 30–September 5, 1999.

40. G. Prunier, "L'Ouganda et les guerres congolaises," *Politique Africaine* 75 (October 1999): 47.

41. A Congolese acquaintance of this author compared the fighting in Kisangani to two neighbors breaking into his house and then fighting in his living room over who would steal his television set.

42. Only in the summer of 2003 were the supplies from Rwanda to the UPC cut off through airspace surveillance by the Interim Emergency Multinational Force (AIP, APFO, CSVR, FEWER, "Ituri: Stakes, Actors, Dynamics," September 2003, p. 5).

43. On Rwandan and Ugandan involvement in the Ituri conflict, see, e.g., Human Rights Watch, *Ituri: "Covered in Blood": Ethnically Targeted Violence in North-Eastern DR Congo* (New York: Human Rights Watch, 2003); B. Leloup, "Le contentieux rwando-ougandais et l'Est du Congo," in *L'Afrique des grands lacs. Annuaire 2002–2003,* ed. S. Marysse, F. Reyntjens (Paris: L'Harmattan, 2003), pp. 246–252.

44. Between May and September 2003, a French-led Interim Emergency Multinational Force was deployed by the European Union. It pacified Ituri's capital, Bunia, after which a reinforced Ituri brigade was deployed by the UN peacekeeping mission MONUC.

45. On Rwandan-Ugandan relations in the context of the Congo war, see B. Leloup, "Le contentieux rwando-ougandais et l'ordre politique dans la region des grands lacs d'Afrique," PhD diss., University of Antwerp, 2008.

46. The panel's early work was criticized on account of both its focus on the activities of the rebel groups and their sponsors, and its definition of "illegality." While these criticisms were not unfounded, the value of the panel's work is considerable: it has unearthed a large amount of empirical data and, in its later phase, redressed the balance by inquiring into the predatory practices of the Kabila regime and its allies, Zimbabwe in particular.

47. UN Security Council, *Final Report of the Panel of Experts on the Illegal Exploitation of Natural Resources and Other Forms of Wealth of the Democratic Republic of the Congo*, S/2002/1146, October 16, 2002. The panel produced another "Final Report" in October 2003 (see below).

48. C. Dietrich, *The Commercialisation of Military Deployment in Africa* (Pretoria, South Africa: ISS, 2001); C. Dietrich, *Hard Currency: The Criminalized Diamond Economy of the Democratic Republic of the Congo and Its Neighbours* Occasional Paper #4, Partnership Africa Canada, June 2002.

49. Several reports point to the direct link between the exploitation of resources and the continuation of the conflict. The UN panel noted that the control of mineral-rich areas "could be seen primarily as an economic and financial objective rather than a security objective for Rwanda" (UN Security Council, *Report of the Panel of Experts on the Illegal Exploitation of Natural Resources and Other Forms of Wealth of the Democratic Republic of the Congo*, S/2001/357, April 12, 2001, para. 175); "Most of the fights between Rwandan soldiers and *mai-mai* have occurred in the so-called 'coltan belt'" (ibid., para. 176). Under the title "Rwanda's unusual tactics," the panel found that "attacks (by the RPA) seem to coincide with the period when coltan has been extracted and put in bags for evacuation by the *mai-mai*. Attacked, the *mai-mai* abandon their coltan, which is then taken away by small aircraft" (ibid., para. 177).

50. I. Samset, "Conflict of Interests or Interests of Conflict? Diamonds & War in the DRC," *Review of African Political Economy* 29, no. 93–94, (2002): 477.

51. UN Security Council, *Final Report of the Group of Experts on the Democratic Republic of Congo, Pursuant to Security Council Resolution 1698 (2006)*, S/2007/423, July 18, 2007, para. 37.

52. C. Young, "Contextualizing Congo Conflicts: Order and Disorder in Postcolonial Africa," Clark, *The African Stakes*, p. 25.

53. Indeed, post-1994 Rwanda has been called "an army with a state," rather than a state with an army. In the Kivus, the Rwandan army was nicknamed "Soldiers Without Borders," a wink to the international NGO Médecins sans frontières.

54. Sénat de Belgique, *Rapport fait au nom de la commission d'enquête Grands Lacs par MM. Colla et Dallemagne*, session 2002–3, February 20, 2003, No. 2–942/1, p. 72.

55. UN Security Council, *Report of the Panel of Experts*, para. 130. See note 49.

56. This may seem a modest figure, but in light of the structure of the Rwandan economy, it is gigantic. Indeed in that same year, the production of export crops (mainly coffee and tea) accounted for only 0.4 percent of GDP (International Monetary Fund, *Rwanda: Selected Issues and Statistical Appendix*, IMF Country Report No. 04/383, 2004, p. 80).

57. S. Marysse, "Regress and War: The Case of the DR Congo," *European Journal of Development Research* 15, no. 1 (2003): 88.

58. Of course, it was not really invisible, but the international community preferred to turn a blind eye to these practices. US Ambassador Gribbin, for one, candidly acknowledged this reality: "Rwanda had discovered during the first war that war in Congo was relatively cheap—even profitable. . . . Well connected Rwandans . . . could seize opportunities . . . to accumulate wealth" (Gribbin, *In the Aftermath of Genocide,* pp. 282–283).

59. S. Jackson, "Making a Killing: Criminality & Coping in the Kivu War Economy," *Review of African Political Economy* 29, no. 93–94 (2002): 528.

60. Marysse ("Regress and war," p. 89) added that "as military spending . . . was limited as a condition for access to financial flows provided by the Bretton Woods institutions, . . . wartime plunder has helped finance the conflict." He denounced the "ostrich policy" of a number of bilateral donors and the international financial institutions that, by continuing to fund the invading countries (Rwanda and Uganda) in the knowledge that their aid is fungible, indirectly supported the continuation of the war.

61. The "Congo Desk" had an office called "Production," which oversaw the economic aspects of Rwandan operations in the DRC.

62. UN Security Council, *Report of the Panel of Experts,* para. 126. See note 49.

63. International Crisis Group, *The Kivus: The Forgotten Crucible of the Congo Conflict* (Nairobi and Brussels, January 24, 2003).

64. Many civil society sources in North and South Kivu reported Rwandan troop movements, and MONUC openly suspected the presence of the Rwandan army on Congolese soil (see, for instance, "DRC: MONUC Denounces Obstruction of Verification Missions in East," Nairobi, IRIN, October 29, 2003).

65. UN Security Council, *Final Report of the Panel of Experts on the Illegal Exploitation of Natural Resources and Other Forms of Wealth of the Democratic Republic of the Congo,* S/2003/1027, October 23, 2003.

66. Letter dated October 20, 2003, from Mahmoud Kassem, chair of the panel, to UN Secretary-General Kofi Annan.

67. Para. 2 of the unpublished Section V.

68. UN Security Council, *Report of the Group of Experts on the Democratic Republic of the Congo,* S/2005/30, January 25, 2005, para. 185.

69. Ibid., paras. 199–200.

70. UN Security Council, *Report of the Panel of Experts,* paras. 135–142. See note 65.

71. Sénat de Belgique, *Rapport fait,* p. 119.

72. UN Security Council, *Report of the Group of Experts on the Democratic Republic of the Congo,* S/2005/30, January 25, 2005, paras. 140–146.

73. J. Cuvelier, "Réseaux de l'ombre et configurations régionales: le cas du commerce du coltan en République Démocratique du Congo," *Politique Africaine* 93 (2004): 82–92.

74. I. Taylor, "Conflict in Central Africa: Clandestine Networks & Regional/Global Configurations," *Review of African Political Economy* 30, no. 95 (2003): 48.

75. Ibid., p. 52.

76. The latter category of Rwandans was imported between 1937 and 1955 as workers as a result of deliberate policies by the Belgian colonial authorities, which even set up an agency (Mission d'immigration des Banyarwanda) to that effect.

77. The Tutsi arrived mainly in 1959–1964, 1973, and 1990–1994.

78. The Hutu arrived massively in mid-1994.

79. See J. Gérard-Libois, J. Van Lierde, *Congo 1965* (Brussels, Belgium: CRISP, 1965), pp. 79–80.

80. For details on earlier developments, see, e.g., J.-P. Pabanel, "La question de la nationalité au Kivu," *Politique Africaine* 41 (March 1991): 32–40; A. Guichaoua, *Le problème des régugiés rwandais et des populations banyarwanda dans la région des grands lacs africains* (Geneva, Switzerland: UNHCR, 1992); P. Kanyamachumbi, *Les populations du Kivu et la loi sur la nationalité. Vraie ou fausse problématique* (Kinshasa, Congo: Editions Select, 1993); "Dossier: la 'guerre' de Masisi," *Dialogue* 192 (August–September 1996); F. Reyntjens and S. Marysse, *Conflits au Kivu: antécédents et enjeux* (Antwerp, Belgium: Centre for the Study of the Great Lakes Region of Africa, 1996); J.-C. Willame, *Banyarwanda et Banyamulenge. Violences ethniques et gestion de l'identitaire au Kivu* (Brussels, Belgium, and Paris: Institut Africain-L'Harmattan, Cahiers Africains, No. 25, 1997); P. Mathieu, J.-C. Willame, eds., *Conflits et guerres au Kivu et dans la région des grands lacs. Entre tensions locales et escalade régionale* (Brussels, Belgium, and Paris: Institut Africain-L'Harmattan, Cahiers Africains, No. 39–40, 1999).

81. An important precedent took place in June 1991, when armed Hutu groups attacked state agents in charge of a census of nationals in Masisi. Offices were ransacked and registers destroyed. Already at that stage, the insecurity was linked to the Rwandan conflict: in March 1991, a retired Rwandan army officer, Colonel Aloys Simba, was arrested in Goma while carrying weapons and funds.

82. For details, see Willame, *Banyarwanda et Banyamulenge,* pp. 66–68, 124–131.

83. As seen above, this proportion reached 70 percent in the zone of Masisi.

84. AZADO, *Nord-Kivu: Etat d'urgence*, Kinshasa, April 1996, p. 4; on August 3, 1996, the NGO SIMA-Kivu organized a conference in Brussels around the theme "Zaire-Rwanda-Burundi: Who would profit from the creation of a Hutu-land and a Tutsi-land?"

85. US Committee for Refugees, *Masisi, Down the Road from Goma: Ethnic Cleansing and Displacement in Eastern Zaire* (Washington, DC: US Committee for Refugees, 1996), p. 16.

86. *Africa News Bulletin–Bulletin Information Africaine*, April 1, 1996.

87. S. Autesserre, *The Trouble with the Congo: Local Violence and the Failure of International Peacebuilding* (New York: Cambridge University Press, 2010).

88. Already in 1998, a UN investigative team concluded that "the systematic massacre of those (Hutu refugees) remaining in Zaire was an abhorrent crime against humanity, but the underlying rationale for the decision is material to whether these killings constituted genocide, that is, a decision to eliminate, in part, the Hutu ethnic group" (UN Security Council, *Report of the Investigative Team Charged with Investigating Serious*

Violations of Human Rights and International Humanitarian Law in the Democratic Republic of Congo, S/1998/581, June 29, 1998, para. 96). A mapping exercise conducted on behalf of the UN High Commission for Human Rights, published in 2010, confirmed and detailed a long list of atrocities uncovered earlier by UN panels, national and international NGOs, and investigative journalists. It concluded that the vast majority of the 617 listed incidents were to be classified as war crimes and crimes against humanity. On the issue of genocide, it noted that "several incidents listed in this report, if investigated and judicially proven, point to circumstances and facts from which a court could infer the intention to destroy the Hutu ethnic group in the DRC in part, if these were established beyond all reasonable doubt"; UN Office of the High Commissioner for Human Rights, *Democratic Republic of the Congo, 1993–2003: Report of the Mapping Exercise Documenting the Most Serious Violations of Human Rights and International Humanitarian Law Committed Within the Territory of the Democratic Republic of the Congo between March 1993 and June 2003* (Geneva, Switzerland: United Nations, 2010), para. 31.

89. See, e.g., V. Peskin, "Victor's Justice Revisited: Rwandan Patriotic Front Crimes and the Prosecutorial Endgame at the ICTR," in *Remaking Rwanda: State Building and Human Rights After Mass Violence,* ed. S. Straus and L. Waldorf (Madison: University of Wisconsin Press, 2011), pp. 173–183.

90. The final report of the UN group of experts on the DRC offers ominous reading: UN Security Council, *Letter Dated 29 November 2011 from the Chair of the Security Council Committee Established Pursuant to Resolution 1533 (2004) Concerning the Democratic Republic of the Congo Addressed to the President of the Security Council,* S/2011/738, December 2, 2011.

91. Ibid., paras. 136–158.

92. Ibid., paras. 41–68.

93. F. Reyntjens, *A Volcano with a Lid: Governance in Post-Genocide Rwanda,* forthcoming.

94. UN Security Council, *Letter Dated 29 November 2011,* paras. 115–122, 284–288.

95. Ibid., paras. 484–492. For instance, the panel found that the house in Goma of General Bosco Ntaganda is on a street that crosses the border into Gisenyi, Rwanda, and that the entire area between the official border crossings is controlled exclusively by soldiers loyal to Ntaganda. The minerals are usually brought in vehicles into the neutral zone, after which they are carried to the Rwandan side, where they are loaded onto other vehicles. During smuggling operations, Ntaganda's troops cut off all access to the area. Rwandan soldiers had sentry posts all along the border, and nothing could cross without their knowledge. The panel estimated that Ntaganda made about $15,000 per week by taxing at this crossing point (ibid., paras. 485–487).

APPENDIX 12.1. TIMELINE

1993
October 21. Coup d'état in Burundi; beginning of civil war.

1994
April–July. Resumption of the civil war in Rwanda; genocide against the Tutsi; RPF seizes power; 2 million Hutu, including defeated army and militia, flee to neighboring countries, Zaire in particular.

1995
Fall. Large-scale violence in North Kivu; hit-and-run operations by Rwandan Hutu refugees, operating from Zaire, against targets in Rwanda.

1996
September. Start of the "Banyamulenge rebellion" supported by Rwanda.
October. Creation in Kigali of AFDL, with Laurent-Désiré Kabila as its spokesperson.
October–December. AFDL, supported by Rwanda and Uganda, occupies a buffer zone in eastern Zaire, stretching from Kalémie to Bunia.

1997
February. Angola joins the anti-Mobutu coalition.
May 17. Fall of Kinshasa.
May 29. Kabila sworn in as president of DRC, the new name of Zaire.

1998
August 2. Beginning of a new Congolese "rebellion" masterminded by Rwanda.
August 12. RCD rebel movement formally launched.
August 19. Deployment of Angolan, Zimbabwean, and Namibian troops in support of Kinshasa regime.
August 23. Fall of Kisangani.
November. Creation of another rebel movement, the MLC, with Ugandan support.

1999
May–June, August. Fighting between Rwandan and Ugandan armies in Kisangani.
July 10. Signing of the Lusaka Accord.

2000
June 5–10. Heavy fighting between Rwandan and Ugandan armies in Kisangani. Close to 1,000 civilians killed. Widespread destruction.

2001

January 16. Assassination of Laurent-Désiré Kabila.

January 26. Joseph Kabila assumes office.

2002

February 25. Launch of the Inter-Congolese Dialogue in Sun City (South Africa).

September. Rwanda officially pulls out troops from the DRC but retains a covert
   presence.

December 17. Global and Inclusive Accord signed in Pretoria, South Africa.

2003

June. European Interim Emergency Multinational Force deployed in Ituri; replaced by
   MONUC Ituri brigade in September.

June–July. 1+4 presidency, transitional government, and transitional parliament in
   place.

2005

December 18–19. Constitution adopted by referendum.

2006

July 30. First round of presidential elections: Kabila 44.81%, Bemba 20.03%, Gizenga
   13.06%; parliamentary elections: PPRD 111 seats, MLC 64, PALU 34, RCD-
   Goma 15.

October 29. Second round of presidential elections: Kabila 58.05%, Bemba 41.95%.

December 6. Joseph Kabila sworn in as president.

APPENDIX 12.2. MAIN ACTORS

Alliance des Forces pour la Libération du Congo-Zaïre (AFDL): Rwanda- and Uganda-backed rebel group led by Laurent-Désiré Kabila that overthrew the Mobutu regime in May 1997.

Banyamulenge: Congolese Tutsi group living in South Kivu; started the war in September 1996 with the support of Rwanda.

Banyarwanda: Kinyarwanda speakers living in eastern DRC; both Hutu and Tutsi.

Jean-Pierre Bemba: Leader of the MLC rebel movement; unsuccessful presidential candidate in 2006; indicted by the International Criminal Court for war crimes committed in the Central African Republic.

Congrès National pour la Défense du Peuple (CNDP): Congolese Tutsi militia, formally integrated in FARDC, supported by Rwanda; its leader Laurent Nkunda arrested by Rwanda in early 2009, replaced by Bosco Ntaganda.

Forces Armées Rwandaises (FAR): Former Rwandan government army that retreated to Eastern Zaire after its defeat in the summer of 1994, and conducted raids against Rwanda from the refugee camps in 1995–1996.

Forces Armées Zaïroises (FAZ)/Forces Armées Congolaises (FAC)/Forces Armées de la République Démocratique du Congo (FARDC): Successive names of the Zairean/Congolese government army.

Forces Démocratiques pour la Libération du Rwanda (FDLR): Rwandan Hutu rebel movement operating in eastern DRC.

Joseph Kabila: Son of Laurent-Désiré Kabila, who succeeded his father as president in January 2001; elected president in 2006, reelected in 2011.

Laurent-Désiré Kabila: Leader of the AFDL; became president in May 1997; assassinated in January 2001.

Paul Kagame: Leader of the RPF/RPA; de facto ruler of Rwanda since 1994; became president in 2000; elected in 2003, reelected in 2010.

Mai-mai: Local militias operating in North and South Kivu; claim to protect local populations against "invaders."

Mobutu Sese Seko: President of Zaire from 1965 to 1997; overthrown by Laurent-Désiré Kabila in May 1997; died a few months later in exile in Morocco.

Mouvement de Libération du Congo (MLC): Uganda-backed rebel movement created in November 1998; its leader, Jean-Pierre Bemba, unsuccessfully stood for president in 2006.

Yoweri Museveni: President of Uganda since 1986.

Bosco Ntaganda: Leader of the CNDP and general in the FARDC; indicted by ICC for war crimes committed in Ituri.

Rassemblement Congolais pour la Démocratie (RCD): Rwanda-backed rebel group that started a war against the Kabila regime in August 1998.

Rwanda Defence Forces: Rwandan national army.

Rwanda Patriotic Front/Army (RPF/A): Tutsi dominated movement that started a rebellion in October 1990 and took power in July 1994; de facto single party.

Uganda People's Defence Forces (UPDF): Ugandan national army.

União Nacional para a Independência Total de Angola (UNITA): Angolan rebel movement defeated in 2008.

Union des Patriotes Congolais (UPC): Main Ituri militia group; its leader, Thomas Lubanga, was the first to be convicted by the International Criminal Court in 2012.

thirteen

The Growth of China in Africa

IAN TAYLOR

The huge growth of Chinese political and business interests in Africa is conceivably the most significant development for the continent since the ending of the Cold War. Published trade figures alone bear evidence to the speed by which the Chinese economic presence in Africa has developed over the past ten years or so: China is now Africa's largest bilateral trading partner. A massive surge in Chinese economic interests in Africa has seen the value of China's trade with Africa increase from US$4 billion in 1996 to US$155 billion in 2011 (Stevens, 2012).

Much of this expansion is underpinned by a desire to obtain sources of raw materials and energy for China's ongoing economic growth and for new export markets for Chinese producers and traders obliged to seek new markets by domestic dynamics within China's economy (see Taylor, 2009). Trade between Africa and China began to conspicuously accelerate around 2000 and between 2001 and 2006, Africa's exports to China rose at an annual rate of over 40 percent (Wang Jianye, 2007: 5). Since 2003 alone, Sino-African trade has increased by nearly 500 percent. Notably, back in 1990, no African countries had trade with China above 5 percent of their GDP; by 2008, nearly two dozen had passed this benchmark. Currently, two-thirds of African nations list China as a top-five trading partner and, in contrast to trade with the West, Chinese economic linkages with Africa demonstrated a strong resilience in the wake of the post-2008 global financial crisis.[1]

CHINA'S AFRICA POLICIES

With the abandonment of Maoism, the reform-era Chinese state has been based on "an unwritten social contract between the party and the people where the people do not compete with the party for political power as long as the party looks after their economic fortunes" (Breslin, 2005: 749). When projected abroad, "foreign policy that sustains an international environment supportive of economic growth and stability in China serves these objectives" (Sutter, 2008: 2). The developing world has long been a noteworthy area where Beijing's foreign policy has been pursued energetically, using the development of "common interests" with the South to raise China's global stature.[2] Africa specifically has emerged as a relatively significant component in Chinese calculations at diverse levels, whether state, provincial, municipal, or individual. While political considerations are important, it is the economics of the relationship that is in the driving seat.[3]

Chinese engagement with Africa is long-standing (see Duyvendak, 1949; Hutchison, 1975; Snow, 1988; Taylor, 2006a), even if not the 2,000–3,000 years of continuous interaction that Chinese spokesmen habitually claim.[4] In the political realm, the continent has been of significance for China since around the late 1950s, when Chinese diplomacy began to emerge from out of the shadow of the Soviet Union (Han Nianlong, 1990: 138–139). During the Maoist period, China's role in Africa was ideologically motivated and included support for liberation movements fighting against colonial and minority rule, as well as direct state-to-state aid, most noticeably with Tanzania (Yu, 1970, 1975). By the mid-1970s, China in fact had a greater number of aid projects in Africa than the United States (Brautigam, 1998: 4), although the extremes of the Cultural Revolution incurred reputational costs that undercut much of the prestige that may have accrued from such largesse.[5]

However, as the Socialist Modernization program picked up under Deng Xiaoping from the late 1970s onward, there was an associated reduction of interest in the continent, although Chinese policymakers and many academics have always refuted this (see Taylor, 1997). The decline in interest in Africa can in part be explained by the fact that "Africa's failure to develop its economies efficiently and open up to the international market militated against Chinese policy aims, and the increasing extraneous role the continent played in global (read superpower) geopolitics resulted in a halt to closer Chinese involvement. Essentially, Beijing not only viewed Africa as largely immaterial in its quest for modernization, but also saw that the rationale behind its support for anti-Soviet elements in the continent was no longer valid" (Taylor, 1998: 443–444). Neglect of Africa by China got to a point where African students in Beijing demonstrated against China's declining interest in Africa and held aloft banners saying "Remember the United Nations in 1971"—a reminder that it was African nations that helped China's entry into the UN (*Agence France-Presse* [Beijing], June 19, 1986). In contrast to the Maoist past, ties with Africa were based on the dispassionate realities of trade and profit, aka "socialism with Chinese characteristics" (*Jianshe you Zhongguo tesede shehuizhuyi*).[6]

However, an event and two processes—one within Africa and the others within China—came together to promote the current interest of Chinese actors in Africa. Firstly, the consequences of the events of June 4, 1989, in and around Tiananmen Square led to Beijing undergoing a critical reevaluation of its policies. While Tiananmen Square occasioned a short-lived crisis in China's relations with the capitalist West, the reactions by many of Africa's elites were far more subdued, if not frankly supportive.[7] As the former Chinese foreign minister, Qian Qichen, put it: "it was . . . our African friends who stood by us and extended a helping hand in the difficult times following the political turmoil in Beijing, when Western countries imposed sanctions on China" (Qian Qichen, 2005: 200). Indicatively, the foreign minister of Angola expressed Luanda's "support for the resolute actions to quell the counter-revolutionary rebellion" (*Xinhua* [Beijing], August 7, 1989), while Namibia's Sam Nujoma dispatched a telegram of congratulations to the People's Liberation Army (*Xinhua* [Beijing], June 21, 1989). As one commentator later remarked, "the events of June 1989 . . . did not affect the PRC's relations with the Third World as it did with the Western world . . . what changed [was] the PRC's attitude towards the Third World countries, which . . . turned from one of benign neglect to one of renewed emphasis" (Gu Weiqun, 1995: 125).

As a consequence, the developing world was raised up in Chinese policy reckoning to become a "cornerstone" of Beijing's foreign policy.[8] Post-1989 the 1970s rhetoric of China being an "all-weather friend" (*quan tianhou pengyou*) of Africa was dusted off and employed with enthusiasm, something that has endured to this day (Taylor, 2004). This posture of mutual affirmation was a restatement of the Five Principles of Peaceful Co-existence, initially articulated in 1954. These Five Principles are viz., mutual respect for each other's territorial integrity; nonaggression; noninterference in each other's internal affairs; equality and mutual benefit; and peaceful coexistence.[9]

The aforementioned two macro-processes were firstly, Chinese state and private actors began to see in Africa great potential economically, partly as a result of economic reform programs that had gained momentum on the continent as the 1990s progressed. This evaluation was centered on the belief that African countries had implemented a raft of measures to advance privatization, open up the domestic economy to international investment, and sign a variety of bilateral and multilateral trading agreements that "locked in" the restructuring. Oftentimes an implicit assumption was that African economies had copied China's reformist policies.[10]

Chinese actors subsequently sought to take advantage of such developments, and in support of this Beijing has officially encouraged joint ventures and economic cooperation at multiple levels. The mid-2000s policy to "go global" (*zouchuqu*), which encouraged Chinese corporations to invest overseas and play a role in international capital markets (see Hong Eunsuk and Sun Laixiang, 2006) was in many respects an attempt by Beijing to catch up with a growing awareness regarding the interconnectedness of the international and domestic settings.[11] This has, in common with much Chinese policies, been sloganized as *yu guoji jiegui,* or "linking up with the international track" (Wang Hongying, 2007). Such an official standpoint couples with the faith held by many Chinese manufacturers and entrepreneurs that the sorts of products (household appliances, garments, and other domestic goods) that Chinese producers make have great potential in Africa, where the economy is relatively underdeveloped and where the consumers are identified as being more receptive to the kind of inexpensive products that a segment of Chinese manufacturers characteristically generate.[12] That the domestic markets of many African countries are comparatively small and that there is relatively little competition means that market share can be substantial almost from day one of operations. Additionally of course, the African continent is seen by both the Chinese government *and* Chinese companies to be abundant in natural resources, many of which are needed by China's burgeoning economy.[13]

The above dynamics then link up with the second macro-process, namely that China's fast-developing economy in itself pushes forward Sino-African commerce. Obviously, China's growth in recent years has been remarkable and does not need repeating here. Yet, what is often disregarded in deliberations on Sino-African ties is that the significance of China to Africa has to be understood in terms of Beijing's own development path. China's real economic growth—on average just under 9 percent annually for the past thirty years—has been based on export figures that have grown by an average of over 17 percent per year. However, growing saturation of China's existing export markets as well as a precipitous rise in the price of imported unprocessed materials into China (due in the main to Chinese demand) makes the African continent increasingly valuable to China's economy. Certainly, as the growth in the net worth of Chinese exports declines, Beijing has to support domestic economic growth through the addition of more Chinese "content" to its exported goods (*Business Day* [Johannesburg], February 22, 2007). Sourcing raw materials to do this is fundamental and is where Africa fits centrally into both Chinese foreign policy *and* domestic necessities.

"ANTI-HEGEMONISM"

On the political front, although preserving cordial ties with Washington is central to Chinese foreign policy, the developing world is increasingly significant. Since the demise of the Cold War, Beijing has often articulated anxiety about the existence of an unchallenged superpower and the hegemonism (*baquanzhuyi*) that this stimulates. Consequently, Chinese official policy has been to argue that it is essential that China and the developing world assist each other and work together to counteract the overweening power of the United States.[14] Central to this position is the assertion that noninterference and respect for the domestic affairs of sovereign states should be the foundations of any international order. This policy is then set alongside an accommodation—but also hedging—with Washington (Foot, 2006).

The above posture then feeds into the long-held position by Beijing that it is the de facto leader of the developing world (formerly, the Third World). Characteristically, when in South Africa in early 2007 President Hu Jintao asserted that while "Africa is the continent with the largest number of developing countries," "China is the biggest developing country" (*Xinhua* [Beijing], February 8, 2007). This is a common refrain in Sino-African relations, as is the assertion "as it is known to all, Western powers, not China, colonized Africa and looted resources there in the history" [*sic*] (*China Daily,* April 26, 2006). This construction of history is then linked to the notion that China and Africa are "natural" partners, given that "as developing regions that . . . once suffered the oppression and exploitation of imperialism and colonialism, China and the African countries . . . easily understand each other's pursuit of independence and freedom and . . . have a natural feeling of intimacy" (Qian Qichen, 2005: 200).

At the global level, as China's leadership has increasingly integrated China into the global capitalist economy and more and more plays by essentially Western-derived rules and norms (epitomized by Beijing's membership in the World Trade Organization), they have worked toward intensifying political ties with the developing world, not least in Africa. This can, in part, be seen as a hedging strategy to balance the international order, construct a defensive diplomatic shield, and develop a support constituency. This milieu can then be deployed when appropriate if and when China's growing internationalization threatens domestic interests. This reality reflects the overall stress in China's diplomacy of practicing both engagement *and* a certain distant coolness vis-à-vis the global order (Breslin, 2007). This posture, and the instinct to "restore" China to its "rightful place" in the world (Mosher, 2000; Scott, 2007) in part by being understood as some sort of mentor of the developing world, while equally acting as a "responsible power" (*fuzeren de daguo*), are important rationales influencing Chinese foreign policy. Indeed, such coalition building partly explains the fresh diplomatic developments in Chinese links to Africa, so vividly demonstrated by the Sino-Africa Forums, which have been held every three years since 2000.

FORUM ON CHINA-AFRICA COOPERATION

The first Forum on China-Africa Cooperation (FOCAC) met in October 2000 in Beijing and was attended by nearly eighty ministers from forty-five African countries. The second ministerial conference was held in Addis Ababa, Ethiopia, in December 2003 and passed the *Addis Ababa Action Plan (2004–2006)*. The FOCAC Summit and the third Ministerial Conference were held in Beijing in November 2006, while the fourth met in Sharm el-Sheikh, Egypt, in 2009.

The background to FOCAC I can be traced to the visit by Chinese Premier Jiang Zemin to Africa in 1996. In early 1996, Jiang Zemin toured Kenya, Ethiopia, Egypt, Mali, Namibia, and Zimbabwe and during this tour, President Jiang publicly unveiled a new and emerging Chinese approach to Africa. The main theme of Jiang's pronouncements was to strengthen solidarity and cooperation with African countries. According to a Chinese report, "The guiding principle that China follows in developing relations with African countries in the new situation is: 'to treat each other as equals, develop sincere friendship, strengthen solidarity and cooperation, and seek common development.'" (*Xinhua*, May 22, 1996).

Interestingly, Chinese sources claim that it was African leaders who initiated and asked for a summit. In his diplomatic memoirs, Tang Jiaxuan, foreign minister of China from 1998 to 2003, wrote that in 1999, Madagascar's foreign minister, who was visiting Beijing at the time, proposed that China and Africa establish a mechanism to strengthen relations. After a feasibility study, China decided to follow up on the suggestion and proposed to hold the first forum in 2000 (Tang Jiaxuan, 2011: 529). In October 1999 President Jiang Zemin wrote to all heads of African states, as well as the Secretary-General of the Organisation of African Unity, to formally propose the convening of a Sino-Africa forum. In his letter he outlined principles for carrying out consultation on an equal footing, enhancing understanding, increasing consensus, promoting friendship, and furthering cooperation. When this was greeted with a favorable reception, the Chinese established a preparatory committee composed of eighteen ministries. The Ministry of Foreign Affairs and Ministry of Foreign Trade and Economic Cooperation were assigned the role of anchor (see Taylor, 2011). An October 2000 forum on China-Africa Cooperation Ministerial Conference in Beijing was held.

The meeting in October 2000 was the first gathering of its kind in the history of China-Africa relations and was attended by eighty ministers charged with foreign affairs and international trade and economic development from forty-five African states. Representatives of international and regional organizations also attended, as did delegates from two African countries that then did not even have diplomatic ties with China (namely, Liberia and Malawi). Discussions at the conference were organized into four separate work sessions: trade; economic reform (with China's program being showcased as a possible model); poverty eradication and sustainable development; and cooperation in education, science technology, and health care.

FOCAC II was held December 15 and 16, 2003, in Addis Ababa. This summit produced the *Addis Ababa Action Plan,* which envisioned an acceleration of Chinese involvement in promoting development on the continent. Apart from the Chinese role in infrastructure building, the plan promised to expand agricultural support to states in Africa via training and technical support and advice. Linked to the issue of development was the question of Sino-African trade, which had jumped by more than 400 percent since FOCAC I. Problematically for Beijing, this huge increase in trade was hugely in favor of China. For instance, the trade relationship between Ethiopia and China in 2004 was 80 percent in favor of China, helping to prompt a recall of Ethiopian ambassadors and diplomats to attend a ten-day orientation on economic diplomacy, held by the Ministry of Trade and Industry and the Export Promotion Agency (*Addis Fortune,* August 8, 2004). To tackle such trade imbalances, the plan advocated the granting of zero-tariff treatment to various commodities from the least developed countries on the continent, while promoting investment.

However, it was the 2006 meeting in Beijing that arguably marked a climax in Sino-African ties, following on from the decision in 2005 to upgrade FOCAC to the status of an official summit between Chinese and African leaders—a meeting of high-level political leaders with a definite program of action on the agenda. Such a decision reflected the growing seriousness with which China's elites held Africa and was part of a wider decision-making process that designated 2006 the "Year of Africa" for China.[15] This Chinese "Year of Africa" began with the release of the *China's African Policy* document in January 2006, aimed at presenting "to the world the objectives of China's policy towards Africa and the measures to achieve them" (Ministry of Foreign Affairs, 2006: 1).

The document was the equivalent of a white paper in which the Chinese government put forward its proposals for cooperation with Africa in various fields in the coming years. The document was the first of its kind in Beijing's diplomatic history with the continent. All through the paper, the Chinese government made repeated reference to the "unequal" relationship that Africa has had with "the West." In contrast, the paper posited that China concretely supports "African countries' independent choice of the road of development" (Ministry of Foreign Affairs, 2006: 2). In addition, Beijing advanced a new style of association with Africa, asserting that, "China will unswervingly carry forward the tradition of China-Africa friendship, and, proceeding from the fundamental interests of both the Chinese and African peoples, establish and develop *a new type of strategic partnership with Africa*, featuring political equality and mutual trust, economic win-win cooperation and cultural exchange" (ibid.). Hours after the white paper was released, Chinese Foreign Minister Li Zhaoxing set out on a nine-day tour of Africa that took him to Cape Verde, Senegal, Mali, Liberia, Nigeria, and Libya. Later, in April 2006, President Hu Jintao toured Nigeria, Kenya, and Morocco, giving Hu an opportunity to propose a five-point plan to forge what he called a "New Type of China-Africa Strategic Partnership" (*Xinhua*, April 27, 2006). Subsequently, in June 2006 Premier Wen Jiabao took part in the World Economic Forum in Cape Town and then proceeded to visit Angola, Congo-Brazzaville, Egypt, Ghana, South Africa, Tanzania, and Uganda. This flurry of activity and official visits was to set the scene for FOCAC III, held in Beijing in November 2006.

One of the key outcomes of FOCAC III was the declaration of the Beijing summit. In a staged and somewhat dramatic setting, Hu Jintao, Ethiopian Prime Minister Meles Zenawi, and Egyptian President Mohammed Hosni Mubarak read aloud the declaration at the end of the two-day meeting. Mubarak read the sections of the declaration that stated that China and Africa would build up a "new strategic partnership" to feature political equality, mutual trust, economic win-win cooperation, and cultural exchanges. Mubarak was quoted as asserting that "we hold that the establishment of a new type of strategic partnership is both the shared desire and independent choice of China and Africa, serves our common interests, and will help enhance solidarity, mutual support and assistance, and unity of the developing countries, and contribute to durable peace and harmonious development in the world" (*Xinhua* [Beijing], November 16, 2006). The declaration called for enhancing South–South cooperation and North–South dialogue to promote balanced and sustainable development of the global economy and to facilitate all countries' sharing in the benefits of common development. It also recommended that the North boost developmental assistance to Africa.

The Ethiopian prime minister read the section of the declaration that stated that "China and Africa enjoy traditional solidarity and cooperation and China-Africa friendship enjoys immense popular support. In the new century China and African countries should enhance their traditional friendship and expand mutually beneficial cooperation to achieve common development and prosperity" (ibid.). This was followed by Hu Jintao's section, where he spoke of

Beijing's assistance to African countries and went on to assert that "China reaffirms its support for the African countries in their efforts to strengthen themselves through unity and to independently resolve African problems, supports the African regional and sub-regional organizations in their efforts to promote economic integration, and supports the African countries in implementing the 'New Partnership for Africa's Development' programs" (ibid.).

The summit also adopted an action plan on China-Africa cooperation for 2007–2009, in which both sides say they are resolved to bolster their companies' joint energy exploration and exploitation under the principle of reciprocity. The document was endorsed by the leaders of China and those of forty-eight African states attending the summit. The outcomes of FOCAC reflect the increased priority China's leadership places on Africa. In the three-year plan, China pledged to double aid to Africa by 2009 (to about $1 billion); set up a $5 billion China-Africa development fund to encourage Chinese companies to invest in Africa; provide $3 billion in preferential loans and $2 billion in preferential buyer credits to African countries; cancel all debt stemming from Chinese interest-free government loans that matured by the end of 2005 for the thirty-one highly indebted and least developed countries (LDCs) in Africa that have relations with China (an amount estimated at around $1.4 billion); further open China's markets to exports from African LDCs by increasing from 190 to 440 the number of products receiving zero-tariff treatment; train 15,000 African professionals, double the number of Chinese government scholarships given annually to Africans (to 4,000), and send 100 senior agricultural experts and 300 youth volunteers; build 30 hospitals, 30 malaria treatment centers, and 100 rural schools (*Africa Renewal,* January 19, 2007). Stemming from FOCAC III, a formal strategic dialogue mechanism was established between China and the African Union (AU), with the first China-AU strategic dialogue being held in Addis Ababa in November 2008.

Equally, the China-Africa Development Fund was officially launched in June 2007 as China's prime investment vehicle in Africa. Established by the China Development Bank (which itself is under the direct jurisdiction of the State Council), by late 2009 the fund was worth $5 billion. However, it has been reported that "the Fund is finding it increasingly challenging to fund infrastructure programs in most African states because of the lack of essential facilities, including sound telecommunications systems." According to Wang Yong, the fund's managing director for the Eastern Africa Investment Department, "We find that they (prospective business partners) expect countries to have basic technology and sufficiently operational ports, airport and roads. . . . Unfortunately these facilities are not necessarily available in some countries on the continent" (*Business Day,* August 31, 2009). Consequently, fund personnel have begun touring Africa actively seeking investment sites. Clearly, establishing the fund and sensibly investing the money was not as easy as foreseen at FOCAC III back in 2006.

The fourth ministerial conference was held in Sharm el-Sheikh, Egypt, November 8–9, 2009. In comparison to the festivities associated with FOCAC III in Beijing in 2006, FOCAC IV was more muted. According to one Chinese source, the conference had two major tasks to perform. One was to review the implementation of the follow-up actions of the 2006 Beijing FOCAC summit and the other was to draw up a new plan of action for cooperation between China and Africa in the next three years.[16] FOCAC IV was, like all its predecessors, a bonanza of developmental assistance projects and loans. Pledges made at FOCAC are invariably implemented by the Chinese, thanks largely due to the various follow-up mechanisms built into FOCAC's frameworks. What was interesting at FOCAC IV was that compared to the proposals that emanated from FOCAC III, cooperation in international relations moved higher up the priority list, replacing economic cooperation, directly next to political cooperation. It was likely that in the context of the ongoing financial crisis, which had hit China and Africa to differing degrees, cooperation at the international level was deemed crucial.

Yet, according to one Chinese commentator, Liu Haifang of the Institute of West Asian and African Studies in Beijing, "the most dramatic change in the new Sharm el-Sheikh Action Plan from the previous Beijing Action Plan [was] the absence in the new plan of any equivalent to the eye-catching pledge in the 2006 document to double China's aid assistance to African countries" (quoted in *Xinhua*, December 17, 2009). Instead, the $10 billion in preferential loans was inserted and devoted specifically to infrastructure, highlighted as a key priority for Sino-African cooperation. While the constraints of the financial crisis no doubt helped explain aspects of this development (the non-appearance of such eye-catching statements as witnessed at FOCAC III), Liu noted that the reason for this also sprang from domestic Chinese processes:

After the 2006 Summit, a common theme in the extensive literature on China's aid assistance to Africa, was criticism of what was seen as inadequate transparency in the application of funds, and questioning of the apparent ambiguity between seeking economic profit and providing development assistance and aid. This may well have led to reflection and readjustment of the definition of China's official development assistance. It seems likely that a deliberate decision has been taken to avoid conspicuous words such as "double aid" that were used in the previous plan and which stimulated too much close attention. (Ibid.)

A further commentator in fact noted the importance of "clarify[ing] the nature of Chinese aid to Africa and to specify its amounts. Indeed, the announcement of a doubling (in flow) of the aid between 2006 and 2009 [did] not refer to any baseline. The lack of clarity surrounding this announcement [was] a double-edged sword for the Chinese: on one hand it [made] it impossible to critically monitor how well commitments are being met, but it also create[d] expectations from recipient African nations. While each country knows what it receives and might expect the doubling of aid on a bilateral basis, the promise of doubling has been made at the continent scale. The issue of aid allocation per country has never been settled and Chinese arbitrations start to make some African countries unhappy" (Guérin, 2008: 6).

Much of the problem stems from the issue of sustainability and the unrealistic expectations of African governments vis-à-vis China. It has become quite clear that some elements of African opinion have already entered into a dependency mind-set with regard to China's rise in Africa.[17] In response, during his 2009 tour to Africa, while Hu Jintao had sought to reassure the continent about Beijing's determination to fulfill its FOCAC III commitments, Wen Jiabao played the role of seeking to fend off the ever-increasing expectations of new aid pledges. The burden of these extremely high expectations, where China is presumed—uncritically—to be the new messiah in Africa, is a very heavy load for Beijing to shoulder. Instead of expecting bountiful largesse from Beijing, Chinese policymakers would much prefer African leaders to focus on commerce and strengthening economic ties.[18]

ECONOMIC RELATIONS

The legitimacy of the Communist Party of China's (CPC) political system today is based upon the Communist Party's ability to sustain economic growth. A problem intimately linked to this is that Beijing faces a long-term decline in domestic oil production (Taylor, 2006b). China's policymakers actively encourage national companies to aggressively pursue oil and other natural resources in Africa. China is the world's second-largest oil importer and the second-largest consumer of African resources. The abundance of natural resources in Africa has thus led Chinese corporations to seek long-term deals with African governments to ensure continued access to all varieties of raw materials and energy in Africa. Because China's national oil companies are largely excluded from the majority of Middle Eastern oil supplies and because Beijing wishes to limit vulnerability to the international oil market, there is a policy to encourage investment in Africa, courting states that the West has overlooked. Consequently, this approach toward securing access to African resources is what Zweig and Bi Jianhai (2005: 31) have dubbed a resource-based foreign policy, which by its very nature has "little room for morality." The potential fallout on the continent that stems from such a milieu has at times damaged China's overall reputation and arguably promoted a growing maturity in policy calculations.

The interest in ensuring its resource security and economic growth through involvement in Africa is by no means restricted to oil, but rather encompasses all natural resources. From investment in copper in Zambia and platinum interests in Zimbabwe to supporting fishing ventures in Gabon and Namibia, Chinese corporations have vigorously courted and pursued the political and business elite in Africa to guarantee continued access, often lubricated with sweetener deals provided by central government. One of the benefits of Chinese interest in African resources is that it has dramatically increased demand and revitalized industries such as Zambia's copper industry. However, the influx of capital into weak and authoritarian governments also has potential for long-term consequences in Africa, as leaders may be tempted to neglect necessary reforms, bolstered by newly perceived economic security from Chinese receipts (see Taylor, 2010).

Yet such a potential negative outcome is not a problem that can be specifically associated with Chinese engagement with Africa and is in fact intimately linked to the nature of the state in much of Africa. In short, African politics must be understood as the utilization of patronage and clientelism and operates within neo-patrimonial modes of governance. "Political instability is . . . rooted in the extreme politicization of the state as an organ to be monopolized for absolute power and accelerated economic advancement" (Fatton, 1988: 35). In this context, the idea that resources should be channeled toward the nebulous concept of "national development" is out of the question in many African states. Productive economic activities and notions of long-term investment are sidelined in favor of immediate consumption, display, and resource diffusion (Chabal and Daloz, 1999). In this regard, Chinese policy is vulnerable to the claim that in dealing only with the state and rigorously adhering to its noninterference strategy, Beijing may exacerbate structural faults in the political economies of a number of African states. Until and unless African elites themselves advance transparency, pro-development policies, and equitable growth (and are prepared and competent enough to put them into force), China at present does little to press them on such issues.

Such a scenario is a problem for China, as the international community, when looking at Chinese activity in Africa, is very often preoccupied with analyzing how China can match its growing commercial influence with responsibility. In turn, Beijing is increasingly zealous in reassuring the world of its desire to be a responsible power. As one commentator noted, "The challenge

is for China . . . to cooperate in defining and addressing the political and social challenges that arise in many of the . . . states of the world" where Chinese
interests are found (Zha Daojiong, 2006: 183).

Indeed, on the one hand one must note that with the exception of oil exports to China, Sino-African trade is generally lopsided in favor of Chinese exporters who are penetrating African markets with cheap household products.
Such imports into Africa have been criticized as doing little to encourage indigenous African manufacturing. Certainly it is the failure of African economies to industrialize and develop postindependence that means they produce
very few processed goods and are a natural target for Chinese exporters.[19] Yet,
much Chinese engagement to date reifies Africa's status as an exporter of raw
materials while an importer of manufactured goods, something that thus far
has consigned the African continent to underdevelopment and a reproduction
of Africa's historical relationship with its former colonial powers. Working
with African countries to overcome such structural weaknesses in Africa's
economies will be a major challenge for Beijing, particularly given Africa's historic economic trajectory.

However, Chinese trade figures with Africa need to be treated with caution.
The part played by Hong Kong as a transit point for Chinese imports and exports makes bilateral figures very dubious when estimating the levels of Chinese trade. A huge proportion of Chinese exports are routed through Hong
Kong. This is important in calculating bilateral trade figures because whether
an export is counted as a Chinese re-export obviously has an enormous bearing on trade statistics. In addition, foreign-owned firms based in China account for just over half of all Chinese trade. Much of Chinese trade is not
actually "Chinese" at all, and if domestic Chinese producers who produce under contract for export using foreign components are included, the figure goes
up. In fact, the majority of Chinese exports are produced by foreign-funded
enterprises, often joint ventures but increasingly wholly foreign owned. The
classic example of this is Wal-Mart, the largest single American importer of
Chinese goods, accounting for 15 percent of total imports of Chinese consumer products into the United States. As one account framed it, "The numbers are huge: over $30 billion in annual imports from China, representing
about 80% of the company's total imports. It would almost be accurate to say
that China doesn't have a trade surplus with the United States; it has one with
Wal-Mart" (Krakoff, 2010).

In addition to the above dynamics, "as Chinese producers can claim a 15
per cent VAT rebate for exports, there is an incentive for producers to overstate the value of exports, or even to totally fabricate exports and sell them at
home instead" (Breslin, 2007: 107). Any visitor to an African market these
days will observe huge amounts of Chinese-made products on sale—that is

not in dispute. The specific (and colossal) figures regarding Sino-African trade provided by Beijing, however, do need to be taken under caution.

Complicating this milieu is the fact that many of the products manufactured in China, but that are sold in African markets, are not actually brought into the continent by Chinese but by African traders. There are now quite elaborate trading networks linking China and Africa, and much of this is centered in the southern province of Guandong, where a relatively large population of African entrepreneurs now live and make deals. Indeed, in Guangzhou city an estimated 20,000 Nigerians alone live and work in the city (*This Day* [Lagos], September 13, 2007). Other African traders have long been established in Hong Kong, primarily based at Chungking Mansions in Tsim Sha Tsui, while Yiwu in Zhejiang Province is now a growing center for export trading to Africa and elsewhere. In fact, Yiwu is perhaps *the* key place where products from China are sold in wholesale quantities to traders from across Africa. African entrepreneurs generally buy in bulk, utilizing Chinese-owned cargo companies, and products are shipped direct to the continent or collected from markets in places such as Dubai.[20]

The point of the above is crucial: Chinese traders are *not* "flooding" the African market with cheap Chinese goods. Rather, African actors are actively facilitating the penetration of Africa by Chinese-made products. Figures do not exist on what proportion of goods sold in Africa's markets were brought in by Chinese entrepreneurs or by African traders, but information gleaned in various interviews and from observations in a variety of African marketplaces suggests that a large percentage was sourced and shipped by Africans. This is somewhat ironic given that condemnation by many African trade unions and civil society organizations of the "Asian tsunami" in cheap products lays the blame squarely on "the Chinese." If the trade pattern between Africa and China is becoming "neo-colonial" in character, it is with the active connivance of many Africans themselves. Yet given this, serious concern must be expressed that a dependent relationship is being crafted. Even if we accept the symbiotic nature of the partnership between the external and domestic, the fact remains that a relationship of dominance and subordination with strong dependent features exists. A certain nonchalance on the part of China regarding such dynamics is apparent. Chinese actors behave as is contextually convenient, with little regard for such complexities in the Sino-African relationship.

A CHINESE MODEL?

Politically as well as economically, China's presence in Africa has been based on the premise of providing an alternate development model for African states and leaders. According to Naidu and Davies (2006: 80), China is seen as "a refreshing alternative to the traditional engagement models of the West. . . . African governments see China's engagement as a point of departure from Western neo-colonialism and political conditions." Of course, this "refreshing alternative" suits incumbent elites. How it may affect and be received by citizens in autocratic African countries is another matter. Thus far, the emphasis China places on respect for state sovereignty and noninterference in its diplomatic rhetoric has meant a willingness to deal with states that have been ostracized by the West. This may appear attractive to some repressive African leaders, but it profoundly challenges the claimed Western vision of a flourishing Africa governed by liberal democracies. In Zimbabwe, for instance, "rumors abound that China has sold Zimbabwe's internal-security apparatus water cannons to subdue protesters and bugging equipment to monitor cell phone networks" (*New York Times*, July 25, 2005). A Zimbabwean analyst commented that "it is important to note . . . that Chinese 'non-interference' policy cannot be permanent. The Chinese are well aware of this themselves. Where deals are signed with unpopular dictatorial regimes that could later be replaced by a new government, it becomes necessary for the Chinese to protect such regimes" (Karumbidza, 2007: 88–89). Despite Chinese protestations to the contrary, supplying governments with equipment to suppress their own citizens *does* constitute a political decision to interfere.[21]

Through political and business summits such as the various Sino-African forums, as well as state visits by high-ranking Chinese political officials, Beijing symbolically and ostentatiously accords Africa equal diplomatic status with the dominant powers. For instance, as an emblematic gesture, it has become a tradition that the first overseas visit that China's foreign minister undertakes each year is to Africa. Equally, African elites are deeply appreciative of being given the red-carpet treatment whenever they turn up in Beijing. A research trip by this author to Beijing once coincided with the visit of Chad's president and it was quite revealing the way the visit was covered (top billing on Chinese television and in the newspapers) and how the Chadian flag was prominently displayed around Tiananmen Square.

In contrast, when an African leader visits London or Washington, unless they are from South Africa or Egypt or one of the few states deemed important, they are barely afforded a few minutes and even then they are more likely to be belabored for their numerous chronic failures in governance than they are to be toasted as "dear friends" and, importantly, credible statesmen. China's leadership realizes this and thus expends energy on massaging the egos of Africa's leaders. And this pays off. Beijing has been successful in gaining African support at institutions such as the United Nations, where the vote of the African bloc has allowed China to block resolutions on domestic human rights abuses. African support also of course helped Beijing in its campaign to host the 2008 Olympics.

Symbolic diplomacy, defined as the promotion of national representation abroad, has become an increasingly important component of Chinese foreign policy in Africa and elsewhere (see Kurlantzick, 2007). As leaders of a developing nation, Beijing's policymakers are very much aware of the importance of prestige projects. In a repeat of what Western powers did in the 1960s, China has been involved in large-scale endeavors that project a particular Chinese image, such as building national stadiums, all over Africa. This approach has proven beneficial to both the ruling elites in Africa, who view these as projections of regime legitimacy and power (and suitably impress the local populations), and to Beijing, as it demonstrates China's rising prominence and presence. Through these kinds of projects, combined with aid packages and the notion that China may be a model for Africa, Beijing is very much asserting itself as an equal of Western powers as well as appealing to the African elite classes. However, while the masses no doubt applaud the building of football stadiums, it is doubtful that the population displacements caused by Chinese projects to build dams in Ethiopia or pipelines in Sudan equally attract mass approval.

This brings us to the very notion of an alternative Chinese model in Africa. Dirlik (2006) notes that the "Beijing Consensus" draws its meaning and appeal not from some coherent set of economic or political ideas à la Ramo, but from its intimation of an alternative pole, from which those opposed to Washington and, by extension, the West can draw inspiration. Certainly, "China's alternative path is partly attractive because of the apparent success of the experience of economic reform. Other developing states might also lean towards the Chinese way not just because China's leaders don't attach democratizing and liberalizing conditions to bilateral relations, but also because China is coming to provide alternative sources of economic opportunities (with non-democratizing strings attached)" (Breslin, 2007: 2). But this does not mean that a coherent alternative has emerged yet.

Indeed, Africa's intellectuals must approach with caution the notion that China offers up an alternative model of development. Firstly, conceptions of Chinese "soft power" built on "the appeal of China as an economic model" (Kurlantzick, 2006: 5) overstate China's ability to project and promote an alternative economic type (Yan Xuetong, 2006). It is true that economic liberalization while preserving an authoritarian political system might appeal to some African autocrats, but this surely has its limits, not least to the Chinese themselves in promoting such a message, given that supporting authoritarian elites in Harare and Khartoum has already stimulated anti-Chinese feelings among African civil society leaders. Furthermore, China's sustained growth not only has taken place with no reference to democracy or transparency, but has also generally shunned policy reforms promoted from outside. This must seem attractive for those African leaders who have no real legitimacy or who are tired of having to fend off criticisms from the IFIs and the wider donor community.

Yet, China's extraordinary economic growth has come about, certainly initially, within the broader context of a capable state and in a region that is itself economically dynamic. Rapid economic growth without democratization as per the East Asian model often required a strong developmental state. Analysis of China within this vein generally confirms such a proposition (Ming Xia, 2000), though with certain caveats (Breslin, 1996). Contrast this milieu with Africa. Granted even the relative declining reach of the Chinese state as liberalization progresses (Wang Hongying, 2003), the type of comparative internal strength and concomitant stability that Beijing is able to enact is beyond the ambition of most—if not all—current African leaders. And this of course assumes that development is on the agenda. As Claude Ake (1991: 319) noted, "One of the most amazing things about the literature on development in Africa is how readily it assumes that everyone is interested in development and that when [African] leaders proclaim their commitment to development and fashion their impressive development plans and negotiate with international organizations for development assistance, they are ready for development and for getting on with it."

Furthermore, the irony is that those who applaud alternatives to Western-dominated IFIs often—sometimes perhaps without realizing so—end up in a position where they support not only the authoritarian status quo in some African states, but also the emerging leadership of China. Opposition to neoliberalism—something that has considerable appeal—can result in the promotion not of social democracy, or even of Keynesian liberalism, but of illiberal authoritarianism. And as Zha Daojiong notes (2005), within China itself there is a debate as to whether the Latin American fate of social polarization, international dependency, and economic stagnation is in China's future unless appropriate policies are implemented. These debates often question the capitalist direction of Beijing's current course, again undermining the notion of a "model" (see Wang Chaohua, 2003; Wang Hongying, 2003). Analyses of the "China miracle" (Wu Yanrui, 2003) that offer up more sober interpretations seem to have been missed by those advocating the Chinese model. Ironically, it is quite noticeable these days how touchy many African intellectuals are to any criticism of China and/or the suggestion that China is possibly *not* the savior of Africa.[22]

CONCLUDING REMARKS

Chinese foreign policy in Africa has been based on several key aims. Beijing has focused on ensuring its regime security through access to crucial resources. By portraying itself as an advocate for the developing world and emphasizing the rhetoric of South–South cooperation, China has arguably sought to offer itself up as an alternative model to Western dominance. However, to achieve its policy goals, Beijing has equally been prepared to defend autocratic regimes, some of which commit gross human rights abuses, such as Sudan and Zimbabwe, as noted. As a repressive government in its own right, the Chinese leadership has been slow to engage with civil society in Africa. Lately some efforts have been made to reach out, but as Kenya's National Council of NGOs chair, Ken Wafula, put it, "issues of human rights violations, attacks on freedom of expression in [China] and its support for repressive regimes will slow us down" in any engagement (*The Nation* [Nairobi], September 9, 2011). When the leadership perceives challenges to Chinese interests, too often Beijing has sided with authoritarian regimes. In this way, China's interactions with the continent fit the pattern of most external actors' intercourse with Africa: beneficial to the ruling elite but disadvantageous over the long term to Africa's peoples.[23]

However, it must be emphasized that China's policies toward Africa are evolving and maturing and Beijing is experiencing a steep learning curve. Recent developments suggest that China is starting to realize that like all other actors in Africa, Beijing needs stability and security in order for Chinese investments to flourish and for its connections with the continent to be coherent.[24] The history and development of Sino-African relations thus far suggest certain patterns, but the relationship is fluid and ever-changing. Indeed, it has to be said that in relative terms, the exponential increase in Chinese trade with Africa from the start of the twenty-first century means that we are in the very early stages of a solidifying Sino-African relationship, even though formal ties between Beijing and Africa go back decades. Thus far the repercussions of this sustained and in-depth political and economic involvement by the Chinese for broad-based development in Africa have yet to be ascertained.

At present, the picture appears mixed—there are instances where the Chinese role in Africa is clearly positive and appreciated. Equally, there are issues where Beijing is, at present at least, playing an equivocal role that arguably threatens to unravel some of the progress made in Africa in recent times on issues of good governance and accountability. Beijing's role in Africa is, like that of all other external actors, diverse, and its effect in the continent varies widely depending on local economic and political circumstance. Studying the diversity of both China and Africa, as well as the nature of the individual African states where Chinese interests operate, is central if we are to have a coherent picture of what is going on and what is likely to play out.

Problematically, the continent lacks a consistent and unified collective policy to connect with Beijing. As a Kenyan report put it, "China has an Africa policy. Africa doesn't have a China policy" (*The Nation* [Nairobi], June 12, 2006). At FOCAC III, for instance, Africa was unsuccessful in developing a combined negotiating approach that might have shaped the debate and been advantageous to the continent. As one commentary at the time noted, "Whereas the FOCAC declaration present[ed] a genuine platform for pragmatic co-operation, to Africa's advantage, Africa's failure to form a unified voice could seriously hamper its ability to determine the terms and general direction of the interaction [because] rather than work as a bloc, Africa continues to negotiate with China on a country-by-country basis" (*Business in Africa* [London], December 20, 2006). Remarkably, there is in fact no official AU view on Sino-African ties, whether positive with regard to their benefits or negative with respect to their downsides.[25] This is partly because China prefers bilateral dealings, which makes constructing a single "China policy" difficult. Furthermore, Beijing has warm relations with Morocco, a non-AU member, but not with the four African states that recognize Taiwan.[26] Consequently, as a collective unit, Africa has little actual negotiating power over China, and most African governments' reactions to the rise of Chinese activity on the continent have been unreflective, ad hoc, and uncoordinated. Thus, to all intents and purposes bilateral arrangement for Sino-African relations have invariably resulted in inexpert African responses to China, be they at the regional or continental level.

Where there is coherence in Sino-African relations, a key intention enunciated by Beijing is to encourage Chinese corporations to invest overseas, play a role in international capital markets, and aid in the policy of ensuring regime security through access to crucial resources. A Chinese Ministry of Commerce statement has in fact averred that Africa is "one of the most important regions for carrying out our 'go outward' strategy" (quoted in Gu Xuewu, 2005: 8). The resulting hike in commodity prices has been potentially good for many of Africa's economies, although the income from this phenomenon is obviously uneven and dependent upon a country's resource attributes. Certainly, in terms of receipts for such commodities, benefits are skewed to only certain economies. South Africa provides iron ore and platinum while the DRC and Zambia supplies copper and cobalt. Timber is sourced from Gabon, Cameroon, Congo-Brazzaville, and Liberia, while various West and central African nations supply raw cotton to Chinese textile factories. However, oil remains China's biggest commercial interest in Africa. Given the nature of the oil industry globally—but particularly in Africa—this has attracted criticism.

Until relatively recently there was an arguable complacency within Beijing about its policies in Africa. The attitude seemed to be that third-party criticism (or even internal African condemnation) was motivated by "China bashing" and could be safely disregarded. Chinese analysts of the older generation (and those Western academics who aspire to the title of "foreign friend" [*waiguo pengyou*]) tend to cling to such a position.[27] However, a flurry of extremely negative articles in the international media about Sino-African ties, as well as incidents on the ground in Africa, has stimulated a rethinking in Beijing. After all, in the past few years, Chinese workers have been kidnapped and/or murdered in Cameroon, Egypt, Ethiopia, Niger, Nigeria, and Sudan, while anti-Chinese riots have occurred in the Congo and Zambia. As Shen Dingli, a professor of international relations at Fudan University in Shanghai, has noted, "Chinese companies go to these dangerous countries without evaluating regional instability and volatile situations. . . . Now we are meeting trouble. This is a big lesson" (*Monitor* [Kampala], February 4, 2012).

Although Beijing obviously objects to being singled out for criticism for its activities in Africa, it can be contended that since China is an emerging power and one that is arguably becoming greater every year, it *has* to acknowledge that it can no longer hide behind the notion of being a poor developing state to whom different rules apply. It is an unarguable fact that once a state becomes a major global player (or at least is supposed by many to be), its policies will be much more under public scrutiny and subject to critical evaluation—whether Beijing likes this or not.

In fact, it is now accepted within Beijing that there is an urgent requirement to publicize the positive side of Chinese diplomacy in Africa.[28] However, this is not without its existential problems. Beijing is finding it increasingly difficult to control what companies, domestic or foreign, do in China, and its own call to "go global" has undermined its former control over many Chinese companies acting overseas.[29] Control over external investment has already been relaxed, and ongoing reforms progressively make it easier for companies to act independently.[30] Although Beijing has made both concerted efforts to educate Chinese traders operating in Africa about local labor laws and safety standards and patriotic appeals to protect the image of China abroad, there is the distinct possibility it has failed on both counts, and reports of irregular treatment of African workers by Chinese companies are commonplace. This is problematic for Beijing policymakers if and when Chinese companies misbehave. FOCAC as an institution was carefully crafted to give the impression that the central state is indeed in charge of operations. Yet developments associated with marketization, combined with deepening corruption at many levels of the Chinese polity, confound any coherent attempts at control from Beijing. When combined with business practices from home that clash with African expectations (never mind the law), a potentially toxic mix is created.

Ultimately, neither Beijing nor Africa's leaders are "in charge" of Sino-African relations. Africa has no credible China policy and China's Africa policy is compromised by the nature of the Chinese state and economy in the way it can—or cannot—direct the multitude of Chinese actors engaging with the continent. This reality makes for an extremely interesting set of dynamics that are likely to play out more and more within the wider framework of Sino-African relations. For students of Africa's international relations, both the connections and contradictions within this relationship are likely to be of immense interest as the continent continues its progress as the twenty-first century unfolds.

NOTES

1. Interview with Luo Xiaoguang, Chinese ambassador to Sudan, Khartoum, Sudan, August 30, 2011.

2. Interview with Shu Zhan, Chinese ambassador to Eritrea, Asmara, Eritrea, June 29, 2006.

3. Interview with the acting head of the Political Affairs Section of the Chinese embassy in Windhoek, Namibia, August 13, 2006.

4. Presentation by Chinese academic at the 13th CODESRIA General Assembly, Rabat, Morocco, December 8, 2011.

5. Interview with Chinese diplomat, Addis Ababa, Ethiopia, May 15, 2007.

6. It is enlightening to look at comments in the chapters on China's links with Africa in post-1985 editions of *Africa Contemporary Record*. In the 1984–1985 edition, we have "a lowering of priorities." The next year, "maintaining a low profile," with 1986–1987 "smooth . . . uneventful" and 1987–1988 "not exceptional or particularly noteworthy." The very year before Tiananmen, the 1988–1989 edition asserted that "once more Africa was low on China's priorities." Such comments give an indication of the tangible decline in Beijing's interest in Africa in the 1980s prior to the Tiananmen affair.

7. Interview with Pentagon official, Washington, DC, United States, April 5, 2007.

8. Conversation with Wang Xuexian, Chinese ambassador to South Africa, Stellenbosch, South Africa, February 13, 1998.

9. Interview with Chinese academic, School of International Studies, Peking University, Beijing, China, September 20, 2007.

10. Interview with Chinese diplomat, Abuja, Nigeria, September 5, 2007.

11. Interview with Chinese academic, School of International Studies, Renmin University, Beijing, China, February 21, 2008.

12. Interview with Xu Mingzheng, general manager of Sierra Leone Guoji Investment and Development Company, Freetown, Sierra Leone, June 8, 2006.

13. Interview with Liu Shangliang, general manager of China Henan International Cooperation Group Co. Ltd., Monrovia, Liberia, November 23, 2009.

14. Interview with Shu Zhan, Chinese ambassador to Eritrea, Asmara, Eritrea, June 29, 2006.

15. Of course, this came after Britain's then–prime minister, Tony Blair, asserted that 2005 was, under his New Labour government, the "Year of Africa," with Africa ostensibly a major policy concern for London.

16. Interview with Zhou Yuxiao, Chinese ambassador to Liberia, Monrovia, Liberia, November 20, 2009.

17. Interview with British diplomat, Accra, Ghana, January 22, 2012.

18. Interview with Luo Xiaoguang, Chinese ambassador to Sudan, Khartoum, Sudan, August 30, 2011.

19. Comments by Rwandan academic at a workshop at the Center for Conflict Management, National University of Rwanda, Kigali, October 14, 2010.

20. Interview with manager, import business, Hargheisa, Somaliland, September 16, 2011.

21. As a somewhat amusing anecdote, at a conference I attended in Beijing recently, a Chinese academic gave the definition of "noninterference" as being that of supporting the recognized government in power and granting its wishes in a nonjudgmental fashion. Stony silence was the response I got after I pointed out that such a position would logically exonerate American support for Chiang Kai-shek and the Guomindang during the Chinese civil war. The Guomindang were, after all, the legally recognized government of China at the time.

22. Interview with Tanzanian academic, Dar es Salaam, Tanzania, December 21, 2011.

23. Interview with Ugandan academic, Mbarara, Uganda, November 2, 2006.

24. Interview with Western diplomat, Abuja, Nigeria, September 3, 2007.

25. Interview with African Union official, Addis Ababa, Ethiopia, May 16, 2007.

26. Interview with Taiwanese diplomat, Banjul, The Gambia, March 31, 2008.

27. In this construction, *any* critique of Chinese activities in Africa, no matter how equivocal, is deemed "anti-China." As the Canadian *Globe and Mail* (July 27, 2008) puts it, "The Chinese authorities always assume that 'friendship' is the ideal relationship between China and well-behaved foreigners. Western scholars, diplomats and journalists are often regarded as either 'friends' or 'enemies' of China, depending on their behavior. The implicit message from the Chinese government [and their academic mouthpieces] is that those who praise the government are 'friends of China' while those who criticize or expose problems are deemed 'unfriendly' or even 'enemies.'" In recent times, there have been attempts by a few of the older Chinese scholar-officials on Africa to divide the academic community who study Sino-African ties into these two stark camps. This has then been supported by some Western-based ac-

ademics eager to denounce criticism of Chinese activities in Africa as racist. For an archaeology of this friend/enemy dichotomy, see Brady (1997).

28. Interview with He Wenping, Chinese Academy of Social Sciences, Beijing, China, September 18, 2007.

29. Interview with British diplomat, Accra, Ghana, January 22, 2012.

30. I am always struck, when interviewing Chinese diplomats in Africa, how little they know (or profess to know) about the range of activities being undertaken by Chinese actors in the host African country and certainly the ability of the diplomats to influence the behavior of said actors. This leads to all sorts of problems and often places the diplomats in the unenviable position of having to clean up after the mess left by irresponsible Chinese businesses. At times, this has been diplomatically damaging to Beijing's public image. It does, however, reflect the subordinate status that the Ministry of Foreign Affairs has vis-à-vis the Ministry of Commerce (aka MOFCOM).

REFERENCES

Ake, C. 1991. "How Politics Underdevelops Africa," in *The Challenge of African Economic Recovery and Development.* Edited by A. Adedeji, O. Teriba, and P. Bugembe. London: Frank Cass.

Brady, A. 1997. "Who Friend, Who Enemy? Rewi Alley and the Friends of China." *China Quarterly* 151.

Brautigam, D. 1998. *Chinese Aid and African Development.* New York: Macmillan.

Breslin, S. 1996. "China: Developmental State or Dysfunctional Development?" *Third World Quarterly* 17, no. 4.

———. 2005. "Power and Production: Rethinking China's Global Economic Role." *Review of International Studies* 31, no. 4.

———. 2007. *China and the Global Political Economy.* Basingstoke, UK: Palgrave.

Chabal, P., and Daloz, J.-P. 1999. *Africa Works: Disorder as Political Instrument.* Oxford: James Currey.

Dirlik, A. 2006. "Beijing Consensus: Beijing 'Gongshi.' Who Recognizes Whom and to What End?" Mimeo.

Duyvendak, J. 1949. *China's Discovery of Africa.* London: Probsthain.

Fatton, R. 1988. "Bringing the Ruling Class Back In: Class, State, and Hegemony in Africa." *Comparative Politics* 20, no. 3.

Foot, R. 2006. "Chinese Strategies in a US-Hegemonic Global Order: Accommodating and Hedging." *International Affairs* 82, no. 1.

Gu Weiqun. 1995. *Politics of Divided Nations: The Case of China and Korea.* Westport, CT: Westview.

Gu Xuewu. 2005. "China Returns to Africa." *Trends East Asia* 9: 8.

Guérin, E. 2008. "Chinese Assistance to Africa: Characterization and Position Regarding the Global Governance of Development Aid." *Global Governance* 3.

Han Nianlong. 1990. *Diplomacy of Contemporary China.* Beijing: New Horizon Press.

Hong Eunsuk and Sun Laixiang. 2006. "Dynamics of Internationalization and Outward Investment: Chinese Corporations' Strategies." *China Quarterly* 187.

Hutchison, A. 1975. *China's African Revolution*. London: Hutchinson.

Karumbidza, J. 2007. "Win-Win Economic Co-operation: Can China Save Zimbabwe's Economy?" In *African Perspectives on China in Africa*. Edited by F. Manji and S. Marks. Cape Town, South Africa: Fahamu.

Krakoff, C. 2010. "Why Wal-Mart Deserves the Nobel Peace Prize." *Emerging Markets Outlook*, November 21.

Kurlantzick, J. 2006. "China's Charm: Implications of Chinese Soft Power." Carnegie Endowment Policy Brief no. 47.

———. 2007. *Charm Offensive: How China's Soft Power Is Transforming the World*. New Haven, CT: Yale University Press.

Ming Xia. 2000. *The Dual Developmental State: Development Strategy and Institutional Arrangements for China's Transition*. Aldershot, UK: Ashgate.

Ministry of Foreign Affairs. 2006. *China's African Policy*. Beijing: Ministry of Foreign Affairs.

Mosher, S. 2000. *Hegemon: China's Plan to Dominate Asia and the World*. New York: Encounter.

Naidu, S., and Davies, M. 2006. "China Fuels Its Future with Africa's Riches." *South African Journal of International Affairs* 13, no. 2.

Qian Qichen. 2005. *Ten Episodes in China's Diplomacy*. New York: HarperCollins.

Scott, D. 2007. *China Stands Up: The PRC and the International System*. London: Routledge.

Snow, P. 1988. *The Star Raft: China's Encounter with Africa*. London: Weidenfeld and Nicholson.

Stevens, Jeremey. 2012. "China Economic Forecast 2012." *Chinafrica* 4 (January 2012): pp. 34–35.

Sutter, R. 2008. *Chinese Foreign Relations: Power and Policy Since the Cold War*. Lanham, MD: Rowman & Littlefield.

Tang Jiaxuan. 2011. *Heavy Storm and Gentle Breeze: Tang Jiaxuan's Diplomatic Memoir*. Beijing: Foreign Languages Press.

Taylor, I. 1997. *China's Foreign Policy Towards Southern Africa in the "Socialist Modernisation" Period*. East Asia Project Working Paper 18, Department of International Relations, University of the Witwatersrand.

———. 1998. "China's Foreign Policy Towards Africa in the 1990s." *Journal of Modern African Studies* 36, no. 3.

———. 2004. "The 'All-Weather Friend'? Sino-African Interaction in the Twenty-First Century." In *Africa in International Politics: External Involvement on the Continent*. Edited by I. Taylor and P. Williams, London: Routledge.

———. 2006a. *China and Africa: Engagement and Compromise*. London: Routledge.

———. 2006b. "China's Oil Diplomacy in Africa." *International Affairs* 82, no. 5.

———. 2008. "Beyond the New 'Two Whateverisms': China's Ties in Africa." *Journal of Current Chinese Affairs* 3.

———. 2009. *China's New Role in Africa.* Boulder, CO: Lynne Rienner.

———. 2010. *The International Relations of Sub-Saharan Africa.* New York: Continuum Publishers.

———. 2011. *The Forum on China-Africa Cooperation (FOCAC).* London: Routledge.

Wang Chaohua, ed. 2003. *One China, Many Paths.* London: Verso.

Wang Hongying. 2003. *China's New Order: Society, Politics, and Economy in Transition.* Cambridge, MA: Harvard University Press.

Wang Jianye. 2007. *What Drives China's Growing Role in Africa?* Working Paper WP/07/211, International Monetary Fund, Washington, DC.

Wu Yanrui. 2003. *China's Economic Growth: A Miracle with Chinese Characteristics.* London: Routledge.

Yan Xuetong. 2006. "The Rise of China and Its Power Status." *Chinese Journal of International Politics* 1, no. 1.

Yu, G. 1970. *China and Tanzania: A Study in Co-operation.* Berkeley: University of California Press.

———. 1975. *China's African Policy: A Study of Tanzania.* New York: Praeger.

Zha Daojiong. 2005 "Comment: Can China Rise?" *Review of International Studies* 31, no. 4.

———. 2006. "China's Energy Security: Domestic and International Issues." *Survival* 48, no. 1.

Zweig, D., and Bi Jianhai. 2005. "China's Global Hunt for Energy." *Foreign Affairs* 84, no. 5.

fourteen

Reconciling Sovereignty with Responsibility

A Basis for International Humanitarian Action

FRANCIS M. DENG

INTRODUCTION

The end of the Cold War was greeted with relief throughout the world. It was assumed that the era of global tension and insecurity was over and that humanity had ushered in a new world order that would guarantee peace, security, and respect for the universal principles of human rights and democratic freedoms. The reverse has been the case. With the disappearance of the bipolar alliance system and control mechanisms of the Cold War, a process of violent disintegration became the plight of many states, especially under formerly oppressive regimes. As the situations in the former Yugoslavia, in the former Soviet Union, and on the African continent testify, since the end of the Cold War, conflicts around the world have resulted in unprecedented humanitarian tragedies and, in some cases, have led to partial and even total collapse of states. A new development that has complicated the situation further has been the emergence of international terrorism, dramatized by the horrific assault on the twin towers of the World Trade Center in New York on September 11, 2001. That event triggered a global war on terror that, while unifying the international community against terror, appears to have polarized the world in a way somewhat reminiscent of the Cold War ideological divide. As was the case in the Cold War, states are also inclined to compromise human rights protection in the name of security from a real or perceived threat of terror.

These developments combined have stimulated a multifaceted trend toward international involvement in weak, impoverished, and conflict-prone countries, both on humanitarian grounds, and to prevent them from providing a fertile ground for international terrorism. The result is a complex situation involving sometimes conflicting motivations: On the one hand, there are mounting pressures for global humanitarian action, sometimes involving forced intervention, with an urgent quest for peacemaking and peacekeeping. On the other hand, there is the ideologically driven war on terror that is polarizing the international community into those accused or suspected of supporting terror and those fighting it. The end result of both forces is the inevitable erosion of traditional concepts of sovereignty, in order to ensure international humanitarian access to protect and assist the needy population and punish actual or potential terrorists. This has in turn generated divergent reactions from the targeted states: cooperation on the part of those governments that stand to benefit from the alliance with the United States and other major allies in the war on terror, and defensive militancy on the part of those perceived as perpetrators or supporters of international terrorism. In both cases, states are becoming fearful of international intervention and are reasserting with a defensive vigor the traditional principles of sovereignty and territorial integrity. The resulting tug-of-war is acquiring a cross-cultural dimension that is confronting the international community with severe dilemmas, as both positions represent legitimate concerns.

Much has been said and written about the processes of economic, political, and cultural globalization that the post–Cold War world was supposedly undergoing. There is, however, a process of fragmentation and localization that is concurrently under way, but which has not received commensurate attention. In Africa and indeed in many parts of the world, the state is undergoing a formidable national identity crisis in which sovereignty is being contested by forces in internal confrontation and by their external supporters. This crisis is rooted primarily in the problems of racial, ethnic, cultural, and religious diversities, rendered conflictual by gross disparities in the shaping and sharing of power, national resources, and opportunities for social, cultural, and economic development.

Indeed, the fate of the state in the post–Cold War international system is essentially dualistic in nature. During the Cold War, there was a tendency to relate all the problems around the world to the ideological confrontation of the superpowers. But in the post–Cold War era, problems are now being better understood in their proper national and regional context, where internal conflicts, violations of human rights, denial of democracy, and mismanagement of the economy are the pressing problem areas. In confronting these problems, the state is being pulled in opposite directions by the demands of various local groups and by the pressures of globalization of the market economy and universalizing political and cultural trends. The assignment of responsibility for addressing these challenges must also recognize the fundamental shift that has taken place in the post–Cold War era. Dependency is being replaced by national responsibility and accountability. This new scenario implies recasting sovereignty as a concept of responsibility for the security and general welfare of the citizens, with accountability at the regional and international levels.

The guiding principle for reconciling these positions is to assume that under normal circumstances, governments that enjoy internal legitimacy are concerned about the welfare of their people, will provide them with adequate protection and assistance, and, if unable to do so, will invite or welcome foreign assistance and international cooperation to supplement their own efforts. The conflict arises only in those exceptional instances when the state has collapsed or the government lacks the requisite capacity and is unwilling to invite or permit international involvement, while the level of human suffering dictates otherwise. This is often the case in civil conflicts characterized by racial, ethnic, cultural, or religious crises of national identity in which the conflicting parties perceive the affected population as part of "the enemy." It is essentially the need to fill the vacuum of moral responsibility created by such cleavages that makes international intervention such a moral imperative.

The paradox of the compelling circumstances that necessitate such intervention is that the crisis has gone beyond prevention and has become an emergency situation in which masses of people have fallen victim to the humanitarian tragedy. Since it is more costly now to provide the needed humanitarian relief than it would have been at an earlier stage, the obvious policy implication is that the international community must develop normative and operational principles for a doctrine of preventive intervention. Such an approach would require addressing the root causes of conflict, formulating normative guidelines, establishing the mechanisms for an appropriate institutional response, and developing strategies for timely intervention.

This is indeed a tall order. The humanitarian crisis resulting from the genocidal war in the western Sudanese region of Darfur, the inability or unwillingness of the Sudanese government to stop the carnage, and the impotence of the international community to intervene effectively to protect the civilian population indicate that, often, the stakes are too high for potential international interveners. There are, however, no easy alternatives but to reaffirm the primary responsibility of the state to protect and assist its citizens and, if it lacks the capacity, to call on the international community to assist in a positive spirit of cooperation. Should it lack the capacity and/or the will to do so, the responsibility to protect must inevitably fall on the international community in its multilevel structures: subregional, regional, global, and alliances of willing and capable states preferably acting collectively, but if need be, acting unilaterally, to stop genocide, mass atrocities, or crimes against humanity. The question is how to make this phased sharing of responsibility effective.

THE MAGNITUDE OF THE CRISIS

The events in the former Yugoslavia, the latest dramatization of which was the horrific situation in Kosovo, and in several hot spots in the former Soviet Union demonstrate that the crisis is truly global. As former UN Secretary-General Boutros Boutros-Ghali observed in his *Agenda for Peace*: "Poverty, disease, famine, oppression and despair abound, joining to produce 17 million refugees, 20 million displaced persons and massive migrations of peoples within and beyond national borders. These are both sources and consequences of conflict that require the ceaseless attention and the highest priority in the efforts of the United Nations."[1]Although the global dimension of the crisis needs to be stressed, it is fair to say that some regions are more affected than others. Africa is perhaps the most devastated by internal conflicts and their catastrophic consequences. During my term as representative of the secretary-general on this issue, of an estimated 20 million to 25 million internally displaced persons worldwide, over 10 million were African, as were the refugees throughout the world. It was in Africa—specifically, Rwanda—that the world witnessed genocide comparable to the horrors of Nazi Germany. In the conflict in the southern region of Sudan, nearly 2 million people are estimated to have died since the resumption of the civil war in 1983; about a quarter perished as a result of war-induced famine and related humanitarian tragedies. The conflict in Darfur has resulted in the death of between 200,000 and 400,000 people, according to varying estimates, displaced over 2 million people, and forced 1 million people to seek refuge in Chad. The Democratic Republic of Congo has also been a theater of massive carnage. In Liberia and Sierra Leone, untold atrocities were perpetrated by all sides to the conflicts. And, of course, the collapse of Somalia stands out as an example of the threat looming over a number of fragile and vulnerable states on the continent. The intervention of Ethiopia, which initially promised to bring peace and stability to Somalia, has proved to be an aggravating factor.

African leaders, diplomats, scholars, and intellectuals have recognized the plight of their countries and their people and are demonstrating a responsiveness commensurate to the challenge. The OAU Mechanism for Conflict Prevention, Management and Resolution, proposed by Secretary-General Salim Ahmed Salim in the 1992 Dakar summit and adopted by the summit in Cairo in June 1993 represented the shift in attitude. In introducing his proposals to the Council of Ministers in Dakar in 1992, the secretary-general said:

> Conflicts have cast a dark shadow over the prospects for a united, secure and prosperous Africa which we seek to create. . . . Conflicts have caused immense suffering to our people and, in the worst case, death. Men, women and children have been uprooted, dispossessed, deprived of their means of livelihood and thrown into exile as refugees as a result of conflicts. This de-humanization of a large segment of our population is unacceptable and cannot be allowed to continue. Conflicts have engendered hate and division among our people and undermined the prospects of the long-term stability and unity of our countries and Africa as a whole. Since much energy, time and resources have been devoted to meeting the exigencies of conflicts, our countries have been unable to harness the energies of our people and target them to development.[2]

The change of the Organization of African Unity (OAU) to the African Union (AU) was more than a change of names. It signified a substantive and procedural shift from the old sacrosanct commitment to the narrow concept of state responsibility, and from noninterference in the internal affairs of states to a more responsible and responsive oversight and constructive involvement to promote peace, security, and stability within state borders. Article 4(h) of the Constitutive Act of the AU provides for "the right of the Union to intervene in a member State pursuant to a decision of the Assembly in respect of grave circumstances, namely war crimes, genocide and crimes against humanity." In promotion and protection of a democratic system of governance, Article 4(p) provides for the "condemnation and rejection of unconstitutional changes of government," implicitly by military coups. To meet the challenge, however, Africa must address sovereignty.

THE ISSUE OF SOVEREIGNTY

Protecting and assisting the masses of the people affected by internecine internal conflicts entail reconciling the possibility of international intervention with traditional concepts of national sovereignty. With the post–Cold War reapportionment of responsibility for addressing these problems, primary responsibility is now placed on the states concerned, with a graduated sharing of responsibility and accountability at the subregional and regional levels and, residually, throughout the international community, both multilaterally and bilaterally. In this emerging policy framework, national sovereignty, as already noted, acquires a new meaning. Instead of being perceived as a means of insulating the state against external scrutiny or involvement, it is increasingly being postulated as a normative concept of responsibility. National sovereignty requires a system of governance that is based on democratic popular citizen participation, constructive management of diversities, respect for fundamental rights, and equitable distribution of national wealth and opportunities for development. For a government or a state to claim sovereignty, it must establish legitimacy by meeting minimal standards of good governance or responsibility for the security and general welfare of its citizens and all those under its jurisdiction. Fulfillment of these standards, in turn, requires the formulation of a normative framework stipulating standards for the responsibilities of sovereignty and a system of accountability at the various interactive levels, from national to subregional and regional to international. The consensus now is that the problems are primarily internal and that, however external their sources or continued linkages, the responsibility for solutions, especially in the post–Cold War era, falls first on Africans themselves. Africans are recognizing that the time has long since come to stop blaming colonialism for Africa's persistent problems.

The irony, however, is that the principal modern agent of Africa's political and economic development and the interlocutor in the international arena is the state, itself a creature of foreign intervention. Although Africans have, for the most part, accepted the state with its colonially defined borders, African states lack the indigenous roots for internal legitimacy. And although democracy has been expanding since the end of the Cold War, it tends to be rather narrowly associated with elections that are often not entirely free and fair; indeed, the state is often not representative or responsive to the demands and expectations of its domestic constituencies. It is important in this context to distinguish between recognizing the unity and territorial integrity of the state and questioning its policy framework, which might be attributable to a regime or might be structural in nature. A structural problem would require a fundamental restructuring of the state to meet both the internal standards of good governance and the international requirements of responsible sovereignty.

Failure on the one level usually implies failure on the other. When a state fails to meet the standards prescribed for membership in the international community, thereby exposing itself to external scrutiny and possible sanctions, it is likely to assert sovereignty and cultural relativism in an attempt to barricade itself against the threat of foreign interference. Sovereignty has evolved enough not only to prescribe democratic representation but also to justify outside intervention. As one scholar of international law observed:

> In the process, the two notions have merged. Increasingly, governments recognize that their legitimacy depends on meeting a normative expectation of the community of states. This recognition has led to the emergence of a community expectation: that those who seek the validation of their empowerment patently govern with the consent of the governed. Democracy, thus, is on the way to becoming a global entitlement, one that increasingly will be promoted and protected by collective international processes.[3]

Another has argued that

> there is a clear trend away from the idea of unconditional sovereignty and toward a concept of responsible sovereignty. Governmental legitimacy that validates the exercise of sovereignty involves adherence to minimum humanitarian norms and a capacity to act effectively to protect citizens from acute threats to their security and well-being that derive from adverse conditions within a country.[4]

During the extensive consultations I conducted in connection with my UN mandate as representative of the secretary-general on internally displaced persons, representatives of several governments commented that national sovereignty carries with it responsibilities that, if not met, put a government at risk of forfeiting its legitimacy. One spokesperson for a major power even went as far as saying, "To put it bluntly," if governments do not live up to those responsibilities (among which he specified the protection of minority rights), "the international community should intervene by force."[5] Similar views have been expressed by representatives of African countries who were voicing a global humanitarian concern.

Such pronouncements have almost become truisms that are rapidly making narrow concepts of legality obsolete. When the international community does decide to act—as it did when Iraq invaded Kuwait, when Somalia descended into chaos and starvation, and (albeit less decisively) when the former Yugoslavia disintegrated, especially in Kosovo—controversy over issues of legality become futile or of limited value as a brake to guard against precipitous change. One observer summarized the new sense of urgency regarding the need for an international response, the ambivalence of the pressures for the needed change, and the pull of traditional legal doctrines as follows:

In the post–Cold War world . . . a new standard of intolerance for human misery and human atrocities has taken hold. Something quite significant has occurred to raise the consciousness of nations to the plight of peoples within sovereign borders. There is a new commitment—expressed in both moral and legal terms—to alleviate the suffering of oppressed or devastated people. To argue today that norms of sovereignty, non-use of force, and the sanctity of internal affairs are paramount to the collective human rights of people, whose lives and well-being are at risk, is to avoid the hard questions of international law and to ignore the march of history.[6]

To intervene is, however, not an easy choice. In 1991 former UN secretary-general Javier Perez de Cuellar highlighted this dilemma when he said, "We are clearly witnessing what is probably an irresistible shift in public attitudes towards the belief that the defense of the oppressed in the name of morality should prevail over frontiers and legal documents." But he also asked, "Does [intervention] not call into question one of the cardinal principles of international law, one diametrically opposed to it, namely, the obligation of non-interference in the internal affairs of states?"[7] In his 1991 annual report, he wrote of the new balance that must be struck between sovereignty and the protection of human rights:

> It is now increasingly felt that the principle of non-interference with the essential domestic jurisdiction of States cannot be regarded as a protective barrier behind which human rights could be massively or systematically violated with impunity. . . . The case for not impinging on the sovereignty, territorial integrity and political independence of States is by itself indubitably strong. But it would only be weakened if it were to carry the implication that sovereignty, even in this day and age, includes the right of mass slaughter or of launching systematic campaigns of decimation or forced exodus of civilian populations in the name of controlling civil strife or insurrection. With the heightened international interest in universalizing a regime of human rights, there is a marked and most welcome shift in public attitudes.
>
> To try to resist it would be politically as unwise as it is morally indefensible. It should be perceived as not so much a new departure as a more focused awareness of one of the requirements of peace.[8]

Preferring to avoid confronting the issue of sovereignty, de Cuellar called for a "higher degree of cooperation and a combination of common sense and compassion," arguing that "we need not impale ourselves on the horns of a dilemma between respect for sovereignty and the protection of human rights. . . . What is involved is not the right of intervention but the collective obligation of States to bring relief and redress in human rights emergencies."[9]

In *An Agenda for Peace,* de Cuellar's successor, Boutros Boutros-Ghali, wrote that respect for sovereignty and integrity is "crucial to any common international progress," but he went on to say that "the time of absolute and exclusive sovereignty . . . has passed," that "its theory was never matched by reality," and that it is necessary for leaders of states "to find a balance between the needs of good internal governance and the requirements of an ever more interdependent world."[10] As one commentator noted, "The clear meaning was that governments could best avoid intervention by meeting their obligations not only to other states, but also to their own citizens. If they failed, they might invite intervention."[11]

But although negative interpretations of sovereignty prevail as "a prerogative to resist claims and encroachments coming from outside national boundaries—the right to say no," the question can be, and has been, posed as to whether erasing the doctrine of sovereignty from the minds of political leaders would reduce those forms of human suffering associated with extreme governmental failure. "Would such an erasure strengthen sentiments of human solidarity on which an ethos of corrective responsibility and individual accountability depends?"[12] The withdrawal of the international community from Somalia once the humanitarian intervention proved costly in American lives, the astonishing disengagement from Rwanda in the face of genocide in 1994, and the indifference to the atrocities and gross human rights violations in Liberia, Sierra Leone, and Sudan, to mention just a few examples—as contrasted to the dramatic, high-tech intervention on behalf of the Kurds in Iraq and the Albanians in Kosovo—prompt a resounding "no" in answer to the question. Selectivity in the manner and scale of response is the fundamental reality.

Boutros-Ghali's successor as secretary-general was even more vocal than his predecessors on the need to curtail the constraints of sovereignty. In an address to the Commission on Human Rights on April 7, 1999, Kofi Annan said, "When civilians are attacked and massacred because of their ethnicity, as in Kosovo, the world looks to the United Nations to speak up for them. When men, women and children are assaulted and their limbs hacked off, as in Sierra Leone, here again the world looks to the United Nations. When women and girls are denied their right to equality, as in Afghanistan, the world looks to the United Nations to take a stand." Emphasizing the expectation of "our global constituency" that the UN will intervene to protect "the tortured, the oppressed, the silenced, the victims of 'ethnic cleansing' and injustice," Annan posed a rhetorical, but pertinent question: "If, in the face of such abuses, we do not speak up and speak out, if we do not act in defense of human rights and advocate their lasting universality, how can we answer that global constituency?"[13]

Although sovereignty as such is no longer a barrier to intervention on human rights and humanitarian grounds, the determining factor is the political will of other states based on national interest, combined with a compelling level of humanitarian concern. However, assertions of sovereignty can also be invoked by powers lacking the will to become involved. Since intervention is often costly in terms of lives and material, it is convenient to avoid it unless imperative national interest dictates otherwise. Sovereignty then elicits benign conformity to the principle of noninterference or provides a convenient excuse for inaction. If the constraints of sovereignty against justifiable intervention are to be circumvented, and more important, if governments and other controlling authorities such as insurgent movements are to be inspired or at least motivated to discharge their obligations, it is necessary to prescribe "normative sovereignty," or "sovereignty as responsibility."[14]

The ambivalence about intervention by the international community arises not only from reluctance to become involved but also from motives for external intervention, which are by no means always altruistic. Self-interest therefore dictates an appropriate and timely action in terms of self-protection. This was the point made by the secretary-general of the Organization of African Unity, Salim Ahmed Salim, in his bold proposals for an OAU mechanism for conflict prevention and resolution. "If the OAU, first through the Secretary-General and then the Bureau of the Summit, is to play the lead role in any African conflict," he said, "it should be enabled to intervene swiftly, otherwise it cannot be ensured that whoever (apart from African regional organizations) acts will do so in accordance with African interests."[15] Criticizing the tendency to respond only to worst-case scenarios, Salim also emphasized the need for preemptive intervention: "The basis for 'intervention' may be clearer when there is a total breakdown of law and order . . . and where, with the attendant human suffering, a spill-over effect is experienced within the neighbouring countries. . . . However, pre-emptive involvement should also be permitted even in situations where tensions evolve to such a pitch that it becomes apparent that a conflict is in the making."[16]

The secretary-general went so far as to suggest that the OAU should take the lead in transcending the traditional view of sovereignty, building on the African values of kinship, solidarity, and the notion that "every African is his brother's keeper."[17] Considering that "our borders are at best artificial," Salim argued, "we in Africa need to use our own cultural and social relationships to interpret the principle of non-interference in such a way that we are enabled to apply it to our advantage in conflict prevention and resolution."[18]

In traditional Africa, third-party intervention for mediation and concilia-tion is always expected, regardless of the will of the parties directly involved in a conflict. Even in domestic disputes, relatives and elders intercede without being invited. Indeed, "saving face," which is critical to conflict resolution in Africa, requires that such intervention be unsolicited. But, of course, African concepts and practices under the modern conditions of the nation-state must still balance consideration for state sovereignty against the compelling hu-manitarian need to protect and assist the dispossessed.

Even in the modern context and sovereignty notwithstanding, as former secretary-general Kofi Annan put it, there is a need for a third party to speak out and say, "Stop, this is enough. This cannot be allowed to happen." Elabo-rating on the role of a third party, Annan said, "the third party has a very im-portant role we should never underestimate, not only in speaking out trying to get help, but it also gives inspiration and strength to those who are caught in the situation."[19] Annan was even more emphatic when he said: "Govern-ments must not be allowed to use sovereignty as a shield to systematically deny their people of human rights and undertake gross systematic abuses of human rights. If that were to happen, shouldn't the international community have some responsibility of going to assist these people?"[20]

The normative frameworks proposed by the OAU secretary-general and the UN secretary-general's *Agenda for Peace* are predicated on respect for the sovereignty and integrity of the state as crucial to the existing international system. However, the logic of the transcendent importance of human rights as a legitimate area of concern for the international community—especially where order has broken down or where the state is incapable or unwilling to act responsibly to protect the masses of citizens—would tend to make inter-national inaction quite indefensible. Even in less extreme cases of acute in-ternal conflicts, the perspectives of the pivotal actors on such issues as the national or public interest are bound to be sharply divided both internally and in terms of their relationship to the outside world. After all, internal conflicts often entail a contest of the national arena of power and, hence, sovereignty. Every political intervention from outside has its internal recipients, hosts, and beneficiaries. Under those circumstances, there can hardly be said to be indi-visible national sovereignty behind which the nation stands united.

Furthermore, it is not always easy to determine the degree to which a gov-ernment of a country devastated by civil war is truly in control when, as often happens, sizable portions of the territory are controlled by rebel or opposing forces. Frequently, though a government may remain in effective control of the capital and the main garrisons, much of the countryside in the war zone will have practically collapsed. How would a partial but significant collapse such as this be factored into the determination of the degree to which civil order in the country has broken down? A government cannot present a clear face to the outside world when it keeps others from stepping in to offer protection and assistance in the name of sovereignty after allowing hundreds of thousands (and maybe millions) to starve to death when food can be made available to them; to be exposed to deadly elements when they could be provided with shelter; to be indiscriminately tortured, brutalized, and murdered by opposing forces, contesting the very sovereignty that is supposed to ensure their security; or to otherwise allow them to suffer in a vacuum of moral leadership and responsibility. Under such circumstances, the international community is called upon to step in and fill the vacuum created by such neglect. If the lack of protection and assistance is the result of the country's incapacity, the government would, in all likelihood, invite or welcome such international intervention. But where the neglect is a willful part of a policy emanating from internal conflict, preventive and corrective interventions become necessary.

As former secretary-general, Kofi Annan argued that the issue is more than the culpability of governments, but the limits to their capacity in the face of the globalizing challenges facing them: "I can understand a nation's right . . . to protect its sovereignty. On the other hand, . . . the traditional concept of sovereignty is being changed by the developments in the world today, from globalization—there are lots of areas governments do not control. They do not control the external factors that affect their economy. They do not control financial flows. They do not control some of the environmental issues. Why should abuse of human rights be the only area that they should insist they should be allowed to control without any interference?"[21]

It is most significant that the Security Council, in its continued examination of the secretary-general's *Agenda for Peace,* welcomed the observations contained in the report concerning the question of humanitarian assistance and its relationship to peacemaking, peacekeeping, and peacebuilding.[22] In particular, the council established that, under certain circumstances, "there may be a close relationship between acute needs for humanitarian assistance and threats to international peace and security";[23] indeed, it "[noted] with concern the incidents of humanitarian crises, including mass displacements of population becoming or aggravating threats to international peace and security."[24] The council further expressed the belief "that humanitarian assistance should help establish the basis for enhanced stability through rehabilitation and development" and "noted the importance of adequate planning in the provision of humanitarian assistance in order to improve prospects for rapid improvement of the humanitarian situation."[25]

Absolute sovereignty is clearly no longer defensible; it never was, but it has now been significantly curtailed. The critical question now is under what circumstances the international community is justified in overriding sovereignty to protect the dispossessed populations within state borders. The common assumption in international law is that such action is justified when there is a threat to international peace. The position now supported by the Security Council is that massive violations of human rights and displacement within a country's borders may constitute such a threat.[26] Others contend that a direct threat to international peace as the basis for intervention under Chapter Seven of the UN Charter has become more a legal fiction than the principle justifying international action, nearly always under conditions of extreme humanitarian tragedies.

To avoid costly emergency relief operations, the international community must develop a response to conflict situations before they deteriorate into humanitarian tragedies. Such a response calls for placing an emphasis on peacemaking through preventive diplomacy, which in turn would require an understanding of the sources of conflicts and a willingness to address them at their roots.

RECASTING SOVEREIGNTY AS RESPONSIBILITY: RECENT DEVELOPMENTS

Recasting sovereignty as responsibility is the fundamental norm that guided my work and dialogue with governments for twelve years as representative of the UN secretary-general on internally displaced persons from 1992 to 2004. Two initiatives helped shape my perspective on the emerging challenge. One was the development of an African Studies Project in the Foreign Policy Studies Program at the Brookings Institution. The other was participating in the initiative of then former head of state of Nigeria and subsequently twice-elected president Olusegun Obasanjo, toward a Helsinki-like Conference on Security, Stability, Development, and Cooperation in Africa (CSSDCA).

In the Brookings Africa Project, we made an initial assessment of conflicts in Africa and the challenges they posed in the post–Cold War era.[27] Next, we undertook national and regional case studies to deepen our understanding of the issues involved.[28] A synthesis of these case studies led to the main conclusion that as conflicts were now being properly perceived as internal, they also primarily became the responsibility of governments to prevent, manage, and resolve. Governance became perceived primarily as conflict management. Within the framework of regional and international cooperation, state sovereignty was then postulated as entailing the responsibility of conflict management. The envisaged responsibility involved managing diversity, ensuring equitable distribution of wealth, services, and development opportunities, and participating effectively in regional and international arrangements for peace, security, and stability. In subsequent work, we tried to put more flesh on the skeleton of the responsibilities of sovereignty, building largely on human rights and humanitarian norms and international accountability. Since internal conflicts often spill across international borders, their consequences also spill across borders, threatening regional security and stability. In the "apportionment" of responsibilities in the post–Cold War era, regional organizations provide the second layer of the needed response. And yet, the international community remains the residual guarantor of universal human rights and humanitarian standards in the quest for global peace and security. Hence, the stipulation of sovereignty as responsibility with implicit accountability to the regional and international layers of cooperation.

The development of the Helsinki process for Africa was motivated by the concern that the post–Cold War global order was likely to result in the withdrawal of the major powers and the marginalization of Africa. It was, therefore, imperative for Africa to take charge of its destiny and observe principles that would appeal to the West and thereby provide a sound foundation for a mutually agreeable partnership. This was found in the Helsinki framework of the Economic and Security Cooperation in Europe, which became the Organization for Security and Cooperation in Europe (OSCE). A series of meetings culminated in the 1991 conference in Kampala, Uganda, which was attended by some five hundred people, including several heads of state and representatives from all walks of life. The conference produced the Kampala Document, which elaborated the four "calabashes," so termed to distinguish them from the OSCE "baskets," and give them an African orientation. The calabashes are security, stability, development, and cooperation. The adoption of the CSSDCA by the OAU was initially blocked by a few governments that felt threatened by its normative principles. Obasanjo's imprisonment by the Nigerian dictator Sani Abacha also removed the leverage needed to exert pressure on the OAU. When Obasanjo returned to power as the elected president of Nigeria, he was able to push successfully for the incorporation of CSSDCA into the OAU mechanism for conflict prevention, management, and resolution.[29]

In connection with these initiatives, I began to focus attention on promoting the need to balance conventional notions of sovereignty with the responsibility of the state to provide protection and general welfare to citizens and all those under state jurisdiction.[30] Given the sensitivity and controversy surrounding my mandate as representative of the UN secretary-general on internally displaced persons, responsible for the protection and assistance of internally displaced populations worldwide, the only way to bridge the need for international protection and assistance for this population and the barricades of the negative approach to sovereignty was to build on the fundamental norm of sovereignty as a positive concept of state responsibility toward its citizens and those under its jurisdiction. Most states discharged this responsibility under normal circumstances, and if they lacked the capacity to do so, called on the international community to assist them in discharging their responsibility. But in the exceptional cases where states failed to do so, the international community needed to assume that responsibility, if necessary, by overriding state sovereignty. In making that argument in my dialogue with governments, I would end by noting that the best way for a state to protect and preserve its sovereignty is to discharge, and be seen to discharge, its responsibility to protect and assist its needy citizens, or call for international assistance to complement its efforts. Otherwise, the world will not watch innocent civilians die or suffer without intervening. As Secretary-General Kofi Annan explained: "If citizens' rights are respected, there will be no need for anyone to want to intervene either through diplomatic means or coercive means. . . . The governments should see it not as a license for people to come in and intervene. We are talking about those situations where there are serious and gross and systematic violations of human rights. I think that governments who protect their citizens and their rights and do not create that kind of situation have no reason to worry that anyone would intervene."[31] The main point, however, was to persuade the governments to accept the positive recasting of sovereignty and the responsibility it entails. This approach was quite effective in the dialogue with governments.

The principle of sovereignty as responsibility has been recast as the responsibility to protect, strengthened and mainstreamed by the Canadian-sponsored Commission on Intervention and State Sovereignty and has continued to gain wide support from the international community.[32] In 2004, the secretary-general's High Level Panel on Threats, Challenges, and Changes also endorsed the principle. This was followed by the secretary-general's creation of the office of the special adviser on the prevention of genocide, also in 2004. In 2005, the secretary-general released his report "In Larger Freedom: Toward Security Development and Human Rights for All." As the UN prepared for its sixtieth-anniversary celebration, the secretary-general pleaded that "we must embrace the responsibility to protect."[33] The World Summit of Heads of State and Government, which convened in New York in September 2005, "stressed the need for the General Assembly to continue consideration of the responsibility to protect populations from genocide, war crimes, ethnic cleansing, and crimes against humanity."[34]

Kofi Annan, who at the beginning of his first term as secretary-general had provoked considerable controversy by calling for the right of humanitarian intervention by the international community, reflected on the progress made in stipulating the responsibility to protect:

The Canadian Commission . . . took the concept further, and in fact gave it a better diplomatic name than I had done. I had referred to humanitarian intervention, and then took up the "responsibility to protect"—that the governments have the responsibility to protect their people, and where they fail or show unwillingness to do that or are incapable of doing it, that responsibility may fall on the international community and the membership at large, the world community, to do something about it.[35]

The challenge that postulating sovereignty as responsibility poses for the international community is that it implies accountability. Obviously, the internally displaced themselves and other victims of internal conflicts trapped within international borders, marginalized, excluded, often persecuted, have little capacity to hold their national authorities accountable. Only the international community, including subregional, regional, and international organizations, has the leverage and clout to persuade governments and other concerned actors to discharge their responsibility or otherwise fill the vacuum of irresponsible or irresponsive sovereignty. A soft, but credible threat of consequences in case of failure to discharge the responsibility of sovereignty, combined with the promise of the benefits of international legitimacy and cooperation, could be an effective inducement.

However, the fact is often that governments of affected countries, even if willing to discharge the responsibility of assisting and protecting their needy populations, lack resources and the capacity to do so. Offering them support in a way that links humanitarian assistance with protection in a holistic, integrated approach to human rights should make the case more compelling and persuasive. No government deserving any legitimacy can request material assistance from the outside world and reject concern with the human rights of the people on whose behalf it requests assistance. Doing so would be like asking the international community to feed them without ensuring their safety and dignity, an implausible logic. Now that the standard of sovereignty as responsibility has been set, the focus of the international community should shift to the need for implementation and persuading the states to honor it as an essential ingredient of their legitimacy, both domestically and internationally.

ADDRESSING THE CAUSES OF CONFLICT

In most countries torn apart by war, the sources and causes of conflict are generally recognized as inherent in the traumatic experience of state-formation and nation-building, complicated by colonial intervention and repressive post-colonial policies. The starting point, as far as Africa is concerned, is the colonial nation-state, which brought together diverse groups that were paradoxically kept separate and unintegrated. Regional ethnic groups were broken up and affiliated with others within the artificial borders of the new state, and colonial masters imposed a superstructure of law and order to maintain relative peace and tranquility.

The independence movement was a collective struggle for self-determination that reinforced the notion of unity within the artificial framework of the newly established nation-state. Initially, independence came as a collective gain that did not delineate who was to get what from the legacy of the centralized power and wealth. But because colonial institutions had divested the local communities and ethnic groups of much of their indigenous autonomy and sustainable livelihood, replacing them with a degree of centralized authority and dependency on the welfare state system, the struggle for control became unavoidable once control of these institutions passed on to the nationals at independence. The outcome was often conflict—over power, wealth, and development—that led to gross violations of human rights, denial of civil liberties, disruption of economic and social life, and the consequential frustration of efforts for development.

As the Cold War raged, however, these conflicts were seen not as domestic struggles for power and resources but as extensions of the superpower ideological confrontation. Rather than help resolve them peacefully, the superpowers often worsened the conflict by providing military and economic assistance to their own allies.

Although the end of the Cold War removed this aggravating external factor, it also removed the moderating role of the superpowers, both as third parties and as mutually neutralizing allies. The results have been unmitigated brutalities and devastation from identity conflicts. It can credibly be argued that the gist of these internal conflicts is that the ethnic pieces that were put together by the colonial glue, reinforced by the old world order, are now pulling apart and that ethnic groups are reasserting their autonomy or independence. Old identities, undermined and rendered dormant by the structures and values of the nation-state system, are reemerging and demanding participation, distribution, and legitimacy. In fact, it may be even more accurate to say that the process has been going on in a variety of ways within the context of the constraints imposed by the nation-state system.

The larger the gap in the participation and distribution patterns based on racial, ethnic, or religious identity, the more likely the breakdown of civil order and the conversion of political confrontation into violent conflict. When the conflict turns violent, the issues at stake become transformed into a fundamental contest for state power. The objectives may vary in degree from a demand for autonomy to a major restructuring of the national framework, either to be captured by the demand-making group or to be more equitably reshaped. When the conflict escalates into a contest for the "soul" of the nation, it turns into an intractable zero-sum confrontation. The critical issue then is whether the underlying sense of injustice, real or perceived, can be remedied in a timely manner, avoiding the zero-sum level of violence.

Viewing the crisis from the global perspective, it is also pertinent to recall the words of UN Secretary-General Boutros-Ghali, who observed in *An Agenda for Peace,* "One requirement for solutions to these problems lies in commitment to human rights with a special sensitivity to those of minorities, whether ethnic, religious, social or linguistic."[36] On the need to strike a balance between the unity of larger entities and respect for the sovereignty, autonomy, and diversity of various identities, the secretary-general further noted:

> The healthy globalization of contemporary life requires in the first instance solid identities and fundamental freedoms. The sovereignty, territorial integrity and independence of states within the established international system, and the principle of self-determination for peoples, both of great value and importance, must not be permitted to work against each other in the period ahead. Respect for democratic principles at all levels of social existence is crucial: in communities, within states and within the community of states. Our constant duty should be to maintain the integrity of each while finding a balanced design for all.[37]

Where discrimination or disparity is based on race, ethnicity, region, or religion, it is easy to see how it can be combated by appropriate constitutional provisions and laws protecting basic human rights and fundamental freedoms. But where discrimination or disparity arises from conflicting perspectives on national identity, especially one based on religion, the cleavages become more difficult to bridge. In some instances, religion, ethnicity, and culture become so intertwined that they are not easy to disentangle. Such is the case in the Sudan, where Islam has gained momentum and is aspiring to offer regionwide and, indeed, global ideological leadership. Islam in the Sudan has been closely associated with Arabism, which also gives the movement a composite ethnic, cultural, and religious identity, even though the Islamists themselves espouse the nonracial ideals of the faith. The composite identity of Islam and Arabism poses the threat of subordination to non-Muslims, who also perceive themselves as non-Arabs. It is consequently resisted, especially in the South.

What makes the role of religion particularly formidable is that there are legitimate arguments on both sides of the religiously based conflict. On the one hand, the Islamists, representing the Arabized Muslim majority, want to fashion the nation on the basis of their faith, which they believe does not allow the separation of religion and the state. The non-Muslims, on the other hand, reject this, seeing it as a means of inevitably relegating them to a lower status as citizens; they insist on secularism as a more mutually accommodating basis for a pluralistic process of nation-building. The dilemma is whether an Islamic framework should be used to encompass a religiously mixed society, imposing a minority status on the non-Muslims, or whether secularism should be the national framework, thereby imposing on the Muslim majority the wishes of the non-Muslim minority. The crisis in national identity that this dualism poses is that there is not yet a consensus on a framework that unquestionably establishes the unity of the country. During the colonial period, the country was governed as two separate entities in one, and since independence, it has intermittently been at war with itself over the composite factors of religion, ethnicity, race, and culture.

If responsibility for Africa's problems is now being assigned to the Africans as represented by their states, the logic should extend down to embrace citizen participation—a process that might be termed the challenge of localization. This process would broaden the basis of participation to include not only the wide array of organizations within the now-popular notion of civil society but also, and primarily, Africa's indigenous, territorially defined, local communities, with their organizational structures, value systems, institutional arrangements, and ways of using their human and material resources.

Given its centrality and pervasiveness, ethnicity is a reality no country can afford to completely ignore. Thus, African governments have ambivalently tried to dismiss it, marginalize it, manipulate it, corrupt it, or combat it in a variety of ways. But no strategic formula for its constructive use has been developed[38]—despite the fact that an overwhelming majority of Africans, however urbanized or modernized, belong to known "tribal" or ethnic origins and remain in one way or another connected to their groups. Indeed, as one African scholar noted, "urban populations straddle the two geographical spaces—urban and rural—with the result [that] the politics of one easily spills into the politics of the other."[39] The other side of this spectrum is flexibility or adaptability that allows considerable room for molding identity to suit changing conditions or serve alternating objectives, some destructive.

Ethnic identities in themselves are not conflictual, just as individuals are not inherently in conflict merely because of their different identities and characteristics. Rather, it is unmanaged or mismanaged competition for power, wealth, or status broadly defined that provides the basis for conflict. Today virtually every African conflict has some ethno-regional dimension to it.[40] Even those conflicts that may appear to be free of ethnic concerns involve factions and alliances built around ethnic loyalties. Analysts tend to hold one of two views regarding the role of ethnicity in these conflicts. Some see ethnicity as a source of conflict; others see it as a tool used by political entrepreneurs to promote their ambitions.[41] In reality, it is both. Ethnicity, especially when combined with territorial identity, is a reality that exists independently of political maneuvers. To argue that ethnic groups are unwitting tools of political manipulation is to underestimate a fundamental social reality and to assume that members of the group lack value judgment on the issues involved. On the other hand, given the emotional fervor and the group dynamics of the identity issues it evokes, ethnicity is clearly a resource for political manipulation and entrepreneurship, which African states are loath to manage constructively.

Ethiopia, after Eritrea's breakaway, can claim credit for being the only African country that is trying to confront the problem head-on by recognizing territorially based ethnic groups, granting them not only a large measure of autonomy but also the constitutional right of self-determination, even to the extent of secession.[42] Ethiopia's leaders assert emphatically that they are committed to the right of self-determination, wherever it leads. But it can also be argued that giving the people the right to determine their destiny leads them to believe that their interests will be safeguarded, which should give them a reason to opt for unity. In fact, the Ethiopian constitution stipulates that the right to independence can be exercised only after following an elaborate process to establish the necessity and appropriateness of that ultimate step, and indeed no ethnic community has so far exercised or demanded the right to independence constitutionally. In contrast to the case of Ethiopia, the 2005 Comprehensive Peace Agreement (CPA) that ended the decades of war in southern Sudan granted the people of the South the right of self-determination through a referendum to be held after a six-year interim period to decide whether to remain in a united Sudan under the interim arrangements of the CPA or become an independent state. The agreement, however, stipulated that during the interim period, efforts would be exerted to make unity an attractive option for the South. In the end the South voted overwhelmingly for independence, which was declared on July 9, 2011, indicating that unity had not been made attractive.

Unfortunately, although Sudan initially received the independence of the South positively, and became the first to recognize the new state, relations have since deteriorated, generating clashes that threaten a return to war. While a number of unresolved issues, such as the sharing of oil revenues, border demarcation, citizenships, and the status of the contested border area of Abyei, account for the tensions, the major source of conflict is the ongoing conflict between Khartoum and the liberation movements in the marginalized regions of the North, some of whom had allied with the South in the war that raged for decades. The vision of a New Sudan freed from any discrimination due to race, ethnicity, religion, culture, or gender, which the southern-based Sudan People's Liberation Movement and Army (SPLM/A) had postulated as the objective of the struggle, not secession, had also inspired these northern groups to join the struggle. Southern independence left them still under the discriminating domination of the old Sudan system. They have therefore reconstituted themselves as SPLM/A-North and have continued the struggle for the new Sudan, hoping for support from the independent South. Sudan has, however, used allegations of support for them from the South not only to justify military incursions into the South, including aerial bombardment of areas where they suspect SPLM/A-North to have bases, but has actively instigated and supported tribal militias to undermine and destabilize the state of South Sudan. While the international community has been calling on both states to stop support for armed opposition groups within each other's territory, what is needed is for Khartoum to negotiate with these groups in good faith, to address their legitimate concerns, and to request South Sudan as their former ally to use its good offices to mediate a just resolution to the conflict.

As the initial hope for a unity vote in the stipulated referendum in the southern Sudan indicated, self-determination does not necessarily mean secession. After all, one of the options of self-determination is to remain within the state. But perhaps even more significant is the reconceptualization of self-determination as a principle that allows people to choose their own administrative status and machinery within the country.[43] It has been noted that internal self-administration "might be more effectively used in a way that would help avoid suffering of the kind that so regrettably become commonplace when communities feel that their only option is to fight for independence."[44] In that sense, self-determination becomes closely associated with democracy and protection of minorities and not conterminous with independence. As Sir Arthur Watts, one of the principal proponents of internal self-determination, has observed, independence is a complicated process that can be traumatic. For many communities, it is not necessarily the best option. Often, no advantage is gained by insisting on independence, excluding other kinds of arrangements, especially if they would grant a community all it wants without the additional burdens of a wholly independent existence.[45]

Ultimately, the only sustainable unity is that based on mutual understanding and agreement. Unfortunately, however, the normative framework for national unity in modern Africa is not the result of consensus. Except for a very few cases, as in postapartheid South Africa, Africans won their independence without negotiating an internal social contract that would forge and sustain national consensus. Of course, the leaders of various factions, ethnic or political, negotiated a framework that gave them the legitimacy to speak for the country in their demand for independence. Political elites certainly negotiated a common ground for independence in Zimbabwe, Namibia, and, with less satisfactory results, Angola. And independent leaders debated over federalism in Nigeria and ethnic representation in Kenya, Uganda, and the Ivory Coast (Côte d'Ivoire). Indeed, in virtually every African country, independence was preceded by intense dialogue and negotiation between various groups, parallel to negotiations with the colonial powers. But these were tactical agreements to rid the country of its colonial yoke and, in any case, were elitist negotiations that did not involve the grass roots, as the South African negotiations did through a broad-based network of political organizations and elements of civil society.

Typically, the constitutions that African countries adopted at independence were drafted for them by the colonial masters and, contrary to the authoritarian modes of government adopted by the colonial powers, were laden with idealistic principles of liberal democracy to which Africa had not previously been introduced and in which it had no experience. The regimes built on these constitutions were in essence grafted foreign conceptualizations that had no indigenous roots and therefore lacked legitimacy. In most cases, they were soon overthrown with no remorse or regrets from the public. But these upheavals involved only a rotation of like-minded elites or, worse, military dictators, intent on occupying the seat of power vacated by the colonial masters. They soon became their colonial masters' images. In the overwhelming majority of countries, the quest for unity underscored the intensity of disunity, sometimes resulting in violent conflicts, many of which have intensified in the post–Cold War era—as evidenced by Burundi, Congo, Liberia, Sierra Leone, Somalia, Rwanda, and Zaire, now the Democratic Republic of Congo. African states must respond to the demands of justice, equity, and dignity by the component elements or risk disintegration and collapse. As Michael Chege noted in a different context, "It is time to bring this highly variegated menu to African statesmen and citizens and to convince them that self-determination of groups need not always lead to the feared disintegration of the present states into a myriad of small ethnic units."[46]

There are four policy options for managing pluralistic identities. One is to create a national framework with which all can identify without any distinction based on race, ethnicity, tribe, or religion. This is clearly the most desirable option. The second option is to create a pluralistic framework to accommodate diversity in nations that are racially, ethnically, culturally, or religiously divided. Under this option, probably a federal arrangement, groups would accommodate each other's differences with a uniting commitment to the common purpose of national identification and nondiscrimination. For more seriously divided countries, the third option may be some form of power sharing, combined with decentralization that may expand federalism into confederalism. Finally, where even this degree of accommodation is not workable, and where territorial configurations permit, partition ought to be accepted.

This is the normative framework in which the crisis in the Sudanese region of Darfur should be addressed. Although Sudan has made appreciable progress in ending the half-century-long war in the South, including the acceptance of self-determination that led to southern secession, Sudan remains challenged by chronic crises of identity that are deeply rooted in its history. It urgently needs to reconcile the injustices of its past with the promise of a national framework that will define a country that all of its citizens can feel the dignity of belonging and enjoy the rights of citizenship on equal footing. The country continues to be challenged by the tragedy in the Darfur region, the tensions that threaten eruption in the eastern Beja region, and the even more violent conflicts in South Kordofan and Blue Nile states, where SPLM/A-North is actively engaged with the center.

In this respect, it is worth noting that the international response to Darfur tends to see the crisis in isolation rather than as an aspect of a national quest for justice and equality that began in the South in the 1950s, extended to the adjacent regions of the North in the mid-1980s, and then to the Beja region in the late 1980s, and finally to Darfur. The response of the dominant Arab center has been to fight ruthlessly to preserve its power against the threats posed by proliferating rebellions in the marginalized and discriminated non-Arab regions of the country.

The appropriate response from the international community should be threefold: provide humanitarian assistance to the needy, protect the civilian population, and press for a political solution to achieve peace with justice. As long as war rages on, the government will continue to use Arab tribal militias, of which the infamous *Janjaweed* are the most notorious, but are only illustrative of a more widespread tool the state uses as a weapon against the rebels. Whatever the government may say in response to the pressure from the international community, it will never rein in the *Janjaweed* and other militias as criminals to be punished. They are allies in the genocidal war for survival. If, on the other hand, emphasis is placed on the search for peace, there is a good chance that all parties may be induced to adopt a more positive and constructive attitude toward international support for the peace process.

THE IMPACT OF THE WAR ON TERROR

The war on terror, in the aftermath of September 11, has created a world order that, to a certain degree, calls to mind the Cold War ideological polarization into Western democratic and Eastern communist blocs, with the United States and the Soviet Union heading these blocs. The difference is that these former superpowers are no longer consistently on opposite sides but indeed are on the same side in the global war on terror. What is still in common with the Cold War ideological divide is that, from a human rights perspective, what was crucial in evaluating the performance of a given country was what bloc it fell into. The tendency was to support any government that was ideologically allied with the superpower concerned, whatever its domestic record on human rights, democracy, or good governance in general. Conversely, the evils of a government on the opposite side were considered legitimate targets for exposure and condemnation.

In a way, a similar polarization appears to have emerged with the global war on terror. This is reflected in a number of ways, including military confrontation in which many innocent civilians fall victim to the cross fire. While the obvious cases are Afghanistan and Iraq, the war against terror is also fueling the hostilities and atrocities of the chronic conflicts in the Middle East. The recent invasion of Somalia by Ethiopia, which aimed at ousting the Islamists deemed as posing a terrorist threat in the region, paradoxically aggravated a situation that seemed to have improved under the dominant Islamic courts. The war on terror is also inducing responses in the United States and other Western democracies that restrict human rights and civil liberties in the name of security, as the controversy over the treatment of prisoners in Guantánamo attests. In the polarization generated by the war on terror, the tendency seems to be that as long as a government is an ally in the war, its own human rights record at home can be overlooked or criticized rhetorically without punitive action. Furthermore, governments opportunistically declare rebel movements as terrorists, however justified their struggle, and expect support, politically and even militarily, from their allies in the war against terror.

The global war against terror has reversed the post–Cold War withdrawal of superpower strategic interests in Africa and turned the continent into a theater of confrontation with Islamic terrorists. As Lieutenant Commander Pat Paterson of the US Navy Special Operations Command in Europe explained in an article titled "Into Africa: A New Frontier in the War on Terror," for the United States, in its war with a growing movement of Islamic fundamentalism, the biggest political and military concern in Africa is terrorism.[47] The dire conditions of border disputes, ethnic conflicts, corruption and mismanagement, famine, and HIV make Africa a fertile breeding ground for Muslim extremism and terrorist recruitment. "On a continent where 50% of the population is under 15 years old and where the population is expected to grow from 800 million to 2 billion by 2050, this vast pool of angry, unskilled youth is a population vulnerable to jihadist sentiment and creates a critical problem demanding immediate attention."[48] Paterson goes on to substantiate the presence and activities of Islamic terrorists on the continent: "The history of al Qaeda in Africa goes back to 1991, when Osama bin Laden used Sudan as his operating base until US and international pressure forced the Sudanese government to withdraw the welcome mat for him in 1996. In August 1998 al Qaeda exploded two massive car bombs outside the U.S. embassies in Dar es Salaam, Tanzania, and Nairobi, Kenya, killing 224 people (including 12 Americans) and injuring 5,000. In response, US Navy warships fired cruise missiles into suspected terror sites near Khartoum later that month during Operation Infinite Reach."[49] Evidence of terrorist activities continues in Paterson's account:

> In 2002, al Qaeda operatives killed 15 people in an Israeli-owned hotel in Mombasa, Kenya, and simultaneously fired surface-to-air missiles at an Israeli passenger jet departing Mombasa's airport. In 2003, four suicide bombers attacked Jewish, Spanish, and Belgian sites in Casablanca, Morocco, killing 33 people. The 11 March 2004 train bombings in Madrid were carried out by African jihadists and killed 191 people and wounded 1,400 others. The 7 July 2005 London bombers who killed 51 people and injured more than 700 were assisted by collaborators from Africa.

In September 2005, the US Department of State listed the African organization Salifist Group for Preaching and Combat (GSPC) as a foreign terrorist organization, putting it on par with al-Qaeda. The GSPC gained notoriety with its June 2003 kidnapping of thirty-two Western tourists in Algeria. Terrorist groups such as GSPC use the vast ungoverned expanses of the Sahara Desert to their advantage, ferrying arms, cash, and contraband along established smuggling routes.[50]

Africans were reported to be fighting the United States in Afghanistan and Iraq: "Pentagon officials estimate that 25% of the foreign fighters in Iraq—estimated to be 5,000–8,000—are Africans. The officials also indicate that a stream of veteran jihadists from the conflicts in Iraq and Afghanistan are returning to Africa to train new soldiers and use insurgent tactics against their native countries."[51]

With Africa emerging as a significant scene, if not actor, in the global war on terror, the US government has quietly opened up a front in East Africa:

> Military spending in the four years following 9/11 doubled the amount expended in the preceding four years. The total spent or allocated for arms, training, and regional peacekeeping operations that focus primarily on train-

ing and arming sub-Saharan militaries in the four-year period from 2002 until the end of 2005 amounted to $597 million, whereas for 1998–2001 it was $296 million. At that rate it was estimated that it would take a comparatively few years to equal the $1.5 billion that some believed was spent during the three decades of the Cold War on arms for African allies.[52]

The new US Africa Command, AFRICOM, which was announced in February 2007 and became operational in the fall of 2008, aimed at working in concert with African partners to create a stable security environment in which political and economic growth could take place. This meant combining humanitarian development assistance with helping Africans pursue the war against terrorism more effectively. As Ryan Henry, principal Defense Department undersecretary for policy, told reporters in June 2007, "AFRICOM will emphasize humanitarian assistance, civic action, military professionalism, border and maritime security assistance, and responses to natural disasters." He added that terrorism was a problem in Africa, and it was something African nations were very concerned about, but "it is clearly not the primary focus" of AFRICOM, which has no intention of committing troops to the continent to pursue terrorists.[53]

Generally speaking, the war on terror poses a threat to human rights and democratic freedoms, as Jennifer Cooke and Steve Morrison pertinently cautioned:

> As Africa has become conspicuously important in the intensified global war on terror and in U.S. efforts to win support within multilateral forums for military action against Iraq, policymakers confront the risk that geopolitical goals may trump locally specific human rights, democracy, and developmental interests. If this risk is not managed effectively, the United States easily could make mistakes reminiscent of the Cold War, in which the United States based strategic partnerships overwhelmingly on African leaders' anticommunist credentials, with enduring negative consequences for African governance and U.S. credibility on the continent.[54]

Even in the Sudan, where the war on terror appeared to have produced positive results in pressuring the parties to end the war in the South, lest they be accused of terror, with severe consequences, contradictory developments have taken place. While the government in Khartoum remains on the State Department's list of states that support terrorism, and Congress continues to be vocally antagonistic to the National Islamic Front, renamed the National Congress Party (NCP) and in control of the government in Khartoum, the Bush administration adopted an ambivalent attitude toward Khartoum, and the NCP shrewdly responded opportunistically to gain Washington's favor. As an observer noted, President Omar al-Bashir's regime, "having hosted Osama bin Laden in Khartoum in the 1990s, has played its hand carefully in the U.S. war on terror. Under pressure from Washington, Khartoum sent its intelligence chief, Salah Abdallah Gosh, to brief Western intelligence officials about al-Qaeda networks in Sudan and beyond."[55] As Greg Miller and Josh Meyer have reported, "Sudan has moved beyond sharing historical information on al-Qaeda into taking part in on-going counter-terrorism operations, focusing on areas where its assistance is likely to be most appreciated."[56] They go on to write:

> Sudan has secretly worked with the CIA to spy on the insurgency in Iraq, an example of how the U.S. has continued to cooperate with the Sudanese regime even while condemning its suspected role in the killing of thousands of civilians in Darfur.
>
> President Bush has denounced the killings in Sudan's western region as genocide and has imposed sanctions on the government in Khartoum. But some critics say the administration has soft-pedaled the sanctions to preserve its extensive intelligence collaboration with Sudan.
>
> The relationship underscores the complex realities of the post–Sept. 11 world, in which the United States has relied heavily on intelligence and military cooperation from countries, including Sudan and Uzbekistan, that are considered pariah states for their records on human rights.[57]

Sudan's cooperation with the United States is said to go beyond Iraq. "Sudan has helped the United States track turmoil in Somalia, working to cultivate contacts with the Islamic Courts Union and other militias in an effort to locate al-Qaeda suspects hiding there" and "has provided extensive cooperation in counter-terrorism operations, acting on U.S. requests to detain suspects as they pass through Khartoum." The paradox is that "at a time when Sudan is being condemned in the international community, its counter-terrorism work has won precious praise. The U.S. State Department recently issued a report calling Sudan a 'strong partner in the war on terror.'"[58] This ambivalent attitude toward Khartoum may be a factor in the contradictory hard-talk, soft-action attitude that the US policy has adopted on international response to the genocidal conflict in Darfur. Indeed, the sanctions announced by the Bush administration in late May 2007 have been described as "window dressing," designed to appear tough while putting little real pressure on the Sudan or the Arab militias, which the country is believed to be using against rebels and civilians alike in Darfur.[59]

Another paradoxical development as a result of the war on terror initially improved relations between the United States and Libya, despite Muammar Gadhafi's controversial human rights record. The United States restored full diplomatic relations with Libya in June 2006 and removed it from the State Department's list of terrorism sponsors, ending long-standing tensions in bilateral relations and US-imposed sanctions. Objectively, it is noteworthy that in later years Gadhafi made significant constructive changes. He began to be viewed as having played a positive role in Africa, his most striking achievement being his initiative and strong support for the African Union. He also took steps to align himself with the United States in an effort to gain Western trust. His government apologized for its past violence, accepted responsibility for the 1988 terrorist attack on an airplane over Lockerbie, Scotland, dismantled its weapons of mass destruction program in 2003, and cooperated with the United States in the war on terror. It is, however, widely contended that

> Libya's track record of human rights abuses was still among the worst in the world, calling into question whether his administration was worthy of US support. Freedom House gave Libya the lowest possible rating in all categories—political rights, civil liberties, and freedom—citing poor prison conditions, arbitrary arrest and detention, torture, domestic violence against women, the prohibition of independent human rights organizations, and the ban on independent press. Any form of political opposition was brutally and unsubtly quelled.[60]

Critics of the US and European shift of policy toward Libya argued that it would entrench Libya's poor human rights record:

> The United States and the European Union face the risk that their new diplomatic partnerships with Libya will help legitimize the regime and perpetuate the country's poor conditions. Libyan dissidents claim that Qaddafi will most likely use this new relationship to consolidate his political base and continue stamping out any possibility for political reform. There are also repercussions in the international arena. The United States has portrayed the war on terror as not only a military conflict but also an ideological struggle; current nation-building processes in Iraq and Afghanistan are inextricably linked with the words and values of "freedom," "liberty," and "democracy." In Libya, Qaddafi's eager suppression of the opposition Libyan Islamic Fighting Group (LIFG), recognized as a terrorist organization, has only reinforced beliefs that U.S. and EU motives are not those of building democracy but of self-interested security. Critics of a Western alliance with the Qaddafi regime claim that this "Western

hypocrisy" further alienates the Muslim world and gives radical Islamists even more ammunition to attack the West.[61]

Of course, this was unsustainable, as Gadhafi's eventual demise in the face of UN-sanctioned NATO intervention in support of internal uprising, part of the "Arab Spring," would demonstrate.

Thus, the global war on terror, while justified by the horrific events of September 11, has triggered a chain of policies and actions that threaten to reverse the progress made in the international promotion and protection of human rights. While hindsight on whether a more targeted pursuit of the individual criminals involved in that incident might have produced different results would be superfluous and futile, there is reason to think carefully about how to pursue the war on terror without compromising the human rights standards that have been painstakingly developed since the end of World War II and the creation of the United Nations. Considering that African states are already prone to the abuse of power and egregious violations of human rights, this development poses a particular danger to be guarded against in the continent.

OPERATIONAL STRATEGIES OF INTERVENTION

Although addressing the issue of sovereignty and the root causes of conflict are critical prerequisites to intervention, formulating credible operation principles is the most pivotal factor in the equation. These principles relate to institutional mechanisms and strategies for action, both preventive and corrective. Ideally, from an institutional or organizational perspective, problems should be addressed and solved within the immediate framework, with wider involvement necessitated only by the failure of the internal efforts. Hence, conflict prevention, management, or resolution progressively moves from the domestic domain to the regional and, ultimately, to the global levels of concern and action.

As already noted, those conflicts in which the state is an effective arbiter do not present particular difficulties since they are manageable within the national framework. The problem arises when the state itself is a party to the conflict. Under those conditions, external involvement becomes necessary. In the African context, it is generally agreed that the next-best level of involvement should be the AU, but there are obvious constraints on its role, as its ineffectiveness in Darfur demonstrated. One such constraint has to do with limited resources, both material and human. But perhaps even more debilitating is the question of political will, since in the intimate context of the region, governments feel they are subject to conflicts arising from the problematic conditions of state formation and nation-building and are therefore prone to resist any form of external scrutiny. And since the judge of today may well be the accused of tomorrow, there is a temptation to avoid confronting such problems. The result is evasiveness and malign neglect. Beyond the AU, the United Nations is the next logical organization, for it represents the international community in its global context. But the UN suffers from the same constraints affecting the AU, though to a lesser degree. It, too, must deal with the problem of resources and the reciprocal protectiveness of vulnerable governments.

As recent events have demonstrated, the role of the major Western powers acting unilaterally, multilaterally, or within the framework of the United Nations—though often susceptible to accusations of selectivity and self-interested strategic motivation—has become increasingly pivotal. The problem in this regard is more one of their unwillingness to become involved or their lack of adequate preparedness for such involvement. Perhaps the most important aspect of the involvement of Western industrial democracies in foreign conflicts is the fact that these nations are often moved to act by the gravity of the humanitarian tragedies involved. Thus, their involvement is both an asset in terms of arresting the tragedy and a limitation in terms of preventing the tragedy at an earlier stage. Even with respect to humanitarian intervention, lack of preparedness for an appropriate and timely response is generally acknowledged as a major limitation.[62]

Nevertheless, some argue that there is a strong presumption that the interests of these countries are powerfully engaged and that they will eventually be driven to uphold and promote such interests through humanitarian intervention in crisis situations. Industrial democracies, they further argue, cannot operate without defending standards of human rights and political procedures that are being egregiously violated. Indeed, they themselves cannot prosper in an irreversibly international economy if large, contiguous populations descend into endemic violence and economic depression. Given these compelling reasons and the lack of preparedness for any well-planned response, the United States and Western European countries are particularly prone to crisis-induced reactions that are relatively easy to execute and, indeed, more symbolic than effective in addressing the substantive issues involved.

There will always be elements in a country who welcome intervention, especially among the disadvantaged groups to whom it promises tangible benefits. But since intervention is, of course, a major intrusion from the outside, resistance on the grounds of national sovereignty or pride is also a predictable certainty. For that reason, the justification for intervention must be reliably persuasive, if not beyond reproach: "The difference between an intervention that succeeds and one that is destroyed by immune reaction would depend on the degree of spontaneous acceptance or rejection by the local population."[63]

To avoid or minimize this "immune reaction," such an intervention would have to be broadly international in character. The principles used and the objectives toward which the intervention is targeted must transcend political and cultural boundaries or traditions and concomitant nationalist sentiments. In other words, it must enjoy an effective degree of global legitimacy. "The rationale that could conceivably carry such a burden presumably involves human rights so fundamental that they are not derived from any particular political or economic ideology."[64]

The strategy for preventive or corrective involvement in conflict should constitute gathering and analyzing information and otherwise monitoring situations with a view toward establishing an early warning system through which the international community could be alerted to act. The quest for a system of response to conflict and attendant humanitarian tragedies was outlined by the then–UN secretary-general Boutros Boutros-Ghali when, referring to the surging demands on the Security Council as a central instrument for the prevention and resolution of conflicts, he wrote that the aims of the United Nations must be:

To seek to identify at the earliest possible stage situations that could produce conflict, and to try through diplomacy to remove the sources of danger before violence results;

Where conflict erupts, to engage in peacemaking aimed at resolving the issues that have led to conflict;

Through peace-keeping, to work to preserve peace, however fragile, where fighting has been halted and to assist in implementing agreements achieved by the peacemakers;

To stand ready to assist in peace-building in its differing contexts: rebuilding the institutions and infrastructures of nations torn by civil war and strife; and building bonds of peaceful mutual benefit among nations formerly at war;

And in the largest sense, to address the deepest causes of conflict: economic despair, social injustice and political oppression. It is possible to discern an increasingly common moral perception that spans the world's nations and peoples, and which is finding expression in international laws, many owing their genesis to the work of this Organization.[65]

The action envisaged to address conflict situations and their humanitarian consequences is a four-phase strategy that would involve monitoring developments to draw early attention to impending crises, interceding in time to avert the crisis through diplomatic initiatives, mobilizing international action when necessary, and addressing the root causes to restore peace, security, and stability.[66] The first step would be to detect and identify the problem through various early-warning mechanisms for information collection, evaluation, and reporting. If a sufficient basis for concern were established, the appropriate mechanism would be invoked to take preventive diplomatic measures and avert the crisis. Initially, such initiatives might be taken within the framework of regional arrangements—for example, the Conference on Security and Cooperation in Europe, the Organization of American States, or the African Union. In the United Nations, such preventive initiatives would naturally fall on the secretary-general, acting personally or through special representatives, to bring the situation to the attention of the Security Council for appropriate action. If diplomatic initiatives did not succeed, and depending on the level of human suffering involved, the secretary-general and the Security Council might decide to mobilize international response, ranging from further diplomatic measures to forced humanitarian intervention not only to provide emergency relief but also to facilitate the search for an enduring solution to the causes of the conflict. A strategy aimed at this broader objective would require a close understanding of the causal link between the conditions and developments leading to the outbreak of the crisis and finding solutions that address the root causes to ensure sustainable peace and stability.

CONCLUSION

Africa's turbulent transformation, initiated by colonial scramble for the continent in the nineteenth century, contained by external domination for much of the first half of the twentieth century, reactivated by the independence movement at the second half of the century, and subdued by the Cold War bipolar control mechanism, is now engaging in a renewed quest of self-liberation from within. While this initially meant more self-reliance with minimum external interference, motivated by the strategic interests of the Cold War era, the global war against international terrorism in the early twenty-first century has reactivated international concern and propensity for varying forms of intervention. The context in which this is taking place is poised delicately between globalization and isolation, initially bordering on the marginalization of Africa, but in the context of the global war on terror, putting Africa back at the center as a potential breeding ground for international terrorism. Paradoxically, ideological withdrawal by the major powers is being counterbalanced by pressures for humanitarian intervention, while the war on terror threatens to relegate human rights to a lower level of concern. This situation calls for a more cost-effective sharing of responsibility, with the Africans assuming the primary role and their international partners lending a comple-mentary affirmative, helping hand. Whether this equation is sustainable or the war on terror will take the upper hand and lead Africa back to intensify-ing dependency remains a question.

Whatever the answer to that question, the policy framework that appor-tions responsibilities in accordance with the emerging scale must place the first tier of responsibility on the state. At the next level up the international ladder, regional actors are increasingly being challenged and motivated by the realization that their own national security is closely connected with the secu-rity of their neighbors. This realization has propelled a range of initiatives in which neighbors offer their good offices for third-party mediation in internal conflicts but, if their counsel is not heeded, intervene unilaterally or collec-tively to achieve their objectives. But as the case of Darfur has shown, regional capacities may be inadequate for the task, and the supportive role of the inter-national community will continue to be a necessity for effective action. The best remedy is internal peace, security, and stability.

A number of African leaders have embraced programs of political and economic reforms that would enhance regional security and stability. Some of their peers remain doggedly committed to authoritarian methods of gover-nance. The international community, weary of shouldering responsibility for Africa's problems, is striving to win the leaders intent on reform, give them the support they need to carry out their programs, and thereby provide them with the incentive to do so in earnest. These measures imply the stipulation of national sovereignty as responsibility with regional and international ac-countability. The way to guard against unwelcome international intervention is to discharge the responsibilities of sovereignty and be seen to be doing so.

An important dimension of such accountability is therefore the reform of state structures, institutions, and processes to be more equitable in their man-agement of diversities. This reform will require pushing the process of revers-ing Africa's international dependency to enhance the autonomy of internal actors, ethnic groups, and members of civil society in order to mobilize and engage them in self-reliant processes of governance and sustainable develop-ment. The state has been the intermediary and often the bottleneck in the chain of Africa's dependent relationship with the outside world. The required reform must broaden the scope of decision making through extensive and genuine decentralization. It must make a more constructive use of indigenous structures, values, and institutions for self-governance and self-sustaining de-velopment from within. Governments genuinely committed to reform should have no difficulty in supporting this approach, whereas those that insist on centralization of authority wittingly or unwittingly expose their authoritarian disposition and risk regional and international scrutiny or admonition and, possibly, condemnation and reprisals.

The time is certainly opportune for reconciling sovereignty with the responsibilities of good governance. In balancing national sovereignty and the need for international action to provide protection and assistance to victims of internal conflicts and humanitarian tragedies, certain principles are becoming increasingly obvious as policy guidelines.

First, sovereignty carries with it responsibilities for the well-being of the population. It is from this precept that the legitimacy of a government derives, whatever the political system or prevailing ideology. The relationship between the controlling authority and the populace should ideally ensure the highest standards of human dignity, but at a minimum it should guarantee food, shelter, physical security, basic health services, and other essentials.

Second, in the many countries where armed conflicts and communal violence have caused massive internal displacement, the countries are so divided on fundamental issues that legitimacy and, indeed, sovereignty are sharply contested. This is why there is always a strong faction inviting or at least welcoming external intervention. Under those circumstances, the validity of sovereignty must be judged, using reasonable standards to assess how much of the population is represented, marginalized, or excluded.

Third, living up to the responsibilities of sovereignty implies that there is a transcendent authority capable of holding the supposed sovereign accountable. Some form of an international system has always existed to ensure that states conform to accepted norms or face the consequences in the form of unilateral, multilateral, or collective action. Equality among sovereign entities has always been a convenient fiction; it has never been backed by realities because some powers have always been more dominant than others and therefore have been explicitly or implicitly charged with responsibility for enforcing the agreed-upon norms of behavior. Considering that hardly any African country has the requisite capacity, "hegemonic stability" has not been a pattern, although Nigeria and South Africa have exercised considerable influence in their subregions.

Fourth, such a role imposes on the dominant authority or power certain leadership responsibilities that transcend parochialism or exclusive national interests and serve the broader interests of the community or the human family, an area where African countries, with their politics of identity, have suffered a deficit.

When these principles are translated into practical action in countries torn apart by internal conflicts, a number of implications emerge. For example, sovereignty cannot be an amoral function of authority and control; respect for fundamental human rights and humanitarian principles must be among its most basic values. Similarly, the enjoyment of human rights must encompass equitable and effective participation in the political, economic, social, and cultural life of the country, at least as a widely accepted national aspiration. This system of sharing must guarantee that all individuals and groups belong to the nation on an equal footing with the rest of the people, however identified; they must also be sufficiently represented and not discriminated against on the basis of the prevailing views of identity.

To ensure that these normative goals are met or at least genuinely pursued, the international community as represented by the United Nations is the ideal authority. The imperatives of the existing power structures and processes may, however, require that authority be exercised by other powers capable of acting on behalf of the international community. Multilateral action may therefore be justified under certain circumstances. Any type of less collective action should be closely circumscribed to guard against selectivity and exploitation for less lofty objectives of a more exclusively national character—objectives that may erode the transcendent moral authority of global leadership for the good of all humankind.

As a polarity emerges between those African governments committed to participatory democracy, respect for human rights, and responsible international partnership and those bent on repression and resistance to reform, the international community should adopt a dual strategy that effectively supports reform with positive incentives and discourages resistance with punitive sanctions. Living up to the responsibilities of sovereignty implies a transcendent authority capable of holding the supposed sovereign accountable. Although the international community has made appreciable progress in responding to humanitarian tragedies, much more needs to be done to ensure that governments adhere to the responsibilities of sovereignty by ensuring the security, fundamental rights, civil liberties, and general welfare of their citizens and all those under their domestic jurisdiction.

Although the world is far from a universal government, the foundations, the pillars, and perhaps even the structures of global governance are taking shape with the emergence of a post–Cold War international order in which the internally dispossessed are bound to benefit. Unmasking sovereignty to reveal the gross violations of human rights is no longer an aspiration; it is a process that has already started. Governments and other human rights violators are being increasingly scrutinized for such violations. What is now required is to make them fully accountable and to provide international protection and assistance for the victims of human rights violations and unremedied humanitarian tragedies within their domestic jurisdiction. In other words, what is called for is not something entirely new but, rather, an intensification and improvement of what has already been unfolding.

The global war on terror is obviously a complication insofar as it creates a Cold War–type of polarization between allies and enemies. However, in the end, just as internal conflicts require internal solutions to ensure just peace, security, and stability, a global alliance against terrorism must also address the internal conditions on which international terrorism breeds. Addressing the symptoms without going to the root causes in the crisis of national identity— acute economic disparities, poverty deprivation, and all forms of indignities in an otherwise flourishing world—experienced not only externally but also internally for the few, will continue to generate internal conflicts in Africa with external ramifications. True security must be comprehensive and inclusive, or those left out will remain a source of instability, internally and globally.

NOTES

1. Boutros Boutros-Ghali, *An Agenda for Peace: Preventive Diplomacy, Peacemaking and Peacekeeping* (New York: United Nations, 1992), p. 7.

2. Boutros Boutros-Ghali, in a statement of his proposals to the Council of Ministers in Dakar, Senegal, in 1992. The main documents in these three areas of African initiative are as follows: *The Kampala Document Toward a Conference on Security, Stability, Development and Cooperation in Africa* (Kampala, Uganda: Africa Leadership Forum and Secretariat of the Organization of African Unity and the United Nations Economic Commission for Africa, 1991); Dent Ocaya-Lakidi, *Africa's Internal Conflicts: The Search for a Response,* Report of an Arusha, Tanzania, High-Level Consultation, March 23–25, 1992, prepared for the International Peace Academy; OAU, Council of Ministers, Fifty-sixth Ordinary Session, *Report of the Secretary-General on Conflicts in Africa: Proposals for an OAU Mechanism for Conflict Prevention and Resolution,* CM/1710 (L.VI) (Addis Ababa: Organization of African Unity, June 22–27, 1992); OAU, Council of Ministers, Fifty-seventh Ordinary Session, *Interim Report of the Secretary-General on the Mechanism for Conflict Prevention, Management and Resolution,* CM/1747 (L.VI) (Addis Ababa: Organization of African Unity, February 15–19, 1993); and OAU, Council of Ministers, Fifty-seventh Ordinary Session, *Report of the Secretary-General,* CM/Plen/Rpt (L.VII) (Addis Ababa: Organization of African Unity, February 15–19, 1993). Also pertinent to the issues involved is UN Secretary-General Boutros Boutros-Ghali's report, *An Agenda for Peace,* originally published as document A/47/277 S/24111, June 17, 1992.

3. Thomas M. Franck, "The Emerging Right to Democratic Governance," *American Journal of International Law* 86 (January 1992), p. 46.

4. Richard Falk, "Sovereignty and Human Dignity: The Search for Reconciliation," in *African Reckoning: A Quest for Good Governance,* ed. Francis M. Deng and Terrence Lyons (Washington, D.C.: Brookings Institution, 1998), p. 13.

5. Francis M. Deng, *Protecting the Dispossessed: A Challenge for the International Community* (Washington, D.C.: Brookings Institution, 1993), p. 14.

6. David J. Scheffer, "Toward a Modern Doctrine of Humanitarian Intervention," *University of Toledo Law Review* 23 (Winter 1992), p. 2.

7. UN press release SG/SM/4560, April 24, 1991; cited in Gene M. Lyons and Michael Mastanduno, *Beyond Westphalia: International Intervention, State Sovereignty and the Future of International Society* (Hanover, N.H.: Dartmouth College, 1992), p. 2. Portions of this statement are also cited in Scheffer, "Toward a Modern Doctrine of Humanitarian Intervention," p. 262.

8. Javier Perez de Cuellar, *Report of the Secretary-General on the Work of the Organization* (New York: United Nations, 1991).

9. Ibid., p. 13.

10. Boutros-Ghali, *An Agenda for Peace,* p. 5.

11. Scheffer, "Toward a Modern Doctrine of Humanitarian Intervention," pp. 262–263.

12. Falk, "Sovereignty and Human Dignity," p. 12.

13. Global Policy Forum, Statement by Secretary-General Kofi Annan, April 7, 1999, at www.globalpolicy.org/nations/kofi2.htm.

14. Francis M. Deng, Sadikiel Kimaro, Terrence Lyons, Donald Rothchild, and I. William Zartman, eds., *Sovereignty as Responsibility: Conflict Management in Africa* (Washington, D.C.: Brookings Institution, 1996).

15. OAU, Council of Ministers, Report of the Secretary-General on Conflicts in Africa.

16. Ibid.

17. Ibid.

18. Ibid.

19. Kofi Annan, interview, *Frontline: Ghosts of Rwanda,* PBS, February 17, 2004, at www.pbs.org/wgbh/pages/frontline/shows/ghosts/interviews/annan.html.

20. Ibid.

21. Kofi Annan, interview, *Online News Hour,* PBS, October 18, 1999, at www.pbs.org/newshour/bb/international/july-dec99/annan_10-18.html.

22. Note by the president of the Security Council, S/25344, February 26, 1993.

23. Ibid., p. 1.

24. Ibid., p. 2.

25. Ibid.

26. Ibid.

27. Francis M. Deng and I. William Zartman, eds., *Conflict Resolution in Africa* (Washington, D.C.: Brookings Institution, 1991).

28. Deng et al., eds., *Sovereignty as Responsibility.*

29. Deng and Lyons, eds., *African Reckoning: A Quest for Good Governance* (Washington, D.C.: Brookings Institution, 1998).

30. Francis M. Deng and I. William Zartman, *A Strategic Vision for Africa: The Kampala Movement* (Washington, D.C.: Brookings Institution Press, 2002).

31. Kofi Annan, interview, *Online News Hour,* PBS, October 19, 1999.

32. For my various contributions to the normative theme of the responsibility of sovereignty, see the following books, chapters, and articles; Deng and Lyons, *African Reck-*

oning; Francis M. Deng, "Sovereignty and Humanitarian Responsibility: A Challenge for NGOs in Africa and the Sudan," in *Vigilance and Vengeance,* ed. Robert I. Rotberg (Washington, D.C.: Brookings Institution and the World Peace Foundation, 1996); Deng, Kimaro, Lyons, Rothchild, and Zartman, eds., *Sovereignty as Responsibility*; Francis M. Deng, "Reconciling Sovereignty with Responsibility: A Basis for International humanitarian Action," in *Africa in World Politics,* ed. John W. Harbeson and Donald Rothchild (Boulder, CO: Westview Press, 1995); F. M. Deng, "Frontiers of Sovereignty: A Framework of Protection, Assistance and Development for the Internally Displaced," *Leiden Journal of International Law* 8, no. 2 (1995).

33. United Nations Report of the High Level Panel on Threats, Challenges, and Changes, *A More Secure World: Our Shared Responsibility,* New York, United Nations, 2004, paras. 199–203; and Kofi Annan, *In Larger Freedoms: Toward Development, Security and Human Rights for All,* UN Doc. A/59/2005, March 21, 2005, para. 135.

34. General Assembly 2005, *World Summit Outcome,* UN Doc. A/60/L1, September 15, 2005, para. 139.

35. Kofi Annan, interview, *Frontline: Ghosts of Rwanda.*

36. Boutros-Ghali, *An Agenda for Peace,* p. 9.

37. Ibid., pp. 9–10.

38. Donald Rothchild, *Managing Ethnic Conflict in Africa* (Washington, D.C.: Brookings Institution, 1997), pp. 20–21.

39. Thandika Mkandawire, "Shifting Commitments and National Cohesion in African Countries," in *Common Security and Civil Society in Africa,* ed. Lennart Wohlgemuth, Samantha Gibson, Stephan Klasan, and Emma Rothschild (Uppsala, Sweden: Nordiska Afrikainstitutet, 1999), p. 15.

40. Roberta Cohen and Francis Deng, eds., *The Forsaken People: Case Studies of the Internally Displaced* (Washington, D.C.: Brookings Institution, 1998).

41. According to one source, ethnicity is important in African politics because it serves as an "organizing principle of sound action," which makes it "basically a political . . . phenomenon." See Naomi Chazan et al., *Politics and Society in Contemporary Africa* (Boulder, CO: Lynne Rienner Publishers, 1988), pp. 110, 120. And as UN Secretary-General Kofi Annan observed in a paper presented to an international conference on "The Therapeutics of Conflict," when he was still undersecretary-general for Peacekeeping Operations: "Many [of the civil wars] have also been perceived as showing strong symptoms of ethnic conflict. Ethnic conflict as a symptom is, at best, extremely difficult to assess. . . . Ethnic differences are not in and of themselves either symptoms or causes of conflict; in societies where they are accepted and respected, people of vastly different backgrounds live peacefully and productively together. Ethnic differences become charged—conflictual—when they are used for political ends, when ethnic groups are intentionally placed in opposition to each other." See Kofi Annan, "The Peacekeeping Prescription," in *Preventive Diplomacy,* ed. Kevin M. Cahill, M.D. (New York: Basic Books, 1996), p. 176.

42. The Constitution of the Federal Democratic Republic of Ethiopia (Addis Ababa, December 8, 1994) provides in Article 39, Number 1, that "every nation, nationality

and people in Ethiopia has an unconditional right to self-determination, including the right to secession." It also states in Article 39, Number 3, that "every nation, nationality and people in Ethiopia has the right to a full measure of self-government which includes the right to establish institutions of government in the territory that it inhabits and to equitable representation in regional and national governments."

43. This is the essence of the proposal that the state of Liechtenstein presented to the General Assembly of the United Nations in 1991—a proposal that aimed at establishing a new international legal framework in which self-determination, defined primarily as self-administration, might be pursued within the existing state framework. See Wolfgang Danspeckgruber and Sir Arthur Watts, eds., *Self-Determination and Self-Administration: A Sourcebook* (Boulder, CO: Lynne Rienner Publishers, 1997).

44. Ibid., p. 1.

45. Sir Arthur Watts, "The Liechtenstein Draft Convention on Self-Determination Through Self-Administration," in *Self-Determination and Self-Administration: A Sourcebook,* ed. Wolfgang Danspeckgruber and Sir Arthur Watts (Boulder, CO: Lynne Rienner Publishers, 1997), p. 23.

46. Cited in a review of Francis M. Deng, "Africa and the New World Disorder," *Brookings Review* (Spring 1993), p. 3. For a more comprehensive discussion of ethnic diversity in the context of democratization, see Chege's article, "Remembering Africa," in *Foreign Affairs* 71, no. 1 (1992), pp. 146–163.

47. Pat Paterson, "Into Africa: A New Frontier in the War on Terror," *United States Naval Institute Proceedings* 132, no. 5 (May 2006), p. 32.

48. Ibid.

49. Ibid.

50. Ibid.

51. Ibid.

52. Sandra T. Barnes, "Global Flows: Terror, Oil, and Strategic Philanthropy," *Africa Studies Review* 48, no. 1 (2005), pp. 1–22; at 1, 6. See also Thomas P. M. Barnett, "The Americans Have Landed," *Esquire,* June 11, 2007.

53. Jim Fisher-Thompson, "New Africa Command to Have Unique Structure, Mission," USINFO, June 22, 2007, at http://iipdigital.usembassy.gov/st/english/article/2007/06/200706221700271ejrehsif0.4897272.html#axzz27af0kJBw. See also "U.S. Africa Command at Initial Operation Capacity," U.S. Africa Command, Stuttgart, Germany, Press Release 08-001, October 1, 2007, at http://iipdigital.usembassy.gov/st/english/texttrans/2007/10/20071003140010xjsnommis0.3377954.html#axzz27af0kJBw.

54. Jennifer G. Cook and J. Stephen Morrison, "Building an Ethic of Public Policy Discourse: An Appeal to African Studies Community," *African Issues* 30, no. 2 (2002), p. 63.

55. "Africa's Year of Terror Tactics," *New York Beacon,* January 11–17, 2007, p. 10.

56. Greg Miller and Josh Meyer, "Sudan Aids CIA's Efforts in Iraq," *Los Angeles Times,* June 11, 2007.

57. Ibid. See also Hans Pienaar, "Spooks, Hacks, Party in Secretive Sudan," *Tribune,* June 10, 2007, p. 14.

58. Miller and Meyer, "Sudan Aids CIA's Efforts in Iraq."

59. Ibid.

60. Samantha Fang, "A Worthy Ally? Reconsidering U.S.-Libyan Relations," *Harvard International Review* 29, no. 3 (Spring 2007), p. 7.

61. Ibid.

62. John Steinbruner, "Civil Violence as an International Security Problem," memorandum, November 23, 1992, addressed to the Brookings Institution Foreign Policy Studies Program staff. See also Chester A. Crocker, "The Global Law and Order Deficit: Is the West Ready to Police the World's Bad Neighbors?" *Washington Post,* December 20, 1992, p. C1.

63. Steinbruner, "Civil Violence as an International Security Problem."

64. Ibid.

65. Boutros-Ghali, *An Agenda for Peace,* pp.7–8.

66. For a more elaborate discussion of these phases as applied to the crisis of the internally displaced, see the UN study in document E/CH.4/1993/35 and the revised version of that study in Deng, *Protecting the Dispossessed.* This study was considered by the Commission on Human Rights at its forty-ninth session, during which its findings and recommendations were endorsed and the mandate of the special representative of the secretary-general was extended for two years to continue to work on the various aspects of the problem presented in the study.

About the Contributors

LOUIS-ALEXANDRE BERG

Louis-Alexandre Berg is a PhD candidate in international relations at Georgetown University. He graduated from Brown University and received his master's degree in public affairs from Princeton University. He has served as an adviser to the US Institute of Peace, the World Bank, and the US Agency for International Development on programs related to justice and security sector development, governance, and conflict mitigation, and was a Jennings Randolph Peace Scholar at the US Institute of Peace from 2009 to 2010.

FRANCIS M. DENG

Francis M. Deng was appointed by UN Secretary-General Ban Ki-moon in May 2007 as the special adviser on the prevention of genocide. Deng served as representative of the UN secretary-general on internally displaced persons from 1992 to 2004, as human rights officer in the UN Secretariat from 1967 to 1972, and as ambassador of the Sudan to Canada, Denmark, Finland, Norway, Sweden, and the United States. He also served as Sudan's minister of state for foreign affairs. After leaving his country's service, he joined a succession of think tanks, universities, and research institutions. Deng holds a bachelor of laws with honors from Khartoum University and a master of laws and a doctor of the science of law from Yale University. He has authored and edited over thirty books in the fields of law, conflict resolution, internal displacement, human rights, anthropology, folklore, history, and politics and has also written two novels on the theme of the crisis of national identity in the Sudan. Among his numerous awards in his country and abroad, Deng is co-recipient with Roberta Cohen of the 2005 Grawemeyer Award for "Ideas Improving World Order" and the 2007 Merage Foundation American

Dream Leadership Award. In 2000, Deng also received the Rome Prize for Peace and Humanitarian Action.

ULF ENGEL

Ulf Engel is professor of African politics at University of Leipzig. He is the editor of *New Mediation Practices on African Conflicts* (2012) and coauthor of *Africa's New Peace and Security Architecture* (2010) and *Respacing Africa* (2009), among other books. Since 2011, he has been a member of the AEGIS (Africa-Europe Group for Interdisciplinary Studies, Leiden) Advisory Council. He is also professor extraordinary of political science at the University of Stellenbosch, a fellow at the Stellenbosch Institute for Advanced Study, and a visiting professor at the Institute for Peace and Security Studies at Addis Ababa University. His research interests include the emerging African Union policies on unconstitutional changes of government, Africa's new peace and security architecture, changing stateness in Africa, and new spatialities of power on Africa.

JOHN W. HARBESON

John W. Harbeson is professor emeritus of political science in the Graduate Center and at City College in the City University of New York and professorial lecturer in the Johns Hopkins University School of Advanced International Studies. He is the author, editor, or coeditor of *Land Reform and National Building in Kenya*; *The Ethiopian Transformation*; *Civil Society and the State in Africa*; *Responsible Government: The Global Challenge*; *The Military in African Politics*; four editions of *Africa in World Politics*; and more than eighty articles and book chapters. He has been a Jennings Randolph Senior Fellow at the US Institute of Peace, and a visiting fellow at Princeton's Center of International Studies, and served as the US Agency for International Development's regional democracy and governance adviser for eastern and southern Africa. He was elected to the American Political Science Association's governing council and cofounded its comparative democratization section and founded its African Politics Conference Group–related group. He serves on the Woodrow Wilson Center's Africa Program Advisory Council.

PRINCETON N. LYMAN

Ambassador (retired) Princeton N. Lyman is US special envoy for Sudan and South Sudan. He has been adjunct senior fellow at the Council on Foreign Relations. From 2003 to 2006, he held the Ralph Bunche Chair for Africa Policy Studies at the Council on Foreign Relations. He is also adjunct professor at Georgetown University. Ambassador Lyman's career in government included assignments as deputy assistant secretary of state for Africa, ambassador to Nigeria, director of refugee programs, ambassador to South Africa, and assistant secretary of state for international organization affairs. Earlier in the US Agency for International Development he was Director of USAID in Addis Ababa, Ethiopia. He has published books and articles on foreign policy, African affairs, economic development, HIV/AIDS, UN reform, terrorism, and peacekeeping.

CARRIE MANNING

Carrie Manning is professor of political science at Georgia State University. She is the coauthor of *Costly Democracy* (2012) and author of *The Making of Democrats: Elections and Party Development in Postwar Bosnia, El Salvador, and Mozambique* (2008) and *The Politics of Peace in Mozambique: Post-Conflict Democratization, 1992–2000* (2002). Her research interests include political party development and party system formation in postconflict democracies, local governance and the challenges for postconflict peacebuilding, role of relief and development NGOs in state-building, and rule of law promotion.

ALI A. MAZRUI

Ali A. Mazrui was born in Mombasa, Kenya, in 1933, and educated in Kenya, Great Britain, and the United States. He has a master's degree from Columbia University in New York, and a doctorate from Oxford University in England. He has written more than twenty books and hundreds of articles. One of his latest books is *Islam Between Globalization and Counterterrorism* (Oxford: James Currey Publishers, and Trenton, NJ: Africa World Press, 2006). He is best known for his television series *The Africans: A Triple Heritage* (BBC/PBS, 1986). Mazrui is currently director of the Institute of Global Cultural Studies, State University of New York, Binghamton; senior scholar in Africana studies, Cornell University, Ithaca, NY; chancellor, Jomo Kenyatta University of Agriculture and Technology, Nairobi, Kenya; senior fellow, Prince Alwaleed bin Talal Center for Muslim-Christian Understanding, Georgetown University, Washington, DC; and Albert Luthuli Professor at Large, University of Jos in Nigeria. Mazrui has received honorary doctorates in subjects ranging from divinity to humane letters and from African studies to development studies. Mazrui is married and has five sons, one daughter, and several grandchildren.

TODD MOSS

Todd Moss is vice president for programs and senior fellow at the Center for Global Development. He is also an adjunct professor at Georgetown University. He is the author of *African Development: Making Sense of the Issues and Actors* (2011) and *Adventure Capitalism: Globalization and the Political Economy of*

Stock Markets in Africa (2003). At the Center for Global Development, Moss directs the Emerging Africa Project, focusing on US-Africa relations and financial issues facing sub-Saharan Africa. Previously he led the center's work on Nigerian debt, Zimbabwe's economic recovery, and the African Development Bank.

WILLIAM RENO

William Reno is professor of political science at Northwestern University. He is the author of *Corruption and State Politics in Sierra Leone* (1995), *Warlord Politics and African States* (1998), and *Warfare in Independent Africa* (2011). His research interests include investigations to explain variations in the organization and behavior of armed groups in complex conflicts, and the role of patronage networks and other nonformal relationships in influencing the decisions of leaders of armed groups. He also is interested in the relationships between states and armed groups in sub-Saharan Africa and how these relationships shape the nature of counterinsurgency efforts on the part of bureaucratically weak states with disorganized militaries.

FILIP REYNTJENS

Filip Reyntjens is professor of African law and politics at the Institute of Development Policy and Management, University of Antwerp. He is the author of *The Great African War: Congo and Regional Geopolitics, 1996–2006* (2010). He is a full member of the Belgian Royal Academy of Overseas Sciences and a board member of the International Third World Legal Studies Association (New York) and the Development Research Institute IVO (Tilburg). His studies focus on the law and politics of sub-Saharan Africa, especially the Great Lakes region.

DONALD ROTHCHILD

The late Donald Rothchild was professor of political science at the University of California at Davis from 1965 until his death in January 2007. His university awarded him a distinguished professorship in 2003. He was the author or editor of more than two dozen books and over seventy articles over a career spanning almost fifty years. He wrote extensively and authoritatively on a wide range of topics including conflict mediation, international political economy, US foreign policy toward Africa, ethnic politics, international regimes, international security, and Africa's place in contemporary world politics. He also wrote important work on Ghana, civil society, Afro-Marxist regimes, and state-society relations. He was elected twice to the presidency of the International Political Science Association's Research Committee on Ethnicity and Politics.

IAN TAYLOR

Ian Taylor is professor of international relations and African politics in the School of International Relations of St. Andrews. He is the author of *The Forum on China-Africa Cooperation (FOCAC)* (2011), *The International Relations of Sub-Saharan Africa* (2010), and five other books. He has edited *China's Rise in Africa: Perspectives on a Developing Connection* (2012) and seven other books. He is also chair professor in the School of International Studies, Renmin University of China, professor extraordinary in political science at the University of Stellenbosch, South Africa, and honorary professor in the Institute of African Studies, Zhejiang Normal University, and has taught at universities in Botswana, South Africa, and Uganda.

AILI MARI TRIPP

Aili Mari Tripp is professor of political science and gender & women's studies at the University of Wisconsin–Madison. She is also director of the Center for Research on Gender and Women. Tripp has published *Museveni's Uganda: Paradoxes of Power in a Hybrid Regime* (2010), coauthored a book with Isabel Casimiro, Joy Kwesiga, and Alice Mungwa titled *African Women's Movements: Transforming Political Landscapes* (2009), and is author of *Women and Politics in Uganda* (2000) and *Changing the Rules: The Politics of Liberalization and the Urban Informal Economy in Tanzania* (1997). Tripp has edited and coedited four other volumes and has published articles and book chapters on gender and politics in Africa, global feminism, civil society in Africa, women in postconflict African countries, and democratization in Africa. She coedits a book series with Stanlie James on *Women in Africa and the Diaspora* for the University of Wisconsin Press. Born in the UK, she lived for fifteen years in Tanzania and has dual citizenship in the United States and Finland. She has carried out fieldwork in Tanzania, Uganda, Liberia, and Angola. She has served as president of the African Studies Association and as vice president of the American Political Science Association.

CRAWFORD YOUNG

Crawford Young is Rupert Emerson and H. Edwin Young Professor Emeritus of Political Science at the University of Wisconsin–Madison, where he taught from 1963 to 2001. He also served as visiting professor in Congo-Kinshasa, Uganda, and Senegal. His major works include *Politics in the Congo* (1965), *The Politics of Cultural Pluralism* (1976), *Cooperatives and Development: Agricultural Politics in Ghana and Uganda* (with Neal Sherman and Tim Rose, 1981), *Ideology and Development in Africa* (1982), *The Rise and Decline of the Zairian State* (with Thomas

Turner, 1985), *The African Colonial State in Comparative Perspective* (1994), and most recently *The Postcolonial State in Africa* (2012). *The Politics of Cultural Pluralism* won the Herskovits Prize of the African Studies Association and was co-winner of the Ralph Bunche Award of the American Political Science Association; *The African Colonial State in Comparative Perspective* won the Gregory Luebbert Prize of the Comparative Politics Section of the APSA. He is a fellow of the American Academy of Arts and Sciences.

I. WILLIAM ZARTMAN

I. William Zartman is the Jacob Blaustein Professor Emeritus of International Organization and former director of the Conflict Management Program at the Paul Nitze School of Advanced International Studies of Johns Hopkins University (SAIS). For twenty years he was director of the SAIS African Studies Program. Previously he taught at the University of South Carolina, American University in Cairo, and New York University. He has been Olin Professor at the US Naval Academy and Halevy Professor at the Institute of Political Studies in Paris. He is a past president of the Middle East Studies Association and of the American Institute of Maghrib Studies and is president of the Tangier American Legation Institute for Moroccan Studies. He is the author, coauthor or editor of more than twenty books, the most recent of which include *The Global Power of Talk*; *Negotiation and Conflict Management: Essays on Theory and Practice*; *Engaging Extremists*; *The Slippery Slope to Genocide*; *Getting In: Mediators' Entry into the Settlement of African Conflicts*; *Cowardly Lions: Missed Opportunities to Prevent Deadly Conflict and State Collapse*; and *Rethinking the Economics of War: The Intersection of Need, Creed and Greed*. He has a PhD from Yale and an honorary doctorate from the Louvain.

Index